Betting Thoroughbreds

*A Professional's Guide for
the Horseplayer*

Betting Thoroughbreds

A Professional's Guide for
the Horseplayer
REVISED EDITION

Steven Davidowitz

E. P. Dutton / *New York*

For information contact:
E.P. Dutton, Inc., 2 Park Avenue, New York, N.Y. 10016

Library of Congress Catalog Card Number: 82-74072
ISBN: 0-525-48046-3

10 9 8 7 6 5 4

Acknowledgments

And special thanks to *Turf and Sport Digest* for the use of its Racing Library in the preparation of this book.

To my father,
my mother
my wife,
and my son

Contents

Foreword
by Andrew Beyer

One of the luckiest moments in my life as a horseplayer occurred in 1971 when, by sheer chance, I sat next to Steve Davidowitz on a bench at Saratoga Racetrack. At the time I viewed racing the way many readers of this book probably do now. I desperately wanted to be a successful handicapper. But I wasn't convinced that this was possible, and I had no idea how to achieve my goal.

After striking up a conversation with Steve, I associated with him throughout that Saratoga season and got the opportunity to watch a consummate professional in operation. I was impressed not only by his success at the betting windows but also by his unique understanding of the nature of the game.

One aspect of Steve's approach to racing struck me as original and helped show me the way to win at the track. Steve was not a dogmatist. Most handicappers, even the good ones, define themselves by the primary methods they use. There are speed handicappers—pace handicappers—class handicappers—angle handicappers—and so on.

Steve perceived that there is a time and place for all these approaches. He swore by none and discarded none. The key to winning at the track was not to find one all-powerful secret, but to learn the right tools to use at the right time.

Most handicapping books purport to offer their readers all-encompassing formulas that will work anywhere. But, in practice, the horseplayer at Aqueduct and the horseplayer at Cahokia Downs are playing very different games. *Betting Thoroughbreds* recognizes their different needs and helps them both.

Steve's chapter on class at minor tracks explair.s an approach to the game which, as far as I know, has never appeared in a book before. Steve explains that the $1,500 claiming ranks at a cheap track may in fact include a half dozen different class stratifications. A handicapper who appreciates those differences will be able to find outstanding bets that elude almost everyone who reads the *Daily Racing Form*. For the bettor at any minor racetrack, that chapter alone is worth the price of the book.

For the handicapper who follows major-league racing, Steve's perceptions about the bias of the racing surface and his analysis of the way good trainers handle their horses are both invaluable. Those were the first things he taught me that summer at Saratoga. We examined a set of past performances and Steve said, "Let's train this horse." He then reviewed the horse's record race by race, considered what the trainer was trying to do with the animal, and determined whether the horseman was succeeding. By the time we came to the most recent race we had a very good idea of what the horse was likely to do that day, as well as insight into the trainer's methodology and competence.

This is a far cry from the approach of the dogmatists who distill the art of handicapping into neat, inflexible rules. But it is the only intelligent, realistic way to tackle the game. Steve's guidance pointed me in the right directions and ultimately enabled me to become a winning horseplayer and to beat him into print as the author of a handicapping book.

A book that examines all the complexities of handicapping may not sell in Peoria. Casual racetrack gamblers generally want systems and rules that will enable them to get rich quick without expending much effort. *Betting Thoroughbreds* offers no such simplistic strategies. But Steve's teachings will be a revelation for the handicappers who, like me in 1971, truly want to learn how to beat the game.

Introduction

For some horseplayers, the romance of the track is linked only to the number of trips made to the cashier's window. For others, it is the spectacle of a Secretariat or a Saratoga or the chance to root away the frustrations of daily living in 1:11²/₅.

But for numerous racing fans—the ones for whom this book is written—Thoroughbred horseracing is all of the above and one of the most intellectually challenging pastimes man has ever invented. Through the art/science of handicapping and the wagering instrument, the fan in the stands is as much a participant as the horse itself. Armed with a copy of the *Daily Racing Form*, the horseplayer becomes a detective, and there are many mysteries to be solved.

How important are speed-pace-class-distance-track condition-weight-jockey-and-trainer? What role do they play in determining the outcome of a race? Are there patterns of predictability? Is the game based on logic or ruled by chance? What about drugs and year-round racing? And, at rock bottom, is it possible to play the game well enough to overcome the stiff 20 percent betting tax and still show a profit for the effort?

Virtually every serious or semi-serious fan has endured periods of frustration and self-doubt while trying to find workable answers to these and other racetrack riddles. The path is littered with thousands of torn-up pari-mutuel tickets. The clues are complex, sometimes contradictory. The secrets of the game are subtle and elusive. And there is just so much bad advice floating around.

Dozens of ads promise to make the racing game easy pickings but in every instance fall way short of the mark. Indeed, the racetrack experience is such that there are no absolute truths to memorize, no ironclad list of dos or don'ts, no simplistic three-rule systems that do your thinking for you.

It may sound like good advice to avoid playing a filly against colts, or to demand a recent race from a potential contender; but it has been my experience that the people who give such advice, and sell it too, have rarely had a winning season in their lives.

Along every step of the handicapping process the player must learn to make well-thought-out judgments: to separate contenders, to eliminate also-rans, to detect relevant information hidden in the hieroglyphics of the *Daily Racing Form*'s past performance records, and to glean valid insights from the fast-paced action on the track.

To acquire that kind of reality-based insight, most successful horseplayers have had to discard the majority of popular handicapping notions, substituting in their place more flexible concepts gained through practical experience, intensive private research, and conversations with the best players in the game.

I would love to assure you that reading this book will automatically make you a winner. But I can't. The truth is you may not have the competitiveness, the patience, or the inclination to follow the steps necessary to improve your game.

It is my belief, however, that thousands, perhaps even tens of thousands, of racing fans could win at the races but are presently unable to do so because they do not know what skills are important, what sources of information are reliable, and what tools are most useful for the task. Thousands more, maybe millions, gain considerable pleasure in their initial outings to the track but for lack of good teachers and other aids find the experience too expensive to pursue. And there are others, too many in fact, who continue to play the game without knowing some of the strategies that could reduce the cost considerably.

The purpose of this book is to lend a hand and fill the void. It is a sourcebook, not about Thoroughbred horseracing per se, but about ideas, concepts, tools, and suggestions taken from twenty-two years of personal and professional racetrack experience. It is designed so that any player, regardless of past history or present skill, can gain sufficient insights to build a solid plan of attack. Good luck, and I hope it helps your game.

Betting Thoroughbreds

*A Professional Guide for
the Horseplayer*

1.
Through the
Looking Glasses

Secretariat ✕ — Ch. c (1970), by Bold Ruler—Somethingroyal, by Princequillo.
Breeder, Meadow Stud, Inc. (Va.). 1973 12 9 2 1 $860,404
Owner, Meadow Stable. Trainer, L. Laurin. 1972 9 7 1 0 $456,404

Oct28-738WO mc 1⅝ 2:41⅘fm 1-5 ▲117 21½ 15 11 12 16½ MapleE12 WfaS 96 Secretariat117 BigSpruce GoldenDon 12
Oct 8-737Bel Ⓣ 1½ 2:24⅘fm 1-2 ▲121 11½ 11½ 13 15 T'c'teR3 WfaS 103 Secretariat 121 Tentam Big Spruce 7
Sep29-737Bel 1½ 2:25⅘sy 1-3 ▲119 21½ 1h 21½ 24½ Turc'teR5 WfaS 86 ProveOut126 Secretariat CougarII. 5
Sep15-737Bel 1 1-8 1:45⅖ft 2-5e▲124 54 3½ 12 13½ T'rc'teR7 InvH 104 Secretariat124 RivaRidge Cougar II. 7
Aug 4-737Sar 1 1-8 1:49⅕ft 1-10 ▲119 44 2½ 2h 21 Turc'teR3 AlwS 94 Onion 119 Secretariat Rule by Reason 5
Jun30-738AP 1 1-8 1:47 ft 1-20 ▲126 13 12½ 16 19 Turc'tteR4 InvA 99 Secretariat 126 MyGallant OurNative 4
Jun 9-738Bel 1 1-2 2:24 ft 1-10 ▲126 1h 120 128 131 Tur'teR1 ScwS 113 Secretariat126 Twice aPr'ce MyGal'nt 5
May19-738Pim 1 3/16 1:54⅖ft 1-3 ▲126 45½ 12½ 12½ 12½ Turc'teR3 ScwS 98 Secretariat 126 Sham Our Native 6
May 19—Daily Racing Form Time, 1:53⅖.
May 5-739CD 1 1-4 1:59⅖ft 3-2e▲126 118¾ 2½ 1½ 12½ T'tteR10 ScwS 103 Secretariat 126 Sham Our Native 13
Apr21-737Aqu 1 1-8 1:49⅘ft 1-3e▲126 75½ 55½ 45½ 34 T'rc'teR6 ScwS 83 Angle Light 126 Sham Secretariat 8
Apr 7-737Aqu 1 1:33⅖ft 1-10 ▲126 31 12 1½ 13 T'rc'teR3 AlwS 100 Secret'riat126 Ch'mp'gneCh'rlie Flush 6
Mar17-737Aqu 7 f 1:23⅕sy 1-5 ▲126 56 53 1h 14½ Tur'tteR4 AlwS 85 Sec'tar't126 Ch'pagneCh'lie Impec'n's 6
Nov18-728GS 1 1/16 1:44⅖ft 1-10e▲122 69½ 33 11½ 13½ Tur'teR6 ScwS 83 Secretariat122 AngleLight StepNicely 6
Oct28-727Lrl 1 1/16 1:42⅘sy 1-10e▲122 614 53 15 18 T'rc'teR5 ScwS 99 Secretar't122 St'p t'eM'sic AngleL'ht 6
Oct14-727Bel 1 1:35 ft 2-3e▲122 1113 53½ 1½ 12† Tur'teR4 ScwS 97 Secr'tar't122 St'p theM'sic St'pNic'ly 12
†Disqualified and placed second.
Sep16-727Bel 6½ f 1:16⅖ft 1-5 ▲122 65½ 53½ 12 11¾ Turc'teR4 ScwS 98 S'cr't'r't122 St'p t'eMusic Sw'tC'rier 7
Aug26-727Sar 6½ f 1:16⅕ft 1-3 ▲121 96½ 1h 14 15 Turc'teR8 SpwS 97 Secretariat121 Fl't toGl'y St'p theM'c 9
Aug16-727Sar 6 f 1:10 ft 3-2 121 54 42 1½ 13 Turc'teR2 SpwS 96 Secr't'riat121 L'da'sCh'f N'thst'rD'c'r 5
Jly 31-724Sar 6 f 1:10⅘ft 2-5 ▲118 73¾ 3½ 1h 11½ TurcotteR4 Alw 92 Secretariat 118 Russ Miron Joe Iz 7
Jly 15-724Aqu 6 f 1:10⅗ft 6-5 ▲113* 66½ 43 1½ 16 Felic'noP8 Mdn 90 Secret'riat113 M'sterAch'v'r BetOn It 11
Jly 4-722Aqu 5½ f 1:05 ft 3 ▲113*107 108¾ 75½ 41¼ Felic'noP2 Mdn 87 Herbull 118 MasterAch'v'r Fl't 'nR'y'l 12
Oct 5 Bel tc 5f fm :56⅘h Sept 25 Bel tc 1m yl 1:38h Sept 21 Bel tc 4f sf :48⅗b

Thanks to television's coverage of the 1973 Triple Crown races, almost every person with the vaguest interest in horseracing knows that the horse whose lifetime record is shown above was one of a kind, a champion of his age, if not, in fact, one of the greatest racehorses ever to appear on this planet.

As a two-year-old, before the TV cameras discovered him, Secretariat was just as spectacular to watch, officially winning eight races in ten starts, including a defeat only the stewards could hang on him in the Champagne Stakes. But it is his other defeat I want to tell you about. His first lifetime start.

Secretariat 113 Ch. c (1970), by Bold Ruler—Somethingroyal, by Princequillo.
Breeder, Meadow Stud, Inc. (Va.). 1972 0 M 0 0 (—)
Owner, Meadow Stable. Trainer, L. Laurin.
June 29 Bel 3f ft :35h June 24 Bel 6f sly 1:12⅘h June 15 Bel 5f ft 1:00⅕hg

One, two, three strides out of the starting gate with inexperienced Paul Feliciano barely able to stay in the saddle, Secretariat was welcomed to the sport of kings with a bang. Make that two bangs. One from the left and one from the right.

"Forget *that* horse," I said to console myself and made a mental note to see him a bit later in the race. Ten lengths to the front, a pack of expensively bred two-year-old maidens were trying to win the first race of their careers. It was time to see how the race was taking shape.

I love two-year-old racing. I'm fascinated by its freshness and its promise, and I've gained valuable insights about speed, class, distance potential, and trainers through watching these young horses progress from race to race. Besides, the better ones run fast, very formfully, and provide some of the best bets in all of racing.

When the great filly Ruffian, for example, made her debut in 1974, I was absolutely astonished to get a $10.40 payoff. Her trainer, Frank Whiteley Jr., is one of the deadliest trainers of first-time starters in the history of racing—a man who wins upward of 40 percent of all such attempts, a man who trains horses like they are put together with Swiss-clockwork efficiency.

Not only did Ruffian score by fifteen lengths in track record time, but she was the third straight first-time starter Whiteley put over in three early season attempts. It also turned out to be a typical Ruffian performance.

THIRD RACE	5 ½ FURLONGS. (1.03) MAIDEN SPECIAL WEIGHTS. Purse $9,000. Fillies, 2-year-olds, weights, 116 lbs.

Belmont

MAY 22, 1974

Value of race $9,000, value to winner $5,400, second $1,980, third $1,080, fourth $540. Mutuel pool $144,330, OTB pool $47,785. Track Exacta Pool $182,574. OTB Exacta Pool $83,829.

Last Raced	Horse	Eqt.A.Wt PP St	¼	½	Str	Fin	Jockey	Odds $1
	Ruffian	2 116 9 8	1³	1⁶	1⁹	1¹⁶	Vasquez J	4.20
	Suzest	2 113 3 3	3hd	2⁴	2⁵	2⁵	Wallis T³	1.50
	Garden Quad	2 116 10 9	5²	4½	4³	3½	Baltazar C	26.20
	Fierce Ruler	2 116 7 5	6¹½	5¹	3¹	4³½	Rivera M A	20.80
	Flower Basket	2 116 8 6	8³	7½	5½	5½	Turcotte R	45.30
	Curlique	b 2 116 5 7	7½	8⁴	6³	6nk	Maple E	14.10
4May74 6CD¹²	Funny Cat	2 116 6 10	10	10	8½	7⁵	Hole M	32.70
14May74 4Bel³	Merrie Lassie	2 116 4 4	9⁶	9⁵	9⁴	8⁴½	Gustines H	13.90
	Precious Elaine	2 116 1 1	2hd	3¹	7½	9⁶½	Castaneda M	4.50
28Feb74 3GP²	Great Grandma Rose	2 116 2 2	4²	6¹½	10	10	Cordero A Jr	4.60

OFF AT 2:32 EDT. Start good, **Won ridden out**. Time, :22⅖, :45, :57, 1:03 Track fast.

Equals track record.

$2 Mutuel Prices:

9–(L)–RUFFIAN	10.40	4.60	3.80
3–(D)–SUZEST		3.20	3.00
10–(M)–GARDEN QUAD			7.00

$2 EXACTA 9–3 PAID $35.20.

dk b or br. f, by Reviewer—Shenanigans, by Native Dancer. Trainer Whiteley F Y Jr. Bred by Janney Jr Mrs & S S (Ky).

RUFFIAN, rushed to the front from the outside at the turn, quickly sprinted away to a good lead and continued to increase her advantage while being ridden out. SUZEST, prominent from the start, was no match for the winner while easily besting the others. GARDEN QUAD hustled along after breaking slowly, failed to seriously menace. FIERCE RULER had no excuse. FUNNY CAT was off slowly. PRECIOUS ELAINE had brief speed. GREAT GRANDMA ROSE was through early.

Owners— 1, Locust Hill Farm; 2, Olin J M; 3, Irving R; 4, LaCroix J W; 5, Reineman R L; 6, Calumet Farm; 7, Whitney C V; 8, T–Square Stable; 9, Brodsky A J; 10, Five Friends Farm.

Trainers— 1, Whiteley F Y Jr; 2, Stephens W C; 3, Johnson P G; 4, Toner J J; 5, Freeman W C; 6, Cornell R; 7, Poole G T; 8, Cincotta V J; 9, Conway J P; 10, Donato R A.

Scratched—Cross Words; Footsie (14May744Bel4); French Rule.

Throughout her two-year-old season Ruffian was never defeated, never threatened, never pushed to race any faster than she was willing to give on her own. But I'm not at all sure that pushing would have produced anything more than she was already willing to give.

Ruffian's striding action was very much like that of Valery Borzov, the Russian "doctor" of the sprint who won the gold medal in the 1972 100-meter dash at the Munich Olympics. Perfect rhythm. Maximum efficiency. Ruffian just came out of the gate running and never stopped, never missed a beat. Indeed, at six furlongs (three-quarters of a mile), I am convinced she could have beaten any horse that ever lived, including Secretariat, the fast-working son of Bold Ruler I had come to watch and bet in his debut, the colt we left in a tangle three steps out of the starting gate.

A few inches more to the left, a few more pounds of pressure, and we might never have heard about Secretariat. My notebooks are full of horses whose careers were terminated by less severe blows. But somehow this greenhorn kept his balance and settled slowly into stride far back of his field in the run down the backstretch.

On the turn I could see all the horses clearly at once, but the image I remember is that of the reddish brown colt going by three horses so fast it made me blink. Twice he changed gears to avoid further trouble. Twice more Feliciano choked him down to avoid running up on the heels of a tandem of horses that looked cloddish by comparison.

At the top of the stretch he moved again, into a higher gear, angling sharply to the inside, looking for room, shifting leads to gain better traction, losing precious time in the bargain. "A freak," I said to myself, but I had barely completed the thought when the red colt exploded in midstretch with a force that jiggled my binoculars right out of focus. He finished fourth, beaten by one and a half lengths. But it was the most electric exhibition of acceleration power I had seen since the mighty Kelso exploded seventy yards from the wire to gobble up Malicious in a stakes race eight years earlier.

It was only the beginning, only the tip of the iceberg; but being there, watching the race, knowing WHAT I was watching was a thrill—the kind of thrill that reaches the mind bringing awareness and awe.

Maybe your aim is to become a successful handicapper. Or perhaps you are reading this book just to improve your understanding of horseracing, putting it on a par with your comprehension of other hobbies and sports. In either case, the quickest, straightest line to the goal begins with the race itself and how to watch it. Unfortunately, all too many racing fans, it seems to me, do not know how to do that.

There are three simultaneous disciplines involved.

For one thing, you must see as much of the race as possible—the development of it, the flow of it, and the battle to the wire down the stretch. For another, your mind controls a switch for a focusing device like the zoom lens of a camera. You must train your mind to operate that switch—to zoom in and zoom out—the moment anything unusual hits the retina.

Combining these two disciplines into a smooth two-gear transmission takes practice. You will have to learn when to switch away from the action in the front of the pack or away from the horse your money is riding on.

There are different ways to facilitate the learning process; but because the inclination of most horseplayers is to watch their bet, I suggest starting with that.

When the field hits the turn, when your grandstand vantage point makes it easy to see the entire field, without moving your binoculars, pull back on the zoom lens in your mind and see if you can spot the fastest-moving horses, the horses in trouble, the horses on the rail, the horses stuck on the outside.

Don't be concerned if you are not able to identify more than a couple of horses at once. Later you can use the videotape replays and result charts to put it all together.

In my judgment, the turn is the most important part of the race. It is the place where the majority of races are won and lost, the place where jockeys show their greatest skill and commit the most atrocious errors, the place where the fan can glean the most knowledge for the future.

Horses get into the most trouble on the turn. Centrifugal force pulls them naturally to the outside, and the ones that are weakly ridden, out of shape, or hurting are unable to hold their line as they turn the corner into the stretch.

Sometimes the player will see a horse who was by far the best, but was simply unable to get free of traffic. Sometimes a good or bad effort can be explained by the way the rider uses (or doesn't use) his whip.

On the turn, every well-meant horse in the race should be making its move or else trying to hold its position. On the turn, a jockey in the race may show if he is afraid to go inside, or if he has a particular strength or weakness.

Does the horse only do its best when it's given lots of running room? Does the jockey do his best only when he's aboard a front-running type? Is the horse in the clear, or suspiciously placed behind a wall of horses?

These observations will help the player in his quest for solid insights. They will provide meaningful clues to compare contenders. But even more important, as described later in greater detail, the action on the turn often reveals the true nature of the racetrack as it tends itself to influence the ultimate result.

There is no need for me to describe any further steps in the process of learning how to watch a race properly. If you master the turn, your ability to focus and shift focus to significant happenings will be firmly established. You will be able to use that skill anytime—at the start or in the stretch—at any stage of the race. After some practice you will even find yourself doing it automatically. Believe me, no other racetrack skill will ever be more useful.

The third discipline you need to master while watching races has nothing to do with the function of sight. And in all sincerity it is what the rest of this book is about. It is the discipline that all your racetrack judgments are based on—the discipline of enlightened insight.

Watching a race properly is only one of the ways you can acquire greater knowledge about particular horses. But to make maximum use of the skill, to put yourself in a position to recognize the unusual, important things that take place, you must first have some clear ideas about the limits of Thoroughbred performance, some understanding of the relative importance of track condition, trainers, class, and all the other pieces that make up the racetrack puzzle.

As I hinted in the introduction, most of the better players in the game have acquired that kind of knowledge only after many years of struggle. For some the effort was roughly equivalent to the pursuit of a college-level education. My own education was a case in point. And I mean that literally.

2.
A B.A. in Handicapping

The first race in my life took place at Aqueduct on April 18, 1960. I was an eighteen-year-old freshman at Rutgers University and I needed $100 to make it to Fort Lauderdale for spring recess. But I only had $42.

A few of my friends paid for the bus ticket, pushed me through the turnstiles, and armed me with a program and Jack's Little Green Card (a tout sheet). I bet $5 to show on Jack's best bet of the day—Happy Lion in the first race—but when I realized that wouldn't get me past the Delaware Memorial Bridge, I went back and bet a wheel in the daily double. Twice.

Of course, when Happy Lion sent me and my crazy friends barreling down the pike to a week of girl chasing in the Florida sun, I thought I had found the secret to a rich and easy life. Naturally, I became a devout believer in Jack's Little Green Card.

But the romance didn't last very long. Every time I skipped classes to go out to the track, Jack's Card would surely have three or four winners listed; but who could figure which of the three choices per race would turn out to be the right choice. It was my misfortune that the winner was rarely the top choice.

So I switched cards; bet the secret code selections of Ken Kling in the New York *Daily Mirror;* made a system founded on *Racing Form* consensus picks; bet repeaters; bet the top speed rating; followed the "horses to watch" list in *Turf and Sport Digest;* bought an assortment of systems and other gadgets at $5, $10, and $20 a pop; and then began to bet with a bookie.

At minus $1,200, it didn't take much of a handicapper to predict where I was headed; but the final straw was a last-place finish by my old friend Happy Lion. The irony of it all did not escape me.

My father, bless his heart, picked up the tab with the New Brunswick bookie and made me promise never to bet another horserace again. It was a promise I wasn't sure I wanted to keep, but I knew there wasn't much future in going out to the track just to lose. I was determined to find out if, in fact, it was possible to win.

For the next six months I stayed away from the track and bought, borrowed, and read everything I could find about the inner workings of the sport.

The history of it was fascinating enough: the stuff about Man O' War and Citation, Arcaro and Shoemaker. But I was appalled at the lack of good material in the field of handicapping. So much of it was so badly written, so illogical, so poorly documented that I became discouraged and abandoned the project. I was convinced that racing was nothing more than a game of roulette on horseback, a sucker's game of pure chance, and I might very well have held that view forever. An assignment my statistics professor handed out a few weeks later changed my mind. "Analyze the winning tendencies of post positions at Monmouth Park," he said. And the irony of *that* did not escape me either.

The task, simple enough, revealed very little useful information the first time through. But when I introduced track condition and distance into the equation, there were powerful indicators that suggested the need for more intensive research. My statistics professor—no fool, to be sure—probably took the hint and spent the rest of the summer buried in his *Racing Form*.

He wasn't the only one.

I looked up horses', trainers', and jockeys' records. I studied result charts and workouts diligently and kept a file on all the best horses and stakes races on the East Coast. I made endless comparisons and was not surprised when some patterns began to emerge, patterns that were never mentioned by the so-called experts who were publishing and selling their empty-headed systems and books to a starved racing public.

I discovered that each type of race had its own set of key clues, its own major factors. I discovered that some trainers were consistently more successful than others and that most successful trainers were specialists who tended to repeat winning strategies. These strategies, I found, were frequently revealed in the past performance records of the horses they trained. By comparing these horses—comparing the dates between races, the workout lines, the distance and class manipulations—I began to gain some important insights into the conditioning process. The effort also cost me a failing grade in German 201, and I damn near flunked out of school. But it was worth it. I had begun to realize that there was a logic to the sport, and I suspected that I would be able to put all this time and effort to good use in the not-too-distant future. And I didn't have to wait very long to test out my thesis.

In late spring 1961 I spotted a horse named Nasomo in the past performance charts for Gulfstream Park. The half-mile workout from the starting gate attached to the bottom of his chart (.47bg) leaped off the page at me.

Nasomo hadn't shown such gate speed in any of his prior workouts, a deficiency he was content to carry over into his races. By habit he was a slow-breaking, Silky Sullivan-type whose late burst of speed had earned him absolutely nothing in eight tries. But my research into workout patterns had already convinced me that such a dramatic change in behavior on the training track invariably meant a vastly improved effort in competition. Barring bad racing luck—which is something that frequently plagues slow-breaking types—I was sure Nasomo would run the race of his life.

At 28–1 Nasomo turned in a spectacular performance, a nose defeat by the stakes prospect Jay Fox. Although that didn't score too many points with Nasomo's betting friends at the track, it was the first time I had ever felt confident about the performance of a horse before a race, the first time I began to think seriously about racing as a career.

Several weeks and several silent winning picks later, I broke my maiden on a horse called Flying Mercury. He was a retread sprinter that had once met top-class stock, but few people in the stands were able to appreciate his virtues (six outstanding workouts stretching back over a four-week period, all but one missing from the past performance records). Flying Mercury paid $78 to win, and I bought back my promise to my father with the proceeds of a $40 wager.

For the next two years I continued my studies into the mysteries of handicapping, keeping my losses to a minimum and my bets in perspective. But the Rutgers Dean of Men was not very pleased about my ragged classroom attendance, and he gave me a year off from school in September 1962, at the beginning of my senior year. In the true sense of the cliché, it turned out to be a blessing in disguise.

I visited racetracks in West Virginia, Louisiana, Ohio, Florida, New England, Michigan, Arkansas, Illinois, Maryland, California, New York, and New Jersey. Through those varied exposures and continued research, I detected two basic racetrack realities that seemed fundamental to handicapping. Yet I was sure that too few people in the stands were giving either of them the thought they deserved.

In the first place, I was surprised to learn that at many racetracks there was no way to measure the true class of horses by the claiming prices or race labels.

At most minor tracks, for example, a careful reading of result charts and race eligibility conditions suggested that there were five, six, or even seven separate class levels lumped into each claiming price. Moving up in company within a particular claiming price was frequently more difficult than ascending to the next claiming level.

At the major one-mile racetracks I frequently observed variations of this phenomenon in lower-level claiming events, maiden races, and nonclaiming (allowance) races. Very often these observations pointed out winners that were not otherwise discernible.

Secondly, because each racing surface—man-made and considerably different—had specific peculiarities, some race results were predetermined, or at least heavily influenced, by those characteristics.

In sprints at Monmouth Park, for example, post positions were of no consequence on fast-track racing days, but following any rain the track did not (and still does not) dry out evenly.

On days like that the rail was so deep and tiring that posts one, two, and three were at a terrible disadvantage. Stretch runners breaking from the outer post positions won everything. (At the Fair Grounds in New Orleans, where water can be found less than ten feet below the surface, the drainage system created precisely the opposite effect.)

Indeed, at every racetrack on my itinerary I noticed an influential track bias at work at one or more distances. And at some tracks a particular bias was so strong and so predictable that all handicapping questions had to be directed toward finding out which horse would be helped, hurt, or eliminated by the peculiarities of the running surface.

Of course, most handicappers seemed well aware of the difference between sloppy, fast, and other moisture-related track conditions, and a few even knew that Aqueduct in July favored speedy, front-running types while Belmont in September seemed to be deeper, slower, and kinder to stretch runners; but my observations about track bias suggested a stronger relationship between the track and actual horse performance. What I discovered was a relationship that sometimes eliminated the best horse in the race from contention, or else helped to promote an otherwise modestly qualified contender into a logical race winner.

By thinking first in these terms, before trying to compare the relative talents of the horses in a specific race, I found myself consistently able to recognize solid horses at every racetrack, horses that frequently went to post at generous odds. *It was also possible to interpret results and past performance lines more accurately when these horses ran back at a later date.*

With the first consistent profits of my handicapping career, I returned to Rutgers full of confidence.

On May 24, 1964, I finally did graduate from Rutgers, with a B.A. in psychology; but in truth it was only through the grace of my music professor, who raised my cumulative average to the passing level by changing a C to a B on the final day. Three weeks earlier the two of us accidentally met at Garden State Park, and he had a $280 reason to remember the event.

"I'm not doing this as a reward for your touting services," Professor Broome said while making the change of grade, "but I think you deserve some academic credit for your racing studies and this is the best I can do."

It was just enough.

3.
The Horseplayer's Bible

In the early morning hours at racetracks coast to coast, from January to December, thousands of horses of varying abilities are out on the training track. In the afternoons and evenings thousands more compete in races for fillies, colts, sprinters, routers, maidens, claimers, allowances, and stakes. Some races are on the grass course, some on the dirt. Some tracks are fast; some are sloppy, muddy, or something in between. The possibilities are endless, the data voluminous. And at $1.75 per copy, most of it is all there in the *Daily Racing Form* in black and white.

Frankly, I have always wished that the *Daily Racing Form* would sharpen its editorial policy to include more investigative reporting and more constructive commentary on issues affecting the everyday racing fan. But for hard racing news, statistics, and daily track poop, the *Daily Racing Form* is unequivocally the best publication of its kind in the world. (And it has improved noticeably since it began to supplement its comprehensive past performance profiles with grass-racing records and lifetime earnings.) Simply put, the *DRF* is an indispensable source of information for the horseman and the horseplayer. Properly used, it is more valuable than all the rest of racing literature put together.

Royal Roberto — **Dk. b. or br. c. 3, by Roberto—Princess Roycraft, by Royal Note**

Own.—Key West Stable — **126** — **Br.—Key West Stable (NY)** — **Tr.—Iselin James H**

1982	**9**	**2**	**2**	**1**	**$84,885**
1981	**2**	**2**	**0**	**0**	**$18,600**
Turf	**1**	**1**	**0**	**0**	**$7,800**

Lifetime 11 4 2 1 $103,485

28May82-7Bel	7f	:22^{1}	:45	1:22^{3}ft	*1	113	6^{14}	6^{11}	1$^{\frac{1}{2}}$	1$^{3\frac{3}{4}}$	Cordero A Jr^{5}	Aw23000	89	Royal Roberto, Keiran, Will OfIron	8
1May82-8CD	1¼	:46^{1}	1:37^{1}	2:02^{2}ft	9¼	126	18^{16}	17^{17}	14$^{7\frac{1}{4}}$	14^{14}	Rivera M A^{5}	Ky Derby	71	GatoDelSol,LaserLight,Reinvested	19
24Apr82-8CD	1	:45	1:09^{3}	1:36^{1}ft	3¼	112	8^{13}	5$^{8\frac{1}{2}}$	4$^{4\frac{1}{2}}$	3$^{1\frac{1}{2}}$	RiverMA^{9}	Derby Trial	86	Listcapade,StarGllnt,RoylRoberto	10
15Apr82-7Kee	7f	:22^{2}	:45^{1}	1:22^{4}ft	8¾	120	9$^{9\frac{3}{4}}$	8$^{9\frac{1}{2}}$	3$^{2\frac{1}{2}}$	2$^{\frac{1}{2}}$	Rivera M A^{7}	Aw30200	91	Linkage, Royal Roberto, CenterCut	9
3Apr82-9GP	1⅛	:47^{1}	1:11^{1}	1:49^{3}ft	11	122	6^{13}	6^{12}	4^{7}	4^{11}	Samyn J L^{4}	Fla Derby	73	TimelyWriter,StarGallnt,OurEscpde	7
6Mar82-10Hia	1⅛	:46^{2}	1:10^{4}	1:49^{3}sy	4¼	122	15^{12}	12^{11}	7^{7}	6$^{5\frac{3}{4}}$	Samyn J L^{16}	Flamingo	78	TimelyWriter,NewDiscovry,LDnsur	16
13Feb82-10Hia	1⅛	:46^{1}	1:10^{2}	1:48^{4}ft	4½	114	6^{13}	5$^{9\frac{1}{2}}$	3^{nk}	1$^{1\frac{1}{2}}$	Fell J^{7}	Everglades	88	RoylRobrto,NwDiscovry,VictorinLn	8
5Feb82-8Hia	1$\frac{1}{16}$	:48	1:12^{1}	1:44 ft	*1	116	8$^{5\frac{1}{4}}$	6^{7}	3$^{4\frac{1}{2}}$	2$^{1\frac{1}{4}}$	Fell J^{3}	Aw15000	82	Bold'nCold,RoyalRoberto,OurBoss	10
12Jan82-8Hia	7f	:23	:45^{3}	1:23^{4}ft	4½	116	11^{13}	8^{17}	7^{6}	4$^{1\frac{3}{4}}$	Fell J^{11}	Aw14000	82	ShootngDuck,H'sAnAngl,ShrpFutr	12
14Nov81-5Med	170 Ⓣ	:48^{1}	1:13	1:42^{1}gd	*8-5	117	8^{10}	6^{8}	4^{3}	1no	Perret C^{8}	Aw13000	79	RoylRoberto,RedBrigde,JsonThRcr	8
15Oct81-4Aqu	6f	:23	:46^{4}	1:12^{3}ft	4	118	10$^{6\frac{1}{4}}$	7$^{3\frac{3}{4}}$	5$^{1\frac{1}{4}}$	1$^{1\frac{1}{4}}$	Fell J^{12}	ⓈMdn	78	RoylRoberto,CtchMe,QuitOldFrind	12

●May 18 Mth 6f ft 1:13^{2} h   May 14 Mth 3f ft :39 b   ●Apr 9 GP Ⓣ 5f fm 1:01^{2} h (d)

Most racegoers have no trouble recognizing the importance of past performance profiles. The p.p. shown above is a season's worth of racing history at a glance. The date, distance, track, and track condition for every start; the fractional times of the leader and finishing time of the race winner; the odds, the weight, the running line, the beaten lengths, and finishing position; the jockey, post position, class of race, speed rating, top three finishers, and size of field. An incredible amount of information. But it is not enough. Indeed, it is not even the complete picture provided by other sources of information published in the very same newspaper. The result chart is far more comprehensive, far more valuable.

While every race is being run in North America, a sharp-eyed *DRF* employee known as the "Trackman" gives a horse-by-horse call of the fast-paced action on the track to an attentive assistant. Presto, the result chart is born. Flash, it's over the wires to Hightstown, New Jersey; Los Angeles, California; Chicago, Illinois; and other cities where editions of the *Form* are put together.

At the chart desk at *DRF* offices each horse's running line is extracted from the chart and then added to its past performance profile.

What many fans do not realize about this process hurts them every time they go out to the track.

Because of space limitations much important information is lost in the transmission from chart to profile. And even more of that information is lost if the profile is scheduled for publication in the *Form*'s tabloid-size Western editions. But whichever edition we consider (in this book all past performance examples are taken from the smaller Western editions), there is no reason any of this information should be lost to the player.

Saving a set of chronologically dated result charts for the track(s) in your area is all that's required to fill in the spaces. While each edition of the *Form* publishes complete result charts for all tracks covered by the past performances, the cost-conscious, once-a-week horseplayer can still keep pace with doings at his favorite track through the condensed charts appearing in the sport section of a good local newspaper. Moreover, by not paying some attention to these charts, you will forfeit your best chance to advance your game.

Foolish Pleasure **126** B. c (1972), by What a Pleasure—Fool-Me-Not, by Tom Fool.
Breeder, Waldemar Farm Inc. (Fla.).

Owner, J. L. Greer. Trainer, L. Jolley.

1976	6	3	0	1	$127,260
1975	11	5	4	1	$716,278

5Jly76	8Aqu		1 3/16	:4741:1121:552ft	2¾	125	11½	11½	11	1no	MapleE4	HcpS	85	FoolishPleasure125		Forego	4
20Jun76	8Hol		1¼	:4541:10 1:584ft	9-5	126	69½	74¼	76	56½	PincyLJr1	HcpS	90	PayTribute117		Avatar	8
6Jun76	8Hol		1⅛	:4621:1021:471ft	2-3	▲128	33	42½	42	33¾	PincyLJr2	HcpS	92	Riot inParis122		PayTribute	5
27Mar76	9GP	Ⓣ	1 1/16	:4641:0941:401fm	3-5	▲129	21½	22	32½	84¼	BaezaB3	HcpS	99	StepForward117		LordHenham	9
6Mar76	9GP		7 f	:22 :4431:212ft	1-3	▲129	43	63¾	1½	13½	BaezaB2	HcpS	97	FoolishPleasre129		PackrCaptn	10
4Feb76	7Hia		7 f	:23 :4541:222ft	1-3	▲119	42¼	43	1h	17	BaezaB4	Alw	93	FoolshPleasure119		Dashboard	7
10Oct75	8Bel		1 1/16	:4641:11 1:413ft	1-5	▲120	21½	11½	1h	2no	CordroAJr6	Alw	94	Stonewalk126		FoolishPleasure	6
13Sep75	8Bel		1¼	:4721:1042:00 ft	2¾	121	54	66½	66	510	CrdroAJr4	InvH	89	Wajima119		Forego	7

July 22 Bel 4f ft :46⅖h July 19 Bel 7f ft 1:26⅗b July 15 Bel 4f ft :46b

When Foolish Pleasure invaded the West Coast in late spring 1976, he was probably unaware of his unpopularity with the top stock at Hollywood Park. Maybe they remembered the way Avatar and Diabolo were "bounced" right out of contention during the stretch run of the 1975 Kentucky Derby. Maybe they wanted to chase Leroy Jolley and his horse back East on the next plane. In any case, Foolish Pleasure's first race at Hollywood Park, on June 6, was much like his second race at Hollywood, on June 20. I think the chart and the Trackman's comments for the latter race tell the story quite graphically.

Bettors at Aqueduct on July 5, 1976, probably needed no

EIGHTH RACE
Hollywood
JUNE 20, 1976

1 ¼ MILES. (1.58⅕) HOLLYWOOD GOLD CUP. Purse $250,000 Guaranteed. A handicap for 3-year-olds and upward. By subscription of $150 each, to accompany the nomination, $750 to pass the entry box and $2,000 additional to start, with $150,000 guaranteed to the winner, $40,000 to second, $30,000 to third, $20,000 to fourth, and $10,000 to fifth. Weights, Sunday, June 13. Starters to be named through the entry box by closing time of entries. A Gold Cup of original design will be presented to the owner of the winner. Trophies will be presented to the winning trainer and jockey. Closed Wednesday, June 9, 1976, with 21 nominations.
Value of race $250,000, value to winner $150,000, second $40,000, third $30,000, fourth $20,000, fifth $10,000. Mutuel pool $372,617. Exacta Pool $285,230.

Last Raced	Horse	Eqt.	A.	Wt	PP	¼	½	¾	1	Str	Fin	Jockey	Odds $1
6Jun76 8Hol2	Pay Tribute		4	117	7	31½	31	3½	31	11½	13¼	Castaneda M	13.90
12Jun76 6Hol1	Avatar	b	4	123	8	52	51	6hd	61½	2½	22	McHargue D G	7.50
6Jun76 8Hol1	Riot in Paris	b	5	123	3	4hd	41	41	41	52	3¾	Toro F	a-2.40
31May76 8Hol1	Dahlia		6	121	4	21	22½	21	2½	41	4½	Shoemaker W	a-2.40
6Jun76 8Hol3	Foolish Pleasure		4	126	1	72½	6hd	71½	73	74	52¾	Pincay L Jr	1.80
23May76 8Hol1	Ancient Title	b	6	127	5	61	73½	5½	5hd	61	6no	Hawley S	1.70
29May76 6Hol1	Our Talisman	b	4	115	6	12	14	11	1hd	3hd	73½	Olivares F	a-2.40
31May76 8Hol6	Top Command		5	116	2	8	8	8	8	8	8	Mena F	a-2.40

a-Coupled: Riot in Paris, Dahlia, Our Talisman and Top Command.
OFF AT 5:53 PDT Start good, Won ridden out. Time, :23⅕, :45⅘, 1:10, 1:34⅗, 1:58⅘ Track fast.

$2 Mutuel Prices:	4–PAY TRIBUTE	29.80	9.40	3.40
	5–AVATAR		9.00	3.60
	1–RIOT IN PARIS (a–entry)			2.40

$5 EXACTA 4–5 PAID $360.00.

Ch. c, by High Tribute—Drummer Girl, by Tompion. Trainer McAnally Ronald. Bred by Elmendorf Farm (Ky).

PAY TRIBUTE taken in hand after a clean break dropped behind the early leaders went up gradually into the far turn, attended the pace to the three sixteenths pole, drew out and into a clear lead under coaxing then stretched his margin in the last sixteenth under a hand ride. AVATAR raced unhurried early, moved nearer leaving the far turn, entered the stretch from between horses in the middle of the track to rally and prompted the winner then lost his full punch. RIOT IN PARIS saving ground raced close enought to the three furlong pole, remained inside pointing for a hole approaching the furlong pole but had to take up when blocked, steered out and around but could not regain his full momentum. DAHLIA broke alertly to be closest the early lead, rallied on the far turn to share the lead to the upper stretch and faded. <u>FOOLISH PLEASURE placed on the rail while being outrun early, checked when blocked into the far turn, remaned without room passing the quarter pole, swung wide for a clear path then could not make up the needed ground.</u> ANCIENT TITLE showed little early speed and came out from the quarter pole while perhaps in light contact with AVATAR and lacked a late rally. OUR TALISMAN set the pace and faltered. TOP COMMAND was always outrun.

Owners— 1, Elmendorf; 2, Seeligson A A Jr; 3, Bradley & Whittingham; 4, Hunt N B; 5, Greer John L; 6, Kirkland Ethel Estate Of; 7, Murty Farm & Schwartzman (Lessees); 8, Martin Mr-Mrs Q & Murty Farm.

Trainers— 1, McAnally Ronald; 2, Doyle A T; 3, Whittingham Charles; 4, Whittingham Charles; 5, Jolley Leroy; 6, Stucki Keith L; 7, Rettele Loren; 8, Whittingham Charles. ¹

Scratched—Mateor (23May76 7Hol10).

---

introduction to Foolish Pleasure. When you win a Derby and $1 million in two racing seasons it's hard not to make an impression. But only chart savers at Aqueduct would have known that Foolish Pleasure's two California races were not as bad as they appeared in the past performances. The Hollywood Gold Cup chart, along with many of the nation's most important stakes race result charts, appears regularly in all editions of the *Daily Racing Form*. I strongly recommend saving these charts too. You will pick winners from them. In the modern age of Thoroughbred racing a trainer will not hesitate to ship a good horse 3,000 miles and back again for a weekend shot at a stakes-class purse.

Fine-line decisions are intrinsic to the handicapping process, and result charts invariably present more clues to the right side of the line than the "p.p.'s." Sometimes these additional clues provide an insight or an excuse for a recent defeat, or force a reappraisal of a horse's physical condition. And sometimes they point out an extra dimension of quality not otherwise detectable from the past performances. The following two race result charts speak volumes to the point I am making. The first is one of my personal favorites. The salient points are underlined.

SIXTH RACE
Garden State
NOVEMBER 9, 1972

1 1/16 MILES. (1.41) ALLOWANCE. Purse $6,000. 3-year-olds and upward which have not wontwo races of $5,200 at a mile or over since June 15. 3-year-olds, 119 lbs. Older 122 lbs. Non-winners of three races of $4,225 at a mile or over since May 15 allowed 3 lbs. such a race of $3,900 since then, 5 lbs. such a race of $4,225 since April 15, 7 lbs. (Maiden, claiming and starter races not considered). (Originally carded to be run at 1 1/16 Miles, Turf.)

Value of race $6,000, value to winner $3,600, second $1,200, third $660, fourth $360, fifth $180. Mutuel pool $114,235.

Last Raced	Horse	Eqt.A.Wt	PP	St	¼	½	¾	Str	Fin	Jockey	Odds $1
23Oct72 ^{8}GS^{5}	Laplander	b 5 119	5	5	6	5^{hd}	5^{6}	4^{4}	$1^{3\frac{1}{2}}$	Barrera C	2.70
21Oct72 ^{9}CT^{5}	Test Run	6 119	3	1	2^{2}	2^{3}	4^{hd}	2^{hd}	$2\frac{1}{2}$	Keene J	20.50
21Oct72 ^{8}Lrl^{2}	Seminole Joe	4 119	4	3	$3^{1\frac{1}{2}}$	4^{5}	$1\frac{1}{2}$	$1\frac{1}{2}$	3^{1}	Iannelli F	7.30
21Oct72 ^{6}Lrl^{1}	Duc by Right	b 5 119	2	2	1^{2}	1^{2}	$2\frac{1}{2}$	3^{hd}	$4\frac{1}{2}$	Moseley J W	4.40
27Oct72 ^{8}GS^{6}	Warino	b 4 119	7	4	4^{2}	$3\frac{1}{2}$	$3^{1\frac{1}{2}}$	5^{6}	5^{5}	Hole M	3.30
27Sep72 ^{8}Atl^{6}	Roundhouse	b 4 119	1	6	5^{2}	6	6	6	6	Tejeira J	16.70
23Oct72 ^{5}Aqu^{3}	Prince of Truth	b 4 122	6	7	—	—	—	—	—	Blum W	2.20

Prince of Truth, Lost rider.

Time, :23⅘, :47⅕, 1:12⅘, 1:39⅕, 1:45⅘ Track slow.

$2 Mutuel Prices:			
5-LAPLANDER	7.40	4.20	2.80
3-TEST RUN		11.00	4.60
4-SEMINOLE JOE			4.20

B. g, by Assemblyman—Reindeer, by Polynesian. Trainer Kulina J. Bred by Fowler A (Md).
IN GATE AT 2:55; OFF AT 2:55 EASTERN STANDARD TIME Start Good For All But PRINCE OF TRUTH Won Driving

LAPLANDER, forced to steady and steer wide to avoid a loose horse inside of him entering the clubhouse turn, fell back, recovered gradually nearing the end of the backstretch, circled rivals rallying into the stretch, again steadied and moved inside to miss the loose horse, gained command leaving the furlong grounds and gradually drew clear. TEST RUN pressed the early pace, reached close contention from the inside in upper stretch was in tight a furlong out and faltered. SEMINOLE JOE was forced to check lightly by the loose horse entering the clubhouse turn, recovered quickly, reached the lead from the outside nearing the stretch, came in when intimidated by the loose horse a furlong out, was straightened away and faltered. DUC BY RIGHT went to the front at once, drew clear and was tiring when placed in close quarters between horses by SEMINOLE JOE in the drive. A claim of foul lodged by the rider of DUC BY RIGHT against the rider of SEMINOLE JOE was not allowed. WARINO was forced wide into the first turn, was taken in hand, rallied to reach close contention from the outside entering the stretch and tired. ROUNDHOUSE was never a factor. PRINCE OF TRUTH stumbled and unseated his rider at the start, raced with his field and caused repeated interference.

Owners— 1, Buckingham Farm; 2, Oliver & Stanley; 3, Sugar Mill Farm; 4, Haffner Mrs H Y; 5, Nesbitt H J; 6, Brandywine Stable; 7, Tucker J R.
Trainers— 1, Kulina J; 2, Oliver D; 3, Stirling W Jr; 4, Wahler C; 5, Cocks W; 6, Raines V W; 7, Jennings L W.
Scratched—Best Go (18Sep72 ^{8}Atl^{6}); Vif (27Oct72 ^{8}GS^{8}).

On the day Laplander was playing tag with a riderless horse at Garden State Park, a claiming horse named Third Law was giving Maryland racing fans a first-class impersonation of O. J. Simpson.

Armed with the Trackman's notes about the winner in each of these two races, we should have no difficulty imagining that Laplander and Third Law were able to step up sharply in

FOURTH RACE
Laurel
NOVEMBER 9, 1972

7 FURLONGS. (1.22⅕) CLAIMING. Purse $7,150, of which $650 to breeder of winner. 3-year-olds, Registered Maryland-Breds. Weights, 122 lbs. Non-winners of two races since September 18, allowed 2 lbs. A race since then, 4 lbs. A race since September 11, 6 lbs. Claiming price $12,500; for each $1,000 to $10,500, 2 lbs. (Races where entered for $9,500 or less not considered.)

Value of race $7,150, value to winner $3,900, second $1,430, third $780, fourth $390; $650 to Breeder of Winner. Mutuel pool $87,225.

Last Raced	Horse	Eqt.	A.Wt	PP	St	¼	½	Str	Fin	Jockey	Cl'g Pr	Odds $1
20Oct72 ^{4}Lrl^6	Third Law		3 116	7	2	7^{hd}	7½	4½	1^1	Jimenez C	12500	40.60
29Sep72 ^{8}Bel^6	Admiral Kelly	b	3 118	1	8	2½	1^{hd}	2^2	2½	Turcotte R L	12500	4.10
24Oct72 ^{5}Lrl^1	All Above		3 119	3	1	1^{hd}	$2^{1\frac{1}{2}}$	1^{hd}	3^{hd}	Feliciano B M	12500	1.40
24Oct72 ^{5}Lrl^7	Rigel	b	3 116	4	6	5½	3½	3^{hd}	4¾	Passmore W J	12500	6.10
4Nov72 ^{4}Lrl^1	Gunner's Mate	b	3 113	8	3	6^4	6^2	6^3	5^1	Cusimano G	10500	4.90
24Oct72 ^{5}Lrl^8	Go Bet		3 116	2	4	3½	4^{hd}	5^{hd}	$6^{2\frac{1}{4}}$	Kurtz J	12500	22.70
2Nov72 ^{8}Lrl^5	Hoosier Grand		3 116	6	7	8	8	7^3	$7^{3\frac{1}{2}}$	Wright D R	12500	6.40
3Nov72 ^{5}Lrl^7	Sky Flight		3 116	5	5	4½	$5^{2\frac{1}{2}}$	8	8	Alberts B	11500	12.90

Time, :23⅗, :47, 1:13, 1:26 Track fast.

$2 Mutuel Prices:

7-THIRD LAW	83.20	20.60	5.80
1-ADMIRAL KELLY		5.80	3.60
3-ALL ABOVE			3.20

B. g, by Quadrangle—Flighty Jane, by Count Fleet. Trainer Green P F. Bred by Kelly Mrs L C (Md). IN GATE AT 2:28; OFF AT 2:28 EASTERN STANDARD TIME. Start Good. Won Driving.

THIRD LAW, away in good order but without early speed, had to check stoutly behind horses on the stretch turn, went to the rail entering the stretch, responded strongly when set down, had to pull sharply outside ADMIRAL KELLY for racing room a furlong out but continued strongly to gain command and draw clear in the final seventy yards. ADMIRAL KELLY, away a bit slowly, was hustled up to force the pace inside all above before a quarter, got the lead leaving the backstretch, lost and regained it inside all above in the stretch, then could not resist the winner's closing bid while tiring near the end. ALL ABOVE set or forced the pace outside ADMIRAL KELLY throughout but hung slightly near the end. RIGEL, always in contention, responded between horses in the final quarter but was not good enough. GUNNER'S MATE did not threaten with a mild closing response. GO BET gave an even effort. HOOSIER GRAND showed little. SKY FLIGHT had only brief early speed.

Owners— 1, Master's Cave; 2, Audley Farm Stable; 3, Lee C; 4, Leonard R A; 5, Green Lantern Stable; 6, DiNatale J; 7, Hunt R R; 8, Berry C T Jr.

Trainers— 1, Green P F; 2, Thomas G; 3, Lee C; 4, Hacker B P; 5, Delp G G; 6, Bannon J T; 7, Vogelman R E Jr; 8, Simpson J P.

Overweight: Gunner's Mate 1 pound.

company and win with ridiculous ease shortly thereafter. It is not stretching the point to say that a few equally revealing charts a season could more than pay for the cost of a subscription to the *Form*. Frankly, I could fill the rest of this book with four-star Trackman comments that pointed out horses who gave better showings than the past performance profiles revealed. But there are other important result chart clues that never find their way into the past performance profiles. Let's go out to Aqueduct racetrack for an everyday example.

Liederkranz

Own.—Swan T J Jr **124**

Ch. g. 4, by Vitriolic—Au Gratin, by Groton
Br.—Perco A (Fla)
Tr.—Skiffington Thomas **$15,000**

1982	3	M	1	0	$1,760
1981	0	M	0	0	

Lifetime 3 0 1 0 $1,760

~~26Mar82-4Aqu~~	~~1~~	~~:47^1 1:14^1 1:42^{1}ft~~	~~6¾~~	~~120~~	~~5^5~~	~~4^3~~	~~4^3~~	~~$6^{3\frac{3}{4}}$~~	~~Molina V H^1~~	~~M20000~~	~~51~~	~~Solidify, Beagle, Savage Gesture~~	~~14~~
11Mar82-2Aqu	6f	⊡:22^4 :46^{2}1:12^{2}ft	21	124	3^4	$3^{3\frac{1}{2}}$	$3^{2\frac{1}{2}}$	2^3	Molina V H^7	M20000	79	Kid'sNoBluffr,Lidrkrnz,CptnMrbls	13
1Mar82-3Aqu	1⅛	⊡:49^{3}1:14^{3}1:53^{2}ft	17	113^5	4^7	5^{11}	6^{14}	6^{23}	Avalon WAIII^5	M45000	56	HlfIced,CornishConqueror,AlvinJck	7

Apr 9 Bel tr.t 4f gd :48^4 h   Mar 20 Bel tr.t 5f ft 1:03 b   Mar 10 Bel tr.t 3f ft :38^3 b   Feb 28 Bel tr.t 3f ft :37 b

FOURTH RACE
Aqueduct
MARCH 26, 1982

1 MILE. (1.33⅘) MAIDEN CLAIMING. Purse $9,500. 3-year-olds and upward. Weight, 3-year-olds, 112 lbs. Older 124 lbs. Claiming price $25,000; for each $2,500 to $20,000 2 lbs.

Value of race $9,500, value to winner $5,700, second $2,090, third $1,140, fourth $570. Mutuel pool $129,807, OTB pool $129,209. Quinella Pool $179,188. OTB Quinella Pool $164,171.

Last Raced	Horse	Eqt.	A.	Wt	PP	St	¼	½	¾	Str	Fin	Jockey	Cl'g Pr	Odds $1
6Mar82 ^{1}Aqu^{10}	Solidify	b	5	115	3	7	3^3	$2^{1\frac{1}{2}}$	$1^{\frac{1}{2}}$	1^{hd}	$1^{1\frac{1}{4}}$	Buscemi S^5	20000	1.70
28Feb82 ^{4}Aqu^8	Beagle	b	4	124	14	1	$1^{\frac{1}{2}}$	1^2	2^2	$2^{1\frac{1}{2}}$	$2^{\frac{1}{2}}$	McCarron G	25000	12.50
2Mar82 ^{7}Aqu^{13}	Savage Gesture	b	3	105	13	3	$9^{\frac{1}{2}}$	9^4	$8^{\frac{1}{2}}$	6^5	3^{nk}	White J R^7	25000	56.30
17Mar82 ^{9}Aqu^5	Marquez		3	107	5	8	$7^{\frac{1}{2}}$	8^4	$3^{\frac{1}{2}}$	$3^{1\frac{1}{2}}$	$4^{1\frac{1}{4}}$	Gomez E R^5	25000	7.60
17Mar82 ^{9}Aqu^4	Damascinian		3	108	12	4	4^{hd}	$4^{\frac{1}{2}}$	5^5	$5^{1\frac{1}{2}}$	$5^{\frac{1}{2}}$	Montoya D	20000	12.80
11Mar82 ^{2}Aqu^2	Liederkranz		4	120	1	12	$6^{\frac{1}{2}}$	$5^{\frac{1}{2}}$	4^{hd}	$4^{\frac{1}{2}}$	6^1	Molina V H	20000	6.70
4Mar82 ^{9}Aqu^4	All Cash	b	3	108	2	14	14	14	14	$11^{\frac{1}{2}}$	$7^{\frac{3}{4}}$	Borden D A	20000	23.00
5Mar82 ^{6}Aqu^5	Eastern Music		3	112	7	11	$13^{\frac{1}{2}}$	13^1	13^2	10^{hd}	$8^{2\frac{3}{4}}$	Beitia E	25000	5.50
11Mar82 ^{6}Aqu^6	Bronze Metal	b	3	114	10	13	12^3	12^{hd}	12^{hd}	12^3	9^{hd}	Fell J	25000	f-12.80
17Mar82 ^{9}Aqu^{10}	Another Wonder		3	112	9	5	10^3	$11^{1\frac{1}{2}}$	11^2	8^{hd}	$10^{1\frac{1}{4}}$	Santiago A	25000	f-12.80
26Feb82 ^{6}Aqu^8	Pink Party	b	3	112	8	9	11^2	10^2	10^2	9^{hd}	11^2	Venezia M	25000	10.60
20Mar82 ^{1}Key^7	Alive at Five	b	3	112	6	10	8^2	7^{hd}	$6^{\frac{1}{2}}$	7^1	12^2	Santagata N	25000	43.60
14Mar82 ^{2}Aqu^9	Hey Kennedy	b	3	114	4	6	$2^{\frac{1}{2}}$	3^1	$9^{1\frac{1}{2}}$	13^2	13^4	Skinner K	25000	19.90
18Mar82 ^{2}Aqu^6	Zack Carr		4	122	11	2	$5^{1\frac{1}{2}}$	$6^{\frac{1}{2}}$	7^{hd}	14	14	MacBeth D	22500	19.50

f—Mutuel field.

OFF AT 2:35 Start good, Won driving. Time, :23⅖, :47⅕, 1:14⅕, 1:42⅕ Track fast.

$2 Mutuel Prices:			
3-(C)-SOLIDIFY	5.40	3.80	3.20
11-(O)-BEAGLE		9.40	7.00
10-(N)-SAVAGE GESTURE			20.40

$2 QUINELLA 3–11 PAID $45.00.

B. h, by Exclusive Native—Lost Control, by Never Bend. Trainer Hough Stanley M. Bred by Gilroy B W (Ky).

SOLIDIFY close up early while saving ground, came out to take over nearing the stretch and outfinished BEAGLE. The latter saved ground while showing speed to the stretch and held on well. SAVAGE GESTURE finished well while racing wide. MARQUEZ rallied from the outside leaving the turn, was lugging in when the rider got his whip hung up in the tail of SOLIDIFY momentarily approaching the final sixteenth and hung. DAMASCINIAN well placed to the stretch, was steadied slightly between horses near the final furlong and lacked a late response. A foul claim against MARQUEZ by the rider of DAMASCINIAN for alleged interference through the stretch but lacked a late response. ALL CASH broke slowly. EASTERN MUSIC was never close. HEY KENNEDY was finished soon after going a half. ZACK CARR tired badly.

Owners— 1, Harbor View Farm; 2, Murty Farm; 3, Rafsky J K; 4, Brodsky Elaine M; 5, Gannon W; 6, Swan T J Jr; 7, Bay View Stable; 8, Sheikh S M; 9, King J.D; 10, Baer R; 11, Malmstrom I W; 12, Martucci W; 13, Shapiro T; 14, Schwartz B K.

Overweight: Bronze Metal 2 pounds; Hey Kennedy 2.

Scratched—Nathan Detroit (22Oct81 ^{6}Aqu^{11}); Diplomat Darren (17Mar82 ^{9}Aqu^6); Deo Volante (8Mar82 ^{3}Aqu^5); Anjun-Sun (18Mar82 ^{2}Aqu^9).

If you give a careful reading to the chart and compare it with Liederkranz's March 20 running line, you will discover several missing facts:

1. Specific eligibility conditions for the race ($25,000–20,000 maiden claiming; weights: three-year-olds, 112 pounds, older, 124 pounds, and so on).
2. Fractional times for each quarter-mile split (p.p.'s show only two splits).
3. Position at the start of the race (missing from the p.p.'s).
4. Position at the first quarter-mile split (missing from the p.p.'s).
5. Blinkers or no blinkers (available in Eastern-edition p.p.'s).
6. Exact age, weight, odds, jockey, owner, running pattern, and finishing position for entire field (weight and margins of top three finishers available in Eastern-edition p.p.'s).
7. Index date, track, and race number of most recent start by each member of the field.
8. Purse value of the race (missing in maiden and claiming races, now available for allowance races in all editions).
9. Trackman's commentary on the way the race was run. (Abbreviated comment available in Eastern edition.)

NOTE: In result charts the margins at each call refer to the horse's margin in front of the *next* horse. In past performance profiles the margins indicate lengths behind the *leader*. Also in the Eastern *DRF* the class of race includes several designations not available in other editions. These designations include (S) for state bred or other restricted races and 3↑ which indicates that the race was carded for three-year-olds and older. A sample past performance profile taken from the Eastern edition is reproduced in the Appendix along with a guide to all the symbols found in *Daily Racing Form* past performances.

Ordinarily, trackman Jack Wilson includes a salient comment for each and every prominent horse in the race, be it a major stakes or a cheap maiden claimer. But for no apparent reason, no comment appears in the chart for Liederkranz, a colt who moved to within three lengths of the leader turning for home, despite getting off to a sluggish start from the inside post.

I should say that Jack Wilson is one of the very best chart callers in the country. He, along with Jay Woodward who used to work the California circuit, Dick Carroll who used to do the Midwest, and Bill Phillips who still writes a *Daily Racing Form* column from Florida, are the four most precise chart callers I have ever had the pleasure of reading. In fact, the only unreliable trackman I have ever read in the *DRF* has retired and died. May he rest in peace. As for result charts, we have just scratched the surface. With a little research and a few investigative tools, we can use this added information to obtain even more substantial clues, clues that can increase our understanding of the horse, the track, and the nature of the game itself.

4.
The Bias of
the Racing Surface

Suppose someone walked up to you and said he knew a roulette wheel in a Las Vegas casino that was rigged in the player's favor. The wheel paid the customary 32–1 odds for a correct number but seldom stopped on any number higher than 20. I am sure you would have trouble believing it.

With a few important variations, that is precisely what I am about to tell you about the majority of racetracks in America. *Some numbers rarely win.*

At Pimlico racecourse in Baltimore, Maryland, where the first turn is less than a stone's throw from the starting gate in 1$\frac{1}{16}$-mile races, horses with sprint speed and inside post positions have a ready-made shot at saving ground and a clear-cut winning edge. Conversely, horses forced to break from post positions nine, ten, eleven, or twelve in such races have to be far superior and perfectly ridden to remain in contention. And there are many racetracks in America with a bias like that. Aqueduct in New York (1$\frac{1}{8}$ miles on the main track, 1$\frac{1}{16}$ miles on the new inner dirt track) is a well-known example. But the Fair Grounds in New Orleans and Churchill Downs in Louisville are rarely considered in a similar light.

Most players approach two-turn races at these two racetracks with an eye toward the fast-closing distance-type runner. It's hard to think otherwise while the two longest stretch runs in American racing are in full view. (Each is over 1,300 feet.) But these are two extremely elongated racetracks, with radically sharp turns. And the starting gate is frequently positioned so close to the first bend that the race is over before the stretch comes into play. A player who knows that about the Fair Grounds and Churchill may not pick the winner of every two-turn race, but very often he will be able to plot the way a race is likely to be run. In addition, he will catch many well-meant speed types outrunning their apparent distance limitations.

And there are other kinds of biases worth knowing about. At Keystone racetrack in Pennsylvania, and at all other cold-weather tracks, extra layers of topsoil are frequently mixed with antifreeze agents to keep the racing surface from turning into a sheet of ice. The effort is usually successful, but not always; sometimes the rail is like a paved highway, and sometimes it's a slushy path to a quick and certain defeat.

No doubt it would be superfluous to spell out the impact such aberrant track conditions have on horse performance, so I won't. But I will say that a handicapper will probably think about throwing away his *Racing Form* if he doesn't take note of them. Indeed, if there is one pervasive influence on the handicapping experience, track bias comes very close to filling the bill. While it isn't fair to say that all races are won and lost because of the influence of a biased racing strip, the player can hardly hope to make consistently accurate predictions without weighing its significance. For instance, take Saratoga, the beautiful track in upstate New York that annually runs a twenty-four-day August meet.

A decade ago Saratoga had a soft racing surface that was biased in the extreme toward stretch runners and outer post positions. This may have contributed to a considerable extent to the track's reputation as a "graveyard for favorites." Confronted with a typical Saratoga race, most players were naturally impressed with recent winners shipping up from Aqueduct, a track that still tends to get pasteboard hard and front-running fast during July. At Saratoga very few of those horses were able to duplicate their prior good form; and race after race went to horses with the best late kick. In the 1960s observant horseplayers could eliminate a lot of short-priced, front-running horses at Saratoga; they can't do that anymore.

In 1974 a new, faster racing strip was installed, turning historic Saratoga into a front runner's paradise. Suddenly the game changed dramatically; the player had to respect Aqueduct form. The two tracks were nearly identical. Both favored fast-breaking types—horses able to get a clear trip on the faster rail path.

This tendency toward front runners is not unusual at many

American racetracks, especially where a thin track cushion is packed down further to speed up final times. And at Saratoga, the bias existed without a major variation for the balance of the decade.

But in 1982, with more racing dates inserted into the Saratoga racing schedule and the track in constant use for training purposes throughout the spring and summer, tons of new topsoil were added to the upper crust of the track, which created a racing rarity: a temporarily unbiased racing strip, a strip in transition.

Naturally, through added use, a brand-new track bias (or an old one) will surely assert itself in coming seasons as it has in prior cycles. And once again the player will have to take notice or be left shaking his head.

Track biases are crucial to the proper understanding of everyday racing. In fact it is virtually impossible to handicap races effectively without some knowledge of the particular bias at work. But at the same time, there is no rule of nature that commands a bias to remain the same from one season to the next.

When Calder racetrack (Florida) was going through its growing pains with the only artificial racing surface in American Thoroughbred racing, a horse capable of running half a mile on the lead in 46 seconds and change, which is not especially fast time at most racetracks, was a horse in fantastic shape. He couldn't win very many races at Calder—the track was powerfully tilted toward stretch-running speed—but when and if the stable was able to keep such a speedball fit enough to get a crack at Hialeah or Gulfstream Park, it was fat city.

Today the Calder-to-Gulfstream angle still works because Gulfstream has the kind of racing surface that speed horses dream about. At the same time, a fit front runner at Calder is no longer an automatic throwout. Times change, people change, and so do track biases.

Every racetrack has its peculiarities. Some are small in circumference, some have pasteboard-hard running surfaces, some card races that place a premium on early speed or post position. And nothing can help to change or create a bias as effectively as a shift in weather conditions. A sudden rainstorm on an otherwise normal racetrack is odds on to force a premium on early speed. On the other hand, a few days of rain, a sudden frost, or extreme heat can have totally unpredictable effects. It's wise to hold onto your money during such drastic changes in weather—unless, of course, you are able to see what is happening firsthand.

Out at the track, any racetrack, it is relatively easy to spot a track bias if you:

Watch the turns.
Observe the running patterns. Are horses able to make up ground going to the outside or is the rail the only place to be?
Watch the break from the gate. Are horses in certain post positions always a bit late getting into the hunt?
Watch the run to the first turn (especially in route races). Are horses able to settle into contending positions from outer post positions without undue effort?
And watch the top jockeys. Do they consistently steer their horses to one part of the track over another? (Frankly, I'm not at all sure I should mention jockeys in this context, because all but a handful seem unable to recognize a bias until they have lost a bunch of races because of it. Of course, there are exceptions; and if you happen to be at a track where Sandy Hawley, Jorge Velasquez, Angel Cordero Jr., Willie Passmore, Mike Venezia, or Alfredo Smith are riding, watch them. They will spot a favorable path on the racing strip in two or three runs of the course.)

If you are unable to attend races regularly or are planning an assault on a new track, the only way to spot a bias is through careful reading of the result charts. But even if your on-track observations have detected a bias—it's hard not to notice the presence of one when six races in a row are won wire to wire— you will need to refer to the charts to note those horses that were stuck on the outside, blocked, left at the gate, or handed the race on a silver platter.

A horse stuck on the rail on a dead rail day will have a ready-made excuse. A speed horse that cruised to a front-running victory because it drew into a favorable post may not be as good as it seems. By way of example I am including trackman Jack Wilson's comments and the charts for the first four main-track races run at Saratoga on August 21, 1976. If the player had reviewed charts from preceding days, the front-running accent would have been hard to miss. (During a rainy spell earlier in the meet, speed held up, but the inside was a bog.) On August 18, 19, and 20 the inside part of the racetrack was faster than the outside. The charts for August 21 indicate that the tendency toward inside speed was overpowering.

FIRST RACE
Sar
August 21, 1976

6 FURLONGS. (1:08). MAIDENS. CLAIMING. Purse $7,500. Fillies. 2-year-olds. Weight, 119 lbs. Claiming price, $20,000; 2 lbs. allowed for each $1,000 to $18,000.
Value to winner $4,500; second, $1,650; third, $900; fourth, $450. Mutuel Pool, $93,694.
Off-track betting, $82,077.

Last Raced	Horse	EqtAWt PP St	1/4	1/2	Str Fin	Jockeys	Owners	Odds to $1
13 Aug76 [1]Sar[3]	By by Chicken	b2 115 8 1	$1\frac{1}{2}$	2^3	1^h 1^h	JVelasquez	Harbor View Farm	1.70
13 Aug76 [1]Sar[9]	Sun Bank	b2 119 5 2	2^h	1^h	2^2 $22\frac{1}{4}$	MVenezia	B Rose	b-4.30
13 Aug76 [1]Sar[8]	Mean Katrine	b2 115 1 3	5^2	$5\frac{1}{4}$	4^2 $3\frac{3}{4}$	ASantiago	Robdarich Stable	7.50
	Peach Flambeau	2 117 4 5	4^h	$41\frac{1}{4}$	$3\frac{1}{2}$ $41\frac{3}{4}$	DMcHargue	J W LaCroix	a-7.40
	I Gogo	b2 112 6 9	6^h	$6\frac{1}{4}$	6^1 $52\frac{1}{2}$	KWhitley[7]	Brookfield Farm	18.50
13 Aug76 [9]Sar[6]	Good Party	2 115 3 4	3^2	$3\frac{1}{4}$	$5\frac{1}{4}$ 6no	EMaple	N A Martini	12.50
25 Jly 76 [2]Del[5]	Tootwright	b2 119 2 10	$7\frac{1}{4}$	7^3	7^4 7^5	PDay†	D Sturgill	3.00
	North Ribot	2 115 7 8	8^2	8^1	$8\frac{1}{2}$ 8^h	MPerrotta	Betty Rose	b-4.30
27 Jun76 [9]Bel[8]	Hot Dogger	b2 117 9 6	9^1	$9\frac{1}{2}$	$91\frac{1}{4}$ $9\frac{1}{2}$	TWallis	Judith McClung	21.20
13 Aug76 [9]Sar[4]	Behavingaise	b2 117 10 7	10	10	10 10	RTurcotte	J W LaCroix	a-7.40

†Seven pounds apprentice allowance waived.
b-Coupled, Sun Bank and North Ribot; a-Peach Flambeau and Behavingaise.
OFF AT 1:30 EDT. Start good. Won driving. Time, :22⅖, :46⅗, 1:12⅗. Track fast.

Official Program Numbers ↘

$2 Mutuel Prices:

7-BY BY CHICKEN	5.40	3.40	2.80
2-SUN BANK (b-Entry)		4.60	3.40
3-MEAN KATRINE			3.60

B. f, by The Pruner—Chicken Little, by Olympia. Trainer, Lazaro S. Barrera. Bred by Carl L. Broughton (Fla.).

BY BY CHICKEN saved ground while vying for the lead with SUN BANK and prevailed in a stiff drive. The latter raced outside BY BY CHICKEN while dueling for command and narrowly missed. MEAN KATRINE finished evenly while saving ground. PEACH FLAMBEAU rallied approaching midstretch but hung. I GOGO failed to seriously menace while racing wide. GOOD PARTY tired from her early efforts. TOOTWRIGHT, off slowly, failed to be a serious factor. NORTH RIBOT was always outrun. BEHAVINGAISE showed nothing.
Claiming Prices (in order finish)—$18000, 20000, 18000, 19000, 20000, 18000, 20000, 18000, 19000, 19000.
Scratched—Lots of Flair.

SECOND RACE Sar August 21, 1976 — 1⅛ MILES. (1:47). CLAIMING. Purse $8,500. 3-year-olds and upward. 3-year-olds, 117 lbs.; older, 122 lbs. Non-winners of a race at a mile and a furlong or over since Aug. 1 allowed 3 lbs.; of such a race since July 15, 5 lbs. Claiming price, $12,500; 2 lbs. allowed for each $1,000 to $10,500. (Races when entered to be claimed for $8,500 or less not considered.)

Value to winner $5,100; second, $1,870; third, $1,020; fourth, $510. Mutuel Pool, $131,999. Off-track betting, $95,870.

Last Raced	Horse	EqtAWt	PP	St	¼	½	¾	Str	Fin	Jockeys	Owners	Odds to $1
7 Aug76 ^{1}Sar^{6}	Tingle King	b4 114	1	3	2½	3^{4}	$1^{1½}$	1^{5}	1^{6}	RTurcotte	Vendome Stable	5.40
7 Aug76 ^{1}Sar^{4}	O'Rei	7 113	4	5	4^{h}	4^{h}	4^{4}	3^{3}	2^{4}	TWallis	Mrs L I Miller	3.40
13 Aug76 ^{3}Sar^{1}	Mycerinus	b5 122	8	7	7	7	6^{2}	4^{7}	3no	MVenezia	Audley Farm Stable	3.40
7 Aug76 ^{2}Sar^{7}	Good and Bold	5 117	5	2	3^{4}	2½	2^{3}	2½	$4^{9½}$	EMaple	S Sommer	4.00
18 Aug76 ^{7}Sar^{8}	Slaw	3 107	7	4	6^{2}	6½	7	5^{2}	5^{8}	RD'g'diceJr^{5}†	Betty Anne King	26.40
7 Aug76 ^{1}Sar^{9}	Gene's Legacy	b4 106	6	6	5^{1}	5^{6}	$5^{1½}$	6^{1}	$6^{6½}$	KWhitley^{7}	Beau-G Stable	10.40
13 Aug76 ^{3}Sar^{2}	Mister Breezy	4 113	3	1	$1^{1½}$	1½	$3^{1½}$	7	7	JCruguet‡	M M Garren	2.50

†Two pounds apprentice allowance waived. ‡Five pounds apprentice allowance waived.

OFF AT 2:05 EDT. Start good. Won handily. Time, :23⅗, :47, 1:11⅕, 1:36⅘, 1:50⅖. Track fast.

$2 Mutuel Prices:			
2-TINGLE KING	12.80	5.80	4.20
3-O'REI II.		5.20	4.00
7-MYCERINUS			3.40

B. c, by Bold Legend—Miss Tingle, by Avant Garde. Trainer, Flint S. Schulhofer. Bred by D. Shaer (Md.).

TINGLE KING raced forwardly into the backstretch, took over while saving ground into the far turn and drew away while being mildly encouraged. O'REI II., never far back, finished well to be second best without menacing the winner. MYCERINUS, void of early foot, passed tired horses. GOOD AND BOLD, a factor to the stretch, tired. MISTER BREEZY stopped badly after showing speed to the far turn.

Overweight—Tingle King, 1.

Claiming Prices (in order of finish)—$10500, 10500, 12500, 12500, 12500, 10500, 10500.

Scratched—Campaigner.

Daily Double (7-2) Paid $56.60; Double Pool, $303,256; OTB Pool, $515,166.

THIRD RACE Sar August 21, 1976 — 6 FURLONGS. (1:08). CLAIMING. Purse $9,000. 3-year-olds and upward. 3-year-olds, 117 lbs.; older, 122 lbs. Non-winners of two races since Aug. 1 allowed 3 lbs.; of a race since then, 5 lbs. Claiming price, $20,000; 2 lbs. allowed for each $1,000 to $18,000. (Races when entered to be claimed for $16,000 or less not considered.)
Value to winner $5,400; second, $1,980; third, $1,080; fourth, $540.
Mutuel Pool, $157.960. Off-track betting, $94,849. Exacta Pool, $158,817. Off-track betting Exacta Pool, $231,460.

Last Raced	Horse	EqtAWt	PP	St	¼	½	Str	Fin	Jockeys	Owners	Odds to $1
26 Apr76 ^{6}Aqu^{8}	Gabilan	4 117	7	2	1^{h}	1^{2}	1^{5}	1^{3}	EMaple	S Sommer	6.20
7 Aug76 ^{2}Sar^{2}	Rare Joel	b4 117	1	7	$7^{1½}$	7½	6½	2^{h}	JVelasquez	Elysa M Alibrandi	5.40
25 Jly 76 ^{3}Aqu^{5}	Snappy Chatter	b4 117	5	5	5^{h}	4^{1}	2½	3¾	JAmy	May-Don Stable	8.80
7 Aug76 ^{2}Sar^{1}	Commercial Pilot	b4 113	2	4	4½	5^{2}	3^{h}	$4^{1¾}$	DMcHargue	Lovir Stable	6.50
10 Jly 76 ^{2}Aqu^{6}	Odds and Evens	5 108	8	8	8	6^{h}	$7^{1½}$	5^{3}	RDelg'riceJr^{5}	Colvie Stable	17.10
7 Aug76 ^{4}Sar^{2}	Native Blend	b6 108	4	3	3^{3}	2^{1}	4^{1}	6^{3}	KWhitley^{7}	Hobeau Farm	1.60
23 Jun76 ^{7}Bel^{9}	Chaulky Long	b4 118	3	6	6^{5}	8	8	$7^{2½}$	BBaeza	A Rosoff	4.40
7 Aug76 ^{4}Sar^{4}	What A Lucky Star	b4 117	6	1	2½	3^{2}	5^{1}	8	PDay	J W LaCroix	14.90

OFF AT 2:45 EDT. Start good for all but ODDS AND EVENS. Won ridden out. Time, :21⅘, :44⅗, 1:09⅘. Track fast.

$2 Mutuel Prices:			
7-GABILAN	14.40	6.20	4.20
1-RARE JOEL		6.00	4.40
5-SNAPPY CHATTER			5.20

$2 EXACTA (7-1) PAID $89.60.

Dk. b. or br. c, by Penowa Rullah—Little Buzzy, by Royal Coinage. Trainer, Frank Martin. Bred by L. P. Sasso (Md.).

GABILAN sprinted clear approaching the stretch and, after opening a good lead, was ridden out to hold sway. RARE JOEL, void of early foot, finished full of run. SNAPPY CHATTER rallied from the outside entering the stretch, lugged in near the final furlong and continued on with good energy. COMMERCIAL PILOT split horses nearing midstretch but lacked the needed late response. ODDS AND EVENS broke in the air. NATIVE BLEND, a factor to the stretch, gave way. CHAULKY LONG was always outrun. WHAT A LUCKY STAR stopped badly after entering the stretch.

Overweight—Chaulky Long, 1.

Claiming Prices (in order of finish)—$20000, 20000, 20000, 18000, 18000, 19000, 20000, 20000.

FOURTH RACE **Sar** **August 21, 1976**

6 FURLONGS. (1:08). MAIDENS. SPECIAL WEIGHTS. Purse $9,000. Fillies and mares. 3-year-olds and upward. 3-year-olds, 117 lbs.; older, 122 lbs. Value to winner $5,400; second, $1,980; third, $1,080; fourth, $540. Mutuel Pool, $223,335.

Last Raced	Horse	EqtAWt	PP	St	¼	½	Str	Fin	Jockeys	Owners	Odds to $1
	Love for Love	3 117	2	4	2^{1}	2½	$2^{2½}$	1^{2}	PDay	Rokeby Stable	1.10
13 Aug76 ^{5}Sar^{7}	Solo Dance	3 117	1	3	7^{2}	$7^{1½}$	5½	2no	JVelasquez	Elmendorf	5.60
13 Aug76 ^{5}Sar^{8}	Ready Again	b3 117	5	1	1^{2}	1^{1}	1^{h}	$3^{1¼}$	MVenezia	Dogwood Stable	21.10
13 Aug76 ^{5}Sar^{3}	Cornish Pet	3 117	6	6	5½	3½	3½	4^{h}	JCruguet	Verulam Farm	5.00
	Skater's Waltz	3 117	4	5	3½	4^{1}	6^{1}	5^{h}	RCSmith	A G Vanderbilt	16.60
13 Aug76 ^{5}Sar^{2}	Like for Like.	3 117	3	2	4½	$5^{1½}$	4½	6no	JARodriguez	Waldemar Farm	6.10
	Naivasha	3 110	8	8	6^{1}	8	$7^{1½}$	$7^{6¾}$	KWhitley^{7}	King Ranch	28.50
13 Aug76 ^{5}Sar^{4}	Artful Levee	3 117	7	7	8	6½	8	8	RLTurcotte	Whitney Stone	5.90

OFF AT 3:21½ EDT. Start good. Won handily. Time, :22⅗, :46⅖, 1:12⅕. Track fast.

$2 Mutuel Prices:			
2–LOVE FOR LOVE	4.20	3.20	3.40
1–SOLO DANCE		4.80	4.40
5–READY AGAIN			6.40

Dk. b. or br. f, by Cornish Prince—Rare Exchange, by Swaps. Tr., Elliott Burch. Bred by Mellon Paul (Va.).

LOVE FOR LOVE prompted the pace into the stretch, took over from READY AGAIN just inside the final furlong and proved clearly best under confident handling. SOLO DANCE, eased back along the inside early, finished well to gain the place. READY AGAIN saved ground while making the pace and weakened under pressure. CORNISH PET made a bid from the outside leaving the turn but hung. SKATER'S WALTZ, between horses much of the way, lacked a late response. LIKE FOR LIKE rallied along the inside leaving the turn but failed to sustain her bid. ARTFUL LEVEE failed to be a serious factor.

I must confess that I was not at Saratoga on August 21, 1976. I was home writing this book. In fact, I missed the entire Saratoga meeting, which is something I'd rather not do again. Saratoga is a special place, a racetrack where the trees outnumber the people, where the best of racing is on display for twenty-four glorious summer days. Oh, it gets hot in Saratoga Springs. Very hot. But with a track bias like the one you just got a peek at, with races and bets like the one you are about to contemplate, a good player will tell time by the coming of the Saratoga season. Frankly, I've enjoyed the experience of writing this book—I might even do another. But I'll be damned if I ever do one during August again.

6th Saratoga

AUGUST 21, 1976

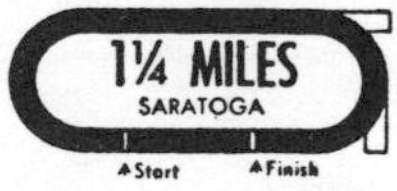

1¼ MILES. (2:01). 107th running TRAVERS. SCALE WEIGHTS. $100,000 added. 3-year-olds. Weight, 126 lbs. By subscription of $200 each, which shall accompany the nomination; $500 to start, with $100,000 added. The added money and all fees to be divided: 60% to the winner, 22% to second, 12% to third, and 6% to fourth. The winner shall have his name inscribed on the Man o' War Cup and a gold plated replica will be presented to the owner. Trophies will also be presented to the winning trainer and jockey. Closed with 22 nominations.

McKenzie Bridge 126
B. c (1973), by Le Fabuleux—Nanticious, by Nantallah.
Breeder, Carver Stable (Ky.).
Owner, Mrs. Douglas Carver. Trainer, J. S. Dunn.

1976 . . 9 2 1 1 $82,566
1975 . . . . $9,626

11 Aug76	8Sar	1$\frac{1}{8}$:46^{11}:103^1:484gd	3	114	10^{17}	96$\frac{3}{4}$	42$\frac{1}{2}$	4^3	McHeDM^6	AlwS 88	FatherHogan114 DanceSpell 10
27 Jun76	8Hol	1$\frac{1}{8}$:45^{2}1:093^1:59^{1}ft	5$\frac{3}{4}$	114	9^{12}	66$\frac{1}{2}$	5^6	59$\frac{1}{4}$	McHeDG^5	AlwS 86	MajsticLight114 CrystlWatr 9
5 Jun76	7Bel	1$\frac{1}{8}$:47 1:11^{1}2:29 ft	6$\frac{1}{2}$	126	9^{22}	7^{12}	37$\frac{1}{2}$	2nk	McHgeD^2	ScwS 75	BoldForbes126 McKzeBrdge 10
24 May76	7Bel	1$\frac{1}{16}$:46^{2}1:104^1:42^{3}ft	3	113	77$\frac{1}{2}$	6^6	51$\frac{1}{2}$	12$\frac{1}{2}$	VasquezJ^7	Alw 89	McKnzieBridge113 FthrHgn 7
2 May76	6Hol	Ⓣ 1$\frac{1}{16}$:47^{1}1:124^1:424fm	3-2	118	5^5	21$\frac{1}{2}$	54$\frac{1}{2}$	53$\frac{3}{4}$	ShoakerW^6	Alw 81	Delta Junction 121 Lean To 6
17 Apr76	8Hol	1$\frac{1}{8}$:46 1:09^{3}1:48^{2}ft	152	122	9^{13}	7^8	66$\frac{1}{2}$	44$\frac{1}{2}$	AlvarezF^9	SpwS 85	CrystalWater122 Life'sHope 11
28 Mar76	8SA	1$\frac{1}{8}$:46 1:10^{1}1:48 ft	16	120	8^{13}	9^9	9^{15}	9^{21}	HawleyS^6	SpwS 71	An Act 120 Double Discount 9
17 Mar76	8SA	1$\frac{1}{8}$:47^{1}1:11^{4}1:48^{4}ft	3-2	118	81^2	63$\frac{1}{2}$	5^5	36$\frac{3}{4}$	ShakerW^3	SpwS 81	June's Blazer 118 Pindoro 8
24 Jan76	6SA	1$\frac{1}{16}$:45^{4}1:104^1:43 ft	3$\frac{1}{2}$	114	4^{10}	4^1	2h	1^4	ShoakerW^7	Alw 87	McKenzieBrdge114 Spoonwd 7
2 Nov75	8SA	1$\frac{1}{16}$:46^{1}1:104^1:43^{3}ft	21	118	8^8	86$\frac{1}{4}$	6^7	56$\frac{3}{4}$	OlivresF^7	SpwS 77	Telly'sPop118 Imcrnishprnce 8
25 Oct75	6SA	6$\frac{1}{2}$ f :21^4 :444^1:16^{1}ft	4$\frac{1}{2}$	118	7^{10}	4^5	42$\frac{1}{2}$	24$\frac{3}{4}$	ToroF^1	Alw 87	PntedWgn115 McKnzieBdge 7

Aug 19 Sar 4f ft :48$\frac{3}{5}$b   Aug 10 Sar 4f sy :50$\frac{1}{5}$b   Aug 5 Sar 4f ft :49b

Quiet Little Table 126
Gr. g (1973), by Mr. Leader—Grey Table, by Grey Sovereign.
Breeder, Meadowhill (Ky.).
Owner, Meadowhill. Trainer, P. G. Johnson.

1976 9 5 1 2 $104,781
1975 1 1 0 0 $5,400

11 Aug76	8Sar	1$\frac{1}{8}$:46^{11}:103^1:484gd	2$\frac{1}{2}$	▲123	57$\frac{1}{2}$	3^1	63$\frac{1}{2}$	68$\frac{3}{4}$	MapleE^8	AlwS 82	FatherHogan114 DanceSpell 10
10 Jly76	8Aqu	1$\frac{1}{8}$:46^{4}1:36^{1}1:49 ft	2$\frac{1}{2}$	▲111	2h	1$\frac{1}{2}$	1^5	12$\frac{1}{2}$	MapleE^7	HcpS 90	Quiet Lttle Tble 111 Sir Lstr 8
30 Jun76	8Aqu	1 :45^{1}1:084^{1}1:34^{1}ft	2	114	3^2	5$\frac{1}{2}$	3^2	1^2	TurctteR^1	AlwS 93	Dance Spell 114 Zen 6
5 Jun76	8Bel	1$\frac{1}{16}$:45^{2}1:10 1:42^{1}ft	4$\frac{1}{2}$	119	1$\frac{1}{2}$	1$\frac{1}{2}$	1^4	12$\frac{3}{4}$	MapleE^4	Alw 91	QuietLittleTable119 KirbyLe 7
26 May76	6Bel	1$\frac{1}{16}$:46 1:10^{3}1:49^{1}ft	3$\frac{1}{2}$	112	2^4	2^1$\frac{1}{2}$	1h	1nk	MapleE^4	Alw 81	QuietLittleTable112 Christn 5
17 May76	5Bel	1 :45^{3}1:094^1:35^{1}ft	4-5	▲115	22$\frac{1}{2}$	2^1$\frac{1}{2}$	11$\frac{1}{2}$	1^3	MapleE^5	Alw 92	QuietLittleTble115 RdAnchr 8
10 May76	6Bel	1$\frac{1}{16}$:46 1:10 1:42^{3}ft	6	111	2$\frac{1}{2}$	1h	2$\frac{1}{2}$	2^2	MapleE^8	Alw 87	Sawbones110 QuietLttleTble 8
20 Apr76	8Aqu	6 f :22^2 :45^{11}:10^{1}ft	1	▲110	4^2	4^5	3^4	11$\frac{3}{4}$	MapleE^4	Alw 92	QuietLittleTble110 Balancer 7
10 Apr76	5Aqu	Cf :22^3 :46^{11}:10^{4}ft	3$\frac{1}{2}$	▲117	4^4	4^4	44$\frac{1}{2}$	33$\frac{1}{4}$	MaplcE^5	Alw 86	Bonge 117 Distinctively 9
5 Oct75	5Bel	6 f :23 :46^{3}1:14^{4}ft	2	122	3$\frac{1}{2}$	2h	1$\frac{1}{2}$	1^2	CstedaM^2	Mdn 83	Quie^{1}LittleTable122 PvtThts 9

Aug 18 Sar 6f ft 1:12$\frac{2}{5}$h   Aug 5 Sar 1$\frac{1}{8}$m ft 1:53$\frac{3}{5}$b   July 26 Bel 6f ft 1:14$\frac{1}{5}$h

Majestic Light 126
B. c (1973), by Majestic Prince—Irradiate, by Ribot.
Breeder, O. M. Phipps (Ky.).
Owner, Ogden M. Phipps. Trainer, John Russell.

1976 .13 6 1 3 $229,123
1975 . 7 1 0 2 $8,400

7 Aug76	8Mth	1$\frac{1}{8}$:46 1:10 1:47 ft	5$\frac{1}{2}$	122	7^{12}	5^4	1$\frac{1}{2}$	1^6	HawleyS^3	InvH 105	MajesticLight122 Appssnato 10
18 Jly76	8Hol	Ⓣ 1$\frac{1}{8}$:48 1:12 1:48^{1}fm	2	▲121	78$\frac{1}{2}$	6^4	2$\frac{1}{2}$	1^1	HawleyS^5	HcpS 95	MajesticLight121 L'Heureux 10
4 Jly76	6AP	Ⓣ 1$\frac{1}{8}$:48^{1}1:122^1:49^{1}fm	2$\frac{1}{2}$	121	10^9	85$\frac{1}{2}$	35$\frac{1}{2}$	2$\frac{1}{2}$	CrdoAJr^1	HcpS 89	Ffth Mrine 121 Mjstic Lght 11
27 Jun76	8Hol	1$\frac{1}{8}$:45^{2}1:09^{3}1:59^{1}ft	20	114	7^{10}	5^4	31$\frac{1}{2}$	13$\frac{1}{4}$	HawleyS^7	AlwS 95	MajesticLight114 CrystlWatr 9
5 Jun76	7Bel	1$\frac{1}{8}$:47 1:11^{1}2:29 ft	14	126	6^{16}	59$\frac{1}{2}$	41^2	4^9	VelasqzJ^6	ScwS 66	BoldForbes126 McKzeBrdge 10
15 May76	8GS	Ⓣ 1$\frac{1}{16}$	1:43^{1}fm	6$\frac{3}{4}$	117	9^{15}	79$\frac{1}{2}$	51$\frac{1}{2}$	1$\frac{1}{2}$	BarreraC^9	HcpS 89	Majestic Light 117 Chati 12
5 May76	8GS	Ⓣ 1	1:393fm	2$\frac{1}{2}$	115	75$\frac{1}{4}$	6^4	41$\frac{1}{2}$	13$\frac{1}{4}$	BarreraC^7	Alw 75	MajsticLight115 NobleAdml 8
16 Apr76	5Aqu	1 :46^{11}:10^{2}1:36 ft	27	117	8^9	7^{10}	7^{10}	6^9	BaezaB^6	Alw 77	BestLaidPlns119 Practitionr 8
11 Mar76	8Aqu	1 :46^{4}1:12 1:37^{1}sy	5	113	2$\frac{1}{2}$	21$\frac{1}{2}$	33$\frac{1}{4}$	58$\frac{1}{4}$	CrdroAJr^2	Alw 72	Be-A-Son 113 Cabriolet II. 6
28 Feb76	6Aqu	1 :48^{2}1:13^{3}1:39^{1}ft	7-5	▲117	3^1	2h	1h	11$\frac{1}{2}$	CordroAJr^6	Alw 70	MajesticLight117 Resilient 8
20 Feb76	8Aqu	1 :46^{3}1:13^{1}1:37^{2}ft	6-5	▲119	6^8	4^6	4^4	31$\frac{1}{4}$	CordroAJr^3	Alw 78	Kupper 115 Distinctively 8

Aug 17 Sar 7f ft 1:26b

Honest Pleasure 126
Dk b. or br. c (1973), by What a Pleasure—Tularia, by Tulyar.
Breeder, Waldemar Farms, Inc. (Fla.).
Owner, B. R. Firestone. Trainer, LeRoy Jolley.

1976 8 4 2 1 $229,172
1975 8 6 2 0 $370,227

7 Aug76	8Mth	1$\frac{1}{8}$:46 1:10 1:47 ft	1	▲1$\frac{1}{2}$6	2$\frac{1}{2}$	11$\frac{1}{2}$	2$\frac{1}{2}$	3^6	PerretC^4	InvH 99	MajesticLight122 Appssnato 10
27 Jly76	8Mth	1$\frac{1}{16}$:46 1:10 1:41^{1}ft	1-10	▲115	13$\frac{1}{2}$	11$\frac{1}{2}$	2h	21$\frac{1}{2}$	BaezaB^1	Alw 97	PeppyAddy119 HonestPlsure 6
15 May76	8Pim	1$\frac{3}{16}$:45 1:09 1:55 ft	4-5	▲126	2^2	2^2	4^2	57$\frac{1}{4}$	BaezaB^6	ScwS 87	Elocutionist126 Play theRed 6
1 May76	8CD	1$\frac{1}{4}$:45^{4}1:10^{2}2:01^{3}ft	2-5	▲126	2^5	2$\frac{1}{2}$	2$\frac{1}{2}$	2^1	BaezaB^5	ScwS 88	BoldForbes126 HonestPlesre 9
22 Apr76	8Kee	1$\frac{1}{8}$:48 1:23^1:492ft	1-10	▲121	14	1^5	1^2	11$\frac{1}{2}$	BaezaB^2	SpwS 90	HontPlease121 CertnRoman 7
3 Apr76	9GP	1$\frac{1}{8}$:46^{4}1:10^{3}1:47^{4}ft	1-20	▲122	13	13	13	13	BaezaB^3	AlwS 95	HonestPlsre122 GrtContrctr 6
28 Feb76	9Hia	1$\frac{1}{8}$:45^{4}1:09 1:46^{4}ft	1-3	▲122	12	1^8	1^8	11^1	BaezaB^7	ScwS 98	HonestPleasure122 IncaRoca 8
11 Feb76	9Hia	7 f :23 :45^{2}1:22^{2}ft		122	1^1	14	1^{10}	1^{14}	BaezaB^4	SpwS 93	HonestPlease122 ParcForiln 4

Exhibition race; no wagering.

1 Nov75	8Lrl	1$\frac{1}{8}$:45^{4}1:03^1:42^{4}ft	1-5	▲122	11	13	11$\frac{1}{2}$	12$\frac{1}{2}$	BaezaB^1	ScwS 95	HonestPlsure122 Whtsyrple 7
18 Oct75	8Bel	1 :45 1:10^{11}:36^{2}sy	6-5	▲122	1$\frac{1}{2}$	11$\frac{1}{2}$	1^5	1^7	BaezaB^9	ScwS 86	HonestPlsure122 DnceSpell 14
8 Oct75	8Bel	7 f :22^4 :45^{2}1:22^{3}ft	2$\frac{3}{4}$	121	1^3	14	1^5	1^8	BaezaB^7	AlwS 89	HnstPlsre121 Whtsyrplsure 7

Aug 19 Sar 4f ft :46$\frac{1}{5}$h   Aug 14 Sar 7f ft 1:25h

Romeo **126** **B. c (1973), by T. V. Lark—Gallizzie, by Tiger Wander.**
Breeder, P. Madden (Ky.). **1976 17 3 2 3 $53,760**
Ownre, Mary Lou Cashman. Trainer, Paul Adwell.

7 Aug76	^{7}AP	Ⓣ	1 1/16	:47^{4}1:12^{4}1:44^{1}fm	9	114	12^{10}	74½	7^{10}	8^{11}	GavdiaW^{2}	HcpS	77	Effervescing113	Rule theRge	13
29 Jly 76	^{9}AP		1 1/16	:47^{1}1:12^{1}1:42^{1}sy	6-5	▲115	4^{1}	2^{1}	1½	1¾	GavidiaW^{6}	Alw	101	Romeo 115	Auberge	7
17 Jly 76	^{6}AP	Ⓣ	1 1/16	:48^{1}1:12^{1}1:43^{4}fm	2¼	115	45½	2^{1}	31½	43¼	GavidiaW^{7}	Alw	87	NatvePraise117	Fightmaster	9
4 Jly 76	^{6}AP	Ⓣ	1⅛	:48^{1}1:22^{1}1:49^{1}fm	12e	111	3^{4}	3^{2}	6^{8}	69½	SnyderL^{9}	HcpS	81	Ffth Mrine 121	Mjstic Lght	11
27 Jun76	^{8}Hol		1¼	:45^{2}1:09^{3}1:59^{1}ft	8¾	115	3^{7}	43½	45½	49¼	PincyLJr^{8}	AlwS	86	MajesticLight114	Crystl Wtr	9
13 Jun76	^{8}Hol		1⅛	:46^{3}1:10^{2}1:47^{2}ft	31	115	6^{8}	5^{3}	3^{2}	2^{2}	VergraO^{7}	HcpS	93	L'Heureux 119	Romeo	7
23 May76	^{5}Hol	Ⓣ	1 1/16	:46^{4}1:11^{2}1:42^{3}fm	7¼	118	7^{4}	41¼	2½	1no	VergaraO^{7}	Alw	86	Romeo 118	Electric Flag	12
8 May76	^{2}Hol	Ⓣ	1 1/16	:48^{3}1:12^{3}1:43^{1}fm	2	▲120	4^{3}	3^{2}	4^{2}	43½	McHgeDG^{9}	Alw	79	PrinceBoynton115	GasEnrgy	9
25 Apr76	^{9}Hol	Ⓣ	1 1/16	:47^{2}1:14^{1}1:42^{4}fm	9	120	64½	5^{3}	5^{3}	34½	VergaraO^{5}	Alw	80	Today n'Tmrrw117	HdnWrld	10
17 Apr76	^{5}Hol	Ⓣ	1 1/16	:47^{3}1:13^{1}1:43 fm	7½	120	4^{2}	52½	3^{3}	35½	VergaraO^{9}	Alw	78	DeltaJnctn120	Tody n'Tmrw	12

Aug 18 Sar 5f ft 1:00h **July 28 AP 3f ft :37b** **July 24 AP 6f ft 1:15⅗b**

El Portugues * **126** **Ch. c (1973), by Gallant Romeo—Miss Swoon, by Swoon's Son.**
Breeder, Copelan & Thornbury (Ky.). **1976..20 2 6 2 $66,593**
Owner, E. Ubarri. Trainer, Lazaro S. Barrera. **1975.. 1 M 0 0 $152**

11 Aug76	^{8}Sar		1⅛	:46^{1}1:10^{3}1:48^{4}gd	4¾	114	6^{11}	5^{2}	3½	3^{3}	CrdoAJr^{7}	AlwS	88	FatherHogan114	DanceSpell	10
31 Jly 76	^{8}Aqu	Ⓣ	1⅛	:47^{2}1:12^{1}1:49^{2}fm	8	112	38½	5^{10}	59½	69¼	VelasqzJ^{5}	HcpS		Mcdred 117	Dream 'n BeLky	7
17 Jly 76	^{8}Pim		1⅛	:46^{3}1:10^{4}1:48^{4}ft	7¼e	110	7^{6}	5^{8}	53¾	43¾	VelezRI^{4}	HcpS	89	AmericanTradr109	OnTheSly	7
4 Jly 76	^{6}AP	Ⓣ	1⅛	:48^{1}1:22^{1}1:49^{1}fm	15	114	76¾	74½	9^{11}	9^{10}	GvidiaW^{10}	HcpS	81	Ffth Mrine 121	Mjstic Lght	11
27 Jun76	^{10}Tdn		1⅛	:46 1:10^{3}1:49^{4}ft	5½e	112	53¼	3½	3^{1}	4^{3}	VelezRI^{14}	AlwS	88	Return of a Native115	Cojak	14
14 Jun76	^{8}Bel		1 1/16	:47 1:11^{3}1:43^{4}ft	3-5	▲110	52¼	3^{3}	3^{3}	23¾	CordroAJr^{1}	Alw	79	Brown Cat 117	El Portugues	6
23 May76	^{8}Bel		1	:45^{3}1:10^{1}1:36 ft	8-5	▲116	64¾	5^{3}	51¾	2½†	CrdroAJr^{6}	AlwS	87	Sir Lister114	El Portugues	9
†Disqualified and placed third.																	
8 May76	^{8}Bel		1	:45^{3}1:10 1:35 ft	8¼	126	6^{7}	5^{4}	2^{2}	2½	CrdroAJr^{2}	ScwS	92	Sonkisser 126	El Portugues	6
1 May76	^{6}Aqu		1	:45 1:09 1:34^{3}sy	5½	110	53¼	45½	3^{8}	28½	AmyJ^{7}	Alw	84	Cinteelo 104	El Portugues	7
24 Apr76	^{6}Aqu		1	:45^{2}1:09 1:35 ft	9½	113	58½	57½	56½	54¾	VelasquzJ^{3}	Alw	86	NewCllection112	Cplet'sSng	7

June 24 Tdn 5f ft 1:02b

Legendaire **126** **Ch. c (1973), by Le Fabuleux—Native Guide, by Raise a Native.**
Breeder, W. P. Little (Ky.). **1976.. 8 2 1 0 $15,157**
Owner, Silk Willoughby Farm. Trainer, J. P. Conway. **1975.. 4 1 0 0 $5,400**

11 Aug76	^{8}Sar		1⅛	:46^{1}1:10^{3}1:48^{4}gd	19	114	9^{16}	108¾	98¾	7^{10}	TurctteR^{4}	AlwS	81	FatherHogan114	DanceSpell	10
31 Jly 76	^{6}Aqu	Ⓣ	1⅛	:47^{2}1:12 1:50 fm	11	112	3^{3}	1^{h}	66¼	63¾	TurctteR^{1}	HcpS		FabledMonrch114	Effrvscing	8
10 Jly 76	^{8}Aqu		1⅛	:46^{4}1:36^{1}1:49 ft	9	112	67½	7^{11}	7^{16}	7^{15}	VasquzJ^{4}	HcpS	75	Quiet Lttle Tble 111	Sir Lstr	8
26 Jun76	^{8}Bel		1 1/16	:46^{2}1:11 1:42 ft	6	113	74¼	3^{1}	1^{1}	12¾	VasquezJ^{2}	Alw	92	Legendaire113	RedAnchor	7
13 Apr76	^{7}Kee		1 1/16	:47^{1}1:11^{1}1:43^{1}ft	7	113	63¾	6^{9}	6^{12}	6^{20}	BrumfldD^{5}	Alw	70	No Link 121	Inca Roca	6
24 Mar76	^{8}GP	Ⓣ	a 1	1:39 fm	6	116	89½	63½	53¾	4^{4}†	MarquzC^{5}	Alw	82	Hall ofRean114	Fightmaster	10
†Placed third through disqualification.																	
6 Mar76	^{6}GP		1 1/16	:47^{2}1:12^{1}1:43^{4}ft	2¼	▲122	4^{5}	3^{3}	2½	1¾	RuaneJ^{5}	Alw	82	Legendaire122	ArchieBmish	11
20 Feb76	^{7}Hia		7 f	:22^{4} :46^{1}1:24 ft	62	115	10^{9}	6^{6}	31½	2^{nk}	MapleE^{3}	Alw	85	Sonkisser 122	Legendaire	11
21 Nov75	^{7}Aqu		1	:44^{4}1:08^{4}1:34^{4}sy	11	122	9^{18}	9^{30}	9^{32}	9^{40}	CastandaK^{5}	Alw	52	Cinteelo 117	Play the Red	9

Aug 17 Sar 1 ft 1:43b **Aug 10 Sar 3f sy :36b** **Aug 7 Sar 5f ft 1:07b**

Dance Spell **126** **B. c (1973), by Northern Dancer—Obeah, by Cyane.**
Breeder, Christiana Stables (Ky.). **1976.. 7 3 1 1 $72,702**
Owner, Christiana Stables. Trainer, J. W. Maloney. **1975..10 2 6 1 $93,846**

11 Aug76	^{8}Sar		1⅛	:46^{1}1:10^{3}1:48^{4}gd	3½e	121	2^{5}	1^{1}	1^{h}	2^{1}	VasquzJ^{5}	AlwS	90	FatherHogan114	DanceSpell	10
10 Jly 76	^{8}Aqu		1⅛	:46^{4}1:36^{1}1:49 ft	3½	117	3^{1}	2½	3^{5}	32¾	CrdoAJr^{8}	HcpS	87	Quiet Lttle Tble 111	Sir Lstr	8
30 Jun76	^{8}Aqu		1	:45^{1}1:08^{4}1:34^{1}ft	3¼e	114	1½	1^{1}	1^{2}	11¼	CdroAJr^{3}	AlwS	95	Dance Spell 114	Zen	6
12 Jun76	^{6}Bel		6 f	:22^{3} :45^{3}1:09^{3}ft	2¾	112	21½	3^{2}	6^{8}	6^{11}	CruguetJ^{3}	Alw	83	QueenCityLd115	VlidAppeal	6
8 May76	^{8}Bel		1	:45^{3}1:10 1:35 ft	1	▲126	2½	2½	4^{4}	4^{9}	CruguetJ^{3}	ScwS	84	Sonkisser 126	El Portugues	6
21 Apr76	^{6}Aqu		7 f	:22^{4} :45^{4}1:22 ft	2¼	110	21½	21½	11½	12¾	CruguetJ^{1}	Alw	91	DanceSpll 110	GabeBnzur	7
31 Mar76	^{7}Aqu		7 f	:23 :45^{4}1:22^{3}ft	8-5	▲111	31½	1^{h}	1^{h}	1½	CruguetJ^{3}	Alw	88	DanceSpel 111	Kohoutek	7
29 Nov75	^{8}Aqu		1⅛	:46^{3}1:10^{4}1:49^{1}ft	9-5	▲113	3^{5}	31½	22½	2½	CrugutJ^{10}	AlwS	88	Hang Ten 116	Dance Spell	12
19 Nov75	^{8}Aqu		6 f	:22^{1} :45^{1}1:09^{4}ft	2½	115	21½	2^{h}	22½	22¼	CruguetJ^{3}	AlwS	92	LordHenribee117	DanceSpell	6
1 Nov75	^{8}Lrl		1 1/16	:45^{4}1:10^{3}1:42^{4}ft	7½	122	31½	33½	33½	3^{6}	CruguetJ^{7}	SpwS	93	HonestPlsre122	Whatsyrplse	7

Aug 20 Sar 3f ft :36b **Aug 17 Sar 5f ft :58⅗h** **Aug 8 Sar 5f sy 1:02⅕b**

While it's not necessary to handicap this prestigious stakes race in depth to select Honest Pleasure as a front-running stickout, I am also including (page 38) the chart of the Monmouth Invitational, the race Majestic Light won over Honest Pleasure by six lengths. The Trackman's comments clearly show that Honest Pleasure was regaining his early season form.

Leroy Jolley wisely stopped on Honest Pleasure after the Preakness debacle (May 15) and was patiently reestablishing the horse's speed and staying power. The recent workouts indicate further progress.

Majestic Light is a slow-breaking, fast-closing three-year-old that appreciates true distance racing. Trainer John Russell has done an excellent job, and there is very little doubt that Majestic Light is fit enough or good enough to win. Thus, a good performance, despite the bias, is possible; however, it's not likely. Much depends on whether Majestic Light can get clear sailing on the rail for an uninterrupted rally. Unfortunately, he will need an unusual degree of cooperation from the rest of the field to get that kind of running room. Finally, he will still have to run faster than Honest Pleasure, who is on the improve and likely to have the rail and the lead for the entire race!

Quiet Little Table, a well-managed speed horse, would have a fine winning chance in any good field. But with Honest Pleasure in the race, Quiet Little Table has virtually no chance at all. It is further doubtful that he has enough speed to stop Honest Pleasure from getting a clear lead over the field in the run to the first turn. That's important for two reasons: (1) most front-running types tend to race better when they are able to relax in front of the pack; (2) everything in Honest Pleasure's record says he is a horse that improves dramatically when he is able to make the lead without undue stress.

Dance Spell has generally good form and cannot be completely eliminated.

The shipper Romeo is a stretch runner that has never beaten a good field.

EIGHTH RACE Mth August 7, 1976 1⅛ MILES. (1:48). Ninth running MONMOUTH INVITATIONAL HANDICAP. Purse $100,000. 3-year-olds. by invitation only, with no nomination or starting fees. The winner to receive $65,000, with $20,000 to second; $10,000 to third; and $5,000 to fourth. A representative field of those weighted will be invited to participate. The Monmouth Park Jockey Club reserves the right to reassign weight to any horse after the release of the weights. Owner of the winner to receive a trophy.

Value to winner $65,000; second, $20,000; third, $10,000; fourth, $5,000. Mutuel Pool, $349,197.

Last Raced	Horse	EqtAWt	PP	St	¼	½	¾	Str	Fin	Jockeys	Owners	Odds to $1
18 Jly 76 ^{8}Hol^{1}	Majestic Light	3 122	3	2	7^{2}	7^{2}	$5^{1\frac{1}{2}}$	$1^{\frac{1}{2}}$	1^{6}	SHawley	O M Phipps	5.30
31 Jly 76 ^{8}Aqu^{5}	Appassionato	3 113	7	9	$9^{1\frac{1}{2}}$	9^{2}	9^{2}	$5^{1\frac{1}{2}}$	2no	RHernandez	F A Luro	27.10
27 Jly 76 ^{8}Mth^{2}	Honest Pleasure	3 126	4	1	2^{2}	2^{4}	$1^{1\frac{1}{2}}$	$2^{2\frac{1}{2}}$	$3^{\frac{1}{2}}$	CPerrtt	B R Firestone	1.10
17 Jly 76 ^{8}Pim^{3}	Zen	3 118	6	7	6^{h}	$5^{1\frac{1}{2}}$	$4^{\frac{1}{2}}$	3^{3}	$4^{2\frac{1}{2}}$	JVasquez	Pen-Y-Bryn Farm	3.10
25 Jly 76 ^{8}Del^{1}	On The Sly	3 115	2	8	8^{7}	8^{6}	8^{6}	4^{2}	$5^{1\frac{1}{2}}$	GMcCarron	Balmak Stable	6.00
31 Jly 76 ^{8}Aqu^{2}	Dream 'N Be Lucky	3 114	5	10	10	10	10	7^{5}	6^{6}	MSolomone	G A Zimmerman	33.00
17 Jly 76 ^{8}Mth^{6}	Wardlaw	b3 115	1	3	3^{h}	$3^{2\frac{1}{2}}$	3^{2}	6^{h}	7^{4}	JTejeira	D Lasater	39.30
27 Jly 76 ^{7}Mth^{1}	Best Bee	b3 113	10	6	$5^{1\frac{1}{2}}$	$6^{1\frac{1}{2}}$	$7^{\frac{1}{2}}$	8^{4}	8^{6}	RWilson	Dixiana	65.10
31 Jly 76 ^{7}Aks^{2}	Joachim	b3 117	8	5	$4^{2\frac{1}{2}}$	4^{1}	6^{2}	9^{h}	9^{h}	SMaple	E Pratt-J C Van Berg	18.90
17 Jly 76 ^{8}Pim^{1}	American Trader	b3 114	9	4	1^{3}	$1^{1\frac{1}{2}}$	2^{h}	10	10	AAgnello	Mrs B Cohen	19.60

OFF AT 5:57 EDT. Start good. Won driving. Time, :22⅗, :46, 1:10, 1:34⅗, 1:47 (new track record). Track fast.

4–HONEST PLEASURE 2.80

B. c, by Majestic Prince—Irradiate, by Ribot. Trainer, J. W. Russell. Bred by O. M. Phipps (Ky.).

$2 Mutuel Prices:

3–MAJESTIC LIGHT	12.60	6.80	4.20
7–APPASIONATO		19.40	6.20

MAJESTIC LIGHT, taken in hand after the start, angled to the outside leaving the clubhouse turn, remained outside when roused under a flurry of right-handed whipping at the far turn, brushed lightly with ZEN on the stretch turn but continued strongly to gain the lead in the upper stretch, swerved out when struck left-handed at the eighth-pole but continued to draw off with authority and was under only mild encouragement in the final seventy yards. APPASSIONATO, outrun for three-quatrers, rallied gamely outside the leaders when roused for the drive but could not threaten the winner. HONEST PLEASURE, reserved off the early pace outside AMERICAN TRADER, moved willingly to the lead when asked at the far turn, resisted the winner gamely in the stretch but hung in the closing yards. ZEN rallied just inside MAJESTIC LIGHT at the far turn, brushed with that one but finished with good courage. ON THE SLY did not reach contention with a mild closing rally. JOACHIM and AMERICAN TRADER were finished after three-quarters.

Overweight—Dream 'N Be Lucky, 1 pound.

In summary, what we have here is a fit front-running racehorse of obvious quality getting a track he should absolutely relish. The betting crowd made the wrong favorite.

SIXTH RACE Sar August 21, 1976 1¼ MILES. (2:01). 107th running TRAVERS. SCALE WEIGHTS. $100,000 added. 3-year-olds. Weight, 126 lbs. By subscription of $200 each, which shall accompany the nomination; $500 to start, with $100,000 added. The added money and all fees to be divided: 60% to the winner, 22% to second, 12% to third, and 6% to fourth. The winner shall have his name inscribed on the Man o' War Cup and a gold plated replica will be presented to the owner. Trophies will also be presented to the winning trainer and jockey. Closed with 22 nominations.

Value of race $108,400. Value to winner $65,040; second, $23,848; third, $13,008; fourth, $6,504. Mutuel Pool, $328,104. Off-track betting, $342,517.

Last Raced	Horse	EqtAWt	PP	¼	½	¾	1	Str	Fin	Jockeys	Owners	Odds to $1
7 Aug76 ^{8}Mth^{3}	Honest Pleasure	3 126	4	1^{2}	1^{6}	1^{4}	1^{2}	1^{3}	1^{4}	CPerret	B R Firestone	2.10
7 Aug76 ^{7}AP^{8}	Romeo	b3 126	5	$5^{1\frac{1}{2}}$	$5^{1\frac{1}{2}}$	5^{1}	4^{1}	2^{h}	$2^{1\frac{1}{2}}$	BBaeza	Mary L Cashman	49.30
11 Aug76 ^{8}Sar^{2}	Dance Spell	3 126	8	4^{1}	4^{1}	$3^{1\frac{1}{2}}$	$3^{\frac{1}{2}}$	3^{1}	3^{3}	JCruguet	Christiana Stable	14.70
11 Aug76 ^{8}Sar^{6}	Quiet Little Table	3 126	2	3^{1}	$3^{1\frac{1}{2}}$	2^{1}	$2^{1\frac{1}{2}}$	4^{2}	4^{nk}	EMaple	Meadowhill	12.50
11 Aug76 ^{6}Sar^{3}	El Portugues	b3 126	6	2^{1}	2^{h}	$4^{1\frac{1}{2}}$	$5^{\frac{1}{2}}$	$5^{\frac{1}{2}}$	$5^{1\frac{1}{2}}$	JVelasquez	E Ubarri	23.60
11 Aug76 ^{8}Sar^{4}	McKenzie Bridge	3 126	1	8	$7^{\frac{1}{2}}$	7^{3}	7^{12}	7^{24}	$6^{\frac{3}{4}}$	DMcHargue	Mrs D Carter	4.60
7 Aug76 ^{8}Mth^{1}	Majestic Light	3 126	3	$7^{\frac{1}{2}}$	$6^{\frac{1}{2}}$	6^{2}	$6^{1\frac{1}{2}}$	$6^{\frac{1}{2}}$	7^{30}	SHawley	O M Phipps	1.00
11 Aug76 ^{8}Sar^{7}	Legendaire	b3 126	7	6^{h}	8	8	8	8	8	RTurcotte	Silk Willoughby Fm	64.40

OFF AT 4:34 EDT. Start good. Won ridden out. Time, :23⅖, :46⅗, 1:10⅖, 1:35, 2:00⅕ (new track record). Track fast.

$2 Mutuel Prices:

4–HONEST PLEASURE	6.20	5.00	4.20
5–ROMEO	2 .1 00		6.80
8–DANCE SPELL			5.40

Dk. b. or br. c, by What a Pleasure—Tularia, by Tlyar. Trainer, LeRoy Jolley. Bred by Waldemar Farms, Inc. (Fla.).

HONEST PLEASURE dropped over to save ground after outrunning QUIET LITTLE TABLE into the turn, quickly opened a long lead, made the pace while going easily, was roused soon after entering the stretch and drew away under a hand ride. ROMEO, unhurried early, rallied along the inside leaving the far turn and finished with good energy to be second best. DANCE SPELL, reserved early while saving ground, moved outside QUIET LITTLE TABLE to launch a bid at the far turn, raced forwardly into the stretch but weakened during the drive. QUIET LITTLE TABLE, well placed early, went after HONEST PLEASURE approaching the stretch but had nothing left for the drive. EL PORTUGUES, hustled along after the start, was finished approaching the end of the backstretch. McKENZIE BRIDGE was never close. MAJESTIC LIGHT, void of early foot, was sent up outside horses midway of the far turn but lacked a further response. LEGENDAIRE wasn't able to keep pace.

As a footnote to the Travers result chart, you might be interested to know that Dance Spell—the colt that moved outside to launch his bid against the Saratoga bias—came back to win the Jerome Mile in his next start, paying $17.60. That price was inflated by Dance Spell's number-one post position, generally interpreted by most Belmont fans as an unfavorable post. I can well understand that interpretation because the rail is usually dead at Belmont during the fall meeting. Nevertheless, it is my experience with track biases that logic still prevails in such conditions.

A dead rail only eliminates horses that race on the dead rail.

A front runner breaking from post one should be automatically downgraded if not eliminated under such conditions.

A stretch runner breaking from post one may have to give up a length or two at the start. That of course is frequently reason enough to eliminate many stretch runners.

Horses like Dance Spell those that have tractable speed, speed that frequently permits maneuverability—may yet get trapped along the rail if the jockey is not alert. That's a smaller risk factor, but it cannot be overlooked. Several issues must be balanced against that risk:

How superior is the horse breaking from post one?
How many horses figure to break with him?
How good is the jockey?

Have most of the riders been breaking toward the outside in order to avoid the rail, thus leaving post one with room to maneuver?

What kind of odds are available for the risk?

In my judgment, a set of encouraging answers to these questions, especially to the first and last questions, would suggest buying into the risk.

EIGHTH RACE
Bel
Septemb'r 6, 1976

1 MILE. (1:33⅗). One hundred and seventh running JEROME HANDICAP. $100,000 added. 3-year-olds. By subscription of $100 each, which shall accompany the nomination; $500 to start, with $100,000 added. The added money and fees to be divided: 60% to the winner, 22% to second, 12% to third and 6% to fourth. Trophies will be presented to the winning owner, trainer and jockey. Closed with 30 nominations.

Value of race $111,000. Value to winner $66,600; second, $24,420; third, $13,320; fourth, $6,660. Mutuel Pool, $560,376. Off-track betting, $193,704.

Last Raceu	Horse	EqtA	Wt	PP	St	¼	½	¾	Str	Fin	Jockeys	Owners	Odds to $1
21 Aug76 ^{6}Sar^{3}	Dance Spell	3	117	1	4	$3\frac{1}{2}$	$2\frac{1}{2}$	1^{1}	$1^{1\frac{1}{2}}$	$1^{3\frac{3}{4}}$	RHernandez	Christiana Stable	7.80
30 Aug76 ^{6}Bel^{3}	Soy Numero Uno	3	117	7	2	$4\frac{1}{2}$	4^{1}	$3^{1\frac{1}{2}}$	$3^{1\frac{1}{2}}$	2no	PDay	Strapro Stable	3.00
26 Aug76 ^{8}Sar^{1}	Clean Bill	3	112	5	10	1^{1}	1^{2}	2^{h}	2^{1}	3^{2}	JImparato	Tartan Stable	30.60
19 Aug76 ^{8}Mth^{3}	Full Out	3	116	4	1	5^{h}	5^{h}	5^{h}	$4\frac{1}{2}$	4^{nk}	DMontoya	Buckland Farm	61.90
17 Jly 76 ^{8}Rkm^{6}	Life's Hope	3	117	3	7	$7\frac{1}{2}$	$6\frac{1}{2}$	$4\frac{1}{2}$	$5\frac{1}{2}$	5^{h}	MSolomone	Harbor View Farm	31.50
21 Aug76 ^{6}Sar^{4}	Quiet Little Table	3	117	2	3	2^{h}	$3\frac{1}{2}$	6^{1}	$6\frac{1}{2}$	6^{3}	EMaple	Meadowhill	7.20
18 Aug76 ^{6}Sar^{1}	Sawbones	3	113	10	8	10	$9\frac{1}{2}$	$8^{1\frac{1}{2}}$	7^{1}	$7\frac{3}{4}$	HGustines	Greentree Stable	5.20
18 Aug76 ^{8}Mth^{2}	Sonkisser	3	122	6	6	$6\frac{1}{2}$	7^{h}	$9\frac{1}{2}$	9^{1}	8^{h}	BBaeza	H I Snyder	3.10
30 Aug76 ^{6}Bel^{2}	Kirby Lane	3	112	8	5	$8^{1\frac{1}{2}}$	8^{1}	$7\frac{1}{2}$	$8\frac{1}{2}$	$9\frac{1}{2}$	ACorderoJr	Gedney Farms	6.30
11 Aug76 ^{8}Sar^{1}	Father Hogan	b3	115	9	9	9^{h}	10	10	10	10	MVenezia	Sea Spray Farms	8.00

Uncoupled for betting purposes: LIFE'S HOPE and KIRBY LANE.

OFF AT 5:53½ EDT. Start good. Won driving. Time, :23⅘, :46⅗, 1:10⅗, 1:35. Track fast.

$2 Mutuel Prices:			
1-DANCE SPELL	17.60	7.60	4.60
7-SOY NUMERO UNO		6.00	3.60
5-CLEAN BILL			9.00

B. c, by Northern Dancer—Obeah, by Cyane. Trainer, James W. Maloney. Bred by Christiana Stable (Ky.).

DANCE SPELL, away in good order, moved to the fore when ready while racing well out in the track approaching the stretch and drew away under brisk handling while continuing wide. SOY NUMERO UNO, reserved behind the early leaders, made a bid while racing wide nearing the stretch, lugged in slightly approaching the final furlong and was just up for the place. A foul claim against SOY NUMERO UNO by the rider of FULL OUT, for alleged interference through the stretch, was not allowed. CLEAN BILL, off slowly, rushed through along the rail to take over before going a quarter, remained a factor to midstretch and weakened. FULL OUT, never far back, remained a factor into the stretch but lacked a late response while drifting out. LIFE'S HOPE made a mild bid along the inside leaving the turn but hung. QUIET LITTLE TABLE tired from his early efforts. SAWBONES, outrun early, was sent up between horses leaving the far turn but failed to be a serious factor. SONKISSER, steadied along while in close quarters between horses approaching the end of the backstretch, lacked a further response. KIRBY LANE failed to seriously menace while racing very wide. FATHER HOGAN showed nothing.

Scratched—Fighting Bill.

Dance Spell's next start was in Forego's Woodward Stakes on September 18. Honest Pleasure was also in the field, making his first start since the Travers. Honest Pleasure drew the rail, Dance Spell the extreme outside post in a ten-horse field. There was really no betting issue involved. Forego was a stickout with a tempting 1–1 price, considering his tendency to go off at 1–2. But there is just no margin for profit or error playing horses at those odds.

Because of the post position draw, the second-best horse looked convincingly like Dance Spell; the third choice depended on how much post one would actually cost Honest Pleasure. As the chart below indicates, the Woodward was no less formful than the other two races we have examined in this series of Saratoga-Belmont stakes races.

EIGHTH RACE
Bel
Sept'ber 18, 1976

1⅛ MILES (chute). (1:45⅖). Twenty-third running WOODWARD HANDICAP. $150,000 added. 3-year-olds and upward. By subscription of $100 each, which shall accompany the nomination; $500 to pass the entry box, $1,500 to start, with $150,000 added. The added money and all fees to be divided 60% to the winner, 22% to second, 12% to third and 6% to fourth. Mrs. William Woodward has donated a trophy to be presented to the owner of the winner and trophies will also be presented to the winning trainer and jockey. Closed with 27 nominations.
Value of race, $173,200. Value to winner $103,920; second, $38,104; thirds, $15,588 each. Mutuel Pool, $550,396.

Last Raced	Horse	EqtA	Wt	PP	St	¼	½	¾	Str	Fin	Jockeys	Owners	Odds to $1
21 Aug76 ^{8}Mth^{3}	Forego	6	135	2	10	7^{h}	7^{h}	7^{2}	4^{3}	$1^{1¼}$	WShoemaker	Lazy F Ranch	1.10
6 Sep76 ^{8}Del^{4}	Dance Spell	3	115	10	1	6^{4}	$5^{1½}$	$2^{½}$	1^{h}	$2^{2¾}$	RHernandez	Christiana Stable	7.10
21 Aug76 ^{6}Sar^{1}	DH Honest Pleasure	3	121	1	2	1^{1}	$1^{1½}$	1^{1}	3^{2}	3	CPerret	B R Firestone	2.10
14 Sep76 ^{4}Bel^{1}	DH Stumping	b6	109	4	7	5^{1}	6^{2}	5^{1}	5^{7}	$3^{½}$	JAmy	Hobeau Farm	27.80
6 Sep76 ^{8}Bel^{2}	Soy Numero Uno	3	112	5	4	3^{1}	$3^{½}$	3^{2}	$2^{½}$	$5^{8¼}$	EMaple	Strapro Stable	11.20
21 Aug76 ^{8}Mth^{1}	Hatchet Man	b5	114	3	9	10	10	$8^{½}$	7^{1}	6no	HGustines	Greentree Stable	11.30
21 Aug76 ^{8}Mth^{8}	El Pitirre	4	112	7	5	9^{4}	$9^{½}$	9^{h}	$6^{½}$	7^{3}	ASantiago	E Ubarri	29.20
6 Sep76 ^{8}Del^{4}	Dancing Gun	b4	112	8	2	$2^{1½}$	2^{h}	6^{h}	$8^{½}$	8^{h}	JVelasquez	Gedney Farms	37.30
6 Sep76 ^{8}Bel^{8}	Sonkisser	3	117	6	8	$4^{½}$	$4^{½}$	4^{2}	$9^{1½}$	9^{nk}	BBaeza	H I Snyder	37.40
7 Sep76 ^{8}Bel^{8}	Right Mind	5	114	9	6	8^{h}	8^{5}	10	10	10	RTurcotte	Deronjo Stable	70.90

DH Dead-heat.

OFF AT 5:45 EDT. Start good. Won ridden out. Time, :23, :45⅗, 1:09⅕, 1:33⅘, 1:45⅘. Track fast.

$2 Mutuel Prices:

2–FOREGO	4.20	3.00	2.20
11–DANCE SPELL		5.40	3.00
1–HONEST PLEASURE (Dead-heat)			2.20
4–STUMPING (Dead-heat)			2.80

B. g, by Forli—Lady Golconda, by Hasty Road. Trainer, Frank Y. Whitley, Jr. Bred by Lazy F. Ranch (Ky.).
FOREGO, unhurried after breaking slowly, was steadied along while racing along the inside to the turn, eased out for room approaching the three-eighths pole, moved fast while continuing wide after entering the stretch, caught DANCE SPELL inside the final sixteenth and drew clear under good handling. DANCE SPELL, eased back after breaking in front, moved fast to make his bid while racing well out in the track leaving the turn, took over from SOY NUMERO UNO with a furlong remaining but wasn't able to withstand the winner while besting the others. HONEST PLEASURE sprinted to the front along the inside soon after the start, made the pace while racing well out from the rail, held on well to midstretch and finished on even terms with STUMPING while weakening. STUMPING, never far back, finished with good energy. SOY NUMERO UNO, reserved behind the early leaders, moved through along the inside to gain a narrow advantage nearing the stretch, remained prominent to the final furlong and gave way. HATCHET MAN was always outrun. EL PITIRRE was never close. DANCING GUN was finished soon after going five furlongs. SONKISSER gave way after racing forwardly for six furlongs. RIGHT MIND was always outrun.

Track bias is one of the fundamental realities of racing. There really is a logic to the race, a surprisingly consistent stream of logic. But it can rarely be appreciated without understanding the role of the racetrack itself as it influences the flow of the action from start to finish.

A SAMPLE RACE. The Schuylerville Stakes, July 29, 1974. Opening day at Saratoga. Five of the first six races were main-track sprints and all were won wire to wire. Not one horse made a move on the outside all day and no horse was passed in the stretch. The logical front runner in this race paid $22.40. I'll give you one guess. The winner will be revealed in Chapter 12.

7th SARATOGA **JULY 29, 1974**

6 FURLONGS. (1:08) Fifty-seventh running SCHUYLERVILLE (1st Division).

My Compliments **116** B. f (1972), by Delta Judge—Granny's Pride, by Roman.
Breeder, R. L. Reineman (Ky.). 1974 3 2 1 0 $11.580
Owner, R. L. Reineman. Trainer, W. C. Freeman.
Jly 20-743Mth 5½ f 1:05⅕sft 9-5 *119 42 2½ 1h 12¾ RuaneJ5 Alw 91 ⒻMyComplim'ts119 Q Up Myst'ryM'd 6
Jly 6-743Aqu 5½ f 1:05 ft 6-5 *117 1½ 13 13 12 VeneziaM6 Mdn 88 ⒻMyC'mpliments117 Aware Q'n'sTurf 7
Jun25-743Aqu 5½ f 1:05 ft 15 117 63¾ 63¼ 3½ 2no VeneziaM8 Mdn 88 ⒻLadyP'tia117 MyC'plim'ts M'lyB'ne 10
July 27 Sar 4f ft :49⅗b July 17 Aqu 4f ft :47⅗h July 13 Aqu 4f ft :51b

Our Dancing Girl **116** B. f (1972), by Solo Landing—Amber Dancer, by Native Dancer.
Breeder, Elcee-H Stable (Fla.). 1974 5 1 1 2 $11,793
Owner, Elcee-H Stable. Trainer, J. Rigione.
Jly 10-748Aqu 5½ f 1:02⅘sft 11 115 31 39 314 321 HoleM3 AlwS 78 ⒻRuff'n118 L'gh'gB'dge OurD'c'gGirl 4
Jly 1-747Mth 5½ f 1:06 ft 7¾ 117 14 1h 21 33 GallitanoG6 Alw 84 PropMan118 Prev'ler OurDanc'gGirl 7
Jun15-743Bel 5½ f 1:06 ft 3¾ 116 14 15 16 14½ HoleM4 Mdn 85 ⒻO'rD'c'gG'l 116 Tricks Bl'de ofR's's 10
Jun 7-743Bel 5½ f 1:05⅗sft 3¼ 116 12 12 11½ 21 HoleM2 M40000 86 ⒻCur'ique116 OurD'c'gG'rl SwiftImp 10
May30-743Bel 5½ f 1:06 ft 4½ 114 31 11 21½ 47½ HoleM3 M35000 77 ⒻCurtainCall 116 M'snM'se Cl's'gM't 8
July 24 Bel 5f ft :59⅘h July 8 Bel 4f ft :47⅖h June 29 Bel 4f ft 48⅗b

La Bourresque **116** Dk. b. or br. f (1972), by Victoria Park—Nearanna. by Nearctic
Breeder, J. L. Levesque (Can.). 1974 6 1 2 2 $7,164
Owner, J. L. Levesque. Trainer, J. Starr.
Jly 14-746WO 6 f 1:11⅗sft 8e 119 54 55½ 54¾ 2no TurcotteN1 Alw 86 R'son'bleWin119 LaB'r'sque Dap'rS'dy 12
Jly 6-746WO 6 f 1:11⅗sft 15 112 3nk 1h 2½ 32½ D'tfashH4 HcpS 83 ⒻDeepstar112 M'dowsw't LaB'r'sque 8
Jun27-746WO 6 f 1:13⅗sl 9½ 116 5 253¼ 56 59¾ RogersC4 InvH 65 P'sleyPal 117 H'pe forS'Shine Petrus 7
Jun 8-744WO 5½ f 1:04⅗sft 1 *119 3½ 32 33½ 39 RogersC6 Alw 87 ⒻKn'tlyPr's119 M'd'sw't LaB'r'sque 6

Some Swinger **116** Ch. f (1972), by Tirreno—Batting a Thousand, by Hitting Away.
Breeder, H. T. Mangurian, Jr. (Ky.). 1972 4 2 0 1 $6,475
Owner, H. T. Magurian, Jr. Trainer, T. F. Root, Sr.
Jly 8-746Crc 6 f 1:13⅘sft 4-5 *118 4¾ 41¾ 2½ 14 GuerinE1 Alw 85 ⒻSomeSw'g'r118 B'PrineR'se Whirl It 8
Jun29-749Crc 5 f 1:00⅘sft 17 118 85¾ 83½ 53 31½ GuerinE5 HcpS 89 ⒻMyM'mN'h113 W'd a.L't'g S'eS'g'r 12
Jun17-742Crc 5½ f 1:07⅘sft 9 118 3nk 11½ 14 13 Gr'nst'nB3 Mdn 91 ⒻS'eS'g'r118 Fl'daN'dles H'K andEye 10
Jun 5-742Crc 5½ f 1:07⅘ssy 18 118 910 911 916 913 StLeonG3 Mdn 78 ⒻSoloRoyal 118 Sm'l theRoses OldH'n 9
July 25 Bel 4f sy :46hg July 21 Bel 6f ft 1:16b July 17 Bel 3f ft :37b

---

Secret's Out **119** **Lt. ch. f (1972), by Royal Saxon—Secret Verdict, by Clandestine.**
Breeder, Mrs. M. W. Schott (Fla.). 1974 4 3 0 0 $24,503
Owner, Marcia Schott. Trainer, J. E. Picou.

Jun19-74^{8}Mth 5½ f 1.04 ft 6 119 2^{1} $7^{4\frac{3}{4}}$ $6^{9\frac{3}{4}}$ $5^{9\frac{1}{4}}$ B'mf'ldD^{2} AlwS 88 Ⓕ F'rWind 115 Copernica Fant'ticMiss 7
May26-74^{9}Suf 5 f 1:00⅖sm 3-5 ▴121 $1^{\frac{1}{2}}$ 1^{2} $1^{3\frac{1}{2}}$ $1^{3\frac{1}{4}}$ W'dh'eR^{9} HcpS 85 Secret'sOut121 Inchiq'lah Wh't aT'k't 9
Apr24-74^{7}Kee 4½ f :53⅕sft 1 ▴119 2 1^{3} 1^{1} $1^{4\frac{1}{2}}$ B'f'ldD^{1} AlwS 89 Ⓕ S'cr't'sOut119 Fl'lPrinc's Ain'tE'sy 8
Mar15-74^{3}Hia 3 f :33⅖sy 2¼ ▴117 3 1^{1} $1^{3\frac{1}{4}}$ W'dh'seR^{1} Mdn 95 Ⓕ S'cr't'sO't117 Ebonide W'tATrink't 14
July 17 Bel 6f ft 1:12⅘h **July 11 Bel 6f ft 1:13h** **June 29 4f ft :48⅘b**

Precious Elaine **112** **Dk. b. or br. f (1972), by Tom Fool or Advocator—Imgoinaway, by**
On-and-On. Br., Mrs. J. R. Pancoast (Fla.) 1974 3 M 1 0 $1,980
(Formerly named Idontlikehim).
Owner, A. J. Brodsky. Trainer, J. P. Conway.

Jly 15-74^{3}Aqu 6 f 1:13 ft 10 117 $1^{1\frac{1}{2}}$ $1^{1\frac{1}{2}}$ $1^{\frac{1}{2}}$ $2^{1\frac{3}{4}}$ S'nt'goA^{1} Mdn 76 Ⓕ GoldB'x117 Pr'ciousE'l'ne G'rd nQu'd 11
Jun12-74^{8}Bel 5½ f 1:03 ft 18 112 6^{4} 6^{11} 6^{23} 6^{30} Cast'daM^{5} AlwS 70 Ⓕ Ruffian 117 Copernica Jan Verzal 6
May22-74^{3}Bel 5½ f 1:03 ft 4½ 116 2^{3} 3^{9} 7^{21} 9^{34} Cast'daM^{1} Mdn 66 Ⓕ Ruffian 116 Suzest Garden Quad 10
July 24 Bel 4f ft :49b **July 10 Bel 5f ft 1:00⅕h** **July 5 Bel 3f ft :36⅘b**

But Exclusive **116** **Ch. f (1972), by Exclusive Native--Royal Bit, by Alcibiades II.**
Breeder, L. Combs II. (Ky.). 1974 3 1 2 0 $9,470
Owner, W. A. Levin. Trainer, D. A. Imperio.

Jly 12-74^{4}Aqu 5½ f 1:05⅖sft 3 118 $6^{5\frac{1}{2}}$ $4^{7\frac{1}{2}}$ 3^{6} 2^{4} VeneziaM^{1} Alw 82 Ⓕ Sc't'shM'l'dy118 B'tExcl've C's'nlvy 8
Jun22-74^{3}Bel 5½ f 1:05⅕sft 3-2 ▴116 $6^{4\frac{1}{4}}$ 3^{2} $2^{\frac{1}{2}}$ 1^{h} VeneziaM^{5} Mdn 89 Ⓕ ButExclu've116 Aw're Sc't'shM'l'dy 9
Jun10-74^{4}Bel 5½ f 1:05⅕sft 7¾ 116 $5^{7\frac{1}{2}}$ 4^{6} 4^{5} $2^{3\frac{1}{2}}$ Ven'ziaM^{1} Mdn 85 Ⓕ FrenchR'le116 B'tExcl've M'ryB'l'tine 10
July 26 Bel 4f ft :48⅕h **July 19 Bel 4f ft :47⅖hg** **July 11 Bel trt 3f ft :35⅘h**

5.
The Money Tree

Trainer Glenn C. Smith will never make the Hall of Fame at Saratoga. But I doubt seriously that he cares.

Mr. Smith, never more than a part-time claiming-horse trainer with few horses and no following, did quite well during the winter meets at Bowie a decade ago. He also helped to teach a particular struggling student of handicapping an important lesson: You can't really understand this game without taking the role of the trainer into account.

It was February 1, 1963, and I had just had a miserable afternoon at Bowie, a zero-for-nine afternoon, and I was not enjoying the four-hour bus ride back to New Jersey one bit. My handicapping had been awful, but the fellow in the back of the bus who had done considerably better was bent on giving me a headache. He was succeeding more than I cared to admit. In exasperation, I opened up the *Racing Form*—half to punish myself, half to get out of his range. What I saw is what you see below—Trojan Seth, the wire-to-wire winner of the sixth race. A 3–1 stickout trained by Mr. Smith.

Trojan Seth * **112** B. h (1958), by Trojan Monarch—Cedquest, by Alquest. Breeder C B. Caldwell.

Owner, G. C Smith. Trainer, G. C Smith. $7.500

1962	8	4	0	4	$10.422
1961	13	2	3	1	$7.240

Apr27-62^{7}Lrl	7 f 1:24⅖ft	5	114•	1^{2}	1½	2^{2}	3^{2}	AddesaE^{5}	10000	88	Cycount103 C'ch a'dF'r109 Troj'nSeth	6
Apr18-62^{6}Lrl	6 f 1:12⅘ft	3¼	114•	1½	2½	2h	3¾	AddesaE^{5}	10000	90	Klinkh'se116 C'h andF'r108 Tr'j'nSeth	10
Apr 7-62^{6}Lrl	6 f 1:11⅕sy	3	114•	2h	2½	2½	3^{2}¼	AddesaE^{1}	12000	97	Adorette115 Polyn'nB'ly115 Tr'nSeth	7
Mar28-62^{7}Bow	6 f 1:11 ft	6-5	112‡	1^{5}	1^{6}	1^{6}	1^{5}	AddesaE^{1}	Alw	96	Tr'j'nS'th112 S'r andC'm107 En'shS'le	6
Mar17-62^{7}Bow	6 f 1:11⅘ft	3-2e	113	1h	2½	2^{1}	3^{4}†	McKeeC^{2}	Alw	88	Yeuxdoux115 Adorette119 TrojanSeth	7
†Dead heat.												
Mar 5-62^{7}Bow	5½ f 1:05⅖ft	2½	▲117‡	1^{2}	1½	1h	1no	AddesaE^{2}	9000	92	TrojanSeth 117 Dollmaker 117 OleKel	6
Feb20-62^{7}Bow	6 f 1:14⅖m	2¾	▲113‡	1^{3}	1^{1}½	1h	1¾	AddesaE^{6}	8000	79	Trojan Seth 113 Dollmaker 112 Ji-Jo	6
Feb14-62^{7}Bow	6 f 1:14 sy	6-5	▲108‡	1^{1}½	1^{4}	1^{1}	1^{2}½	AddesaE^{2}	7000	81	TrojanSeth108 Dalsax1°4 Tourdan	8
Dec13-61^{6}P.m	6 f 1:13 m	12	107‡	2^{1}	2^{2}	4^{3}½	5^{6}	AddesaE^{5}	9000	79	Ano rArt114 Giewith116 Barb'raLeeG.	7

Jan 30 Bow 1m ft 1:45⅖b

According to all the rules of traditional handicapping theory, Trojan Seth should have been a throwout on the grounds of physical condition. The colt had not been out on the track for a race in over nine months. The workout, a single slow mile just two days before the race, could hardly have sharpened the colt's speed. And as the race shaped up, it was not an easy spot.

There were four recent winners shipping in from the South and two confirmed $8,500 horses dropping down in class. Now, when it was too late, the bottom two races in Trojan Seth's chart barked out their message.

Instantly, it was clear that Trojan Seth was not a horse that needed to be raced into shape. Was Smith, I wondered, the kind of man who made a habit of such doings?

The answer, along with the cure for my headache, came later that night when I compared the past performance records of all Smith's starters from the previous winter. Nine horses. Thirty-two starts. Ten total victories. An excellent 30 percent win record. But there was more, much more. I checked back over the prior year just to be sure.

There was no doubt about it; this little-known trainer brought considerable skill to his craft. Smith had a pattern. An amazing 60 percent win record with first-time starters and absentees, only one of which was a post-time favorite. But the most astounding part of the pattern was the long, slow workout that accompanied six out of his seven absentee winners. All were sprinters, all showed early speed in their past performances, and all but one scored after several months of inactivity.

The lone exception raced in a route, finished out of the money, and then came back five days later to score in a sprint at 16–1. Mr. Smith was a horseplayer's dream. A veritable money tree. He trained all his horses back on the farm, away from the prying eyes of the clockers and the competition. And the long, slow workout was just the final touch of a well-thought-out training regimen.

Each year Smith invaded Bowie with a stableful of razor-sharp claimers, got the money, went back to the farm, and smiled a lot.

I was smiling too. By meeting's end Smith won nine more races to lead the Bowie trainers. His overall win record was an excellent 30 percent. But he was five for nine with the pattern, and I was four for eight. But the moral of the story is not complete without sharing one additional detail.

One of the nonpattern horses that won for Mr. Smith was a cheap but useful three-year-old named Cedar Key. Smith lost him via the claim box for $5,000, took him back for $6,500, and then lost him again at the end of the meeting for $6,500 to Don McCoy, the same trainer who had taken him away from Smith the first time.

McCoy wanted this colt as badly as Smith, but for a very different reason. McCoy's New York client owned a bakery shop with the identical name—the Cedar Key Bakery. Of such motives are champions made.

Over the next two years, while Smith was breaking his back to win $100,000 in purses with his band of hobbled platers, Cedar Key was winning nearly $200,000 in turf stakes coast to coast. That may be one reason Mr. Smith will never make the Hall of Fame at Saratoga. For what it's worth, he has my vote.

6.
Coaching Counts

There are many successful trainers like Glenn C. Smith. Every racetrack has its aces, and each horseman brings to his craft one or more special skills (or winning strategies) that separate him from the rest of the crowd.

Some are small-time operators, patient men who spend months getting cheap, sore-legged horses fit enough to deliver one or two sharp efforts. Others travel the racing circuit first class, commanding large armies of horses on several fronts. And there are a few—throwbacks to the days when racing was truly the sport of kings—who deal only with the best-bred racing stock money can buy.

Because of these vastly different economic situations, because different trainers have rather personal methods, preferences, and skills, there is no single, simplistic formula that can be applied to a reading of physical condition. Although we all tend to forget it from time to time, the Thoroughbred racehorse is an athlete in the purest sense of the word. And to a far greater degree than most people think, the trainer is its coach.

From dawn until well after dusk, 365 days a year, the trainer must watch over the feed tub, consult the veterinarian, study the *Racing Form*, plan the workout schedule, saddle the horses, watch the days's races, make travel arrangements, supervise the stable help, reassure the owners, select the class, distance, jockey, equipment, and date of the race. The horse is a wonderfully fast, woefully fragile creature, and it takes considerable skill, timing, and patience to keep it in competition. (It also costs the owner about $11,000 a year per horse.)

"I can usually tell when a horse is a race away from losing its form," said Allen Jerkens, master horseman and the best coach a thoroughbred athlete could possibly want. No other trainer in racing is more dangerous with recently acquired stock and no other trainer is more in touch with the subtle day-to-day changes of the horses in his barn.

"There are many signs," explained Jerkens. "Every horse has his own habits. You get to know them pretty well. The ankle doesn't respond as quickly, or the hair on the coat begins to lose its sheen, or he leaves some feed in the tub. You've got to look them over very carefully. Any change makes an impression." Later, Jerkens added, "If you want to save a horse for future racing, the time to stop on him is *before* he stops on you."

A handicapper who happens to be a reporter can learn a lot touring the backstretch.

"A great many good horses are abused at an early stage in their careers," said articulate John Russell, the versatile horseman in charge of the blue-blooded Phipps Stable, a man with a strong winning history with lightly raced horses stretching out in distance, stakes-class three-year-olds, turf routers, and shippers.

Russell amplified his point. "It's a complex dilemma. First, you have to get a two-year-old to develop a little confidence, train him hard enough to be fit so he gets some benefit out of his racing. Second, the money is out of this world for a good two-year-old; and when you've got one, you have to decide how much potential the horse has to remain sound, how far you think he will want to run, and how much you can afford to push him.

"Frankly," Russell added, "I'm not opposed to breaking a horse's maiden in a first or second start—an early win is a magnificent confidence builder, the best in fact—but I'm more concerned with having a horse reach its natural peak in the spring or summer of its three-year-old season."

Not all trainers can afford the luxury of long-range planning. Where cheap horses are concerned, most goals begin and end with the here and now. Nevertheless, at each racetrack there are a few claiming-horse trainers who seem to have more patience and a better sense of timing than many stakes-class horsemen. One such trainer is Richard E. Dutrow, who has been a major force on the Maryland racing scene since leaving minor-class racing in West Virginia a dozen years ago. Another is King Leatherbury, who has been no less a force on the same circuit for a quarter century. Between them, Leatherbury and Dutrow win approximately 400 of the 2,100 races run in Maryland each season. In a very real sense they are at war with each other, but they conduct their operations in the spirit of détente.

Very rarely do they claim from each other. Very rarely do they compare notes or share insights or anything else. But they respect each other's talent and they learn from each other by competing tooth and nail throughout the long Maryland season.

Dutrow used to have difficulty stretching horses out in distance. Leatherbury is an ace at that. Leatherbury used to win most of his races with horses dropping in class. Dutrow likes to push his horses up the class ladder. Today each trainer has incorporated a few of his rival's methods. Leatherbury still has an astounding 60 percent win record with dropdowns coming back after thirty or more days' rest. But he wins more often with repeaters stepping up in class than he used to. Dutrow still wins one race in every four attempts, a record only the top twenty or thirty trainers in America can claim, but he now wins them at any distance with all types of horses.

"I'm not a claiming-horse trainer," Dutrow said to a bleary-eyed reporter one morning. "At least I'm not anymore. Right now I'm training two-year-olds, stakes horses, turf horses, and as many allowance-class runners as I have claimers." What Dutrow didn't say was that most of the allowance horses in his care started out as claimers before he solved their problems and moved them up in class.

King Leatherbury has more than a few allowance runners in his barn too, but it is still the cheap, sore-legged horse that brings out the man's best work. "When you're dealing with cheap horses, you have to be part horseman, part businessman," he explained. "You have to have the patience to wait on a horse; you can't be too aggressive, too forceful, but you can't waste a whole lot of time either. Once the horse begins to respond, you can't be thinking about next year or next week; you've got to put it in a race where it can win . . . dropping it down a notch or two in class is like taking out insurance."

"I agree," said Johnny Campo, the ebullient, oft-quoted, New York-born and -based horseman who decided he wanted to become a trainer the day he saw a Hopalong Cassidy movie in his youth, Campo is the closest thing to a Damon Runyon character on the New York backstretch, and the Belmont Stakes "Alibi Breakfast" would not be the same without him. Almost unnoticed, or perhaps partially obscured by his deceivingly clownish reputation, Campo is one of the most effective trainers of two-year-old fillies in the country, and he has nearly as much skill with allowance-class routers on the main track as with claimers of every age and sex. While Campo is not the most patient trainer of a promising three-year-old, he did show great skill with Pleasant Colony in the 1981 Triple Crown events and has trained a pair of juvenile champions—Talking Picture and Protagonist—and has ranked among the top five trainers in New York since the day he took out a trainer's license in 1970.

"I can't tell you how interesting it is to be a trainer," Campo said in a serious moment. But that didn't stop him from trying. By the third sentence he was in high form.

"Every horse is different. Some need a long-drawn-out program to get them to do anything; others will kick down the barn to get in a race or a work every three days. But don't get me wrong," he added, "I'm no genius or anything. I don't do nothing special. I just work hard, harder than most, especially on the legs. I learned a lot about legs from working for Eddie Neloy when he had all those top two-year-olds for Wheatley in the sixties. Don't let anybody tell you that top horses don't have leg problems. All horses have leg problems. That's one thing at least that all horses have in common. Fact is," he continued, "the biggest leg problem I've ever seen was on the best horse I've ever had—Protagonist—and not getting him to the Derby was my biggest disappointment so far. He would've won it. I know he would've won it. But I'll get another chance; I've got some pretty good two-year-olds in my barn right now. But what was that question you asked, something about claimers?"

"Yes, claimers, Johnny—what about claimers? Do you like to drop them in class as often as King Leatherbury?"

"Well, it works both ways," Campo responded. "A drop in class has to help most horses. That's just plain common sense. But sometimes I'll drop a horse in class because I'm praying somebody'll take the stiff off my hands. I'm sure Leatherbury does the same thing. It's like poker. Sometimes you've got to bluff and sometimes you're laying there waiting with the best hand at the table."

Phil Johnson, a first-rate public stable trainer who wins most of his races with two-year-old maidens, first-time starters, fillies, turf specialists, and high-priced claimers, had more to say on this subject: "As a rule, I'm very suspicious about dropdowns. There are few bargains and too many bargain hunters. I much prefer to take a horse that has come to life and is being stepped up a notch or two in company. You can always drop it back a bit later, but a sound, improving horse is where the money is."

Anthony Doyle, who trained the rugged Avatar to a victory in the 1975 Belmont Stakes via a series of demanding workouts at various distances, had some poignant insights into the trainer's dilemma a few hours before his greatest victory. "If you see a horse show some speed when you didn't train it hard enough to expect it, that's the time to think you might have something special," said the Irish-born Doyle, a West Coast-based horseman whose winners at every class level usually telegraph their potential via improved workouts. "But," he added, fully aware that Avatar was going to put up or shut up later in the day, "if you do train a horse hard and draw a blank, the horse is telling you something. Maybe you've made a mistake; maybe blinkers would help or a change of scenery or a switch in distance. Maybe you pushed too hard, or not hard enough. Sometimes you have to guess, sometimes the jockey will give you a clue, and sometimes the answer comes in the middle of the night."

In the middle of the night Charles Town ace Wade Johnson is usually just returning from the track. "By the time I get to work with a horse," said Johnson, "it's had maybe ten, twenty, or thirty starts, four or five different trainers, a couple of major injuries, a lot of medication, and everything has been tried already. But every horse has its hole card and every horse—even a sore-legged, eight-year-old, $1,500 claimer—can be treated with patience and respect.

"When I claim a horse like that, I'm betting my time and money that I can straighten it out fast."

Leroy Jolley, controversial, talented, and every bit as articulate as John Russell, was not talking much during Honest Pleasure's troubles in the 1976 Triple Crown chase. But in a calmer period the previous summer he offered several insights into the pressures faced by the trainer of a million-dollar horse. "If you're shooting for a major race like the Derby or the Travers or the Jockey Club Gold Cup, you can't start thinking about it two weeks beforehand," said the trainer of Foolish Pleasure, Honest Pleasure, Genuine Risk, and General Assembly.

Jolley continued: "You have to know your horse and know what you are trying to do. Every workout, each race, must have a purpose. Good horses tend to be precocious workers and you have to let them test their limits; get them tired and move them out in distance or up in company step by step. The biggest problem," Jolley said with emphasis, "is not getting them fit but *keeping* them fit. One unlucky break or bad step can ruin a month's worth of training or even end a horse's career. I suppose I've been pretty lucky so far, but I've also been very careful."

"I don't know about the Derby. I've never had a horse good enough to think about it," said Ida Mae Parrish, a Midwestern-based horsewoman who annually demolished the Massachusetts fair circuit (40 percent winners) over a ten-year period. "But to get a stableful of cheap claimers ready to win, you have to freshen them up, give them a lot of long, slow gallops, a decent work or a prep race, and crack down hard at the first sign of improvement. If you get too cute or wait too long to put them in a sensible spot, you'll never pay the feed bills, much less win a race."

According to the American Racing Manual and other authoritative sources, there are approximately 11,500 licensed trainers in North America.

More than 2,000 failed to win a single race in 1981.

A thousand more failed to win as few as ten races, and another thousand failed to win twenty.

Looking at this picture from the opposite perspective, the top 500 trainers have won approximately 25 percent of all the purse money distributed in each of the past three calendar years. Barely more than 125 were good enough to win one race in every five attempts.

For his own protection alone, the player should know which trainers have winning skill, what that skill is, and which ones can't train their way out of a paper bag.

7.
The Trainer's Window

In the hands of one trainer, a horse with good recent form might be an excellent wager; in the care of another, the horse might be ready to fall apart at the seams.

In the hands of an ace, a horse stepping up sharply in company or stretching out in distance might well be expected to handle the task; in the care of a lesser talent, such a maneuver might only be an experiment or an unnecessary risk.

Naturally, the vast majority of trainers like to bet to overcome their financial difficulties or to take advantage of their skill; but the player is misled if he thinks they are any better at handicapping than they are at their chosen craft. The horse may have a fine turn of speed or suddenly show signs of life; but if the trainer is impatient, sloppy, or incompetent, he will find a way to lose control of the horse and blow the best of opportunities.

Maybe the horse is crying for a route race on the turf, or perhaps he needs a better jockey or a change in equipment or a shorter resting period between starts. Maybe the horse has been too ambitiously placed too often or has left his race on the training track. You'd be amazed how many horses are mismanaged in that fashion.

The positive and negative impact of the trainer on horse performance is all too rarely taken into account by the average horseplayer, who at best glances at the leading trainers' list and automatically assumes universal competence.

But the mistake is easily corrected, and it is great fun.

After all, the past performance profile is not only a summation of horse performance but a window through which the talents, habits, and strategies of the trainer can be seen.

For example, by comparing the past performance records of a dozen or so winners (and losers) trained by Woody Stephens, the player will know for a certainty that the man is an absolute master with an improving three-year-old as well as with stakes-class fillies and mares on and off the grass course. Stephens is the winningest trainer of stakes in the history of American racing and he didn't reach that plateau without going to school on the job.

His approach, like the approach of many of the best horsemen who have graced the twentieth-century racing scene, has been to mix extraordinary patience with the boldness of a bank robber. When Woody Stephens sets a horse down for a series of hard races, the signs are unmistakable and the horse will nearly always fire *two, three,* or *four solid efforts in succession.* No task is deemed impossible, but no horse is ever asked to do what is physically beyond its capabilities.

The remarkable but predictable development of Conquistador Cielo is an example worthy of careful study.

Below are this great horse's past performances as they appeared prior to his track record victory in the Metropolitan Mile, a prestigious handicap for three-year-olds and up, contested around one turn at Belmont Park, May 31, 1982.

Conquistador Cielo			B. c. 3, by Mr Prospector—K D Princess, by Bold Commander					
			Br.—Iandoli L E (Fla)		1982	4	3 0 0	$46,300
Own.—deKwiatkowski H		**111**	Tr.—Stephens Woodford C		1981	4	2 0 1	$49,668
			Lifetime	8	5 0 1	$95,968		
19May82-7Bel	1 :45⁴ 1:09⁴ 1:34¹ft	*2-3 113	1hd 13 17 11¹	Maple E⁴	Aw35000	95	ConqstdorClo,SwngngLght,BchlorB 7
8May82-7Pim	1⅛ :47³ 1:11³ 1:44¹ft	*1-2 112	2² 2¹ 11½ 1³	Maple E³	Aw27000	84	ConquistdorCielo,DoubleNo,SixSils 5
26Feb82-7Hia	7f :22⁴ :45¹ 1:22¹ft	*3-5 116	1½ 11½ 12½ 1⁴	Maple E¹	Aw14000	92	ConquistdorCilo,Hostg,MysticSqur 7
16Feb82-9Hia	7f :22³ :44³ 1:23 ft	5½ 116	53½ 67½ 44 47½	Maple E¹	Aw14000	81	Star Gallant, CutAway,Rex'sProfile 7
12Aug81-8Sar	6f :21³ :45 1:11¹gd	3½ 122	64½ 78 54½ 4nk	Maple E²	Sanford	84	Mayanesian,ShippingMgnte,Lejoli 10
3Aug81-8Sar	6f :22¹ :45³ 1:10³ft	8½ 117	63¾ 2hd 1hd 1½	Maple E²	Sar Spec'l	87	ConqstdorCl,Hrschlwlkr,TmlyWrtr 10
10Jly81-6Bel	5½f :23 :46⁴ 1:05 ft	*8-5 118	3² 21 13 1⁸	Saumell L7	Mdn	90	ConquistdorCilo,HghAscnt,Grrs'Ldr 9
29Jun81-4Bel	5½f :22⁴ :46⁴ 1:06²ft	4½ 118	44½ 53 23 33½	Saumell L9	Mdn	82	AntgBrd,Commodty,ConqstdorClo 10
● May 26 Bel 6f ft 1:10² h		● May 16 Bel 5f ft :59 h		May 6 Bel 4f ft :47 h		May 2 Bel 5f ft 1:00 h		

Stephens knew he had an outstanding colt in the summer of 1981, when C.C. ran a great race to finish fourth, despite suffering a minor fracture and a world of traffic trouble.

Instead of rushing his prize colt into the Triple Crown chase, Woody took special care to give C.C. lessons in a variety of racing situations, including a race around two turns at Pimlico one week prior to the Preakness and a rather convincing win over older horses in an allowance race at Belmont, May 19.

Following his awesome victory in the Met, Stephens became characteristically aggressive, throwing a razor-sharp, budding superhorse into the grueling 1½-mile Belmont Stakes five days later.

(At 4–1, the betting public and most of the public handicappers seemed to rely far too much on doubts about C.C.'s apparent breeding limitations, and in the process they ignored the colt's overpowering final quarter-mile splits, already displayed in three straight winning races at one mile or longer.)

This kind of horse training is literally textbook material, and it would serve the player well to take special note of every nuance, every last ounce of information. The same can be said for the work of other outstanding horsemen who, like Stephens, have gained their knowledge over years of trial and error.

Frank Whiteley Jr. and his son David are two horsemen in particular who fit into this category. By comparing the past performances of the champion Forego with those of Sarsar, Near East, and Highland Blade, the player will know for certain that every horse these two men send to the post is a dangerous contender.

There are no frills, no tricks, no wild experiments.

A sprinter is kept sprinting, a stakes horse is given a balanced, well-spaced campaign, and a first-time starter is well prepared and well meant.

Mistakes are made; but they are seldom repeated. Experiments are tried; but if they do not produce improvement or satisfactory results, the horse is promptly returned to familiar conditions.

You can learn a lot about good horsemanship by looking through the Whiteleys' window.

Forego **137** B. g (1970) by Forli—Lady Golconda by Hasty Road.
Breeder. Lazy F Ranch (Ky.). 1976 7 5 1 1 $321,481
Owner, Lazy F Ranch. Trainer, Frank Y. Whiteley, Jr. 1975 9 6 1 1 $429,521

18 Sep76	^{8}Bel	1⅛	$:45^3 1:09^1 1:45^4$	ft	1	▲135	7^6	$7^{6\frac{1}{2}}$	$4^{2\frac{1}{2}}$	$1^{1\frac{1}{4}}$	ShmkrW^2	HcpS	98	Forego 135	Dance Spell	10
21 Aug76	^{8}Mth	1¼	$:47^2 1:11^2 2:00^3$	ft	3-5	▲136	3^3	2^2	2^1	3^1	VasquzJ^7	HcpS	98	HatchetMan112	IntrepidHro	8
24 Jly 76	^{8}Aqu	1¼	$:46^4 1:11^1 2:01^1$	ft	2-3	▲134	$6^{8\frac{1}{2}}$	$2^{1\frac{1}{2}}$	2^h	1^2	CustinsH^4	HcpS	90	Forego 134	Lord Rebeau	8
5 Jly 76	^{8}Aqu	1$\frac{3}{16}$	$:47^4 1:11^2 1:55^2$	ft	2-5	▲134	$3^{2\frac{1}{2}}$	$2^{1\frac{1}{2}}$	$3^{1\frac{1}{2}}$	2no	GustinsH^2	HcpS	85	Foolish Pleasure 125	Forego	4
13 Jun76	^{8}Bel	1⅛	$:47^2 1:11^2 1:48^3$	ft	4-5	▲132	$4^{2\frac{1}{2}}$	3^2	1^h	$1^{2\frac{3}{4}}$	VsquezJ^1	HcpS	84	Forego 132	El Pitirre	5
31 May76	^{8}Bel	1	$:45^3 1:09^2 1:34^4$	ft	1	▲130	$5^{4\frac{1}{2}}$	4^4	$4^{1\frac{1}{2}}$	1^h	GustinsH^4	HcpS	94	Forego 130	Master Derby	6
20 May76	^{8}Bel	7 f	$:23^4 :46^4 1:22$	ft	1-3	▲126	$4^{1\frac{1}{2}}$	$3^{\frac{1}{2}}$	1^h	$1^{1\frac{1}{4}}$	GustinesH^2	Alw	92	Forego 126	Wishing Stone	4

Oct 1 Bel 4f sy :46h **Sept 27 Bel 1f ft 1:43⅘b** **Sept 25 Bel 5f ft 1:05b**

Sarsar **117** Ch. f (1972), by Damascus—Durga, by Tatan.
Breeder, A. B. Hancock, Jr. (Ky.). 1974 0 M 0 0 (——)
Owner, W. H. Perry. Trainer, D. A. Whiteley.
Juiy 15 Bel 5f ft :58h **July 9 Bel 4f ft :49bg** **July 4 Bel 4f ft :47⅕h**

Near East — Gr. g. 5, by Damascus—Shenanigans, by Native Dancer
Br.—Janney Mr-Mrs S S Jr (Ky) — 1981 8 6 0 0 $84,000
Own.—Locust Hill Farm — **116** — Tr.—Whiteley David A — 1980 0 M 0 0
Lifetime 8 6 0 0 $84,000

24Sep81-8Bel	1 1/16	:47^1	1:11^1	1:41^{4}ft	*7-5	117	1^{hd}	1^2	1^9	1^{11}	Vasquez J^7	Aw35000	93	Near East, Globe, Fiddle Faddle	7
26Aug81-8Bel	1	:45	1:08^4	1:33^{4}ft	12	112	3^1	5^8	5^{11}	5^{15}	MacBeth D^4	Forego H	84	Fppino,HerbWter,GuiltyConscience	5
4Aug81-9Mth	1	:46^1	1:10^1	1:35^{3}ft	3¼	116	5^{3½}	8^{8½}	11^{15}	10^{15}	VasquezJ^{11}	Sal Mile H	80	ColonelMoran,SunCtcher,Pikotzo	12
11Jly81-7Bel	1	:45^2	1:09^4	1:35^{2}ft	*1-2	115	2^{1½}	1^{hd}	1^{hd}	1^{½}	Vasquez J^4	Aw35000	91	NerEst,DiplomticNot,ThLibrlMmbr	8
10Jun81-7Bel	7f	:23^3	:47	1:22^{1}ft	8-5	119	1^{1½}	1^2	1^3	1^6	Vasquez J^4	Aw23000	91	NerEst,VoodooRhythm,PintedShild	5
22May81-6Bel	6f	:22^3	:46	1:11 ft	*2¼	117	2^1	2^{½}	1^{1½}	1^2	Vasquez J^3	Aw20000	87	Near East, Sly Flyer,Caesar'sWorld	7
4Feb81-3GP	6f	:22^4	:46^1	1:11^{2}ft	*1-2	122	2^{hd}	1^{hd}	2^{hd}	1^{hd}	Vasquez J^9	Aw14000	82	Near East, Lunarian, Cheverdeen	9
14Jan81-4GP	6f	:22^4	:46	1:10^{3}ft	*6-5	122	1^{hd}	1^{½}	1^1	1^{1½}	Vasquez J^7	Mdn	86	NearEast,WillieByrd,Triggs'zAsset	10

Jun 8 Bel 5f ft 1:01^1 b — Jun 5 Bel 5f gd 1:03^2 b — Jun 2 Bel 4f sy :50^3 b — May 15 Bel 6f ft 1:13^4 h

Highland Blade — Dk. b. or br. c. 4, by Damascus—Misty Bryn, by Misty Flight
Br.—Pen-Y-Bryn Farm (Ky) — 1982 3 3 0 0 $102,000
Own.—Pen-Y-Bryn Farm — **125** — Tr.—Whiteley David A — 1981 10 4 2 1 $206,813
Lifetime 17 8 2 1 $322,013 — Turf 10 7 0 0 $170,607

29May82-8Bel	1¼ [T]	:50^2	1:41	2:06^{2}sf	2½	124	8^{6¾}	3^{½}	2^{½}	1^{¾}	VsquzJ^8	Red Smith H	62	HighlandBlde,DomMenotti,OpenCll	8
6May82-7Aqu	1 (T)	:48^1	1:11^4	1:36^{2}fm	*9-5	115	8^5	6^{3¾}	1^{hd}	1^{1¾}	Vasquez J^2	Aw35000	96	HighlandBlade,OpenCall,Mr.Dremer	8
13Feb82-8Hia	a1⅛ (T)			1:47^{4}fm	*7-5	119	12^{9½}	8^5	4^{1½}	1no	Vasquez J^2	Aw20000	93	HighlandBlade,Robsphere,DatSwp	12
3Oct81-8Bel	1⅜ (T)	:48^4	1:37^4	2:14^{4}fm	*9-5	121	6^{11}	6^{7½}	6^{7½}	6^{6¾}	VasquezJ^5	Man O War	81	GlxyLibr,MtchTheHtch,‡NtivCourir	6
19Sep81-8Bel	1 1/16 [T]	:49^1	1:13^4	1:46^{1}sf	*4-5	113	7^{7¼}	6^{4¼}	1^{½}	1^{3¾}	Vasquez J^4	Aw35000	70	HighlandBlade,Mr.Dreamer,NoBend	7
18Jly81-8Bel	1½	:49^2	2:01^3	2:26 ft	*2¼	113	4^5	5^2	5^{5½}	6^{9¼}	VasquezJ^4	Brooklyn H	81	Hechizdo,TheLiberlMmbr,PtMoss	10
4Jly81-8Bel	1¼	:47^3	1:36	2:02 sy	6¼	113	8^{13}	5^{5½}	4^4	3^{¾}	VsquezJ^8	Suburban H	89	TmprncHill,RingofLight,HighlndBld	8
6Jun81-8Bel	1½	:48^2	2:04	2:29 ft	13	126	9^7	2^4	2^3	2^{nk}	Vasquez J^2	Belmont	75	Summing,HighlndBld,PlsntColcny	11

Jun 11 Bel 4f ft :49^1 b — Jun 6 Bel 4f sy :51 b — Jun 3 Bel 4f ft :49^4 b — May 27 Bel 4f ft :49^2 b

NOTE: *Honorable Miss' past performance profile is on page 132.*

If you were to perform a similar study on Jack Van Berg, probably the busiest and best trainer in the Midwest, you would also find unmistakable patterns staring you in the face.

Like Whiteley, Van Berg gives stakes horses consistent, thoroughly professional management. But with claimers and modest class allowance stock, Van Berg operates with an arsenal of maneuvers that produces one winner in every four attemps at a half dozen racetracks. (For six straight seasons in the 1970s Van Berg averaged over 350 winners a year!) It is astounding, perhaps, but Van Berg's three most productive winning patterns account for almost half his total victories and would have produced a flat bet profit over the past ten years. Along with Robert Frankel, Wayne Lucas, Mike Mitchell, the father and son team of F. W. and Gary Jones (California), Daniel Hasbany (New England), Richard Hazelton and Frank Brothers (Illinois), Allen

Jerkens, Howard Tesher, Laz Barrera, Joe Trovato (New York), Dewey Smith (Louisiana), Dale Baird (West Virginia), Ronald Alfano, Dick Dutrow (Maryland), Mike Sedlacek, Efrain Garcia, Henry Carroll, W. A. Croll Jr. (New Jersey), and several other fine horsemen, Van Berg is deadly with repeaters going up in class as well as with recent claims. On the other hand, a Van Berg winner attempting a repeat victory at the same class level or lower is usually a poor risk (approximately one win for every eight attempts). The same is true for most of the other horsemen who tend to win going up the ladder.

Obviously, it takes considerable horsemanship to know that a horse is fit enough and fast enough to beat better competition. And it takes no less skill to spot genuine value in another man's horse. It costs money to claim a horse. Not Monopoly money— *real* money: $5,000, $10,000, $20,000 and up. If a trainer at your favorite track seems particularly skillful with recent claims, it would be worthwhile to pull out a few past performance profiles and compare them. Possibly he likes to give his recent claims a few weeks off, or else break them in with an easy race. Some trainers prefer to wait out the thirty-day "jail" period which most states require. (After a claim, the trainer is forced to race the horse at a price at least 25 percent higher for a period of thirty days.) Perhaps you will conclude that there is no apparent pattern. Don't believe it. That is rarely the case. You're probably not looking at the right clues. For example, the third and most significant Van Berg pattern has nothing to do with past performance records as they appear in the *Daily Racing Form*. It merely has to do with where he is!

To a far greater extent than any horseman I have ever seen, Jack Van Berg is prone to go on incredible winning binges, seemingly at will. In amazing Ripley-like fashion, these streaks invariably coincide with his travel itinerary.

Van Berg has many horses under his wing and operates at two or three tracks simultaneously, often leading the trainers' standings at each racetrack. But if he is not on the grounds to personally supervise the training regimen of his stock, only his recent claims and repeaters win more than their share of races. If he is on the grounds, however, and has indicated control over the situation by winning two races back to back or three out of five, the odds say he'll win fifteen more before he saddles thirty or thirty-five to the post. Sometimes such a streak will last a month or more; sometimes it will be the only clue a player will get.

During the 1970s, Van Berg orchestrated at least three dozen such explosions at racetracks all over the country. And aside from the extraordinary reliability of his repeaters stepping up in company, there was no concrete theory of handicapping or insight into the conditioning process that explained some of his wins. But don't say I didn't warn you.

Can you imagine the kind of bet Lucky Principio was when he came back April 2 to attempt a repeat victory in the middle of a Van Berg streak?

Lucky Principio **112** **Dk. b. or br. g (1972), by Sir Ivor—Spar Officer, by Round Table.**
Breeder, Carver Stable (Ky.). **1976 4 2 0 0 $19,500**
Owner. P J. Luckino. Trainer, J. Van Berg. **1975 7 3 2 0 $14,744**

2 Apr76	8OP	6 f	:21^4 :45^1 1:09^3	ft	14	115	$6^{8\frac{3}{4}}$	$6^{6\frac{1}{4}}$	$5^{2\frac{1}{2}}$	1no	WhitedDE1	Alw	97	LckyPrncpo115	ChnceLndng	7
27 Mar76	5OP	6 f	:21^3 :45^1 1:11	ft	11	119	$6^{3\frac{1}{4}}$	$5^{2\frac{3}{4}}$	2^h	1no	WhitdDE1	25000	90	LuckyPrincipio119	King'sCre	12
19 Mar76	7OP	6 f	:21^4 :44^4 1:11	ft	28	110	6^{10}	$6^{8\frac{1}{2}}$	6^6	$7^{3\frac{1}{2}}$	MiceliM4	33000	86	JustAWondr112	MilingoEstr	8
28 Feb76	7Hia	6 f	:22 :45 1:09^4	ft	14	117	$6^{3\frac{1}{2}}$	$6^{3\frac{1}{2}}$	$8^{5\frac{3}{4}}$	$10^{8\frac{3}{4}}$	FieslmnJ4	25000	85	LoveReality115	LucayanBrze	10
29 Nov75	9HP	6½ f	:23^2 :49^1 1:23	sy	3½	110	$1^{\frac{1}{2}}$	2^h	3^3	$4^{9\frac{1}{2}}$	JonesK5	HcpS	56	Ske theAnvl 118	Dr'sEnjyDs	6
22 Nov75	3HP	6½ f	:23^2 :48 1:20^2	gd	2	▲119	1^1	$1^{\frac{1}{2}}$	1^6	1^{10}	JonesK4	Alw	79	LckyPrincipio119	I CanHcktt	8
13 Nov75	7HP	6 f	:24^3 :49^3 1:16	ft	1-2	▲119	$2^{1\frac{1}{2}}$	1^1	1^4	1^5	JonesK6	Alw	72	LkyPrincipio119	BelmrLanes	7
7 Nov75	8HP	4 f	:22^4 :47^4	ft	1	▲114	5	3^3	2^2	1no	JonesK5	Alw	86	LkyPrincpio114	Whps aDaisy	10
1 Apr75	4OP	6 f	:21^4 :45^1 1:11^2	ft	3½	113	$7^{5\frac{3}{4}}$	$5^{5\frac{1}{2}}$	$5^{1\frac{1}{4}}$	$2^{2\frac{1}{2}}$	LivelyJ4	Mdn	85	BeauMatt113	LckyPrincipio	11
26 Mar75	4OP	6 f	:22^1 :45^3 1:11^1	ft	1	▲113	2^h	2^h	4^1	$4^{4\frac{1}{2}}$	StrassRO1	Mdn	84	Galley Ho 113	Beau Matt	12

April 9 HP 4f ft :49⅗b **March 10 HP 4f gd :53b**

Winding River (below) was a Van Berg claim on March 27. There was no streak going at Sportsman's Park on April 8, but there was a repeater pattern. Thirteen to one is mind bending. In today's race Winding River remains at the same $8,500 class level. I hope there is something else worth playing in this race because Winding River is going to be the favorite. He may win, but Van Berg knows this horse is not as sharp as he looks. Otherwise he would step him up in class again.

Winding River ✻ **116** Dk. b. or br. h (1971). by Crafty Admiral—Santa's Creek, by River War.
Breeder, S. Cohn (Md.).

				1976	7	2	0	2	$8,640
			$8,500	1975	14	0	5	3	$9,383

Owner, J. Van Berg.   Trainer, J. Van Berg.

8 Apr76	9Spt	1 :4841:1511:411ft	⑬	115	33	2h	11	121	TurctteRL5 8500 74 WindgRivr115 Sctch andSda 10
27 Mar76	6FG	1 1/16 :4741:1311:463ft	31	114	67	36	221	1nk	GuajdoA2 ©500 82 WindingRiver114 FowlLuck 8
21 Mar76	7FG	6 f :22 :4541:11 ft	19	112	871	77	541	551	GuajrdoA5 8000 84 Kerry Debby 104 Timoteo 8
10 Mar76	7FG	6 f :222 :4621:114ft	15	114	751	65	331	541	GuajrdoA3 8000 81 Bandwagon114 NationalNote 8
18 Feb76	9FG	140 :4641:1221:403ft	71	113	561	341	431	39	PowerJ10 c6250 81 Sctch andSda113 CurusKitn 10
7 Feb76	3FG	1 1/16 :4821:1411:46 ft	31	113	411	1h	21	341	DayP8 6500 80 Tumizon 116 Tioo Ke' 8
31 Jan76	5FG	6 f :222 :4621:12 ft	41	115	851	911	917	910	TrosclrR5 7500 75 SpanishState117 FuelPrince 9
14 Sep75	6LaD	6 f :23 :4611:122ft	81	116	67	571	351	511	DupasR3 1300C 101 Peerless Prince 120 Truxton 9
6 Sep75	7LaD	6 f :234 :4741:272sl	21	▲116	67	671	611	591	FrominM2 1500 89 Amberope118 WindingRiver 6
30 Aug75	6LaD	6 f :231 :4731:134ft	2	116	48	49	37	271	FrominM5 16000 88 Bill'sCmet116 Run to theWe 8

April 16 Spt 5f ft 1:03b   April 5 Kee 5f ft 1:02b

The following horse is one of eight stakes winners trained by
Jack Van Berg during the first six months of 1976. Looks like
Frank Whiteley's work, doesn't it? Obviously, the man knows
how to read a condition book and is not afraid to go hunting.

Summertime Promise **119** B. f (1972), by Nijinsky II.—Prides Promise, by Crozier.
Breeder, P. Mellon (Va.).

			1976	9	3	5	1	$139,250
			1975	8	2	1	2	$65,300

Owner, K. Opstein. Trainer, J. Van Berg.

7Jly 76	8AP	⊤ 1 :4731:1141:38 fm1-2	▲122	11	14	14	11	SnyderL7 Alw 85 ⒻSmrtmePmise122 Ksaptmus 7
19May76	8Hol	⊤ 1 1/16 :4721:1131:414fm	21	▲119	21	21	2h	32	LivelyJ7 HcpS 88 ⒻMiaAmore116 Bastonerall. 7
8May76	8Haw	⊤ 1 :4921:1421:404sf 4-5	▲120	121	1h	13	13	LivelyJ3 HcpS 67 ⒻSmrtimePmise120 MiniGift 10
17Apr76	8Pim	⊤ 1 1/16 :4731:1121:421fm	31	117	1h	1h	1h	2nk	MHeDG9 HcpS 100 ⒻDese duVI 119 SmtmePmse 9
31Mar76	8OP	170 :4621:1121:403ft	2	119	21	21	12	1nk	McHeDG2 HcpS 93 ⒻSumertmePrmise119 Baygo 9
29Feb76	8SA	11 :4821:1231:492ft	17	114	11	31	2h	2no	McHgeDG5 InvH 85 ⒻFscntgGrl 115 SmrtmePmse 8
14Feb76	9Hia	⊤ 11	1:482hd 31	114	21	211	21	21	McHgeD1 HcpS 91 ⒻYsDrMggy116 SmrtmePmse 14
4Feb76	9Hia	⊤ 1 1/16	1:414fm 41	115	12	111	12	2no	McHeD12 HcpS 89 ⒻRedndcy117 SmrtmePrnse 12

No streak, no claim, no repeat, no step-up in class. No play.

Nowata Pride **117** Gr. c (1973), by Thermos—Swing Time Too, by Leisure Time.
Breeder, C. E. Stewart (Okla.).

			1976	2	1	0	0	$6,400
			$12,500	1975	3	1	1	0	$3,768

Owner, Mrs. J. Potrykus.   Trainer, J. Van Berg.

11 Mar76	10P	6 f :221 :4621:13 ft	2	▲122	42	32	421	513	MapleS7 15000 78 Two Rivers 115 Quen Boy 12
24 Feb76	10P	6 f :214 :46 1:113ft	12	116	11	11	131	11	MapleS1 15000 87 NwataPride116 RunForClem 12
22 Nov75	10HP	61 f :232 :4741:222gd	41	113	1216111612241223	StraussR8 HcpS 46 Alastair 122 Tidoc 12
11 Nov75	1HP	6 f :25 :4911:161ft 3-5	▲120	11	12	13	15	StraussR1 Mdn 71 NowataPre120 NationlArmr 8
29 Oct75	1HP	4 f :233 :483ft	33	120	4	441	471	25	StraussR7 Mdn 77 SenatrKiddoo120 NowataPde 10

Feb 8 OP 4f ft :493/5b

Van Berg isn't the only trainer who goes on winning streaks.

All good trainers tend to get hot from time to time. It's important to be able to detect such patterns in the making.

Sometimes a trainer will point for a particular meeting, à la Glenn C. Smith or Iva Mae Parrish. Sometimes he must sacrifice a month or two of racing to get ready.

When Frank Martin, a hard man to pin down, went to California for the 1974–1975 winter racing season, he obviously had Aqueduct on his mind. Martin won only two races in fifty-odd starts at Santa Anita, but he returned to New York with a barnful of tigers. Three weeks into his 1975 Aqueduct winter invasion Martin had nineteen winners; eight weeks later he had fifty. An astute player in California or New York who was willing to look through Frank Martin's window might well have gotten the message by the third racing day.

Just as the best trainers tend to get hot, they also suffer occasional losing streaks. Fortunately, the player can often spot such losing patterns in the making.

Has the trainer abandoned a successful pattern or strategy? Perhaps he has had to push his horses very hard of late in pursuit of extra victories. Maybe horses and trainer need a rest. Or maybe the horseman is trying to shake off the effects of tough recent defeats or a disastrous break. A few years ago John Parisella, a fine horseman, lost most of his horses by fire. Even when he got new stock it took him a full year to get back into a winning groove.

Naturally, some trainers will emerge from such difficulties with added confidence, while others will never be heard from again. And there are also a few who do not need a disaster or an emotional trauma to bring out their worst. A trio of well-known trainers from the recent past—Del Carroll, John Gaver Sr., and Reggie Cornell—are interesting cases in point.

All three had more than their share of stakes victories; all knew their way to the winner's circle and all were in the 20 percent winner's bracket. But even so, all three had great difficulty coping with certain circumstances and frequently tele-graphed their defeats through glaring mistakes of judgment.

Carroll, extremely well liked by most of his peers, was a prominent winner with allowance-class fillies, turf runners, and lightly raced maidens. But he had a hole in his game and some of the best horses he trained had very short careers.

When his Bee Bee Bee upset the Preakness field in 1972, leaving Key to the Mint and Riva Ridge in his wake, the sloppy track helped, but the result was no fluke. Bee Bee Bee was a very fast, very strong racehorse, one who might have become cham-pion, but he was never given a settled program to follow.

In 1970 Carroll got an improving runner named Bushido ready to score a well-deserved but predictable "upset" in the John B. Campbell Handicap at Bowie. At the time the Campbell was one of the most prestigious handicap races on the national racing calendar, a race that had been won by numerous Hall-of-Famers, including the mighty Kelso, Mongo, and Tosmah. Bushido looked very impressive on the day of his biggest lifetime victory, but afterward he was never heard from again.

And then in 1974 Carroll had an opportunity to deliver a solid one-two punch in the important Triple Crown classics, with Better Arbitor and Eastern Lord, two extremely fast horses in a year that sorely lacked depth and quality. With all of these very good horses, Carroll ducked a variety of logical spots, changed strategies, tried the grass course, pointed for meaningless races, worked his already fit horses too fast and too often, and won very few races.

As a rule, Carroll was always dangerous with a longshot in a stakes race, but once his best horses reached their peak, they would often lose their edge mysteriously, sometimes without any apparent warning. The bottom line is that no trainer can hope to get the most out of a good horse through tentative management. A good horse needs the best of handling and when it finally does get to its maximum potential, the trainer must pursue a solid strategy to get the desired results.

Although Del Carroll did seem to have his difficulties in keeping good horses on target, I doubt seriously that any trainer ever had more problems in this regard than Reggie Cornell. After gaining a noteworthy reputation in 1958 as the man behind the incredible Silky Sullivan (would you believe that Silky once won a 6½-furlong race at Santa Anita after breaking *forty-seven lengths behind his field!*), Cornell won some and lost some during the next twelve years without stirring up much of a fuss. In the early 1970s, however, he was given the top training post at fabled Calumet Farms, once the nation's premier racing stable. It turned out to be a disastrous relationship.

Calumet had been in decline for much of the 1960s, but began a strong comeback under Henry Forrest in 1968, with Forward Pass and other promising horses. Cornell inherited a stable on the rebound, a stable that was destined to provide him with more top-class racing prospects during the next few years than most trainers get to work with in a lifetime: Horses like Gleaming, Bold and Able, Eastern Fleet, Prince Turian, Turn to Turia, and the freakishly fast Raise a Cup.

All these horses signaled their championship potential by winning at least one stakes race very impressively, and at least half a dozen other horses showed similar ability in their first or second start. Every spring Calumet seemed loaded for bear, ready to dominate the racing calendar. But by August almost every last horse worthy of note was on the sidelines for repairs or on the verge of breaking down. Most, it seems to me, were kept out of races that were all too obviously theirs to win and were instead pushed to the breaking point on the training track. With first-time starters and absentees, Cornell was a solid 20 percent winner his whole working life. But two or three races or a dozen fast workouts later, and the player would read the predictable note in the *Daily Racing Form* announcing the horse's sudden departure from competition.

John Gaver Sr., a genuine Hall-of-Famer, was another who seemed to put excessive pressure on his horses in the morning.

Notwithstanding his lifetime record, which included some out-standing achievements with the likes of Stagedoor Johnny and Stop the Music, I am three-quarters convinced the man thought every horse in his barn was the reincarnation of Tom Fool, the rugged handicap champion Gaver developed in the early 1950s.

Tom Fool would often work near track record time between starts and then on race day he'd run his eyeballs out, winning twenty-one out of thirty lifetime starts, including his last eleven in succession under 126–136 pounds.

Some horses thrive on the kind of training regimen that pushes them constantly against their limits. Most, however, will buckle under the punishment and sulk or break down, losing their interest or giving in to pain, never to be heard from again.

Frankly my mind boggles at the number of races a patient trainer like Frank Whiteley Jr. or his son would have won with some of the horses trained by Gaver, Cornell, and Carroll, horses that showed signs of brilliance, horses you and I will never hear about.

The player has to be on guard with trainers who have problems that repeat themselves. The horses they train will go off form or lose races they should win.

On the other hand, give a promising young horse to a trainer like Elliott Burch or Charles Whittingham, and you may see an early win, but it is doubtful you will see the true ability of the horse until it turns three on New Year's Day. Burch, Whit-tingham, and a few other scattered horsemen are from a com-pletely different orientation than the trainer who seeks glory with two-year-olds in five- and six-furlong stakes.

Burch trains horses to run far and to last from one season to the next.

Fast workouts? Definitely. But each workout is designed to complement the horse's progress in actual races—to advance it toward a longer distance, sharpen its speed, or just keep it within range of Burch's control between important engagements. Once top form has been achieved, Burch will decrease the frequency, the speed, or the distance of the workouts (or all three) in direct proportion to the horse's actual racing opportunities. With that kind of sensible management, Elliott Burch frequently gets two, three, or four wins in a row out of his best-grade stock. And he is just as liable to do that with a good grass horse as he is with a three-year-old colt or filly. The player who knows that about Burch's training skill can string along for a very profitable ride.

Glowing Tribute **121** **B. f (1973), by Graustark—Admiring, by Hail to Reason. Breeder, P. Mellon (Va.).**

Owner, Rokeby Stable. Trainer, E. Burch.

1976	9	5	1	1	$91,825
1975	5	1	1	1	$8.460

6 Aug76	^{8}Sar	Ⓣ $1\frac{1}{16}$	:46	1:10^1	1:41^1	fm	6-5	▲113	$2^{1\frac{1}{2}}$	2^1	1^h	1^2	DayP^8	HcpO	91	ⒻGlowgTribte113	Assmblyn	10
17 Jly 76	^{6}Aqu	Ⓣ $1\frac{1}{8}$	:49	1:13	1:49^1	gd	$3\frac{1}{2}$	110	1^h	2^h	$1^{\frac{1}{2}}$	$1^{\frac{3}{4}}$	DayP^4	HcpS		ⒻGlwngTribute110	Bubbling	6
10 Jly 76	^{7}Aqu	Ⓣ 1	:47^2	1:12^1	1:36^1	fm	4-5	▲111	1^1	$1^{1\frac{1}{2}}$	1^4	$1^{2\frac{3}{4}}$	DayP^4	Alw		ⒻGlwngTrbute111	StdntLdr	8
31 May76	^{6}Bel	Ⓣ $1\frac{1}{16}$	:46^2	1:10^1	1:41^1	fm	10	112	1^2	$1^{1\frac{1}{2}}$	1^3	1^5	DayP,	Alw	94	ⒻGlowngTrbte112	StdntLdr	9
4 May76	^{7}Bel	6 f	:22^4	:45^3	1:11	ft	11	111	$8^{6\frac{1}{4}}$	$9^{8\frac{1}{2}}$	$7^{5\frac{3}{4}}$	3^3	GustinesH^8	Alw	84	ⒻFurling 113	Desert Boots	10
9 Apr76	^{7}Aqu	6 f	:23	:46^2	1:11^4	ft	$4\frac{1}{2}$	121	$5^{2\frac{3}{4}}$	$3^{5\frac{1}{2}}$	4^7	4^5	GustinesH^5	Alw	79	ⒻIn theOffing114	DesertBts	6
29 Mar76	^{6}Aqu	7 f	:23	:46^1	1:23^4	ft	3	121	5^5	$5^{4\frac{1}{2}}$	4^3	$4^{4\frac{1}{4}}$	VasquezJ^6	Alw	78	ⒻFrlssQueen118	In theOffng	9
5 Mar76	^{6}Hia	6 f	:22^1	:46	1:11^2	ft	$4\frac{3}{4}$	116	5^5	$3^{3\frac{1}{2}}$	1^1	1^5	GustinesH^9	Alw	86	ⒻGlowingTrbte116	PlsntTne	10
21 Feb76	^{5}Hia	6 f	:22^1	:46^1	1:12^1	ft	$5\frac{3}{4}$	116	$3^{\frac{3}{4}}$	$4^{\frac{3}{4}}$	2^h	2^1	GustinesH^2	Alw	81	ⒻSecretGss111	GlwingTrbte	9
4 Nov75	^{6}Bel	7 f	:23	:46^4	1:24^3	ft	$7\frac{3}{4}$	113	1^3	$1^{1\frac{1}{2}}$	$4^{3\frac{1}{2}}$	$7^{9\frac{1}{4}}$	MontoyaD^5	Alw	70	ⒻZookalu 116	Dalton Road	8
10 Oct75	^{3}Bel	7 f	:22^3	:45^2	1:24^4	ft	1	▲121	1^h	2^3	$5^{3\frac{1}{2}}$	6^9	MontoyaD^6	Alw	69	ⒻDancer'sVixen121	FstSaw	7

Aug 3 Sar 4f ft :48b **July 7 Bel 5f ft 1:01b** **July 2 Bel 6f ft 1:13b**

Here are the past performances of Arts and Letters as they appeared in early 1969. The workout line shows that Burch was beginning to crank this horse up for major improvement. He got it. Ten months later Arts and Letters was voted Horse of the Year over one of the best crops of three-year-olds I've ever seen.

Arts and Letters **113** **Ch. c (1966), by Ribot—All Beautiful, by Battlefield. Breeder, P. Mellon (Va.).**

Owner, Rokeby Stable. Trainer, E. Burch.

1969	1	0	0	1	$550
1968	6	2	1	0	$18,898

Jan25-69	^{6}Hia	7 f	1:22⅗	ft	$3\frac{1}{2}$	119	$5^{4\frac{1}{2}}$	4^5	3^6	3^6	CruguetJ^4	Alw	89	AckAck117	Dist'ctive119	A'ts a'dL't'rs	9
Nov 2-68	^{8}Lrl	$1\frac{1}{16}$	1:44	ft	$2\frac{3}{4}$	122	$4^{2\frac{1}{2}}$	2^2	3^2	$4^{1\frac{1}{4}}$	Vel'q'zJ^7	ScwS	96	King Emperor 122	Dike 122	Mr. Leader	8
Oct15-68	^{6}Bel	1	1:36⅖	ft	9-5	▲122	$2^{\frac{1}{2}}$	1^2	1^3	$1^{2\frac{1}{2}}$	Vel'squezJ^9	Alw	92	A'ts a'dL'rs122	Hyd't122	K'g of t'eC'e	9
Sep25-68	^{5}Bel	7 f	1:24⅕	ft	3	▲122	6^3	3^3	1^h	$1^{3\frac{1}{2}}$	Velasq'zJ^9	Mdn	86	A'ts a'dL't'rs122	H'd'l'g't122	W'c'tH'ls	12
Sep18-68	^{1}Bel	6 f	1:11⅕	ft	$3\frac{3}{4}$	122	3^3	$2^{1\frac{1}{2}}$	$2^{\frac{1}{2}}$	2^3	Vel'quezJ^2	Mdn	86	K'g of t'e S'a122	A's a'd L's122	El'tW'k	14
Sep11-68	^{4}Aqu	6 f	1:12⅖	sy	2	▲122	$5^{7\frac{1}{2}}$	5^6	$4^{5\frac{1}{2}}$	$4^{4\frac{3}{4}}$	TurcotteR^6	Mdn	76	Royal Tom 122	Full of Gin 119	Izaak	12
Aug 9-68	^{5}Sar	$5\frac{1}{2}$ f	1:04⅘	ft	5	122	$3^{\frac{1}{2}}$	2^1	$3^{3\frac{1}{2}}$	4^7	PincayLJr^1	Mdn	86	DixieGus122	Ch'nHarb'r122	B'uBr'm'l	12

Feb 14 Hia 3f ft :35h **Feb 11 Hia 5f ft :59h** **Feb 8 Hia 1m ft 1:37h**

And just to show that Mr. Burch has not lost his touch with a good horse, here are the past performances of Silver Buck as they appeared July 4, 1982—the day he began a winning streak of his own in topflight Handicap company. Again note the sharply improved workout that telegraphs an improved performance.

Silver Buck — Own.—Whitney C V — **110**

Gr. c. 4, by Buckpasser—Silver True, by Hail to Reason
Br.—Whitney C V (Ky) — 1982 2 1 1 0 $49,860
Tr.—Burch Elliott — 1981 10 4 0 2 $98,376
Lifetime 12 5 1 2 $148,236

31May82-8Bel	1	:45	1:09	1:33 ft	4	111	85¼	56	46½	27¼	HrnndR3	Metroplt'n H	94	ConquistdorCilo,SlvrBuck,StrGllnt	14
7May82-8Aqu	1⅛	:501	1:14	1:503ft	*4-5	119	31½	1½	11½	11	Maple E5	Aw27000	82	Silver Buck, Rahway II, NicePirate	6
12Nov81-6Med	1¼	:471	1:363	2:022ft	3½	114	97¼	710	67¼	65¼	HrnndzR7	Med Cup H	84	Princelet, Niteange, Peat Moss	14
31Oct81-8Aqu	1⅛	:473	1:113	1:484ft	*9-5	112	105¾	76	44½	31¾	HrndR9	Stuyvesant H	89	Idyll, Spoils Of War, Silver Buck	12
22Oct81-7Aqu	1⅛	:483	1:124	1:502ft	*1-3	114	47½	34½	1hd	1nk	Hernandez R4	Aw22000	83	SilverBuck,SpoilsOfWr,NphwScott	6
10Oct81-8Bel	1½	:48	2:021	2:282ft	8½	121	76¼	32½	31½	41	VlsqzJ9	J C Gold Cup	77	John Henry, Peat Moss, Relaxing	11
23Sep81-7Bel	1	:473	1:12	1:361ft	*2-3	118	52	42½	1½	12¾	Hernandez R5	Aw21000	87	SilverBuck,SpoilsOfWar,TroonRoad	7
6Sep81-6Bel	1⅛	:473	1:114	1:481ft	*3-5	114	31½	2hd	15	113	Hernandez R6	Aw20000	86	Silver Buck, Piling, MyFriendWillie	7

●Jly 1 Bel 6f ft 1:113 h ●Jun 25 Bel 6f ft 1:141 h Jun 20 Bel 5f ft 1:02 b Jun 16 Bel 4f ft :491 b

When Lou Rondinello puts a first-timer on the track, anytime, anywhere, a 93 percent losing record says throw the horse out.

Mackenzie Miller, an ace with fast-working two-year-olds, is even better than that with grass-racing stock of all ages. Miller has few peers on the turf, and his win record with newcomers to the infield is better than 33 percent. Again, there is no theory of handicapping that will explain Miller's uncanny success on the turf with horses that look like Student Leader and Fun Forever. But knowledge of the man's special talent can surely help us evaluate their chances when we see them.

Student Leader **115**

Dk. b. or br. f (1973), by Personality—Class Is Out, by Outing Class.
Breeder, K. Frazheim II. (Ky.). — 1976 3 1 0 0 $6,600
Owner, K. Franzheim II. Trainer, M. Miller. — 1975 3 1 0 1 $6,480

16 May76 6Bel	Ⓣ 1	:453	1:093	1:36 fm	5	111	41¾	34½	22	11½	VelsquezJ6	Alw	91	StudentLeadr111	PrmsdOne	9
3 May76 4Bel	6 f	:224	:463	1:111ft	8¼	114	812	810	87	64½	VelsquezJ1	Alw	81	ⒻDesiree 114	Light Frost	8
24 Apr76 5Aqu	6 f	:222	:452	1:11 ft	6	114	54¼	66½	711	814	VelsquezJ1	Alw	74	ⒻFurling 118	Swim	8
19 Nov75 3Aqu	7 f	:234	:472	1:251ft	6-5	*1195	2½	1h	1h	11¾	VelasquzJ3	Mdn	75	ⒻStudentLeadr119	InteOfg	7
29 Oct75 1Bel	6 f	:23	:464	1:113ft	5	119	88½	76½	45	34¾	VelasquzJ7	Mdn	79	ⒻSweetBernice119	InteOfg	12
13 Oct75 4Bel	6 f	:224	:463	1:112ft	3	121	917	1012	611	612	VelasqzJ12	Mdn	73	ⒻZooKaly 121	Bite the Dust	12

May 27 Bel trt 5f ft 1:02⅖b May 22 Bel trt 4f ft :49h May 13 Bel trt 3f ft :36⅗b

J. M. Bollero, P. G. Johnson, Mary Edens, Flint Shulhofer,

Fun Forever **117** B. f (1973), by Never Bend—Fairway Fun, by Prince John.
Br., L. Combs II. & Wm. Floyd (Ky.). 1976 7 1 1 2 $10,960
Owner, W. Floyd. Trainer, Mac Miller.

20 Aug76 2Sar	Ⓣ 1 1/16	:463 1:114 1:422 fm	4 1/2	117	21 1/2	11 1/2	13	17 3/4	VelasqzJ4	Mdn 85	ⒻFunFrvr117	Two fr theShw	11
11 Aug76 6Sar	1 1/8	:471 1:121 1:504 gd	3-2	▴117	33	23	413	421	VelsqezJ2	Mdn 60	ⒻTable Hopper 110	Bashful	8
26 Jly 76 5Aqu	6 f	:222 :454 1:12 ft	6 1/2	116	65 1/2	44	25	22 3/4	MartnsG12	Mdn 80	ⒻIronPromise116	FunForver	12
29 May76 2Bel	1 1/16	:462 1:114 1:444 ft	7	1105	2 1/2	32	717	922	MartensG9	Mdn 56	ⒻLaughingKys115	TbleHppr	9
12 May76 9Bel	1 1/16	:48 1:123 1:443 ft	8-5	▴114	4nk	31 1/2	67	714	VelsqezJ3	Mdn 62	ⒻDonaMaya114	TbleHopper	10
30 Apr76 4Aqu	6 f	:221 :453 1:11 ft	1	▴114	65 1/2	56	37 1/2	34 1/2	VelasqzJ4	Mdn 83	ⒻSisterJulie112	MissPrism	8
19 Apr76 2Aqu	6 f	:22 :45 1:104 ft	2e	▴112	44 1/2	46	53 1/2	32 1/4	VelquezJ2	Mdn 87	ⒻShnghaiMry114	Qn'sGmbt	10

Aug 17 Sar tc 3f fm :36 2/5 h   Aug 10 Sar 3f sy :34 4/5 h   Aug 7 Sar trt 4f ft :48 1/5 h

T. J. Kelly, W. A. Croll, and Joe Pierce are trainers who do well in grass races, especially in allowance and stakes company, and there are others, far too many in fact for me to list, for grass racing has become very popular in recent seasons. Which introduces a digression of sorts.

There is a booklet on the market that follows up a turf-racing research study published in the mid-seventies. This booklet catalogues the outstanding sires of grass horses.

The only problem with it (ignoring the $20.00 price) is that the game has changed over the past decade. Turf racing is no longer the rarity it was in the 1960s and 70s. Today nearly every racecourse has a turf course and cards upward of a dozen grass races a week.

A few years ago, knowledge of grass breeding was all a good handicapper needed to pick live contenders and longshot winners on the turf. But grass racing is no longer a one-dimensional game. Sure, knowledge of the most potent turf sires is helpful, but that is easily attainable through simple observation of a month's worth of results. Yes, you can pick winners on the grass by spotting a Stagedoor Johnny colt or a son of Raise a Native, or Rock Talk, or Tom Rolfe making his first or second start on the green, but it is far better to pay attention to the special talents of expert trainers and to watch the way actual races are run, or to study the workout line or to use horse by horse comparisons as per all racing situations.

Whereas it used to be possible to eliminate three-fourths of all horses entered in a given grass race on the basis of wrong blood or poor turf form, today the majority of grass races include experienced turf performers and others who have close relatives who were stakes winners in top grass company. To successfully handicap turf races in the 1980s, you need more than a master sires list (see Chapter 13), you need a solid foundation in race-watching skills and all the other tools required for every other type of race. End of digression.

Of all the 11,500 trainers in North America, there is one man who seems to be in a class by himself. He is an incredible talent named Allen Jerkens.

In the early 1960s Jerkens revved up a sprint-type named Beau Purple to take the measure of the mightly Kelso, not once, but three times.

Later in the decade he took Handsome Boy, another sprinter, and developed him into a winner of four straight $100,000 route races.

During that period he was the leading trainer in New York. More wins, more money won, more stakes, highest win percentage. But no trainer has ever had the kind of year that Jerkens had in 1973.

In the early spring Jerkens cranked up a $25,000 claiming filly named Poker Knight to win an allowance sprint. The result was a surprise, for Jerkens had not trained the filly for speed. Building her stamina through long, slow training gallops, he had hoped to stretch her out in distance at a later date. By virtue of her surprising victory, Jerkens realized that Poker Knight was going to be a much better horse than he had thought.

On April 3 Jerkens entered her in another allowance sprint. Another win. He then stepped up his program, working her a mile in modest time four days later—a work too slow to make the clocker's tab. April 10, another sprint race, this time against the fastest three-year-old filly in the country—the undefeated Windy's Daughter.

"I was more curious to see what she would do than thinking she would win," said Jerkens later that summer. What she did was come within a length of beating Windy's Daughter, closing ground in the stretch.

Two weeks later Jerkens was convinced that Poker Knight could beat any filly in the country at a mile or more. In successive races the ex-claimer proved him right, beating Numbered Account and Summer Guest, the two top fillies in America.

A few months later Jerkens was at it again. Onion to beat Secretariat, paying $13.60; although I've made larger wagers, this was the most painful, most professional bet I have ever made.

Onion came into the Whitney Stakes on the first Saturday in August 1973 with a superior sprint race win over the track on the first Tuesday. The great Secretariat came into the same race with subpar workouts, a signal that had tipped off his subpar performance in the Wood Memorial at Aqueduct in April. Onion was the speed of the field, a four-year-old getting a weight concession from a three-year-old. (That's a big edge, bigger than most people know; see page 132.)

Secretariat drew the rail, which was as dead as I had ever seen it at Saratoga. The few horses that had made moves hugging the rail on the far turn during the preceding week of racing were all eligible to improve dramatically in their next starts.

In all my handicapping experiences I have rarely encountered a situation that was more ripe for an upset. But I was torn and I was angry. Secretariat was the most compelling horse I had ever seen. Every race he ran was different, each more dynamic than the one before. I was emotionally involved with this horse. I rooted for him just like I root for other superior athletic talents— not only the ones that hit the home runs, leap higher than anyone else, or shoot the eyes out of the basket, but the ones that step into another dimension of performance when nothing less than that will get the job done. Damascus, Dr. Fager, Kelso, Majestic Prince, and Canonero II had shown me that kind of talent a few times each. Secretariat did it better than any of them, and he did it repeatedly: in his debut, in his second start, in the Sanford Stakes, in the Hopeful Stakes, in each of the Triple Crown races (and later in the Man O' War Stakes on the grass). I was angry because I was spoiled. I did not want to see him at anything less than his best.

Cold logic said the race was even up. Onion and Jerkens versus a potentially subpar Secretariat and Lucien Laurin. No other result seemed possible. But the tote board said Onion.

Actually Secretariat put in a fine race, gaining three lengths along the deepest part of the track on the final turn. At the top of the stretch it looked like he was going to drive past Onion and win by daylight. My schizophrenia was showing. I forgot about my bet and screamed for him to do it. But he never uncorked his explosive move. Onion stayed in the middle of the track the whole trip and pulled away in the final five strides. I cashed all my tickets save one.

But Jerkens was hardly through. Days later he bought Prove Out, who had been an allowance-class sprinter for the better part of three seasons. Under Jerkens the horse needed but three weeks to begin a new career as the biggest giant killer of them all.

On the next-to-last day at Saratoga, Jerkens cut him loose to defeat Forego in a seven-furlong allowance race, posting a new track record.

Two weeks later Prove Out tied the Belmont Park track mark for $1\frac{1}{16}$ miles. Two weeks after that he was at Bowie, facing the improving True Knight, a bona-fide handicap horse. I was there too, and of course I bet Prove Out even though he went to post at 8–5 odds. By now I was as mesmerized as everyone else. At the top of the stretch Prove Out was in front and beginning to tire when he bounced off the inner rail. There went some of my Onion money.

One week later I decided to skip a Secretariat race for the first time in his career. It was the Woodward Stakes, and Prove Out put in a superior performance, one of the top ten races of the past twenty years. Secretariat ran just a bit below his exceptional Kentucky Derby form and got his head handed to him. Jerkens again. Incredible.

For an encore, Prove Out showed he was no fluke by beating the other half of the Meadow Stable's team, Riva Ridge, in the two-mile Jockey Club Gold Cup.

In day-to-day racing at Aqueduct, Belmont, and Saratoga, Jerkens is a 25 percent winning trainer overall, but he does have a pattern that produces better than 40 percent winners.

What does Allen Jerkens do with an improving horse? Move it up in company as soon as possible. Or stretch it out in distance or put it on the turf course.

How does one spot a ready-set-go Jerkens runner? Very fast recent trials or a sharp race within the past seven days.

Arcadio II. ★   **114**   Dk. b. or br. h (1971), by Granadero II.—Aretina, by Bell Hop.
Breeder, Haras La Companaia (Chile).   1976 6 2 1 2 $17,508
Owner, Hobeau Farm.   Trainer, H. Allen Jerkens.   1975 21 3 4 3 $2,448

24 Aug76	8Sar	⊕ 1¹⁄₁₆ :46¹¹:11¹¹:41⁴fm	4¹⁄₂	115	44¹⁄₄ 4¹¹⁄₂ 2¹⁄₂	1ⁿᵒ	HerndezR⁴	Alw 88	Arcadio II. 115	Blue Times 7
17 Aug76	5Sar	6 f :22³ :45³¹:10¹ft	17	115	2¹ 2¹¹⁄₂ 3²¹⁄₂ 3²¹⁄₂	RolonJ⁴	37500 86	JacksnSqre117	BldandStrmy 8
18 Apr76	6CIH	⊕ a 1¹⁄₄		2:02²fm	3¹⁄₂e 132	Chilie	10	UlloaP	Stk Jadar 132	Poccardi 10
7 Apr76	4HCh	a 6¹⁄₂ f		1:19 ft	7¹⁄₂ 134	Chile	3³	UlloaP	Stk Piche 134	Venezuela 10
21 Mar76	7Val	⊕a 1²⁄₄		1:55⁴fm	4¹⁄₂ 106	Chile	2¹	UlloaP	Hcp Royal Fun 110	Arcadio II. 13
4 Jan76	7CiH	⊕a 1¹⁄₁₆		1:41³fm	1 ▲121	Chile	1¹¹⁄₄	RiveraC	Hcp Arcadio II. 121	Espionaje 8
25 Dec75	7CIH	⊕ a 1		1:34²fm	3 106	Chile	2²	GnklezF	Hcp Retraido 132	Arcadio II. 9
14 Dec75	5CIH	⊕ a 1¹⁄₄		2:01⁴fm	† 134	Chile	1²¹⁄₂	UlloaP	Hcp Arcadio II. 134	Mesurado 5

†No Pari-mutuel wagering.
Aug 22 Sar 3f f :36b   Aug 12 Sar 3f ft :37²⁄₅b   Aug 4 Sar 4f ft :47¹⁄₅hg

---

Tell Me All   **121**   B. f (1973), by Cyane—Lead Me On, by Native Dancer.
Breeder, Mooring Stable (Md.).   1976 8 5 1 0 $57,355
Owner, Hobeau Farm.   Trainer, H. A. Jerkens.   1975 1 M 1 0 $1,760

5 May76	8Bel	7 f :22³ :45³¹:23¹ft	6³	113	3² 2¹ 2ʰ 1¹	RuaneJ⁴	AlwS 86	Ⓕ TellMeAll 113	DrlyPrcious 5
26 Apr76	4Aqu	1 :46³¹:10³¹:35 ft	3-2	▲109	11¹⁄₂ 12 17 11¹	RuaneJ¹	Alw 91	Ⓕ TellMeAll 109	BusySaxon 5
12 Apr76	5Aqu	6 f :23⁴ :47²¹:112ft	4-5	▲109	1ʰ 1ʰ 1¹ 12¹	RuaneJ¹	Alw 86	Ⓕ TellMeAll 109	FnnyPculiar 6
3 Mar76	9Hia	1¹⁄₄ :46¹¹:10²¹:49³ft	20	114	1¹ 35¹⁄₂ 714 81⁹	RuaneJ⁸	AlwS 65	Ⓣ T.V.Vixen116	AnneCmpbll 10
18 Feb76	9Hia	7 f :23 :46 1:23¹ft	4	112	51¹⁄₄ 75³⁄₄ 66 67³⁄₄	RuaneJ⁶	AlwS 81	T.V.Vixen11	FortyNineSnsts 11
7 Feb76	6Hia	7 f :23⁴ :47 1:24²ft	2-3	▲165	3¹⁄₂ 1ʰ 1¹ 1¹	VelezRl⁸	Alw 83	Ⓕ TellMeAll 116	Cohabitatn 10
24 Jan76	4Hia	7 f :23 :45⁴¹:23²ft	7-5	▲1095	3² 23 1¹ 14	VelezRl³	Alw 88	Ⓕ Tell Me All 109	Polipeg 12
16 Jan76	3Hia	6 f :21⁴ :45¹¹:10²sy	9-5	▲121	21¹⁄₂ 21¹⁄₂ 2¹⁄₂ 2¹	BaezaB⁸	Mdn 90	Ⓕ Misukaw 121	Tell Me All 11
24 Sep75	3Bel	6 f :22³ :46³¹:112sy	3³	121	63³⁄₄ 31¹⁄₂ 24 27³⁄₄	SthRC⁹	M45000 77	Ⓕ XalapaSnrse121	TellMeAll 10

May 21 Bel 3f ft :31¹⁄₅h   May 18 Bel 6f ft 1:12¹⁄₅h   **May 4 Bel 3f ft :31¹⁄₅h**

Clean 'Em Up   **112**   Dk. b. or br. c (1973), by Handsome Boy—Mopkins, by Bolero.
Breeder, Hobeau Farm (Fla.).   1976 4 1 1 0 $7,380
Owner, Hobeau Farm.   Trainer, H. Allen Jerkens.

19 May76	5Bel	6 f :22⁴ :46¹¹:10¹sy	3	114	4³⁄₄ 1ʰ 2ʰ 1³	MapleE⁷	Mdn 91	Clean 'EmUp114	ThirdWorld 8
15 May76	3Bel	7 f :22⁴ :45⁴¹:24²ft	7-5	▲114	2ʰ 1ʰ 14 2³⁄₄	GustinesH⁶	Mdn 79	Azirae 114	Clean 'Em Up 8
26 Jan76	4Hia	6 f :22 :45 1:11 ft	9-5	▲122	65 45 43¹⁄₂ 56³⁄₄	GustinesH⁶	Mdn 81	LittleFishrmn122	Knight ofLve 11
19 Jan76	4Hia	6 f :22² :45³¹:113ft	3³⁄₄	122	73¹⁄₄ 99¹⁄₄ 69 76³⁄₄	GustinesH³	Mdn 78	GaitorRatn122	Knight ofLve 12

May 31 Bel 7f ft 1:24¹⁄₅h   May 26 Bel 1m ft 1:39⅘h   May 25 Bel trt 5f ft 1:02¹⁄₅h

How can a player uncover the special winning abilities of new trainers operating at any racetrack, or simply formulate intelligent judgments about the present form of any horse entered in any race at any track? A single past performance profile may well answer all the fundamental questions. The trick is to recognize the implications of the evidence. The examples in the next chapter may help to crystallize this point.

8.
"What's He Doing in Today's Race?"

The horse has had ten starts; his last race was a strong performance; the trainer is somebody we have never heard of, or somebody who wins a few races now and then but we don't know how he wins them. How do we decide whether the horse is going to improve, run the same race, or fail to make an impression? What clues in the past performances will help us rate this horse in this field today?

The answer is all the clues we can get—the result charts, the workout listings, and the past performance records of other horses trained by this man or woman. If we had occasion to do that kind of research before we came out to the track, we would be able to make a confident assessment.

In a single past performance profile there are important clues about the fitness of the horse, its class, distance capabilities, and soundness. And in fact about the trainer too.

In the following examples, we shall look closely at a handful of individual past performance profiles to glean as much information about the horse as possible, attempting to get a fix on the skill of the trainer and to find the answer to an important question: What's this horse doing in today's race?

6 FURLONGS—MAIDEN SPECIAL WEIGHT, HIALEAH, FEBRUARY 18, 1976

Nancy's Robert **122** **B. c (1972), by Subpet—Sonodra, by Midpassage. Breedtr, H. E. Robinson (Fla.).**

Owner, H. E. Robinson. Trainer, G. Zateslo.

												1976	2 M	0	1		$600
												1975	5 M	0	0		$165
3 Feb76	^{2}Hia	6 f	:22^3	:46	1:10^{3}ft	71	117^5	2^h	6^5	5^4	3$^{4\frac{1}{4}}$	DruryMA^4	Mdn	86	OldFrankfrt122	DbleMerger	10
27 Jan76	^{3}Hia	7 f	:23	:46	1:23^{1}ft	51	122	10^{12}	9^{15}	10^{15}	10^{16}	BrussrdR^9	Mdn	73	SunnyClime122	DoubleTudor	12
10 Oct75	^{1}Mth	6 f	:22^3	:45^4	1:10^{4}ft	36	111^7	3^1	5$^{2\frac{3}{4}}$	5$^{4\frac{3}{4}}$	6$^{5\frac{1}{4}}$	DruryMA^1	Mdn	81	BalTalk118	SparklingSuccs	7
27 Aug75	^{5}Mth	1^{70}	:47	1:13^1	1:44^{2}ft	13	115	4^2	4$^{3\frac{1}{4}}$	5$^{7\frac{1}{2}}$	6^{15}	ThornbgB^5	Mdn	81	Doc Rofus 115	West End	8
20 Aug75	^{3}Mth	6 f	:22^1	:46^1	1:12^{1}gd	42	117	7$^{6\frac{1}{4}}$	7$^{3\frac{3}{4}}$	5$^{8\frac{1}{2}}$	5$^{8\frac{1}{4}}$	ThornbgB^8	Mdn	71	HigherMarks 117	WestEnd	9
13 Aug75	^{3}Mth	6 f	:22^1	:45^2	1:11^{2}ft	37	117	4$^{1\frac{1}{2}}$	5$^{6\frac{1}{2}}$	5^{12}	7^{14}	MacBthD^1	Mdn	69	RoyalPower117	IrishOuting	8

Feb 14 GP 5f ft 1:01⅗h **Jan 25 GP 3f ft :37b** **Jan 16 GP 6f sy 1:15⅗b**

Notice the August 1975 races and the six-week gap until Nancy's Robert was able to get back on the track.

The October 10 race was an encouraging effort; but there was no follow-up race to take advantage of the horse's slight but real improvement. Obviously, this sparsely raced colt has had his physical problems.

On January 27, 1976, Nancy's Robert returned to competition but did very little, running in back of the pack.

Without checking the result chart for the race, we might consider the possibility that there was interference at the start. In any case, this bad trip didn't put Nancy's Robert out of commission again. In fact, his trainer put him back on the track for another race the following week and gave him a five-furlong workout just four days before today's race.

The February 3 race was a marked improvement, the best race of Nancy's Robert's interrupted career. The workout that followed was also good. A positive sign of health, a touch of speed, and a logical move toward better condition.

The evidence says that trainer Zateslo has done a fine job straightening this horse out, and there is every likelihood that Nancy's Robert is on the verge of reaching his peak. We don't know what that peak is, we don't know how long he will be able to hold it, and we don't know whether he will reach it today. But we do know that he is already competitive at this class level and distance, and we have a right to think he's going to run a stronger race, his best to date. Our optimism for this horse's winning chances would be tempered by other strong contenders, but this is a typical maiden race—only two other horses in the field look like they can run. One has had fourteen previous maiden races and three seconds. The other is a well-bred first-time starter that has been training well enough to be dangerous. Nancy's Robert, who should have been a 9–5 favorite, paid $12 to win. The first-timer ran second, beaten by four lengths.

6½ FURLONGS—$8,500 CLAIMING, HAZEL PARK, NOVEMBER 15, 1975

Toolin Around **117** B. g (1968). by Tooley—Saragino by **Cosmic Bomb.**
Breeder. A. J. Algeri (Ky.). 1975 14 2 3 1 $11,073
Owner, Standen Stable. Trainer, A. Blundell. $8.500 1974 4 1 0 1 $8.000

8 Nov75	^{5}HP	4 f	$:22^4$	$:47^4$ft	4	117^5	6	$7^{6\frac{1}{2}}$	$7^{6\frac{3}{4}}$	$7^{7\frac{1}{2}}$	GarciaJR^7	Alw	78	WinsomeWine119	RightPckt	7
1 Nov75	^{5}HP	6½ f	$:22^3$ $:47^1$	$1:20^4$ft	4	112^5	$2^{\frac{1}{2}}$	$1^{\frac{1}{2}}$	1^3	3^1	GarciaJR^4	10000	76	Fast Left 112	I Can Hackett	7
18 Oct75	^{4}HP	6½ f	$:22^3$ $:47^2$	1:20 gd	9-5	▲112^5	$4^{4\frac{1}{2}}$	3^2	1^h	2^4	GrciaJR^3	10000	77	OwnPower119	ToolinAround	6
11 Oct75	^{5}HP	6½ f	$:22^4$ $:46^3$	$1:18^4$ft	3¾	112^5	$5^{4\frac{1}{4}}$	$1^{\frac{1}{2}}$	1^3	$2^{\frac{3}{4}}$	GrciaJR^5	10000	86	Bandwagn117	ToolinAround	9
4 Oct75	^{7}HP	4 f	$:22^1$	$:46^4$ft	26	118	5	$8^{5\frac{1}{4}}$	$7^{5\frac{1}{2}}$	$7^{1\frac{3}{4}}$	MillerS^7	Alw	89	FastTrackMiss115	BoldDggr	9
20 Sep75	^{6}HP	6½ f	:23 $:47^3$	$1:21^1$hy	17	117	4^2	2^3	2^4	6^{10}	MillerS^6	10000	64	LightCharger117	FamsPatrt	8
13 Sep75	^{7}HP	6½ f	$:22^4$ $:46^4$	$1:19^2$ft	15	117	2^h	$2^{\frac{1}{2}}$	$6^{8\frac{1}{2}}$	7^{10}	BreenR^5	12500	74	Brunate 115	Light Charger	8
30 Aug75	^{5}HP	6½ f	$:23^2$ $:48^3$	$1:23^2$m	4¾	117	$5^{5\frac{1}{2}}$	5^6	7^{13}	8^{16}	MillerS^5	10000	48	LightCharger110	Chest Eqle	3
23 Aug75	^{5}HP	6½ f	$:23^2$ $:48^1$	1:21 m	3	120	3^3	3^2	2^3	6^{15}	MapleS^2	12500	61	WavetheFlag115	LdyRchelle	7
9 Aug75	^{5}HP	6½ f	$:22^2$ $:46^2$	$1:18^4$ft	4-5	▲120	$5^{3\frac{1}{2}}$	5^4	4^5	7^{11}	MapleS^1	15000	76	E'Omer 115	Fast Fun	8

Oct 30 HP 3f ft :38⅘b **Oct 2 HP 3f ft :36⅖h**

After two wins and one second no longer appearing in the current past performance profile (see consistency box in upper right corner), Toolin Around was unable to sustain his speed throughout August and September.

Instead of resting this useful gelding, trainer Blundell tried an unusual strategy. If it hadn't worked we might have had reason to think Blundell was off his rocker or at least out of touch with his horse; but the maneuvering did work, so we ought to take a closer look.

On October 4 Blundell ran the already fast-breaking Toolin Around in an ultrashort four-furlong race against some of the fastest-breaking horses on the grounds. The bettors dismissed him at 26–1, and they were right. But one week later Toolin Around was back in top form, the form he maintained without winning in his next two starts at $10,000 claiming.

On November 8, one week before today's race, Blundell repeated the same four-furlong prep race strategy, but this time, unfortunately, the betting public was unaware of the trainer's intentions.

The "go" part of the pattern is today's race, an $8,500 claimer, a slight but important drop in class. This time Toolin Around should (and did) get back on the winning track. Put Mr. Blundell's name down for future reference. He has some unusual methods and was slow to realize the need for a drop in class, but he did use his head with this horse. At $7.60 Toolin Around was a steal.

Roulette Wheel			Dk. b. or br. c. 3, by Key To The Mint—Silly Game, by Sir Gaylord		
			Br.—Greentree Stud Inc (Ky)	1982 4 1 1 0	$14,050
Own.—Greentree Stable		111	Tr.—Reinacher Robert Jr	Turf 1 0 0 0	
			Lifetime 4 1 1 0 $14,050		
16Jun82-6Bel	1¹⁄₁₆ ⑦ :46² 1:10⁴ 1:43⁴ yl	5¾ 112	1hd 1hd 2½ 55 Velasquez J²	Aw20000 72 ThunderPuddls,HuntrHwk,Piroutt 12
16May82-5Aqu	6f :23 :46⁴ 1:11²ft	9-5 113	22½ 2hd 1¹ 1¾ Velasquez J⁴	Mdn 84 RouletteWhel,SmokingGun,SilvrPik 8
21Apr82-6Aqu	7f :23 :46¹ 1:24¹ft	3¾ 112	1hd 2hd 1hd 2¹ Velasquez J⁴	Mdn 79 Faces Up, Roulette Wheel, Fulton 7
22Mar82-4GP	6f :22¹ :45¹ 1:10³ft	3¾ 122	11¹² 9¹⁵ 7¹³ 6¹⁴ Velasquez J⁹	Mdn 72 MortonBy,NorthrnBrbizon,BuBddr 12
Jly 1 Bel ⑦ 5f gd 1:01 h (d)	Jun 25 Bel 5f ft 1:00² h	Jun 9 Bel 7f ft 1:26³ h	May 27 Bel ⑦ 7f fm 1:32² b (d)		

Here we have a lightly raced stakes prospect from the Greentree Stable looking for his second lifetime win.

Trainer Robert Reinacher Jr. is a fresh new face on the national racing scene, and if this horse is any indication of his style, horseplayers would do well to pay him some attention.

Notice that Roulette Wheel did not race as a two-year-old and hardly showed any hint of ability in his first try in Florida, March 22, 1982. A month later, at Aqueduct over the seven-furlong main track, Roulette Wheel made a determined bid from start to finish in a vastly improved performance. Three weeks later the horse was spotted back in a slightly shorter maiden dash and his effort was hard to fault at 9–5.

A full month later, following two seven-furlong workouts, including one on the turf, Reinacher put Roulette Wheel in a longer race, at 1¹⁄₁₆ miles on the infield course. Perhaps a win was a realistic possibility, but it was no demerit against the horse to have tired. It was his first race around two turns, his first attempt on grass. Consider the unfamiliar conditions and the additional possibility that the turf course, labeled *yielding*, might not have been advantageous to horses running on or near the lead. Consider the probable benefit of a race over the course.

For today's race, Reinacher put two more workouts into the colt and entered him back on the turf. It is eighteen days later, at a shorter distance.

The field contains only mediocre horses and no standout speedsters who could take the pace away from Roulette Wheel. Any reasonable improvement would put him right in the thick of things all the way to the wire. Besides, there is nothing wrong with $3.30 to a dollar for a live contender who is running at a distance he figures to love.

Although this horse may or may not turn out to be the second coming of Man O' War, he has been well prepped to run a solid mile on the turf by a horseman who seems exceptionally disciplined toward a sensible training regimen. Robert Reinacher is a relative newcomer who is progressing toward his true potential. On the evidence of such horses as Roulette Wheel, he seems likely to be an important trainer for many years to come.

6 FURLONGS—$20,000 ALLOWANCE PURSE, BELMONT PARK, JUNE 7, 1976

Desert Boots **107** **B. f (1973), by Ridan—Signal Flag, by Restless Wind.**
Breeder, Mrs. Barbara Joslin (Fla.). 1976 . . 7 1 4 1 $16,300
Owner, W. M. Joslin. Trainer, S. DiMauro. 1975 . . 2 1 0 0 $5,940

17 May76 ^{7}Bel	6 f :22	:44^{4}1:10^{3}ft	7¾	106^5	1^{1½}	1^{1½}	1^2	2½	MartinJE^4	Alw 88	ⒻFurling 114	Desert Boots	7
4 May76 ^{7}Bel	6 f :22^4	:45^{3}1:11 ft	6½	105^5	1½	1^h	2^h	2^{1¼}	VelezRI^6	Alw 86	ⒻFurling 113	Desert Boots	10
9 Apr76 ^{7}Aqu	6 f :23	:46^{2}1:11^{4}ft	2	▲113^5	1^2	1^4	1^5	2^h	VelezRI^6	Alw 84	ⒻIn theOffing114	DesertBts	6
15 Mar76 ^{7}Aqu	6 f :22^1	:45^{3}1:11^{1}ft	2½	118	1½	1^2	1^3	3^2	BaezaB^3	Alw 85	ⒻAncntFbles114	Rsn frTrce	9
3 Mar76 ^{8}Aqu	6 f :22^2	:45^{2}1:10^{1}ft	4¾	114	1½	2^h	2^4	7^{8¼}	HoleM^4	AlwS 84	ⒻToughElsie116	LightFrost	13
14 Feb76 ^{6}Hia	6 f :21^3	:44^{3}1:11^{2}ft	4-5	▲116	1½	1^3	1^4	1^{1½}	BaezaB^5	Alw 86	ⒻDesertBoots116	She'sTrble	8
31 Jan76 ^{6}Hia	6 f :22	:45^{1}1:11^{1}ft	2¾	114	1½	1^3	1^{1½}	2^{2½}	MapleE^8	Alw 84	ⒻDaltonRoad114	DesrtBoots	12
1 Sep75 ^{3}Bel	5 f :22^1	:45^{4}1:1^{12}ft	3	▲119	1^{1½}	1^4	1^7	1^{8½}	BracleVJr^9	Mdn 85	ⒻDesertB'ts119	Sw'tB'rn'e	12

June 3 Bel trt 1m ft 1:46⅖b **May 29 Bel trt 1m ft 1:45⅕b** **May 23 Bel trt 1m ft 1:46⅗b**

Returning now to an example from a few years back, take a very close look at the past performances of Desert Boots, a rather quick filly who has been in the money in six of her seven most recent races, with two wins in her nine lifetime starts.

With two champs in the barn (Wajima and Dearly Precious), trainer Steve DiMauro had the best year of his life in 1975. In 1976 things were not all that bad, but this particular horse must have driven him crazy.

Although an apparent money *earner*, Desert Boots is a classic money burner, a one-dimensional speedball who simply refuses to keep something in reserve for the stretch run. DiMauro was trying to solve her problem through a program of long, slow, stamina-building workouts. The prescription was sensible but it didn't work.

Perhaps a route race would have gotten the message across better than workouts alone. But there is a chance too that nothing will help a horse like this. Desert Boots may have congenital wind problems, which will always keep her from beating quality horses at six furlongs.

In a game like racing we have a right to go our separate ways with a fast-breaking horse like Desert Boots. A horse like that is always eligible to keep right on going all the way to the finish. And some players might be willing to give trainer DiMauro the benefit of the doubt, on the evidence of those interesting long workouts.

I prefer not to be so generous, not unless there is a strong speed-favoring track bias operating in the horse's favor. I want proof that the trainer has solved such a serious problem, or insurance if he hasn't—insurance of a track bias, or proof only a recent winning race can provide.

Horses that tire in race after race are notorious money burners.

---

6 FURLONGS—$10,500 CLAIMING, BELMONT PARK, SEPTEMBER 1, 1976

Panda Bear   **113**   B. g (1973), by My Dad George—Gold Threat, by Infidel.
Breeder, Martha Broadbent (Fla.).

Owner, B. Combs II. Trainer, J. Martin.						**$10,500**	1975	3 1 1 1	$5,865	
							1976	7 2 1 1	$12,770	

Date	Track	Dist	Time		Wt					Jockey	Clm	Sp	Finish
11 Aug76	2Sar	6 f :222 :4621:112m	4½	119	32½ 31½ 52½ 53½	BaezaB4	12500	80	Chompchomp 117	I'mProud	7
18 Jly 76	2Aqu	6 f :224 :4631:122ft	8-5 ▲117	31½ 32½ 22 1nk	BaezaB7	10000	81	PandaBear117	TakeYourBts	7
16 Jun76	9Bel	7 f :23 :4641:252ft	3	117	21½ 21½ 3nk 36½	CrdroAJr6	12500	69	Fling 119	Spotted Gem	8
22 May76	9Bel	6 f :223 :46 1:113ft	4½	119	3nk 3½ 42½ 76½	CrdoAJr8	16000	77	Cayman Isle117	Mgie'sPride	11
13 May76	2Bel	6 f :223 :4621:113ft	2½	117	11½ 11½ 1h 1½	CdroAJr5	12500	84	PandaBear117	CaymanIsle	9
8 May76	4Bel	6 f :224 :4611:113ft	2½	▲1125	41¾ 41¾ 52 43	MrtinJE8	14000	81	HowiesHeat117	TakeYrBoots	8
15 Apr76	7Aqu	6 f :223 :46 1:122ft	2¾	▲117	31 1h 2h 21½	HerndzR7	12500	79	Break theLock115	PndaBear	11
12 Jly 75	9Tdn	5 f :232 :48 1:003ft	2½	114	21 1h 3nk 32½	WeilerD3	AlwS	85	FierceRuffian115	HpyMircle	7
2 Jly 75	9RD	5½ f :22 :45 1:041ft	3½	113	2h 21 3nk 27	RieraRJr3	AlwS	87	ChanningRoad113	PndaBear	9
21 May75	3CD	5 f :222 :47 :594ft	5½e	122	2½ 11½ 1½ 1h	RieraRJr7	Mdn	90	Panda Bear 122	Sam's Act	11

Aug 30 Bel trt 3f ft :37b   Aug 24 Sar trt 3f ft :37⅖b   Aug 19 Sar trt 4f ft :54b

---

Although the point of this chapter is to zero in on trainers as they reveal their skill in a single past performance profile, the next three illustrations, including Panda Bear, trained by Jose Martin (Frank Martin's son), also highlight fundamental considerations involved in the claiming game, an integral part of racing from coast to coast.

The claiming game is a game for shrewd business-minded trainers and for poker-playing types too. And if you've never encountered Jose Martin before, the following example should be enough to convince you of his precise mastery over that aspect of the game.

In the spring Panda Bear was a solid $12,000 racehorse. During the summer Martin found out she was able to beat only $10,000 stock.

Up and down the class ladder Panda Bear won two races and $12,770. Each time Martin dropped the horse to her proper level, she delivered an improved effort.

Three workouts on the deeper training track leading up to today's race assure us of Panda Bear's fitness. Today's drop in class tells us Martin is thinking win. If you're thinking the same thing after you get through with the rest of the field, you'll catch a $9 mutuel.

---

6 FURLONGS—$9,500 CLAIMING, BELMONT PARK, SEPTEMBER 1, 1976

Tacky Lady **116** **Ch. f (1973), by Nail—Lady Cavan, by Cavan.**
Breeder, Mrs. W. A. Kelley (Del.). 1976 . . 11 3 1 0 $15,930
Owner, Stu-Al Stable. Trainer, Frank Laboccetta. **$9,500** 1975 . . 2 1 0 0 $2,280

24 Aug76	3Sar	7 f	:23 :463 1:244 ft	3	116	42	22	42	45¾	VelasqzJ8	15000	75	ⓕJrry'sMona116	JyeuxNelll.	8
6 Aug76	2Sar	6 f	:231 :464 1:12 ft	3½	118	62½	63¼	63¾	65½	CdroAJr2	20000	74	ⓕShawi 111	Jerry's Mona	9
15 Jly 76	7Aqu	6 f	:224 :461 1:114 ft	2¼	▲114	32	21½	1h	1no	TurtteR9	19000	84	ⓕTackyLady114	JoyousPlsre	9
4 Jly 76	1Aqu	7 f	:232 :464 1:24 ft	3½	116	22	21	11½	12¾	MapleE10	15000	81	ⓕTackyLady116	FineAsWne	10
20 Jun76	1Bel	6 f	:224 :464 1:113 ft	2½	▲116	1½	1½	11	2no	MapleE1	12500	84	ⓕDela Pet 121	Tacky Lady	7
9 Jun76	3Bel	6 f	:224 :472 1:124 ft	17	113	32	31½	13	13½	MapleE2	7500	78	ⓕTackyLady113	Encapslate	9
13 May76	1Bel	7 f	:231 :463 1:261 ft	5½	114	43	45½	67½	812	TurcotteR4	8500	59	ⓕFiredRed111	NeverFlow	12
4 May76	1Bel	6 f	:232 :473 1:124 ft	3½	116	74	105¼	83¾	67¾	CruguetJ2	8500	70	ⓕGldnSl 113	StkeUp theBnd	10
20 Apr76	7Aqu	7 f	:224 :46 1:251 ft	6	116	117½	1011	109	106½	CrguetJ11	15000	68	ⓕHoldingOn116	FineAsWine	12

Aug 19 Sar trt 5f ft 1:03⅗b **Aug 2 Sar 3f sy :36b** **July 27 Aqu 5f ft 1:02⅗b**

Barely six weeks before today's race Tacky Lady was winning against horses worth twice as much as those she is facing today. Tacky Lady is dropping down sharply in class, and the bettors at the track think she's a mortal lock, a 3–5 betting favorite. If they were willing to question why this horse is being discounted so suddenly they might make her 3–5 to wind up being carted off the track in a hurry-up wagon.

This is what is known in the trade as a negative drop in class. A horse that is deteriorating so fast that the owner and trainer can't wait to get rid of her. The player should not be so hasty; there are some trainers who win races with horses like this, but in this specific case, all the signs are negative.

Tacky Lady's best races came when trainer Laboccetta had confidence in her ability. He successfully stepped her up in company four straight times.

This is the second steep drop in class in two weeks. Instead of resting this horse, trainer Laboccetta can't wait to get rid of her. I don't think his loss of confidence should be taken lightly. Throw the horse out.

1 1/16 MILES (turf)—$10,000 CLAIMING, ARLINGTON PARK, SEPTEMBER 20, 1976

Manager Ed **113** B. c (1973), by Dust Commander—Amberly, by Ambiorix.
Breeder, R. E. Lehmann (Ky.). 1976 5 0 1 1 $2,774
Owner, A. J. Wozneski. Trainer, John C. Wozneski. $10.000 1975 12 1 1 2 $4,798

10 Sep76	^{9}AP	Ⓣ 1	:48^1	1:14^2	1:40^{2}fm	$3\frac{1}{2}$	114	$9^{9\frac{3}{4}}$	9^9	$8^{7\frac{3}{4}}$	8^6	FiresE^9	11500	67	BlckCrw114	Knck'sOlympus	11
26 Aug76	^{5}AP	$1\frac{1}{16}$	:48	1:12^2	1:44^{1}ft	2	▲114	$3^{5\frac{1}{2}}$	$3^{3\frac{1}{2}}$	$3^{\frac{1}{2}}$	$2^{1\frac{1}{4}}$	StoverD^1	11500	90	Lex Legio 112	Manager Ed	7
12 Aug76	^{7}AP	$1\frac{1}{16}$	:47^2	1:14^1	1:43^{4}ft	20	112	$5^{8\frac{1}{2}}$	5^8	4^4	$4^{4\frac{1}{2}}$	StoverD^2	13500	88	Sum Chipper 113	Fleet Flit	8
27 Jly 76	^{7}AP	[T] a $1\frac{1}{16}$	:46^3	1:14^1	1:44^{2}fm	25	107^5	5^{13}	6^{15}	$6^{9\frac{1}{2}}$	$3^{3\frac{3}{4}}$	RdgzDP^1	10500		SumChipper114	UnitdKngdm	7
16 Jly 76	^{6}AP	6 f	:22	:46	1:12^{2}ft	29	108^5	10^{12}	11^{13}	10^{12}	10^{12}	RdrgzDP^4	10000	69	Demon Run 113	Ahga Mag	11
13 Nov75	^{9}Haw	$6\frac{1}{2}$ f	:22^2	:45^4	1:18^{1}ft	$9\frac{1}{2}$	118	8^7	5^6	$2^{1\frac{1}{2}}$	2^{nk}	StoverD^8	7500	82	Key Sa 117	Manager Ed	10
4 Nov75	^{9}Haw	6 f	:22^2	:46^1	1:12 sy	8	118	9^{10}	7^9	7^{11}	$7^{9\frac{3}{4}}$	StovrD^{10}	10000	76	Lil'sTommie117	SumChipper	11
20 Oct75	^{7}Haw	6 f	:22^2	:45^3	1:10^{2}ft	26	114	6^7	6^{12}	6^{14}	6^{20}	CoxR^1	Alw	74	Elocutionist 119	Irish Port	6
14 Oct75	^{3}Haw	6 f	:22^2	:45^4	1:12^{4}ft	13	118	9^{11}	$9^{8\frac{1}{2}}$	$6^{3\frac{1}{4}}$	$4^{4\frac{3}{4}}$	StoverD^9	10000	77	Jim James 116	Rich Passion	9
29 Aug75	^{4}AP	$5\frac{1}{2}$ f	:22^4	:47^2	1:07^{4}sy	6-5	▲122	$4^{1\frac{1}{2}}$	$3^{3\frac{1}{2}}$	2^1	1^{nk}	PatsnG^1	cM7000	76	Manager Ed 122	Kid Louie	12

Sept 20 AP 4f ft :51⅗b **Aug 19 AP 4f ft :50b** **Aug 3 AP 3f ft :36⅘b**

Following eight months of inactivity and a terrible six-furlong race on July 16, Manager Ed delivered a vastly improved performance on July 27. It was Manager Ed's first try beyond a sprint distance, his first try around two turns, and his first attempt on grass. We have no way of knowing whether trainer John Wozneski knew his horse was fit enough to perform as well as it did, but he had a right to feel proud of his work. I suspect, in fact, that it went to his head.

On August 12 Wozneski stepped Manager Ed up in company and switched him back to the main track. The horse ran its best but had to settle for fourth money after failing to gain ground in the stretch. We can excuse the trainer for trying to upgrade his horse on that occasion, but the result was not very encouraging.

On August 26 Wozneski dropped the horse a notch, keeping him on the main track, at a level slightly higher than the prior good race. Again, Manager Ed raced to the full limit of his apparent talent, only to lose momentum in the final yards. He did finish second, but that loss of ground marked the second straight wasted opportunity, a sign that trainer Wozneski misjudged his horse's class or distance capability.

Two weeks and *no* workouts later Wozneski decided to try Manager Ed on the grass again. While everything in the horse's record indicates the preference for a slightly cheaper race, the most plausible explanation for the horse's lackluster performance is that trainer Wozneski has blown it. Today's $10,000 race on the turf is not likely to help this horse's chances. Wozneski had a fit horse on his hands but overestimated its talent. The evidence says this horse has lost its edge in condition and will need every break possible to earn a piece of the purse.

Christmas Past — Own.—Phipps Cynthia — 121
Gr. f. 3, by Grey Dawn II—Yule Log, by Bold Ruler
Br.—Phipps Cynthia (Ky) — 1982 6 3 2 0 $110,034
Tr.—Penna Angel Jr — 1981 2 M 0 2 $4,080
Lifetime 8 3 2 2 $114,114

4Jun82-8Bel	1$\frac{1}{8}$	:45^{4}	1:09^{4}	1:48^{2}ft	7	121	5^{9}	4^{7}	2$^{1\frac{1}{2}}$	2$^{\frac{3}{4}}$	VszJ^{6}	ⒻMother Goose	84	Cpcy'sJy,ChrstmsPst,BlshWthPrd	12
22May82-8Bel	1	:46	1:09^{3}	1:34^{1}ft	4$\frac{1}{4}$	121	5^{3}	4$^{4\frac{1}{2}}$	5$^{6\frac{1}{2}}$	5$^{9\frac{1}{2}}$	Vasquez J^{9}	ⒻAcorn	85	Cupecoy's Joy,NancyHuang,Vestris	9
24Mar82-9GP	1$\frac{1}{16}$	:47^{4}	1:11^{4}	1:44^{1}ft	*2-5	121	4$^{1\frac{3}{4}}$	3^{1}	1$^{1\frac{1}{2}}$	1^{3}	VsqzJ^{2}	ⒻBonnie Miss	80	Christmas Past, Norsan,OurDarling	6
4Mar82-9Hia	1$\frac{1}{8}$	:48^{1}	1:12^{1}	1:49^{2}ft	7$\frac{1}{4}$	113	3$^{1\frac{1}{2}}$	2$^{1\frac{1}{2}}$	1$^{1\frac{1}{2}}$	1^{6}	VsquezJ^{6}	ⒻPoinsettia	85	ChristmasPast,Larida,SmartHeiress	8
1Feb82-6Hia	1$\frac{1}{16}$	:48^{2}	1:13^{3}	1:45^{1}ft	*3-5	120	2^{hd}	1^{3}	1^{6}	1^{11}	Vasquez J^{6}	ⒻMdn	77	ChristmasPast,Friedenau,Sidmzelle	9
18Jan82-4Hia	6f	:22^{2}	:45^{3}	1:10^{4}ft	*7-5	120	7$^{6\frac{1}{4}}$	4$^{8\frac{1}{2}}$	3$^{6\frac{1}{2}}$	2^{9}	Vasquez J^{9}	ⒻMdn	80	Artic Moss, Christmas Past,Pittsy	12
8Oct81-9Bel	6f	:22^{3}	:46^{1}	1:12^{3}ft	*8-5	117	6$^{4\frac{3}{4}}$	5$^{3\frac{1}{2}}$	3$^{4\frac{1}{2}}$	3$^{3\frac{1}{4}}$	Vasquez J^{5}	ⒻMdn	76	IntlEncontr,PshYrLck,ChrstmsPst	12
23Sep81-3Bel	6f	:22^{4}	:46^{2}	1:12 ft	8$\frac{1}{4}$	117	10$^{9\frac{1}{2}}$	8$^{7\frac{3}{4}}$	5$^{4\frac{1}{2}}$	3$^{2\frac{1}{2}}$	Vasquez J^{7}	ⒻMdn	79	Pert, Broom Dance,ChristmasPast	13

● Jun 24 Bel 4f ft :46^{1} h ● Jun 18 Bel 7f ft 1:23^{4} h Jun 12 Bel 3f ft :36^{3} b Jun 3 Bel 3f ft :37 b

In the highest-caliber stakes competition the player is often forced to make comparisons between horses who are shipping in from far-flung locations, or else are stretching out to classic racing distances.

Occasionally, a well-regarded runner will be suited by the extra length of a championship race or seem ready to show additional improvement, while a key rival might now be hard pressed to maintain her edge under significantly heavier weight, or some other noticeable problem.

In the 1982 Coaching Club American Oaks, at 1½ miles, Christmas Past was meeting her arch rival Cupecoy's Joy, a very fast filly who had already won their first two encounters at 1 mile and 1⅛ miles.

Today, Christmas Past is no cinch to avenge those defeats, but she should be given the benefit of the doubt, especially while Cupecoy's Joy is the odds-on favorite. (Cupecoy's Joy's past performances appear in Chapter 11.)

Trainer Angel Penna, Jr., whose father did a successful stint in Europe, is an outstanding world-class trainer, a man who programs his best stock to improve as the distances stretch out.

Christmas Past herself appears to be a natural router who only began to win when she was sent around two turns in her fourth lifetime start. At one mile, she had virtually no chance against the electrifying speed of Cupecoy's Joy. At 1⅛ miles, she seemed no better off, but at the wire she closed like a whirlwind to get within a length of her front-running rival.

Today, the 1½-mile distance will present serious problems to Cupecoy's Joy, who despite her enviable record, has never won a race around two turns and has not shown any inclination to stay a mile and a half. For the first time in their rivalry, Christmas Past figures to be right at home, getting stronger the longer she goes.

What you are seeing on display here is a potential champion being brought to her best form by an ace trainer on the day she had everything in her favor. At 5–2 odds, a good player had a fine chance to share the rewards of her most impressive lifetime win. Christmas Past won by six lengths, going away.

1¼ MILES—$350,000 PURSE, HOLLYWOOD PARK, JULY 20, 1974

Chris Evert **121** Ch. f (1971), by Swoon's Son—Miss Carmie, by T. V. Lark.
Breeder, Echo Valley Horse Farm (Ky.). 1974 4 3 0 1 $159,789
Owner, C. Rosen. Trainer, J. A. Trovato. 1973 5 4 1 0 $93,012

Jun22-748Bel	1 1-2	2:28⅘ft	4-5	▴121	2h	1h	11½	13½	Vel'q'zJ1	ScwS	76	Ⓕ ChrisEvert121	F'staLibre	M'dM'll'r	10
Jun 1-748Bel	1 1-8	1:48⅗sy	2¾	121	32	21½	1h	1½	Vel'ezJ14	ScwS	84	Ⓕ ChrisEvert121	M'dMuller	QuazeQ'lt	14
May11-748Aqu	1	1:36 ft	9-5	▴121	21	43	31½	1¾	Vel'q'zJ1	ScwS	87	Ⓕ ChrisEvert121	ClearC'py	FiestaLibre	9
May 1-748Aqu	7 f	1:24⅖ft	2	▴118	74¾	66¼	67½	34½	Vel'q'zJ10	AlwS	74	Ⓕ ClearCopy113	ShyDawn	ChrisEvert	10
Nov14-738Aqu	1	1:36⅖ft	4-5	▴121	2h	2h	11	11¼	Pi'yLJr11	AlwS	85	Ⓕ ChrisEvert121	Amb'lero	Kh'd'sK'er	11
Nov 3-738CD	7 f	1:25⅕ft	6-5	▴116	911	913	43½	11¼	Pin'yLJr2	AlwS	81	Ⓕ ChrisEvert116	B'ndl'r	KissMeD'rlin	13
Oct 6-737Bel	1	1:36⅘ft	6¼	121	94	31½	41	2¼	Cas'aM11	ScwS	85	Ⓕ Bundler121	ChrisEvert	I'm a Pl's're	14
Oct 2-736Bel	6 f	1:10⅘ft	3	120	52½	44½	3½	12¾	Pinc'yLJr10	Alw	92	Ⓕ ChrisEv'rt120	Symp'th'tic	F'h'gL'dy	10
Sep14-733Bel	6 f	1:11 ft	3½	120	31½	32	2½	1¾	Pin'yLJr10	Mdn	88	Ⓕ ChrisEvert120	M'dMuller	MamaKali	13

July 18 Hol 4f ft :46⅖h July 14 Hol 1m ft 1:38⅖h July 9 Hol 6f ft 1:15b

Chris Evert is another example of a stakes-class filly champion who was extremely well managed.

Here from top to bottom is a well-managed, top-grade racehorse at her seasonal peak. Notice the way trainer Joe Trovato established a solid foundation in 1973 and stretched Chris out in distance with each succeeding start in 1974. A fine piece of work by a man who knows how to get a horse to produce and keep producing.

These were the past performances of Chris Evert prior to her fifty-length "upset" victory over the speedy Miss Musket on July 20, 1974, in one of the richest match races of all time. Although the key to her winning performance was in the workout line, it was not possible to know that without searching for other clues published in that day's edition of the *Form*.

For Saturday stakes races, and especially for championship-caliber events, the *Daily Racing Form*'s reportage is often excellent. For the Kentucky Derby, for instance, Joe Hirsch does an incredible job, logging the daily doings of all the key eligibles for the two months leading up to the race. Every player should take some time to read the news items and columns in the *Daily Racing Form;* there are many useful tidbits and insights that can be gleaned from them.

Deep within the pages of the July 20, 1974, edition of the *Form*, California correspondent Pat Rogerson reported on the fractional times for the latest workouts of both horses. Although he was most impressed with Miss Musket's blazing one-mile training trial in 1:35⅕, the astute player might have noted that Chris' first quarter-mile fraction in her one-mile workout was noticeably faster. On July 17 Miss Musket worked a half-mile in 48 seconds, a relatively slow move compared with Chris' final workout on July 18. "I told Velasquez to break Chris sharply from the starting gate and not to be worried about getting her tired," said Trovato in Rogerson's report. The significance of Trovato's instructions could hardly be lost on the player who knew that 85 percent of all match races have been won wire to wire. The player may not wish to spend his time researching trainer patterns, but he surely can read his *Racing Form* between races at the track.

9.
The Key Race Method

In late October 1972 I was faced with a unique problem. I had just moved to Columbia, Maryland, and was going to conduct a daily five-minute seminar on handicapping over WLMD radio in the Washington-Baltimore area.

Based on my private results, I thought that I could pick 50 percent winners, show a flat bet profit in the thirteen-week test period, and explain handicapping in the process.

The format was simple. I would handicap races at Laurel racetrack and explain the theories behind the best betting opportunities of the day.

There was one catch. I had been to Laurel racetrack only once, on opening day, October 2. And because I had just joined the staff of *Turf and Sport Digest*, I knew I would not be able to go out to the track more than once a week. I had some familiarity with the leading trainers and their patterns; but I didn't know the horses, the track, or very much else about the local conditions. And I only had a week to prepare myself. In desperation, I did further trainer research, studied post positions, pulled out past performance records and workout listings, and studied the result charts as if I were preparing for an examination before the bar.

A brand-new racing surface complicated the problem. Wild upsets were taking place every day as the maintenance crew fought to stabilize conditions. Horses with late speed seemed to have a built-in edge during this period, but it was not easy to tell from the past performance records which horses would be able to produce that late speed. I solved the problem by using a simple research tool I had developed a few years earlier, one that investigates the relationship between a race over the track and future winning performance.

Strange as it may seem, almost every stretch-running Laurel winner with a prior race over the track had displayed one major characteristic: a sign of increased speed on the turn in the previous Laurel race. The implications were too powerful to ignore. The turn was the roughest piece of real estate in Maryland. Any horse in good enough shape to make a move on it was a horse worth tabbing for improvement next time out.

Admittedly, as form settled down and the track stabilized, I was forced to handicap races more thoroughly than that. But I got past the first four weeks with 45 percent winners, including some outrageous longshots. And I was on the air to stay.

It is also true that this was a particularly unusual set of conditions, yet the investigative tool has served me well for many purposes, as it might well serve you. Here is how to set it up. Again you will need to work with a set of chronologically dated result charts.

First, with the most recent race on top, check the index date and race number of the winner's last race: see below, 6Aug76 ${}^{1}\mathrm{AP}^{3}$ Windy City Butch means Windy City Butch last raced in the first race, August 6, and finished third.

THIRD RACE 6 FURLONGS. (1:08$\frac{3}{5}$). MAIDENS. SPECIAL WEIGHTS. Purse $7,000. 2-year-olds. Weight, 119 lbs.
AP Value to winner $4,200; second, $1,400; third, $770; fourth, $420; fifth, $210.
August 23, 1976 Mutuel Pool, $144,583.

Last Raced	Horse	EqtA	Wt	PP	St	¼	½	Str	Fin	Jockeys	Owners	Odds to $1
6 Aug76 ${}^{1}\mathrm{AP}^{3}$	Windy City Butch	2	119	6	5	7^{1}	$6\frac{1}{2}$	5^{3}	1^{nk}	MGavidia	S Berry C Scott	2.80
	Cornucopian	2	119	5	6	5^{h}	$5^{2\frac{1}{2}}$	4^{h}	$2\frac{1}{2}$	GPatterson	E A Cox Jr	a-1.80
14 Aug76 ${}^{3}\mathrm{AP}^{2}$	Hinkston	2	119	3	4	4^{3}	$3\frac{1}{2}$	$1\frac{1}{2}$	3^{5}	EFires	Levitch-Stone	3.30
29 Jly 76 ${}^{5}\mathrm{AP}^{7}$	Bask	2	119	9	3	3^{1}	2^{1}	2^{1}	4^{h}	LSnyder	Reineman Stable Inc	a-1.80
	Wellspoken	2	119	7	9	2	9	7^{2}	5^{h}	RBreen	EJmendorf	20.60
1 May76 ${}^{1}\mathrm{Sun}^{4}$	Knotty Knave	b2	119	1	7	6^{1}	7^{1}	$6^{1\frac{1}{2}}$	$6^{3\frac{1}{2}}$	JLively	M Ross et al	6.30
6 Aug76 ${}^{4}\mathrm{AP}^{7}$	East Union	b2	119	4	2	1^{2}	$6^{2\frac{1}{2}}$	3^{1}	$7\frac{1}{2}$	JPowell	B-G Bromagen	17.20
23 Apr76 ${}^{3}\mathrm{Kee}^{7}$	Count Tumiga	2	119	8	8	8^{2}	8^{1}	8	8^{2}	RSibille	G'ld'n Ch'nce F'm Inc	36.10
11 Aug76 ${}^{3}\mathrm{AP}^{2}$	Debarcation	b2	119	2	1	2^{1}	$4^{1\frac{1}{2}}$	8^{1}	9	JDBailey	S Laser	9.90

Coupled, a-Cornucopian and Bask.
OFF AT 2:53 CDT. Start good. Won driving. Time, :22$\frac{2}{5}$, :46$\frac{2}{5}$, :59$\frac{1}{5}$, 1:11$\frac{4}{5}$. Track fast.

$2 Mutuel Prices:			
6-WINDY CITY BUTCH	7.60	3.40	2.40
1-CORNUCOPIAN (a-Entry)		3.20	2.40
4-HINKSTON			2.60

Ch. c, by Lurullah—Christy Blue, by Porterhouse. Trainer, Clifford J. Scott. Bred by Estate of Charles Cunningham (Ky.).

WINDY CITY BUTCH was unhurried early, rallied wide leaving the upper stretch to run down CORNUCOPIAN in the final strides. The latter was unhurried early, drove inside the leaders leaving the eighth pole to wrest the lead late in tht drive but was unable to contain the winner approaching the finish. HINKSTON circled rivals coming out of the turn to take the lead a furlong out, faltered late in the drive. BASK moved between horses coming out of the turn, lacked a closing rally. WELLSPOKEN had to steady while in tight quarters leaving the gate, rallied mildly late to pass tiring rivals. KNOTTY KNAVE went evenly. EAST UNION sprinted out o a clear lead in the early running, tired leaving the upper stretch. COUNT TUMIGA was always outrun. DEBARCATION was through after a half.

Scratched—Dravir.

Next, thumb back to the date and race number indicated to see what the winner did in his last race. But whatever he did, *circle his name*. That circle will forever mean that Windy City Butch won his *next* start.

FIRST RACE 6 FURLONGS. (1:08⅗). MAIDENS. SPECIAL WEIGHTS. Purse $7,000. 2-year-olds
AP Weight, 119 lbs.
Value to winner $4,200; second, $1,400; third, $770; fourth, $420; fifth, $210.
August 6, 1976 Mutuel Pool, $64,776.

Last Raced	Horse	EqtAWt	PP	St	¼	½	Str	Fin	Jockeys	Owners	Odds to $1
21 Jly 76 5AP8	Fiddlefish	b2 119	4	2	1^h	$1^{3\frac{1}{2}}$	$1^{2\frac{1}{2}}$	$1^{1\frac{1}{4}}$	APatterson	Mary Lou Cashman	5.00
29 Jly 76 1AP6	Barely Safe	2 119	9	6	$5^{\frac{1}{2}}$	$3^{\frac{1}{2}}$	$2^{1\frac{1}{2}}$	$2^{2\frac{1}{2}}$	RSibille	Golden Chance F'm Inc	8.40
21 Jly 76 5AP2	Windy City Butch	b2 119	8	5	$6^{2\frac{1}{2}}$	4^h	$3^{2\frac{1}{2}}$	3^5	WGavidia	S Berry-C Scott	2.00
	Victory Flag	2 119	6	3	$4^{\frac{1}{2}}$	5^1	6^4	$4^{\frac{1}{2}}$	EFires	Elmendorf	14.00
29 Jly 76 1AP5	Gordon Pasha	b2 119	3	1	3^3	2^1	$4^{1\frac{1}{2}}$	$5^{\frac{3}{4}}$	RLTurcotte	D A Hess	2.70
21 Jly 76 5AP5	Beau Dustin	b2 119	7	7	7^8	7^6	$5^{\frac{1}{2}}$	$6^{1\frac{1}{4}}$	CStone	Mary Zimmerman	16.50
	Selaru	b2 119	2	9	9	8^h	$7^{1\frac{1}{2}}$	7^2	PRubbicco	Bar R J's Stable	22.10
	The Stinger	2 119	5	8	8^1	9	8^2	$8^{2\frac{1}{2}}$	HArroyo	R F Salmen	15.90
29 Jly 76 5AP2	Coldwater	2 119	1	4	2^h	$6^{\frac{1}{4}}$	9	9	RBreen	R Russell	9.00

OFF AT 2:00½ CDT. Start good. Won driving. Time, :22⅗, :46⅖, :58⅘, 1:11⅗. Track good.

Official Program Numbers

$2 Mutuel Prices:			
5-FIDDLEFISH	12.00	6.60	4.00
10-BARELY SAFE		7.80	3.80
9-WINDY CITY BUTCH			2.80

Ch. c, by Piko—Noholme's Gal, by Noholme II. Tr., Paul T. Adwell. Bred by Fontainebleau Farm, Inc. (Ky.).

FIDDLEFISH broke alertly to vie for the lead outside two rivals, drew out in the turn and won under a strong hand ride. BARELY SAFE circled rivals coming out of the turn and was gradually getting to the winner. WINDY CITY BUTCH was outrun early, rallied strongly between rivals after a half but was no threat to the top pair. VICTORY FLAG went evenly. GORDON PASHA pressed the early lead while between rivals, faltered leaving the turn. BEAU DUSTIN had no excuses. SELARU and THE STINGER were always outrun. COLDWATER had brief early speed along the rail.

Scratched—Brach's Honey, Promising Dream, Uncle Jett, Restless Rascal.

If you repeat this simple exercise for the most recent fifty or sixty races (you can go back as far as you wish) and if you continue the process every day, you will be adding exceedingly valuable information to dozens of result charts. The data may help you distinguish patterns that are not otherwise detectable.

Maybe you will discover, as I did, that the majority of route race winners at Hazel Park and Latonia racetracks had a prior sprint race for a jumpoff effort. Maybe you will observe that horses shipping from California to New York during the early spring win an astounding percentage of races first crack out of the box. Perhaps you will note that horses coming off the turf course at Delaware Park and other tracks tend to show improved early speed in their next try on the dirt. The possibilities are without limit. Without really trying, you will automatically create the Key Race method, a powerful tool that isolates especially well-run races at every class level.

For example, the three horses circled in the following chart came out of the race to win their very next starts. A Key Race.

FIRST RACE
Aqu
July 15, 1976

1⅛ MILES. (1:47). CLAIMING. Purse $7,500. For 3-year-olds and upward. 3-year-olds, 116 lbs.; older, 122 lbs. Non-winners of a race at a mile and a furlong or over since July 1 allowed 3 lbs.; of such a race since June 15, 5 lbs. Claiming price $8,500; if for less, 2 lbs. allowed for each $250 to $8,000. (Races when entered to be claimed for $7,000 or less not considered.)

Value to winner, $4,500; second, $1,650; third, $900; fourth, $450. Track Mutuel Pool, $106,946. OTB Pool, $87,971.

Last Raced	Horses	Eqt A	Wt	PP	St	¼	½	¾	Str	Fin	Jockeys	Owners	Odds to $1
25Jun76 ^{6}Bel^{3}	Charms Hope	b5	113	1	2	4^{4}	4^{3}	4^{7}	$3^{\frac{1}{2}}$	1^{nk}	MVenezia	J J Stippel	2.50
7Jly 76 ^{1}Aqu^{1}	Finney Finster	b4	117	3	7	6^{8}	5^{2}	$3^{1\frac{1}{2}}$	2^{h}	$2^{1\frac{1}{4}}$	ASantiago	Camijo Stable	5.60
9Jly 76 ^{1}Aqu^{1}	Good and Bold	5	110	4	1	1^{4}	1^{6}	1^{6}	1^{3}	$3^{1\frac{3}{4}}$	BDiNicola^{5}	Emmarr Stable	3.00
9Jly 76 ^{1}Aqu^{6}	Just Like Pa	b3	109	2	4	$3^{\frac{1}{2}}$	$3^{1\frac{1}{2}}$	2^{h}	4^{8}	4^{9}	DMontoya†	Audley Farm Stable	8.50
8Jly 76 ^{1}Aqu^{1}	Wave the Flag	6	115	5	6	7	7	7	5^{6}	$5^{4\frac{1}{2}}$	RHernandez	O S Barrera	3.40
1Jly 76 ^{2}Aqu^{1}	Jolly Mister	b4	113	6	5	5^{1}	6^{7}	$6^{\frac{1}{2}}$	6^{12}	6^{22}	PDay	Stan-Mar Stable	7.30
9Jly 76 ^{3}Aqu^{5}	Acosado II.	4	117	7	3	2^{5}	2^{3}	5^{1}	7	7	JVasquez	Bellrose Farm	11.90

†Five pounds apprentice allowance waived.

OFF AT 10:30 PDT. START GOOD. WON DRIVING. Time, :24; :47⅕, 1:12⅗, 1:39⅗, 1:53⅖. Track fast.

$2 Mutuel Prices

1-CHARMS HOPE	7.00	4.00	2.60
3-FINNEY FINSTER		6.20	3.60
4-GOOD AND BOLD			2.80

B. h, by Abe's Hope—Cold Dead, by Dead Ahead. Trainer, F. J. Horan. Bred by Criterion Farms (Fla.).

CHARMS HOPE, unhurried early, rallied approaching the stretch and outfinished FINNEY FINSTER. The latter, off slowly, advanced steadily to loom a threat near midstretch and continued on with good courage. GOOD AND BOLD tired from his early efforts. JUST LIKE PA rallied leaving the far turn but lacked the needed late response. WAVE THE FLAG was never close. JOLLY MISTER was always outrun. ACOSADO II tired badly.

Charms Hope claimed by M. Garren, trainer G. Puentes; Good and Bold claimed by S. Sommer, trainer F. Martin.

Claiming Prices (in order of finish)—$8000, 8500, 8250, 8250, 8250, 8000, 8500.

Wave the Flag won a $5,000 claimer on July 21. Charms Hope won an allowance race on July 23. Good and Bold won a $10,000–$12,000 claimer on July 31. In addition, Just Like Pa ran fourth on July 29, encountering traffic problems, and won a $9,000 claimer on August 18.

Coincidence might dilute the impact of the added information, but nine out of ten times there is a better explanation. Either this race was superior to the designated class or else it contained an unusually fit group of horses. In either case, that's important information.

Indeed, after Wave the Flag's easy score at $5,000 claiming and Charms Hope's five-length victory in allowance company, the Key Race method would have certainly pointed out the merits of Good and Bold at 9–1 in a six-furlong race on July 31 (note the running line of Good and Bold in the Key Race chart). Observant race watchers and chart readers might similarly have made a strong case for Just Like Pa when he went to the post at 6–1 on August 18.

The Key Race method has many applications, but it is simply sensational in pointing out above-average fields in maiden races and turf events.

Maiden races are a mixed bag. Very few horses entered in such races have established their true class level. Some maidens will turn out to be useful racehorses; others will be little more than walking feed bills. Sooner or later, most often sooner, the best of the maidens wind up in the winner's circle. With deadly precision the Key Race method points out those maiden races that contained the fastest nonwinners on the grounds.

Maybe the winner of a maiden race returns to win a stakes race. Maybe the fifth horse in the maiden race comes back to graduate in its next start. If so, I would begin looking for the second, third, and fourth horses to come out of that maiden race. There could be little question that they had raced against above-average stock. Naturally, I would not suspend the handicapping process. I would still want to know what the rest of the field looked like, whether there was a prevailing track bias, what type it was, what if any trainer patterns were present, and so on. I would, however, surely upgrade the chances of any horse coming out of such a strong field.

Similar logic explains the effectiveness of the Key Race method in classifying turf races. Regardless of a horse's record on dirt, its ability to compete on grass is never established until it has raced on grass. In effect, the horse is a maiden on the turf until it wins on the turf. Again, the Key Race method will isolate the stronger fields.

Every once in a while you will encounter the phenomenon of a result chart with six, seven, or more circled horses—a Key Race in the ultimate sense of the word. My research says this occurs at least once in every 500 races. By the time four horses come out of the same field to win their next starts you should get the message.

The Key Race at Saratoga on August 5, 1972, is my personal favorite. The circles are not included. They aren't necessary. Every last horse provided a winning effort.

EIGHTH RACE
Saratoga
AUGUST 5, 1972

1 $\frac{1}{16}$ MILES.(turf). (1.39 2/5) ALLOWANCES. Purse $15,000. 3-year-olds and upward which have not won three races other than maiden, claiming or starter. Weights, 3-year-olds, 117 lbs. Older, 122 lbs. Non-winners of $7,200 at a mile or over since July 1, allowed 2 lbs. $6,600 at a mile or over since June 17, 4 lbs. $6,000 at a mile or over since May 15, 6 lbs. (Maidens, claiming and starter races not considered inallowances.)
Value of race $15,000, value to winner $9,000, second $3,300, third $1,800, fourth $900. Mutuel pool $128,695, OTB pool $70,388.

Last Raced	Horse	Eqt.A.Wt	PP	St	¼	½	¾	Str	Fin	Jockey	Odds $1
23Jly72 ^{8}Del^{2}	Scrimshaw	4 116	2	2	7^{1}	7½	4^{1}	1^{3}	1^{4}	Marquez C H	2.40
20Jly72 ^{6}Aqu^{4}	Gay Gambler	3 108	8	8	$9^{1\frac{1}{2}}$	9^{5}	9^{8}	$8^{1\frac{1}{2}}$	$2^{1\frac{1}{2}}$	Patterson G	5.60
22Jly72 ^{6}Aqu^{3}	Fast Judge	b 3 111	7	7	6^{2}	6^{1}	6½	4^{hd}	3^{hd}	Velasquez J	10.00
28Jly72 ^{6}Aqu^{1}	Straight To Paris	3 115	9	3	2½	$2^{1\frac{1}{2}}$	2½	2½	4no	Vasquez J	2.70
25Jly72 ^{9}Aqu^{1}	Search the Farm	b 4 116	3	9	$8^{1\frac{1}{2}}$	$8^{1\frac{1}{2}}$	8^{1}	6^{hd}	5no	Guadalupe J	11.20
23Jly72 ^{8}Del^{3}	Chrisaway	4 116	4	6	$5^{1\frac{1}{2}}$	4^{hd}	7½	7½	6^{2}	Howard R	25.30
25Jly72 ^{9}Aqu^{5}	Navy Lieutenant	b 4 116	1	1	3½	5^{1}	3½	5½	7^{4}	Belmonte E	10.90
25Jly72 ^{7}Aqu^{4}	Head Table	b 3 113	10	5	4^{1}	3^{1}	5½	9^{10}	8^{2}	Baeza B	7.50
17Jly72 ^{8}Del^{3}	Mongo's Image	3 111	5	4	$1^{1\frac{1}{2}}$	1½	1^{1}	3^{hd}	9^{10}	Nelson E	28.70
21Jly72 ^{7}Aqu^{5}	Chartered Course	b 4 116	6	10	10	10	10	10	10	Arellano J	16.70

Time, :23⅕, :46⅖, 1:09⅘, 1:34⅗, 1:40⅘ (Against Wind in Backstretch). Course firm.

$2 Mutuel Prices:			
2-(B)- SCRIMSHAW	6.80	3.60	3.20
8-(H)- GAY GAMBLER		7.00	4.80
7-(G)- FAST JUDGE			5.60

B. g, by Jaipur—Ivory Tower, by Hill Prince. Trainer Lake R P. Bred by Vanderbilt A G (Md).
IN GATE AT 5.23; OFF AT 5.23 EASTERN DAYLIGHT TIME. Start Good Won Handily

SCRIMSHAW, taken back after breaking alertly, swung out to go after the leaders on the far turn, quickly drew off and was never seriously threatened. GAY GAMBLER, void of early foot, was unable to split horses entering the stretch, altered course to the extreme outside and finished strongly. FAST JUDGE, reserved behind the leaders, split horses leaving the far turn but was not match for the top pair. STRAIGHT TO PARIS prompted the pace much of the way and weakened during the drive. SEARCH THE FARM failed to menace. CHRISAWAY raced within easy striking distance while outside horses much of the way but lacked a late response. NAVY LIEUTENANT, a factor to the stretch while saving ground, gave way. HEAD TABLE was finished leaving the far turn. MONGO'S IMAGE stopped badly after showing to midstretch.

Owners— 1, Vanderbilt A G; 2, Whitney C V; 3, Wygod M J; 4, Rokeby Stable; 5, Nadler Evelyn; 6, Steinman Beverly R; 7, Sommer S; 8, Happy Hill Farm; 9, Reynolds J A; 10, Camijo Stable.

Trainers— 1, Lake R P; 2, Poole G T; 3, Nickerson V J; 4, Burch Elliott; 5, Nadler H; 6, Fout P R; 7, Martin F; 8, Wright F I; 9, Reynolds J A; 10, King W P.

Overweight: Head Table 2 pounds.

On August 12 Scrimshaw won the first division of the Bernard Baruch Handicap. One half-hour later Chrisaway took the second division at 50–1. A few days later Chartered Course won a daily double race paying $25. On the same card Gay Gambler—probably the best bet of the year—took the sixth race. Straight to Paris shipped to Monmouth for his win; Fast Judge, Search the Farm, and Navy Lieutenant raced out of the money in their next starts at Saratoga but won on the rebound at Belmont in September. Mongo's Image won a high-class allowance race at the end of the Saratoga meeting at 8–1.

The only horse that didn't race back during this period was Head Table. For weeks I hunted through the *Racing Form* hoping to find his name among the entries. I was prepared to fly anywhere. But he never showed up.

Believe it or not, Head Table returned to the races on April 21, 1973, nine months after the Key Race. Yes, you guessed it: Head Table won by six. That's weird.

10.
An Edge in Class

At Charles Town racetrack in West Virginia, where the racing is cheap and the betting action takes exotic forms, the horseplayer seldom has a chance to see a top-drawer horse in action. Nevertheless, the player would be making a serious mistake if he failed to incorporate notions about class into his handicapping.

On a typical racing program at a minor-league track like Charles Town, the majority of races are for $1,500–$2,000 claiming horses—the lowest level of horsedom. These are horses that have seen their better days or are just not fast enough to compete in the higher-class claiming events found at the major one-mile racetracks.

Actually, that is not quite true. A respectable number of Charles Town horses can run fast—and a select few can run very fast—but they are too short-winded or too battle-scarred to be able to sustain their speed in three-quarter-mile races at the majors. After all, there are no four-furlong races for three-year-olds and up at Arlington Park, and there are no six-furlong races for $1,500 horses either.

For all the wrong reasons, major-track handicappers tend to have a snobbish attitude toward their compatriots at the minors, thinking perhaps that the cheaper racing is less formful, less predictable. I can assure you, however, that there are more winning players per capita at "bull ring" tracks like Charles Town than there are at Aqueduct or Hollywood Park.

Far from being the indecipherable mess that it seems on the surface, minor-track racing offers some of the most attractive betting opportunities in all of racing. Examining the class factor will show exactly why this is so, and for the astute player the applications extend to a large body of races at the major tracks as well.

The first step toward success at Charles Town is to use the result charts to construct a record of the eligibility conditions of all the cheapest races. About 90 percent of Charles Town claiming events have restrictive clauses which resemble the eligibility conditions found in allowance (nonclaiming) races at the major one-mile tracks.

For example, the third, sixth, eighth, and tenth races at Charles Town on August 4, 1976, were $1,500 claiming races for three-year-olds and up, but any bettor who assumed that these races were for the same class of horse was on his way to a disastrous evening of betting.

The first $1,500 claiming race was limited to horses "which have not won a race in 1976"; the second, "for nonwinners of three races in 1976"; the third, "for nonwinners of two races lifetime"; and the final $1,500 race, "for nonwinners of a race in 1975 or 1976," the lowest $1,500 race in captivity.

The next evening there were four more $1,500 claiming races with four additional sets of eligibility conditions. Confusing? Perhaps. But it turns out that there is a measurable difference between each of the restricted $1,500-class races. This difference is not only reflected in the average winning times for each separate restricted class but is greater than the difference between the average $1,500 and $2,000 race. In other words, it is more difficult to advance within the same $1,500 claiming class than it is to step up to the $2,000 claiming level!

Whenever a $1,500 horse wins at Charles Town, it loses its chance to compete in the same restricted class. The claiming price remains the same—even the purse tends to be the same—but the horse must now face other horses that have also graduated from the lower restricted level.

Naturally, the next level (within the same $1,500 claiming class) will include other horses with recent victories. This makes for much tougher competition.

Indeed, most Charles Town horses have a very hard time scoring two wins back to back, and some never advance until all the better $1,500 horses win their way into the next level of competition. In a very real sense, the slower horses are hopelessly trapped, and some remain trapped for months.

For the purpose of identification, it is helpful (if not essential) to formulate a classification system for all $1,500 and $2,000 races. (At the major tracks, where allowance races are written with similar restrictive eligibility clauses, the purses attached to each race are scaled in proportion to the quality of the field. A classification code is therefore unnecessary, provided of course that the player refers to the charts to note the purse values. The purse values are in themselves a ready-made classification system.)

CHARLES TOWN CLASSIFICATION CODE FOR $1,500 OR $2,000 CLAIMING RACES

O—open race, unrestricted eligibility (top class)

A—Nonwinners of 2 races in the past two months
or 3 races in the past three months

B—Nonwinners of 2 races in three to five months

C—Nonwinners of 2 races in six to nine months
or 3 races in nine to twelve months

D—Nonwinners of 2 races in nine to twenty-four months

E—Nonwinners of a race in nine to twenty-four months

M—Nonwinners lifetime (maidens)

As you can see, the increments *between* class levels at the same $1,500 claiming price are quite steep. It takes a pretty decent $1,500 horse to make its way up the ladder during a calendar year.

The easiest class jump is maiden to E class (nonwinners of a race in nine to twenty-four months). It is no coincidence that the majority of Charles Town repeaters occur at this rock-bottom level. Most E-class horses have very little ability and are always forced to meet recent maiden graduates. Generally speaking, a recent maiden graduate, especially a lightly raced maiden graduate, is a very dependable Charles Town bet. At the very least, the recent victory is a positive sign of current condition. In the spring of 1976 I charted two months of Charles Town races and found fifteen repeaters of this type in thirty-four E-class races. The average mutuel payoff was $8.60.

With minor revisions, the Charles Town classification code will prove useful at any minor-class racetrack and at any major track where similar eligibility conditions are written into the cheapest races.

Tracks like River Downs, Thistledown, Waterford Park, Pocono Downs, Finger Lakes, Commodore Downs, and others scattered all across the country fit into this category, as do all the fair circuit tracks in California and Massachusetts.

From practical experience at a few of these minor racetracks, I cannot stress enough the value of the classification code. Of course, you might have to set up slightly different categories depending upon the particular eligibility conditions of races in your area, but you will reward yourself many times over for the effort. Some results will in fact astound you.

At Green Mountain Park, for example, where I enjoyed many an evening during the mid-1960s while working as a counselor at nearby Camp Watitoh, one of the most satisfying bets of my entire career came in the first week that I put the classification code to work.

To my amazement I spotted a 14–1 shot in a $2,000 D-class race that had flashed some high early speed in a $1,500 A-class race. Believe it or not, despite the apparent raise in claiming price, the horse was dropping down sharply in company. He won by nine lengths!

And if you're wondering how this classification code works in today's overexpanded racing marketplace, a good friend of mine, Dick White, has been using this method at Charles Town for the past two years, and he confirms that the identical "dropdown" phenomenon takes place every few weeks.

There are other fundamental applications to consider as well. Very often a $1,500 horse will be entered in an A- or B-class race when it is still eligible for a weaker C- or D-class event. Such a horse can be safely and automatically thrown out. The horse is just out for the exercise, or the trainer is purposely trying to darken its form. (If the horse is really that good, the trainer will invariably raise its selling price.)

Conversely, horses that have been showing signs of life in A- or B-class races make excellent wagers when they are properly placed in less demanding D- or E-class events. This type of hidden class maneuver is the most powerful dropdown angle in all of racing, and you can also expect to see it in a slightly different form at the major tracks.

An allowance race at Aqueduct or Santa Anita or any other major track is probably the toughest kind of race for the novice or intermediate horseplayer. In order to handicap such a race properly, the player must have a fix on the local pecking order. He must know which horses on the grounds are the best sprinters, the best routers, the best turf horses, the best three-year-olds, and so forth. He must also know the approximate breaking point when a claiming race is equal to or better than the allowance race in question.

Allowance race conditions like those $1,500 claiming races at Charles Town are restricted events. A two-time stakes winner or a three-time winner of a $10,000 purse is not allowed into any field that is designed to attract winners of a single lifetime race.

Moreover, the major-track trainer of an allowance horse will often do what the Charles Town trainer of a $1,500 claimer does. He will race the horse against more experienced winners and then drop it back to a level where its best race could make it a top contender. Because the major-track trainer can sometimes hide this maneuver by using top-price claiming events ($100,000 in New York and California, $50,000+ in Illinois and New Jersey, $30,000+ in Maryland and Michigan, and so on), he can often fool the unsophisticated bettors into thinking the horse is stepping up in company when it goes from a claiming to an allowance race. Many times over the opposite is true.

SEVENTH RACE 6 FURLONGS. (1.08½) ALLOWANCE. Purse $8,000. 3-year-olds and upward which have
Delaware never won a race other than maiden, claiming, starter or hunt meeting. Weights, 3-year-
olds, 113 lbs. Older, 122 lbs. Non-winners of a race other than claiming since May 7,
JUNE 19, 1982 allowed 3 lbs. Such a race since April 29, 5 lbs.
Value of race $8,000, value to winner $4,800, second $1,760, third $960, fourth $480.

At Delaware Park during the 1982 meeting there were over forty such allowance races. Almost half of them were won by horses that showed good form in claiming races. And it shouldn't surprise you to learn that the purse values for all $22,000 claiming races at Delaware were higher than the purses listed for this category of allowance race. This is important information, information that does not present itself without consulting result charts.

(Beginning with 1982, the *Daily Racing Form* began to publish purse values attached to all allowance races in the past performance profile, but the player must still check result charts to get the purse values for all claiming races.)

I strongly recommend that the player become familiar with the overall purse structure at his favorite track and maintain a general awareness of the relative purses offered at other tracks. (See Appendix for a list of all tracks including a purse-value index.)

Sometimes the player will be faced with tricky assessments regarding shippers. Sometimes the different purse values of out-of-town tracks will be the only legitimate clue to the true class of these strangers.

Moreover, at a given racetrack where form has settled into a regular pattern, the simple comparison of purse values will often isolate a genuine contender who is subtly moving into a softer spot.

A trainer at Santa Anita knows that a fit $75,000 claimer can beat most of the medium-grade allowance horses in California. A trainer at Atlantic City racecourse knows that a sharp $25,000 claimer can handle all but the very best allowance horses on the grounds.

Smart trainers look for spots where they can take a fair run at a purse without jeopardizing their horses for a claim. And the best of them know that the purse structure doesn't always make perfect sense.

What follows is a rather straightforward example of how all this sometimes leads to an easy selection in a competitive race.

```
Caspar Milquetoast   113  Dk. b. or br. c (1973). by Our Michael—Backseat Driver. by Traffic
                           Judge. Breeder. C. Wetherill (Ky.).      1976  12  5  1  2    $45,020
Owner. Leonard Henry.  Trainer Philip G. Johnson.                  1975   5  1  1  0     $7.340
10 Aug76 2Sar    7 f :222 :4511:242sy 8-5 *122  34   35   31  121 MapleE1   60000 83 CsprMilqetst122  Adm'sActn  5
16 Jly 76 6Aqu    1 :4531:1011:354sy 8-5 *113  591  451  21  111 MapleE1   55000 87 CasparMilqtst113  MldNedle  6
2 Jly 76 7Aqu    1 :4641:1111:354ft  33  112  481 441 341 323 SantiagoA4  Alw 84 Political Coverup 112  Bakor  6
24 Jun76 2Bel   7 f :231 :4641:231ft 41e 122  88  612 44  1no MapleE4   40000 86 CasparMilqutst122 Rbrt'sBy  8
6 Jun76 4Bel   7 f :231 :4641:23 ft  33e 117  32  31  1h  1no MapleE6   40000 87 CsprMilqtst117  FnncialWhiz  7
19 May76 6Bel   7 f :232 :47 1:24 sy   4  117  53  43  22  13 VasqezJ3   30000 82 CasparMilqtst117  ArcticLck  8
6 May76 5Bel    1 :4621:1131:371ft   33  117  431 2h  11  21 VasqezJ4   30000 81 Mr.Interntnl117 CsprMilotst  9
23 Apr76 4Aqu   7 f :231 :4631: gd   81  117  66  671 561 413 VsqezJ2   35000 74 ForestStrm117  Drover'sDwn  7
10 Apr76 5Aqu   6 f :223 :4611:104ft  24  115  55  55  551 553 HoleM3    Alw 83 Bonge 117       Distinctively  9
18 Mar76 7Aqu    1 :4531:1021:363ft  61  115  713 711 791 691 HoleM7    Alw 73 HailLiberty115 HenryBrooks  9
6 Mar76 6Aqu    1 :47 1:1131:363ft 8-5 *115  961 761 18  463 CordroAJr3 Alw 77 Resilient 115    Ship Trial  9
        Aug 24 Sar trt 4f ft :49h        July 27 Bel 6f ft 1:142/5h        July 11 Bel trt 4f ft :492/5b
```

The chart below refers to Caspar Milquetoast's most recent race, a $60,000 claiming event with a purse of $15,000. (In 1982, this purse surely would have been $23–25,000.)

SECOND RACE 7 FURLONGS. (1:21). CLAIMING. Purse $15,000. 3-year-olds. Weight, 122 lbs. Non-
Sar winners of a race since July 15 allowed 3 lbs.; a race since July 1, 5 lbs. Claiming
price, $60,000; for each $2,500 to $55,000, allowed 2 lbs. (Races when entered to be
August 10. 1976 claimed for $50,000 or less not considered.)
Value to winner $9,000; second, $3,300; third, $1,800; fourth, $900. Mutuel Pool, $66,701.
Off-track betting, $61,941.

Last Raced	Horse	EqtAWt	PP	St	¼	½	Str	Fin	Jockeys	Owners	Odds to $1
16 Jly 76 6Aqu1	Caspar Milquetoast	b3 122	1	5	32	32	35	121	EMaple	L D Henry	1.60
5 Aug76 7Sar1	Adam's Action	b3 118	2	1	24	1h	11	2nk	JVelasquez	Exeter Stable	2.10
2 Aug76 2Sar1	Austin	b3 113	5	2	1h	25	21	371	ACorderoJr	Harbor View Farm	2.60
1 Aug76 7FE3	Salim Alicum	3 122	3	3	4h	41	41	4	RTurcotte	G R Gardiner	6.00
10 Jly 76 7Aks9	Le Punch	b3 117	4	4	5	5	5	Eased.	RHernandez	E C Cashman	10.00

OFF AT 2:01 EDT. Start good. Won driving. Time, :222/5, :451/5, 1:11, 1:242/5. Track sloppy.

$2 Mutuel Prices:
2-CASPAR MILQUETOAST	5.20	2.80	2.20
3-ADAM'S ACTION		2.80	2.20
6-AUSTIN			2.20

Dk. b. or br. c, by Our Michael—Backseat Driver, by Traffic Judge. Trainer, Philip G. Johnson. Bred by
Cortright Weterill (Ky.).
CASPAR MILQUETOAST raced wide into the stretch while rallying and drew clear after catching ADAM'S
ACTION near the final sixteenth. The latter saved ground while vying for the lead with AUSTIN to midstretch
and weakened. AUSTIN weakened from his eary efforts. SALIM ALICUM was always outrun. LE PUNCH,
outrun to the stretch, was eased during the late stages.
Corrected weight—Salim Alicum, 122.
Claiming Prices (in order of finish)—$60000, 55000, 55000, 60000, 60000.
Scratched—Buttonbuck, Gabe Benzur.

The next chart is the result chart for the race in which Caspar Milquetoast was entered with the past performances as shown at the start of this discussion. Note the $10,000 purse and the restricted conditions of eligibility. (If this race were run in 1982, the purse would have been $19,000, or still lower than the purse for the $60,000 claiming race.) This is a classic illustration of the hidden class-dropdown maneuver, expertly manipulated by trainer P. G. Johnson, who is one of the best all-around trainers in the sport.

SEVENTH RACE
Bel
August 31, 1976

6 FURLONGS. (1:08⅘). WISE MARGIN PURSE. ALLOWANCES. Purse $10,000. 3-year-olds and upward which have never won a race other than maiden, claiming or starter. 3-year-olds, 118 lbs.; older, 122 lbs. Non-winners of a race other than claiming since Aug. 1 allowed 3 lbs.; such a race since July 15, 5 lbs.
Value to winner $6,000; second, $2,200; third, $1,200; fourth, $600.
Mutuel Pool, $138,757. Off-track betting, $96,245. Exacta Pool, $177,505. Off-track betting Exacta Pool, $191,008.

Last Raced	Horse	EqtAWt	PP	St	¼	½	Str	Fin	Jockeys	Owners	Odds to $1
10 Aug76 ^{2}Sar^{1}	Caspar Milquetoast	b3 113	6	5	$7^{1\frac{1}{2}}$	$4\frac{1}{2}$	$2\frac{1}{2}$	$1^{1\frac{3}{4}}$	EMaple	L D Henry	1.90
20 Aug76 ^{7}Sar^{3}	Bold Needle	b3 113	5	4	$4\frac{1}{2}$	5^{1}	5^{5}	$2\frac{3}{4}$	PDay	Willwynee Stable	7.20
28 Jly 76 ^{6}Aqu^{2}	Balancer	4 117	9	1	2^{1}	$2^{1\frac{1}{2}}$	3^{h}	$3\frac{3}{4}$	MVenezia	Mrs D E Kerr	5.10
23 Aug76 ^{7}Sar^{3}	Master Jorge	3 115	8	2	3^{1}	3^{1}	$4^{1\frac{1}{2}}$	4^{1}	JVelasquez	E Ubarri	5.40
23 Aug76 ^{7}Sar^{7}	Private Thoughts	b3 113	2	3	$1\frac{1}{2}$	1^{h}	1^{h}	$5^{5\frac{1}{2}}$	TWallis	R L Reineman	7.40
7 Aug76 ^{9}Sar^{7}	Ferrous	3 113	4	6	8^{2}	8^{3}	$6\frac{1}{2}$	$6\frac{3}{4}$	ACorderoJr	J Allen	6.10
31 Jly 76 ^{4}Aqu^{1}	Irish Era	4 119	1	7	$5\frac{1}{2}$	$6\frac{1}{2}$	7^{2}	7^{4}	RHernandez	V J Cuti Jr	9.30
6 Aug76 ^{1}Sar^{1}	Uphold	b4 117	7	8	6^{h}	7^{h}	8^{2}	$8^{1\frac{1}{2}}$	HGustines	Darby Dan Farm	44.70
20 Aug76 ^{1}Sar^{1}	Iroquois Tribe	3 118	3	9	9	9	9	9	GMartens	T Veale II	18.60

OFF AT 4:38 EDT. Start good. Won ridden out. Time, :23, :46⅗, 1:11⅕. Track fast.

$2 Mutuel Prices:			
6-CASPAR MILQUETOAST	5.80	3.60	2.60
5-BOLD NEEDLE		6.80	3.80
9-BALANCER			3.60

$2 EXACTA (6–5) PAID $49.20.

Dk. b. or br. c, by Our Michael—Backseat Driver, by Traffic Judge. Trainer, Philip G. Johnson. Bred by Cortright Wetherill (Ky.).

CASPAR MILQUETOAST raced wide into the stretch while rallying and proved clearly best under intermittent urging. BOLD NEEDLE, between horses to the stretch, finished with good energy to gain the place. BALANCE raced forwardly to midstretch and weakened. MASTER JORGE made a run between horses leaving the turn but hung. PRIVATE THOUGHTS was used up making the pace. FERROUS raced very wide. IRISH SEA saved ground to no avail.

Corrected weight—Master Jorge, 115.
Scratched—Clean 'Em Up, Kool as Ice.

Occasionally, an aggressive trainer will take a recent graduate or a limited winner and step it right up to top allowance-class or stakes competition. In most cases this is not beneficial to the horse, but unlike the cheap races at Charles Town, the player should not automatically assume that the horse is out for the exercise. That is the most likely explanation, but a careful look at one horse's brief career suggests a different story.

6th Belmont Park — SEPTEMBER 6, 1975

WIDENER TURF COURSE
1 1-16 MILES
BELMONT PARK
START
FINISH

1 1/16 MILES (turf). (1:40⅕). TUDOR ERA PURSE. ALLOWANCES. Purse $20,000. 3-year-olds and upward which have not won four races other than maiden, claiming or starter. 3-year-olds. 118 lbs.; older, 122 lbs. Non-winners of $25,000 at a mile or over since July 12 allowed 2 lbs.; $15,000 at a mile or over since July 2, 4 lbs.; $9,000 at a mile or over since July 26, 6 lbs. (Claiming races not considered in allowances.) 3-year-olds which have never won at a mile or over allowed 3 lbs.; older, 5 lbs.

COUPLED: SHREDDER and DROLLERY; JACQUES WHO and CHRISTOFORO; NALEES RIALTO and BRANFORD COURT.

*Appell II. — 111

B. c (1971), by El Centauro—Amichevole, by Tatan.
Breeder, Haras Arjo (Argentina). 1975 5 0 2 0 $7,136
Owner, Green Mill Farm. Trainer, T. J. Gullo. 1974 9 4 2 0 $19,978

31 Aug75 4Bel 6 f :231 :46 1:103ft 3¼ 116 62½ 63¼ 43 53 TurcotteR3 Alw 86 Ramahorn 113 Townsand 6
6 Aug75 7Sar 7 f :23 :46 1:33 ft 2½ 114 11 3½ 32 66 TurcotteR6 Alw 89 QueenCityLad120 BigMoses 6
28 Jly 75 4Sar 7 f :221 :4421:223ft 2¼ 116 21 21½ 32 53¼ TurcotteR4 Alw 89 OurTalisman112 Christofro 8
17 Jly 75 8Bel 6 f :223 :4531:101ft 8½ 113 21 44½ 42½ 2½ TurcotteR6 Alw 91 NativeB'end 113 Appell II. 8
6 Jan75 9Maro a 1 1:351ft 119 Uruguay 22¼ SangttiV Stk Brac 119 Appell II. 12
24 Nov74 7Pal a 1 1:354ft 3-4 ▲118 Argentina 1nk SangttiV Stk Appell II. 118 Get Sun 6
9 Nov74 6S.I. Ⓣ a 1 1:332fm 3 119 Argentina 54¼ SangttiV Stk Grand Guignol 119 Ctonal 19
1 Sep74 6Pal a 1⅜ 2:15 ft 3 126 Argentina 925 SangttiV Stk El GranCapitan 126 Envite 10
4 Aug74 6Pal a 1 1:353hy 8-5 ▲123 Argentina 41 SangttiV Stk Telefonico 123 Pinino 21
20 Jly 74 6Pal a 7½ f 1:29 ft 2 ▲121 Argentina 15 SangttiV Stk Appell II. 121 Pinino 8
Aug 28 Bel 4f ft :49⅘b Aug 16 Sar 3f ft :36⅕b Aug 14 Sar 3f ft :36⅘b

Shredder — 112

Ch. c (1972), by Stage Door Johnny—Cut It Up, by Tudor Minstrel.
Breeder, Greentree Stud, Inc. (Ky.). 1975 2 1 0 0 $5,400
Owner, Greentree Stable. Trainer, J. M. Gaver. 1974 2 M 0 2 $2,160

23 Aug75 1Sar Ⓣ 1⅛ :47 1:1041:463fm 6¼ 117 11½ 11½ 14 19 BrccleVJr1 Mdn 94 Shredder 117 CopprKingdm 12
16 Aug75 9Sar 6 f :222 :46 1:104ft 9-5 ▲118 75 86 68 513 BracleVJr2 Mdn 73 YuWipi118 SomethingGold 11
Sep 9-743Bel 6 f 1:11⅕ft 1 ▲121 88¾ 64½ 41½ 32¾ Turc'tteR6 Mdn 84 Doug 121 Lucky Limey Shredder 11
Sep 2-743Bel 6 f 1:10⅖sy 7-5 ▲121 1h 1h 2h 34 Turc'tteR7 Mdn 87 Lefty 121 Co Host Shredder 7
Sept 5 Bel 4f ft :47b Sept 1 Bel 5f ft 1:03b Aug 28 Bel 5f ft 1:02b

Candle Stand — 116

B. c (1971), by Round Table—Terentia, by Bold Ruler.
Br., W. H. Perry & Claiborne Farm (Ky.). 1975 6 2 1 0 $19,800
Owner, W. H. Perry. Trainer, D. A. Whiteley. 1974 5 2 1 0 $9,576

31 Aug75 8Bel Ⓣ 7 f :223 :45 1:222fm 12 110 910 98¾ 89¾ 610 WdhuseR5 HcpS 82 BeauBugle113 RibotGrande 10
26 Jly 75 7Bel Ⓣ 1 1/16 :48 1:13 1:463sf 4-5 ▲116 37 42 2½ 1nk VasquezJ3 Alw 68 Candle Stand 116 Meon Hill 6
5 Jly 75 9Bel Ⓣ 1 1/16 :4521:0941:412fm 7 116 59½ 35 63¾ 22 MapleE1 Alw 92 PamperdJbnh116 CndleStnd 10
7 Jun75 5Bel 1 1/16 :47 1:12 1:432ft 5¼ 116 77 64 65½ 66¼ VasquezJ7 Alw 79 Christoforo 116 Co Host 8
15 May75 8Aqu 1 :4521:0921:344ft 7-5 ▲116 48½ 45½ 44½ 44½ VasquezJ2 Alw 87 Hunka Papa 114 Phrenology 6
18 Apr75 8Aqu 6 f :222 :45 1:101ft 8¼ 116 54½ 55 52 11¼ VasquezJ5 Alw 92 Candle Stand 116 Erwin Boy 8
Sep18-742Ayr Ⓣ 1⅜ 2:25⅘sf 6-5 ▲119 Ireland 1½ CarsonW Stk CandleSt'nd108 Jimsun Mids'mer Star 7
Aug13-743Cur Ⓣ 1½ 2:43⅗yl 4½ 108 Scotland 48½ BurnsTP Stk Rich'dGrenville122 ConorPass Mistigri 9
Jun 1-741Leo Ⓣ 1¼ 2:10⅘gd 112 ▲126 Ireland 44 PiggottL Stk Conor Pass 133 Silk Buds Klairvimy 7
May15-743Cur Ⓣ 1½ 2:382gd 14 122 Ireland 2no MurphyT Stk Klairvimy 139 Candle Stand Tameric 6
Apr 6-746Cur Ⓣ 1 1:45 gd 6-5 ▲119 Ireland 11 Pigg'tL Mdn C'dleSt'd126 Archd'eFerd'de Retr'ved 26
Aug 30 Bel 3f ft :37b Aug 28 Bel 3f ft :36b Aug 24 Bel 4f ft :48⅕b

Intrepid Hero — 118

B. c (1972), by Forli—Bold Princess, by Bold Ruler.
Breeder, O. M. Phipps (Ky.). 1975 8 4 2 1 $143,110
Owner, O. M. Phipps. Trainer, J. W. Russell. 1974 1 M 0 0 (——)

2 Aug75 8Mth 1⅛ :4621:1021:493ft 4¼ 115 32 2½ 2h 2nk ShmkerW7 InvH 92 Wajima 118 Intrepid Hero 8
13 Jly 75 8Hol Ⓣ 1½ :4821:1342:29 fm 7¾ 126 13½ 1½ 11½ 1¾ PierceD5 InvSc 83 Intrepid Hero 126 Terete 7
21 Jun75 8Atl Ⓣ 1 1/16 :47 1:1021:413fm 4 110 3½ 2h 11 12 WoodheR2 AlwS 98 IntrepidHero110 King ofFls 8
16 Jun75 7Bel 🅃 1¼ :4911:1412:044gd 3 114 11 1h 1h 2h TurcotteR1 Alw 76 BrianBoru116 IntrepidHero 6
2 Jun75 7Bel 1 1/16 :4611:10 1:421ft 7½ 114 2½ 31 42 35 TejadaV4 Alw 86 Nalee'sKnght118 AllOurHpes 6
30 Apr75 5Aqu Ⓣ 1⅛ :4911:1341:504fm 36 121 31½ 1h 1h 1no TejadaV7 Alw 81 Intrepid Hero 121 Northerly 9
12 Apr75 5Aqu 1⅛ :4821:1221:504ft 6 122 32½ 43 35 47¼ TejadaV2 Alw 74 Old Vic 122 Gunpowder 6
6 Mar75 3Aqu 1 :232 :4531:371ft 23 116 21½ 23 21 1½ TejadaV2 Mdn 80 IntrepidHero116 NobleRctor 7
Dec14-744Aqu 6 f 1:12⅘ft 15 122 77¼ 812 711 711 Mont'yaD8 Mdn 68 Cockbird 122 Alishamar Trounce 8
Sept 1 Bel tc 1f fm 1:39⅗h Aug 22 Sar trt 5f ft 1:07b Aug 17 Sar trt 5f ft 1:03b

Nalees Rialto **112** B. c (1972), by Ribot—Nalee, by Nashua.
Breeder, Mrs. G. M. Humphrey (Ky.). 1975 8 2 2 1 $26,340
Owner, Mrs. G. M. Humphrey. Trainer, E. Burch. 1974 7 1 4 1 $14,620

16 Aug75 8Sar 1⅛ :4721:1121:511ft 2¼ 108 34 33 2½ 13† MontoyaD2 Alw 79 Nalees Rialto 108 First Slice 6
†Disqualified and placed second.
12 Jly 75 8Bel 1⅛ :4531:0931:482sy 7¼ 112 85½ 88½ 710 712 MontyaD8 HcpS 73 Valid Appeal 110 Wajima 8
7 Jun75 7Bel 1½ :48 1:1222:281ft 19 126 55 611 711 817 MntyaD9 ScwS 62 Avatar 126 Foolish Pleasure 9
26 May75 7Aqu 1⅛ :4831:1221:493ft 2 110 13 12 13 12¾ MontoyaD4 Alw 87 Nale'sRlto110 TrmpterSwan 7
17 May75 9Aqu 1⅛ :4721:1121:494ft 2 ▲114 55 42½ 21½ 12½ MontoyaD6 Alw 86 Nalee's Rialto 114 HvnForbd 11
19 Apr75 7Aqu 1⅛ :47 1:1031:483ft 9-5 ▲113 21½ 22 22 22½ MontoyaD1 Alw 89 KaysRoman115 Kp thePmise 8
4 Apr75 9Aqu 1⅛ :49 1:1421:524ft 5½ 114 2h 2½ 2½ 44 MontoyaD8 Alw 67 Media117 Keep thePromise 7
Sept 3 Bel 5f ft :58⅘h Aug 30 Bel 5f ft :59⅘h Aug 27 Bel 3f ft :33⅘h

Drollery **116** Dk. b. or br. g (1970), by Tom Fool—Persian Garden, by Bois Roussel.
Breeder, Greentree Stud, Inc. (Ky.). 1975 11 1 3 4 $61,785
Owner, Greentree Stable. Trainer, J. M. Gaver. 1974 6 1 1 1 $13,800

20 Aug75 8Sar (T) 1⅝ :4831:11 2:42 fm 3 111 21 32 32 32 BccleVJr8 HcpS 77 SnowKnight 118 GoldenDon 8
10 Aug75 8Sar (T) 1⅛ :4831:1231:494fm 7e 112 812 87¼ 54 31¾ BrcceVJr7 HcpS 76 SaltMarsh116 WardMcAlstr 8
5 Jly 75 8Bel (T) 1⅜ :4921:14 2:134fm 9½ 112 24 31½ 69½ 67 BrcleVJr4 HcpS 89 Brigand 112 Prod 9
14 Jun75 8Bel (T) 1½ :51 1:4212:321fm 3¾ 113 52½ 52½ 31½ 21 BrcleVJr5 HcpS 58 Barcas 113 Drollery 6
2 Jun75 8Bel [T] 1¼ :4811:13 2:03 gd 7½ 114 511 69½ 46 21¼ BrcleVJr4 AlwS 84 Telefonico 120 Drollery 9
10 May75 8Pim (T) 1½ :4831:1542:332yl 7¾ 114 1225 912 611 36 BrcleVJr1 HcpS 75 Bemo 114 Outdoors 13
6 Apr75 7SA (T) a 1¾ :4721:1122:521yl 12 115 812 62½ 54 45¾ BracleVJr4 InvH 60 La Zanzara 114 Astray 12
26 Mar75 8SA (T) 1¼ :4741:1232:261fm 3¼ 120 64 42½ 42 2no BrcleVJr2 HcpS 84 El Botija 117 Drollery 6
4 Mar75 9Hia (T) 1½ 2:272fm 9-5e▲111 710 89½ 66¾ 42¾ SmithRC5 HcpS 91 Outdoors 112 Barcas 13
Sept 5 Bel 4f ft :48⅘b Sept 1 Bel 7f ft 1:29b Aug 25 Bel 5f sy 1:02⅖b

---

The conditions for the above race clearly suggest a top-drawer field. It was in fact more than that. The field was loaded with stakes-class stock, including some of the nation's best grass horses, several of which appear along with the race winner.

Shredder, a recent graduate of a maiden race, was a lead-pipe cinch. And the best bettors in the crowd knew it. Coupled in the betting with the multiple stakes winner Drollery, Shredder's mutuel price was naturally reduced by a few points. But on the evidence of his lone turf race win, there was no way he would have paid more than 4–1 no matter what he was going to run against.

Shredder was a freak. A champion that never got crowned. In the Eclipse Award balloting, I voted him the top turf horse of 1975, simply on the basis of his two grass races. And I don't think I overstated his credentials. They were both incredible performances. Let's examine them.

In his maiden victory romp Shredder ran on his own courage throughout, raced to a nine-length victory under wraps. Jockey Bracciale never moved a muscle. And if you weren't there to see it, the following two result charts tell an interesting tale.

24th Day. WEATHER CLEAR. TEMPERATURE 73 DEGREES.

FIRST RACE
Saratoga
AUGUST 23, 1975

1 ⅛ MILES.(turf). (1.45⅖) MAIDEN SPECIAL WEIGHT. Purse $9,000. 3- and 4-year-olds. Weight: 3-year-olds, 117 lbs., 4-year-olds, 122 lbs.

Value of race $9,000, value to winner $5,400, second $1,980, third $1,080, fourth $540. Mutuel pool $101,518.

Last Raced	Horse	Eqt.	A.	Wt	PP	St	¼	½	¾	Str	Fin	Jockey	Odds $1
16Aug75 9Sar5	Shredder		3	117	1	1	1 1½	1 1½	1 1½	1 4	1 9	Bracciale V Jr	6.30
3Aug75 5Sar2	Copper Kingdom	b	3	117	6	12	12	7 hd	3 4	2 1½	2 1½	Cruguet J	2.70
3Aug75 5Sar3	Spasoje		3	117	8	11	10 hd	9½	6 hd	5 2	3 no	Velasquez J	9.50
18Aug75 1Sar2	Braulio		3	117	7	4	4½	5 hd	4 1½	4 1½	4 2½	Amy J	13.90
9Aug75 9Sar7	Count Nijinsky	b	3	117	5	7	11 1½	11½	8½	6 2	5 nk	Turcotte R	a-8.00
13Aug75 1Sar5	Jack Barrett	b	3	117	2	2	3 1½	2½	2 hd	3 1½	6 3¾	Hole M	8.30
13Aug75 1Sar7	Off The Record	b	3	110	3	5	8½	6½	10 1	7 4	7 3	Campanelli T7	a-8.00
4Oct74 6Bel7	Vincent	b	3	117	4	3	7 hd	8½	9½	8 hd	8 1¾	Ruane J	12.20
13Aug75 1Sar2	Blue Cross	b	3	117	12	8	6½	12	12	10 1½	9 1¾	Baeza B	5.10
9Aug75 2Sar4	Sweet Basil	b	3	117	9	10	9 2	10 1	11 2	12	10 nk	Maple E	9.80
13Aug75 1Sar10	Bridaled Tern	b	3	110	11	9	5 1½	4 1	5½	9 hd	11 6	Long J S7	48.00
16Aug75 9Sar3	The Irish Lord		3	110	10	6	2½	3½	7 1	11 1½	12	Martens G7	13.00

a-Coupled: Count Nijinsky and Off The Record.

OFF AT 1:30 EDT. Start good, Won ridden out. Time, :22⅘, :47, 1:10⅘, 1:35, 1:46⅗ Course firm.

Official Program Numbers

$2 Mutuel Prices:				
	2-(B)-SHREDDER	14.60	7.60	5.20
	5-(G)-COPPER KINGDOM		4.60	3.20
	7-(I)-SPASOJE			4.20

Ch. c, by Stage Door Johnny—Cut It Up, by Tudor Minstrel. Trainer Gaver J M. Bred by Greentree Stud Inc (Ky).

SHREDDER sprinted right to the front, made the pace under good handling and drew away rapidly after entering the stretch. COPPER KINGDOM, outrun away from the gate, moved around horses to reach contention racing into the far turn but was no match for the winner. SPASOJE rallied mildly. Barulion, well placed early, lacked a late response. COUNT NIJINSKY, very wide into the stretch, failed to be a serious factor. JACK BARRETT raced forwardly to the stretch and flattened out. OFF THE RECORD saved ground to no avail. BLUE CROSS was through early. SWEET BASIL was always outrun. BRIDALED TERN gave way after going five furlongs. THE IRISH LORD, a factor to the far turn, stopped badkly.

Owners— 1, Greentree Stable; 2, Live Oak Plantation; 3, Tartan Stable; 4, Blum P E; 5, Hexter Stable; 6, Rokeby Stable; 7, Reineman R L; 8, Hobeau Farm; 9, Sturgis J R; 10, Rosenthal Mrs M; 11, Humphrey Mrs G M; 12, Phipps Ogden.

Trainers— 1, Gaver J M; 2, Kelly T J; 3, Nerud J A; 4, Jerkens S T; 5, Freeman W C; 6, Burch Elliott; 7, Freeman W C; 8, Jerkens H A; 9, Veitch S E; 10, Johnson P G; 11, Miller Mack; 12, Russell J W.

Scratched—Paul's Impulse (13Aug75 1Sar11); Special Project (3Aug75 5Sar4); Triple Optimist (9Aug75 9Sar5); Survey (16Aug75 1Sar10); Rapid Transit II (16Aug75 1Sar11); Red Grasshopper (18Aug75 1Sar4).

An allowance race later that day.

SEVENTH RACE
Saratoga
AUGUST 23, 1975

1 1/16 MILES.(turf). (1.39⅖) ALLOWANCE. Purse $15,000. 3-year-olds and upward which have not won three races other than maiden, claiming or starter. Weight: 3-year-olds, 117 lbs., Older, 122 lbs. Non-winners of $9,000 at a mile or over since July 26 allowed 2 lbs., $7,200 at a mile or over since July 12, 4 lbs., $6,000 twice at a mile or over since June 25, 6 lbs. (Claiming races not considered in allowances.) 3-year-olds which have never won at a mile or over allowed 3 lbs.; older, 5 lbs.

Value of race $15,000, value to winner $9,000, second $3,300, third $1,800, fourth $900. Mutuel pool $165,739, OTB pool $82,881. TrackExacta Pool $140,551. OTB Exacta Pool $180,996.

Last Raced	Horse	Eqt.	A.Wt	PP	St	¼	½	¾	Str	Fin	Jockey	Odds $1
6Aug75 3Sar2	Great Above		3 101	5	2	22½	21½	13	12½	1nk	Velez R I7	3.70
28Jly75 6Sar1	One On The Aisle	b	3 115	8	7	7½	41	2½	22	26	Maple E	2.00
16Aug75 6Sar2	American History		3 110	6	4	51½	6hd	61	4½	31¾	Velasquez J	3.00
28Jly75 6Sar3	In The Swing	b	4 116	7	5	41½	3½	32	34	4nk	Bracciale V Jr	13.00
6Aug75 3Sar3	Co Host	b	3 113	4	6	61	8	73	52	55	Vasquez J	5.60
25Jly75 8Bel5	Port Authority		3 111	3	3	12	1hd	5½	63	63	Turcotte R	12.20
8Jly75 7Com1	Montsalvat		3 111	2	8	8	71½	42	74	73½	Ruane J	13.50
6Aug75 3Sar5	Campaigner		4 116	1	1	31	5½	8	8	8	Cruguet J	17.20

OFF AT 4:53, EDT. Start good, Won driving. Time, :23⅘, :48, 1:11⅘, 1:35⅖, 1:41⅗ Course firm (=1:48)

$2 Mutuel Prices:

5-(E)-GREAT ABOVE	9.40	4.80	2.80
8-(I)-ONE ON THE AISLE		3.60	2.40
6-(F)-AMERICAN HISTORY			2.80

$2 EXACTA 5–8 PAID $28.80.

dk b or br. c, by Minnesota Mac—Ta Wee, by Intentionally. Trainer Nerud J A. Bred by Tartan Farms Corp (Fla).

GREAT ABOVE prompted the pace in hand, took over when ready racing into the far turn, quickly sprinted clear and lasted over ONE ON THE AISLE. The latter, unhurried early, rallied from the outside approaching the stretch and finished strongly. AMERICAN HISTORY, steadied along between horses nearing the end of the backstretch, was going well at the finish. IN THE SWING, never far back, made a run approaching the far turn, remained a factor to the upper stretch and flattened out. CO HOST lacked room between horses midway along the backstretch and failed to be a serious factor. PORT AUTHORITY tired badly from his early efforts. MONTSALVAT, sent around horses racing into the far turn, continued wide and lacked a further response.

Owners— 1, Tartan Stable; 2, Rokeby Stable; 3, Mangurian H T Jr; 4, Brookfield Farm; 5, Schiff J M; 6, Cody M; 7, Steinman Beverly R; 8, Garren M M.

Trainers— 1, Nerud J A; 2, Burch Elliott; 3, Root T F; 4, Kelly E I; 5, Kelly T J; 6, Preger M C; 7, Fout P R; 8, Puentes G.

Overweight: American History 2 pounds; Co Host 2.

Scratched—Grand Salute (13Aug75 6Sar6).

On a time-comparison basis, Shredder wins hands down. It was the third fastest 1⅛-mile turf race ever run at Saratoga. Note the final eighth-mile in 11⅗ seconds. That is superhorse time. Most horses are incapable of running the last eighth in 12 seconds flat.

Now let's look at what Shredder did to all those top-drawer stakes horses he met in his next start, his final appearance of the season.

SIXTH RACE
Belmont
SEPTEMBER 6, 1975

1 1/16 MILES.(turf). (1.40⅕) ALLOWANCE. Purse $20,000 3-year-olds and upward which have not won four races other than maiden, claiming or starter. Weights 3-year-olds, 118 lbs.; older, 122 lbs.; non-winners of $25,000 at a mile or over since July 12, allowed 2 lbs.; $15,000 at a mile or over since July 2, 4 lbs.; $9,000 at a mile or over since July 26, 6 lbs. (Claiming races not considered in allowances.) 3-year-olds which have never won at a mile or over allowed 3 lbs.; older, 5 lbs.

Value of race $20,000, value to winner $12,000, second $4,400, third $2,400, fourth $1,200. Mutuel pool $439,287, OTB pool $93,203.

Last Raced	Horse	Eqt.	A.Wt	PP	St	¼	½	¾	Str	Fin	Jockey	Odds $1
23Aug75 ^{1}Sar^{1}	Shredder		3 112	2	2	2^{3}	$2^{1\frac{1}{2}}$	1^{hd}	1^{3}	1^{5}	Bracciale V Jr	a-1.40
31Aug75 ^{8}Bel^{6}	Candle Stand		4 116	4	4	6^{hd}	6^{1}	4^{1}	$4^{1\frac{1}{2}}$	$2^{\frac{3}{4}}$	Vasquez J	12.10
2Aug75 ^{8}Mth^{2}	Intrepid Hero		3 118	5	5	$5^{\frac{1}{2}}$	$4^{1\frac{1}{2}}$	3^{1}	2^{1}	$3^{2\frac{1}{4}}$	Cordero A Jr	1.20
31Aug75 ^{4}Bel^{5}	Appell II		4 111	1	1	$1^{\frac{1}{2}}$	$1^{\frac{1}{2}}$	2^{1}	$3^{\frac{1}{2}}$	$4^{\frac{1}{2}}$	Turcotte R	12.00
29Aug75 ^{8}Bel^{7}	Jacques Who	b	5 111	3	9	9	9	7^{1}	5^{3}	5^{nk}	Martens G5	23.60
20Aug75 ^{8}Sar^{3}	Drollery		5 116	9	6	8^{5}	8^{2}	$6^{\frac{1}{2}}$	7^{12}	6^{4}	Velasquez J	a-1.40
16Aug75 ^{8}Sar^{2}	Nalees Rialto	b	3 112	6	8	7^{2}	5^{hd}	5^{3}	$6^{\frac{1}{2}}$	7^{15}	Maple E	7.40
31Aug75 ^{4}Bel^{6}	Bold and Fancy	b	4 116	7	3	3^{1}	$3^{\frac{1}{2}}$	8^{4}	8^{1}	8^{nk}	Castaneda M	44.80
13Aug75 ^{6}Sar^{6}	Grand Salute	b	4 118	8	7	4^{1}	7^{3}	9	9	9	Ruane J	56.80

a–Coupled: Shredder and Drollery,

OFF AT 4:18, EDT. Start good, Won handily. Time, :22⅘, :46⅖, 1:11, 1:35⅘, 1:41⅘ Course firm.

$2 Mutuel Prices:				
	1–(B)–SHREDDER (a-entry)	4.80	3.60	2.20
	5–(D)–CANDLE STAND		8.80	2.60
	6–(E)–INTREPID HERO			2.20

Ch. c, by Stage Door Johnny—Cut It Up, by Tudor Minstrel. Trainer Gaver J M. Bred by Greentree Stud Inc (Ky).

SHREDDER, eased back off APPEAL II soon after entering the backstretch, moved through inside that rival to take over on the turn and drew off with authority. CANDLE STAND finished with good courage along the inside to gain the place. INTREPID HERO, unhurried early, loomed a threat from the outside approaching the stretch but weakened during the drive. APPELL II tired badly from his early efforts. DROLLERY was always outrun. NALEES RIALTO rallied nearing the stretch but lacked a further response. BOLD AND FANCY was through soon after going a half. GRAND SALUTE showed some early foot.

Owners— 1, Greentree Stable; 2, Perry W H; 3, Phipps O M; 4, Green Mill Farm; 5, Wimpfheimer J D; 6, Greentree Stable; 7, Humphrey Mrs G M; 8, Vogel Marcus; 9, Steinman Beverly R.

Trainers— 1, Gaver J M; 2, Whiteley D A; 3, Russell J W; 4, Gullo T J; 5, Sedlacek W; 6, Gaver J M; 7, Burch Elliott; 8, Barrera L S; 9, Fout P R.

Scratched—Christoforo (31Aug75 ^{8}Bel^{4}); T. V. Newscaster (29Aug75 ^{7}Bel^{6}); Branford Court (31Aug75 ^{8}Bel^{7}).

I would not like to leave this brief look at allowance races with the notion that all winners come from dropdown maneuvers or have Shredder-type records. The truth is in many allowance races neither factor comes into play. Such allowance races cannot be handicapped without considering track bias, trainer patterns, and other relevant data. Nevertheless, the player who appreciates the subtle power of the hidden class dropdown and is able to incorporate purse values, classification codes, and Key Race studies into his handicapping is almost certain to move many lengths ahead of the crowd. And that's what the game is all about.

11.
$E = MC^2$

In the previous chapter I made a point to introduce the importance of time as it relates to class. At Charles Town the cheapest $1,500 claiming race is usually run in slower time than the next step up in the classification code. At Delaware Park an allowance race for limited winners is usually run somewhat slower than a $22,000 claiming race. And at Saratoga Shredder proved he was no ordinary maiden graduate by running the fastest race of the day.

Although this orderly relationship between class and final times extends through every class level at every racetrack in America, it is nevertheless true that the official time of a race is worthless information by itself.

In order to make sense out of time, in order to make it a meaningful piece of information, the player must be able to answer four intriguing questions:

1. What is a good time or slow time for that distance and that class at that track?
2. How fast or slow was the racetrack the day the race was run? That is, to what extent must the time of the race be adjusted to compensate for the speed of the track itself?
3. To what extent, if any, is final time influenced by track bias, by fractional times, or by unusual pace tactics? And to what extent is it possible to detect a fluky time?
4. When is it most useful to know how fast the horse ran and under what conditions is time a waste of time?

Very few fans ever bother to take these questions seriously. It's an understandable failing. The majority of so-called experts don't do it either. Besides, the past performance profiles seem to provide ready-made answers in the track condition labels, in the speed ratings, and in the track variant figures published in some editions of the *Form*.

Cupecoy's Joy ×		**B. f. 3, by Northerly—Lady Abla, by Alsina**		
		Br.—Perez R (NY)	**1982 10 4 4 1**	**\$255,016**
Own.—Ri-Ma-Ro Stables	**121**	**Tr.—Callejas Alfredo**	**1981 8 2 2 3**	**\$91,814**
		Lifetime 18 6 6 4 \$346,830		

4Jun82-8Bel	$1\frac{1}{8}$	:45^4	1:09^4	1:48^{2}ft	*6-5	121	$1^{1\frac{1}{2}}$	$1^{\frac{1}{2}}$	$1^{1\frac{1}{2}}$	$1^{\frac{3}{4}}$	StA^2 ⒻMother Goose	85	Cpcy'sJy,ChrstmsPst,BlshWthPrd	12
22May82-8Bel	1	:46	1:09^3	1:34^{1}ft	$7\frac{1}{2}$	121	$1^{\frac{1}{2}}$	$1^{1\frac{1}{2}}$	1^2	$1^{2\frac{3}{4}}$	Santiago A^5 ⒻAcorn	95	Cupecoy's Joy,NancyHuang,Vestris	9
17May82-8Aqu	7f	:22	:44^3	1:23^{1}ft	*9-5	121	$4^{3\frac{1}{2}}$	$3^{1\frac{1}{2}}$	1^{hd}	$2^{\frac{1}{2}}$	SantigoA^3 [S]Albany H	84	MjesticKt,Cupecoy'sJoy,FdedPostr	9
1May82-8CD	$1\frac{1}{4}$	:46^1	1:37^1	2:02^{2}ft	9f	121	$1^{3\frac{1}{2}}$	$1^{\frac{1}{2}}$	8^3	10^{11}	Santiago A^1 Ky Derby	74	GatoDelSol,LaserLight,Reinvested	19
27Mar82-9Lat	$1\frac{1}{16}$	:46^3	1:11^3	1:44^{3}ft	$9\frac{1}{4}$	115	2^{hd}	2^3	2^5	3^5	SntgA^{10} J Beam Spirl	82	GoodN'Dusty,FstGold,Cpcoy'sJoy	12
17Mar82-8Aqu	6f	:22^4	:46	1:11 gd	8-5	115	3^1	$3^{1\frac{1}{2}}$	3^2	2^{nk}	Santiago A^5 [S]Catskill	86	PayorPly,Cupecoy'sJoy,FdedPoster	7
20Feb82-8Aqu	6f	⊡:22^3	:45^4	1:11 ft	*2	121	2^{hd}	1^{hd}	1^4	2^{hd}	Santiago A^4 ⒻCicada	89	Bold Ribbons,Cupecoy'sJoy,Adept	11
3Feb82-8Aqu	6f	⊡:22^1	:46^4	1:14^{4}sy	*2-3	121	—	—	1^3	1^{nk}	SntA^2 Ⓕ[S]Sag Harbor	70	Cupecoy'sJoy,HstyDmscn,LdyHoot	7

3Feb82—Running positions omitted because of weather conditions.

●Jun 12 Bel 5f ft :58^2 h ●May 30 Bel 5f ft :57^3 h May 11 Bel 5f ft :59^4 b

Unfortunately, a "fast" racetrack can have a wide range of speed conduciveness—from lightning fast to not very fast at all. And despite the good intentions of the *Daily Racing Form* in publishing these speed ratings, they are not good enough for serious students of time.

As a matter of course, the speed ratings earned by Cupecoy's Joy were computed by comparing her times in each race with the appropriate track records for each distance. In the *DRF* speed-rating system, the track record is always worth 100 speed-rating points, and one point is deducted for each fifth of a second slower than the track mark.

On June 4, 1982, Cupecoy's Joy ran a winning race at $1\frac{1}{8}$ miles in $1{:}48\frac{2}{5}$. That was three full seconds slower than Secretariat's track record for the distance. Thus the 85 speed rating.

On May 1, 1982, Cupecoy's Joy finished well back in the pack after running her heart out against colts in the Kentucky Derby. According to the time-honored notion that a length equals a fifth of a second, Cupecoy's Joy earned her 74 speed rating this way:

Churchill Downs track record $1\frac{1}{4}$ miles	=	$1{:}59\frac{2}{5}$	=	100 speed rating
Time of race winner	=	$2{:}02\frac{2}{5}$	=	85 speed rating
Beaten 11 lengths (deduct 11 points)	=	$2{:}04\frac{3}{5}$	=	74 speed rating

Here is a partial list of Belmont Park track records in effect for the fall 1982 racing season. Each track record is worth 100 speed-rating points. Each horse racing at Belmont earned its speed ratings by comparisons with these times. There are several things wrong with this method. Two of the most important appear below the chart.

TRACK RECORDS AT BELMONT PARK					
DISTANCE	HORSE	AGE	WGT.	TIME	DATE
5½ Furlongs	Raise a Cup	2	118	1:03	June 8, 1973
6 Furlongs	Sailor's Watch	5	114	1:08⅖	July 3, 1975
6½ Furlongs	Cohasset Tribe	4	114	1:15⅕	May 19, 1973
7 Furlongs	King's Bishop	4	114	1:20⅖	May 19, 1973
1 Mile	Conquistador Cielo	3	111	1:33	May 31, 1982
1¹⁄₁₆ Miles	Everton II	4	112	1:40⅖	Aug. 28, 1973
1⅛ Miles	Secretariat	3	124	1:45⅖	Sept. 15, 1973

First, some track records are set on extremely fast racing days, by horses of varying ability. Although each track record equals 100 speed-rating points, at Belmont Park it is considerably more difficult for a horse to earn an 85 rating at seven furlongs and 1⅛ miles than it is at any other distance. King's Bishop and Secretariat ran much faster races to establish their track records than Cohasset Tribe and Everton II did to establish theirs.

Second, a length does not equal a fifth of a second at all distances and at all rates of speed. Mathematically speaking, a length equals a fifth of a second only when horses travel a furlong in 15 seconds. The only horses that go that slow charge 10 cents a ride.

Not surprisingly, the same sort of inconsistencies among track records can be shown to exist at most racetracks. And the error is compounded in the editions of the *Form* that feature track variant figures.

These variants—which purport to measure the relative speed of the track—are computed by averaging all winning speed ratings earned at that track that day. The average for the day is then subtracted from 100 to produce the track variant.

If the average winning speed ratings for all races run on June 4 at Belmont were 82, the *DRF* track variant would be listed as 18. In the Eastern edition of the *Form*, Cupecoy's Joy would show her 88 speed rating, but it would read 88–18, to reflect the rating and the variant.

At times these variants provide a few clues about the speed of the track, especially when the variant is very high or very low. A variant above 30 would clearly indicate a slow racing strip and a variant under 10 would suggest a concrete highway.

Otherwise, these variants are too weak and unreliable for serious use, because it is impossible to tell whether a moderate variant is produced by fast horses racing over a slow track, or slow horses racing over a fast one. In a game where fifths of a second are so important, the flaws built into *DRF* speed ratings lead to inaccurate time comparisons. They may even cost unsuspecting players a lot of money.

Frankly, it remains possible to win at the track without paying the subject of time any special attention. There are other windows to look through, other methods to determine which horse is most likely to win. But if you are mathematically inclined and wish to explore the racetrack puzzle from a semi-scientific base, you will need to become familiar with *Speed Figures*—an ingenious process that translates answers to the first two questions about time (see page 112) to a workable set of numbers, par times, and parallel time charts.

SPEED FIGURES

The very best speed-figure method I have ever seen was created by Sheldon Kovitz, a math wiz who divided his time at Harvard in the early 1960s between his classes, the track, and the nearest IBM computer. I never met Kovitz, but my good friend Andy Beyer learned the method firsthand and refined it for practical use ten years later. In its present form, it involves a two-step research project that may seem tedious but will do a great deal to broaden your understanding of the hows and whys of racing in your area. And if you're as crazy about handicapping as I am, you might even love it.

STEP 1: Using a complete set of result charts from the previous meeting, compile a list of all final times recorded on "fast" racetracks at every class level and distance. If back copies of the *Form* are unavailable, or too expensive to consider, a trip to the nearest library file of daily local newspapers will suffice. *Daily Racing Form* chart books, available in microfiche, are another alternative.

For the purpose of this research project you are not concerned with anything but age, sex, class of race, distance, and fast-track final times. But for dependable results you should study a minimum of fifteen races at each class and distance. Obviously, the more races you use to work up the data, the more reliable the data will be.

STEP 2: Obtain the *average* winning time for each class and distance.

Logically, to determine a good time for a six-furlong, $20,000 claiming race, you must determine the *average* time for that class and distance. These averages will then serve as the par, or standard, for each class and distance. The following is a sample of six-furlong average times for New York tracks:

Three years and up stakes.........................1:09²/₅
Three years and up $32,000 allowance..............1:09⁴/₅
Three years and up $40,000 claiming...............1:11²/₅
Maiden special weight (all ages)...................1:11⁴/₅

The average winning times at several distances at another racetrack produced the following results:

$20,000 CLAIMING RACE—KEYSTONE RACETRACK				
6 FURLONGS	6½ FURLONGS	7 FURLONGS	1 MILE, 70 YARDS	1¹/₁₆ MILE
1:11²/₅	1:17⁴/₅	1:24²/₅	1:44²/₅	1:46

These average winning times are the building blocks for establishing an accurate track variant. They are all equal to a single measurement of average speed—the average speed of a $20,000 claiming horse at Keystone racetrack. We may now compare all final times at Keystone with that average or we may go a step further and plot the averages for every class and construct a parallel time chart, a chart that could help us make accurate time comparisons swiftly.

For convenience, Kovitz created a mathematically sound rating system to simplify comparisons between horses running different times and distances. In this rating system the value of a fifth of a second is proportionately greater in faster races and at shorter distances. It also assigns the appropriate number of points for each beaten length.

I will spare you the mathematics behind this idea and refer you to the Appendix for a step-by-step method to compute a satisfactory version of the Kovitz-Beyer speed-figure system. For those of you who are interested in this subject, I strongly recommend Beyer's beautifully written book *Picking Winners*, which is one of the few handicapping books worth serious attention. The time charts, class pars, ratings, and beaten-length charts for New York racetracks included in the Appendix of this book were adapted from *Picking Winners*, reproduced with Andy's special permission. And if you wonder whether the effort to learn how to derive speed figures is worth the trouble, the next chapter should set your head straight.

12.
The Race Is to the Swift

When is time important? How potent is speed-figure handicapping? What about fractional times? Does "pace make the race," as so many handicappers believe?

It is rare that a horseplayer gets a chance to confront a major mystery of the racetrack puzzle. Being naturally bent toward such mysteries helps. I confess. I am always willing to put my most effective handicapping methods aside and experiment with new tools and test out new ideas.

It was in that spirit that I incorporated Andy Beyer's speed figures in my handicapping in 1972, and it was in the same spirit that I stopped using them in the second year of my handicapping broadcasts in 1974.

In the first season the results said 176 winners in 310 picks. Fifty-three percent. A flat bet profit in all categories.

Of course, I relied on numerous handicapping concepts, but so long as speed figures were available on a daily basis, I wasn't sure how much they contributed.

I designed an informal test to find out.

For the first three months of the new season I continued using figures and made note of when they seemed to be the major reason for a selection. For the next three months I operated without using them at all. And for the remainder of the year I used them only when the results of previous use suggested their relevance. Fortunately, I was able to keep my 50 percent win record intact throughout the experiment.

Certainly, a more scientific survey needs to be done here, but in the meantime I think the results I obtained under fire are worth keeping in mind.

These are my present thoughts on the subject.

1. Speed figures, by definition, tell how fast the horse ran at a given racetrack at a given distance on a given day. They do not automatically tell how fast a horse *will* run, especially at a different distance. But the top speed-figure horse in the race does win approximately 35 percent of the time at a slight loss for every $2 wager. With no handicapping at all, speed figures produce more winners than public favorites and at slightly better prices.

2. By computing the *par times* for each distance and class at a specific racetrack, the player will know which claiming horses have been meeting better stock than the allowance horses. He will know at a glance whether a $20,000 claiming race is better than a low-grade allowance race without having to consult the purse values in the result charts. He will also know at what class a field of fillies is faster than colts.

3. By computing speed figures on a regular basis, the player will have an important handicapping tool in the following cases.

When maiden graduates are entered in races for winners, their speed figures will often indicate their suitability to the class. The horse that graduates with a mediocre speed figure is not likely to repeat the feat in higher company. The graduate that has earned a superior speed figure may not be overmatched in any company. Below is the past performance record of a horse that graduated with an extremely high speed figure. Here he is entered in the 1975 Belmont Futurity against the best two-year-olds in the country. He ran the same speed figure as his maiden win and won by daylight.

Soy Numero Uno

122 B. c (1973), by Damascus—Tasma, by Crafty Admiral.
Breeder, Nuckols Bros. (Ky.). 1975 1 1 0 0 $5,400

Owner, J. R. Straus. Trainer, H. C. Pardue.

25 Aug75 4Bel 6 f :22² :45²1:09⁴ft 4-5 ▲120 3¹ 2ʰ 1² 1⁴ VasquzJ¹⁰ Mdn 93 SoyNumeroUno120 SecretCll 10
   Sept 5 Bel trt 3f ft :36⅖b Sept 1 Bel 5f ft :58⅜h Aug 24 Bel trt 3f ft :37⅖b

---

When a field of maidens is mixed between horses with minimum racing experience and first-time starters, the figures for the horses who have already raced will tell how difficult it will be for the first-timer to win. If the horses with racing experience have been producing above-par figures for the class, the first-timer has to be a tiger to compete. If the figures are subpar, a nicely bred, fast-working first-timer could be an excellent wager.

When a horse has consistently produced superior figures—when its *lowest* figure is better than the *best* figure of the competition—it will win at least 80 percent of the time! (This happens approximately once in every 250 races.)

If the top speed-figure horse in the race is also the horse most likely to get a clear early lead, it deserves a solid edge, providing of course it is not racing far beyond its normal distance capabilities or is not pitted against a stretch-running track bias. On a front-running track bias this kind of horse will usually outrun its apparent distance limitations.

4. Speed figures can be used effectively in the following circumstances.

Prior speed figures can be a valuable clue in spotting the inherent weakness of a betting favorite. If the figures are low for the class or low versus the competition, the player must have well-thought-out reasons to select such a horse at short odds—trainer pattern, visual evidence, vastly improved workouts, and so on.

When a horse is stepped up in claiming price, prior speed figures can be an important clue to its winning potential. If it has run fast enough in the past, the class raise may only be an illusion. Most of the time there will be additional evidence to support the class raise. See Chapter 18 for an illustration of the value of speed figures in spotting horses in the above two situations.

5. If a horse is likely to get a clear early lead for the first time in its recent racing record, the player should expect a minimum of two lengths' improvement over its customary speed figures. Even more important, whenever such a horse is in a particularly slow-breaking field or has a bias in its favor, no other horse in the

race can be played with confidence. An example of this type of straightforward betting situation is also presented in Chapter 18.

6. The traditional handicapping notion that "pace makes the race" is only true in special circumstances.

In the vast majority of sprints the early fractional times do not seem to affect the final time of the race winner. But if the pace is contested by two or more horses, regardless of the early fractions, the chances are good that the leaders will tire in the stretch. Some horses, however, respond to competition by running harder, and the player should have no trouble spotting these game creatures in the past performance records.

Aloma's Ruler

Own.—Scherr N

126

Dk. b. or br. c. 3, by Iron Ruler—Aloma, by Native Charger
Br.—Silk Willoughby Farm (Fla)
Tr.—Lenzini John J Jr

		1982	4	3	1	0	$269,894
		1981	4	3	1	0	$30,135

Lifetime 8 6 2 0 $300,029

15May82-8Pim	1$\frac{1}{16}$:48 1:12 1:55²ft	7 126	1¹ 1¹ 11½ 1½	Kaenel J L⁷ Preakness	93	Aloma's Ruler, Linkage, Cut Away	7
8May82-8Aqu	1 :46 1:10¹ 1:35²ft	7 126	2¹ 1½ 1½ 1ⁿᵏ	Kaenel J L⁵ Withers	89	Alom'sRulr,SpnshDrms,John'sGold	6
29Apr82-8Pim	6f :22⁴ :45³ 1:10⁴ft	*1-3 115	1ʰᵈ 1ʰᵈ 1¹ 2ⁿᵒ	BraccialeVJr⁶ Aw16200	92	HppyHoolign,Alom'sRuler,St.Chrisb	6
27Jan82-9Hia	7f :22³ :45¹ 1:22¹ft	3½ 117	32½ 4³ 31½ 1ʰᵈ	CorderoAJr³ Bahamas	92	Alom'sRlr,DstnctvPro,LtsDontFght	9
17Oct81-5Med	6f :22 :45¹ 1:10 ft	2½ 117	2¹½ 2ʰᵈ 1¹ 12¼	Cordero A Jrⁿ Nutley	93	Aloma's Ruler, Obgyn, Sleek Gold	7
28Sep81-5Med	6f :22² :46¹ 1:11²ft	*6-5 120	1ʰᵈ 1ʰᵈ 1ʰᵈ 12¼	Cordero AJr⁵ Aw12000	86	Alom'sRuler,Rjb'sSon,JettingPlsur	8
14Sep81-5Med	6f :22³ :46¹ 1:12¹ft	*6-5 118	31½ 31½ 1² 11½	Cordero A Jr⁷ Mdn	82	Alom'sRuler,Mythology,I'mPurGold	9
29Aug81-4Mth	6f :22³ :46¹ 1:11²ft	11 118	2ʰᵈ 2ʰᵈ 2¹ 2⁴	Kurtz J⁹ Mdn	79	CrftyProspctor,Alm'sRlr,WtAMnt	12

● May 30 Bel 1 ft 1:39⁴ b   May 25 Lrl 5f ft 1:01⁴ b   May 7 Aqu 3f ft :37³ b   ● Apr 27 Lrl 3f m :37¹ b (d)

In route races pace can influence the final time as well as the final result. A very slow early pace may or may not prejudice the final time depending upon the action that follows, but it will help a front runner to reach the stretch with more gas in the tank. Naturally, a very fast or highly competitive pace will frequently bring about the opposite result. The very best horses, however, are prone to use that fast pace as a springboard to track records.

EIGHTH RACE
AP 35688
August 24, 1968

1 MILE (chute). (Buckpasser, June 25, 1966, 1:32$\frac{3}{5}$, 3, 125.) Forty-first running WASHINGTON PARK HANDICAP. $100,000 added. 3-year-olds and upward. By subscription of $100 each, which shall accompany the nomination, $250 to pass the entry box and $750 additional to start, with $100,000 added, of which $20,000 to second, $15,000 to third and $10,000 to fourth. The winning owner to receive a trophy. Closed with 27 nominations.

Value of race $112,700. Value to winner $67,700; second, $20,000; third, $15,000; fourth, $10,000.
Mutuel Pool, $282,271.

Index	Horses	Eq't	A	Wt	PP	St	¼	½	¾	Str	Fin	Jockeys	Cl'g Pr.	Owners	Odds to $1
35524Sar^1	—Dr. Fager		4	134	9	1	6^1	2^h	$1^{\frac12}$	1^3	1^{10}	B Baeza		Tartan Stable	.30
35415AP^1	—Racing Room		4	116	2	7	$4\frac12$	3^2	2^3	$2^{1\frac12}$	$2^{1\frac12}$	J Sellers		Llangollen Farm	10.40
35553AP^4	—Info		4	112	3	6	8^2	6^2	3^1	3^3	3^1	E Fires		Mrs E J Brisbine	37.00
35580AP^1	—Out the Window	b	4	115	5	8	9^6	9^7	7^2	$5\frac12$	4^{nk}	H Moreno		J R Chapman	13.90
35625AP^3	—R. Thomas	b	7	118	1	9	5^1	1^h	4^2	4^2	5^6	J Nichols		Wilson-McDermott	24.80
35553AP^6	—Cabildo		5	114	8	10	10	10	10	10	6no	M Sol'mone		Mrs J W Brown	a-13.60
35625AP^2	—Angelico		5	111	6	5	1^h	$4\frac12$	$5\frac12$	7^3	7^{nk}	L Pincay Jr		Foxcatcher Farm	16.00
35606Atl^2	—Hedevar		6	112	10	2	$3\frac12$	8^h	6^h	6^2	$8^{1\frac14}$	T Lee		Mrs Edith W Bancroft	47.60
35625AP^1	—High Tribute	b	4	112	7	3	$7\frac12$	$7^{1\frac12}$	9^5	9^2	$9^{1\frac34}$	D Brumfield		Elmendorf	18.40
35433AP^3	—Kentucky Sherry		3	112	4	4	$2\frac12$	$5\frac12$	8^1	8^h	10	J Combest		Mrs J W Brown	a-13.60

a-Coupled, Cabildo and Kentucky Sherry.

Time, :22$\frac{4}{5}$, :44, 1:07$\frac{3}{5}$, 1:32$\frac{1}{5}$ (new track and world record). Track fast.

$2 Mutuel Prices:

8-DR. FAGER	2.60	2.20	2.20
3-RACING ROOM		3.80	3.20
4-INFO			5.20

B. c, by Rough'n Tumble—Aspidistra, by Better Self. Trainer, J. A. Nerud. Bred by Tartan Farms (Fla.).
IN GATE—5:36. OFF AT 5:36$\frac12$ CENTRAL DAYLIGHT TIME. Start good. Won easily.

DR. FAGER, away alertly but hard held to be reserved just off the lead, moved with a rush while still under restraint to take command leaving the backstretch, continued slightly wide to shake off RACING ROOM on the final turn, commenced lugging in while drawing off through the stretch run and won with something left.

The reliability of speed figures as a handicapping tool is significantly lower in route races whenever established running styles figure to create a superfast or slow, snail-like pace.

EIGHTH RACE
Bel
June 4, 1976

1⅛ MILES (chute). (1:45$\frac{2}{5}$). Twentieth running MOTHER GOOSE. SCALE WEIGHTS. $75,000 added. Fillies. 3-year-olds. Weight, 121 lbs. By subscription of $150 each, which shall accompany the nomination; $375 to pass the entry box; $375 to start, with $75,000 added. The added money and all fees to be divided: 60% to the winner, 22% to second, 12% to third and 6% to fourth. Trophies will be presented to the winning owner, trainer and jockey. Closed with 14 nominations.

Value of race $80,850. Value to winner $48,510; second, $17,787; third, $9,702; fourth, $4,851. Mutuel Pool, $328,981. Off-track betting, $129,405.

Last Raced		Horse	Eqt	A	Wt	PP	St	¼	½	¾	Str	Fin	Jockeys	Owners	Odds to $1
22 May76	8Bel^4	Girl in Love		3	121	4	5	5	5	5	2^7	$1^{1\frac14}$	JCruguet	Elmendorf	4.00
22 May76	8Bel^2	Optimistic Gal		3	121	2	2	2^5	2^5	1^2	1^2	2^{11}	BBaeza	Mrs R B Firestone	1.00
29 May76	8GS^1	Ancient Fables	b	3	121	5	1	4^{10}	4^8	4^2	$3\frac12$	$3^{6\frac34}$	ACorderoJr	Brazil Stable	18.50
22 May76	8Bel^5	Artfully	b	3	121	3	4	3^2	3^4	3^3	4^2	$4^{3\frac14}$	GPIntels'noJr	R N Webster	30.40
22 May76	8Bel^1	Dearly Precious		3	121	1	3	$1\frac12$	$1\frac12$	2^3	5	5	JVelasquez	R E Bailey	1.20

OFF AT 5:02$\frac12$ EDT. Start good. Won driving. Time, :22$\frac{1}{5}$, :44$\frac{2}{5}$, 1:08$\frac{4}{5}$, 1:35$\frac{1}{5}$, 1:48$\frac{4}{5}$. Track fast.

$2 Mutuel Prices:

4-GIRL IN LOVE	10.00	4.00	4.40
2-OPTIMISTIC GAL		2.60	2.20
5-ANCIENT FABLES			3.80

Ch. f, by Lucky Debonair—Lover's Quarrel, by Battle Joined. Trainer, John P. Campo. Bred by Elmendorf Farm (Ky.).
GIRL IN. LOVE, badly outrun on the backstretch, commenced to rally after going five furlongs, raced wide into the stretch, continued to advance under left-handed pressure and proved clearly best after catching OPTIMISTIC GAL. GIRL IN LOVE pulled up lame. OPTIMISTIC GAL, bothered by DEARLY PRECIOUS while racing outside that rival on the backstretch, took over while racing well out in the track on the turn, quickly opened a clear lead but wasn't able to withstand the winner. ANCIENT FABLES failed to be a serious factor. ARTFULLY raced within striking distance to the stretch and flattened out. DEARLY PRECIOUS ducked out into OPTIMISTIC GAL after the start, made the pace while bearing out into that rival throughout the run down the backstretch and was finished soon after going six furlongs.

7. Except for the top speed figure with front-running tendencies mentioned earlier (see point 3 above), the presence of a powerful, one-dimensional track bias of any kind makes speed figures as irrelevant as the times they are based on.

On a stretch runners' track the final quarter-mile time is somewhat helpful, but the dominant handicapping considerations are stamina, class, condition, and post position.

On a front runners' track the early fractions and early position calls in the running line are the best clues to the cashier's window.

If the bias is also to the inside part of the track, post position is the player's best means of separating contenders.

Virtually every racetrack in America provides aberrant conditions like the ones described here sometime during the racing season. The player who can recognize these prevailing situations and then adjust his handicapping will have the best shot at the equivalent of a perfect game. It's possible to sweep the card on days like that.

NOTE: *The early speed in the Schuylerville Stakes, the sample race exhibited in Chapter 4 (pages 42–43), was Our Dancing Girl. This determination was made by noting the first call position of Our Dancing Girl in her race with the great Ruffian. Post number two didn't hurt either. The next best speed in the race seemed to be Secret's Out and the top closer But Exclusive. This was the result.*

SEVENTH RACE
Saratoga
JULY 29, 1974

6 FURLONGS. (1.08) 57TH RUNNING THE SCHUYLERVILLE. $25,000 Added. 1st Division. Fillies, 2-year-olds. By subscription of $50 each, which shall accompany the nomination; $125 to pass the entry box; $125 to start, with $25,000 added. The added money and all fees to be divided 60% to the winner, 22% to second, 12% to third and 6% to fourth. Weights, 119 lbs. Non-winners of a sweepstakes allowed 3 lbs.; maidens, 7 lbs. Starters to be named at the closing time of entries. A trophy will be presented to the owner of the winner. Closed Monday, July 15 with 30 Nominations. Value of race $27,625, value to winner $16,575, second $6,077, third $3,315, fourth $1,658. Mutuel pool $108,621, OTB pool $46.764. Exacta Pool $79.247. OTB Exacta Pool $98.708.

Last Raced	Horse	Eqt.	A.	Wt	PP	St	¼	½	Str	Fin	Jockey	Odds $1
10Jly74 ^{8}Aqu^{3}	Our Dancing Girl	b	2	116	2	1	1^{2}	$1^{2\frac{1}{2}}$	1^{2}	1no	Bracciale V Jr	10.20
19Jun74 ^{8}Mth^{5}	Secret's Out		2	119	5	3	2^{1}	2^{2}	2^{3}	$2^{2\frac{1}{2}}$	Vasquez J	4.70
12Jly74 ^{4}Aqu^{2}	But Exclusive		2	116	7	7	$6^{\frac{1}{2}}$	5^{4}	5^{5}	3^{1}	Cordero A Jr	3.60
8Jly74 ^{6}Crc^{1}	Some Swinger	b	2	116	4	4	5^{2}	$4^{1\frac{1}{2}}$	$3^{\frac{1}{2}}$	$4^{1\frac{1}{4}}$	Velasquez J	6.00
20Jly74 ^{3}Mth^{1}	My Compliments		2	116	1	5	3^{2}	$3^{\frac{1}{2}}$	4^{hd}	5^{6}	Venezia M	1.60
14Jly74 ^{6}WO^{2}	La Bourrasque	b	2	116	3	6	7	6^{5}	6^{5}	$6^{7\frac{1}{2}}$	Turcotte R	5.90
15Jly74 ^{3}Aqu^{2}	Precious Elaine	b	2	112	6	2	4^{hd}	7	7	7	Santiago A	15.60

OFF AT 4:42 1/2 EDT. Start Good, Won driving. Time, :22⅕, :45⅕, 1:11⅕ Track fast.

$2 Mutuel Prices:				
	2-(B)-OUR DANCING GIRL	22.40	7.00	4.60
	5-(E)-SECRET'S OUT		5.00	4.00
	7-(H)-BUT EXCLUSIVE			3.20

$2 EXACTA 2-5 PAID $80.40.

B. f, by Solo Landing—Amber Dancer, by Native Dancer. Trainer Rigione J. Bred by Elcee H Stable (Fla).

OUR DANCING GIRL quickly sprinted clear, saved ground while making the pace and, after settling into the stretch with a clear lead, lasted over SECRET'S OUT. The latter prompted the pace throughought, lugged in slightly nearing midstretch and finished strongly, just missing. BUT EXCLUSIVE, off slowly, finished well while racing wide. SOME SWINGER rallied along the inside leaving the turn, eased out for the drive but lacked the needed late response. MY COMPLIMENTS had no excuse. LA BOURRASQUE was always outrun after breaking slowly. PRECIOUS ELAINE broke through before the start and was finished early.

Owners— 1, Elcee-H Stable; 2, Schott Marcia W; 3, Levin W A; 4, Mangurian H T Jr; 5, Reineman R L; 6, Levesque J L; 7, Brodsky A J.

Trainers— 1, Rigione J; 2, Picou J E; 3, Imperio D A; 4, Root T Jr; 5, Freeman W C; 6, Starr J; 7, Conway J P.

Scratched—Elsie Marley (30Apr74 ^{4}Aqu^{1}).

13.
Theory vs. Experience

For each and every piece of information in the past performance profile, there is a popular theory purporting to measure its exact significance. The interesting thing about that is I know of no winning player who subscribes to any such rigid approach to any aspect of the game.

WEIGHT

The old saying that "weight will stop a freight train" is true enough. But except for a few special cases, it is pure conjecture that a fit racehorse can be stopped or slowed by the addition of a few pounds. Weight is simply the most overrated factor in handicapping.

Perhaps 105 pounds will help a horse run a fifth of a second faster than 110 pounds and two-fifths of a second faster than 115. But there is no proof to demonstrate the validity of such a rigid relationship. Indeed between 105 and 115 pounds the amount of weight carried by the horse is demonstrably unimportant.

Beyond 115 pounds, the effect of added weight on performance is an individual thing.

Some horses can't handle 120 pounds; others are able to run just as fast and as far with considerably more. Past performance profiles usually provide sufficient clues to make such determinations; but because the betting public tends to automatically downgrade the chances of a top-weighted horse, the reward for a more flexible attitude is generally generous mutuel prices.

Gallant Bob **126** **Dk. b. or br. g (1972), by Gallant Romeo—Wisp O'Will, by New Policy.**
Breeder, J. L. Homan (Ky.). **1975 16 12 1 2 $229,213**
Owner, R. Horton. Trainer, J. D. Morquette. **1974 10 3 4 0 $58,118**

22 Nov75	^{8}Key	6 f	:22^1	:45^1	1:09^{4}gd	3-5	▲119	2½	1½	1½	1$^{1\frac{1}{2}}$	GalltnoG^3	AlwS	93	GallantBob119	BearerBond	8
4 Oct75	^{8}Key	6½ f	:22	:44^4	1:16^{3}ft	2-5	▲119	3½	2^1	1$^{1\frac{1}{2}}$	1^2	GalltnoG^3	AlwS	94	Gallant Bob 119	Talc	6
6 Sep75	^{8}Key	7 f	:21^4	:44^1	1:24 ft	6-5	▲129	3^1	3^2	2^h	1^3	GalltnoG^7	HcpO	89	Gallant Bob 129	Talc	9
13 Aug75	^{8}Mth	6 f	:20^4	:43^4	1:09^{2}ft	2	▲129	2^7	2$^{3\frac{1}{2}}$	2½	1$^{1\frac{1}{4}}$	GalltnoG^5	HcpO	93	Gallant Bob 129	Talc	7
5 Jly 75	^{8}Bow	6 f	:22^3	:45^4	1:10^{2}ft	2-5	▲127	2^h	1$^{1\frac{1}{2}}$	1^3	1$^{3\frac{1}{2}}$	GalltnoG^5	HcpO	91	GallantBob127	FrchWhistler	6
21 Jun75	^{8}AP	7 f	:22	:44^3	1:23^{2}ft	4½	124	1^h	1½	1^2	1^1	GallitnoG^5	AlwS	85	Gallant Bob 124	Doug	11
1 Jun75	^{8}Del	1$\frac{1}{16}$	:46^2	1:12	1:46^{1}ft	3-2	▲117	1^h	1^h	5^6	5^{12}	GallitnoG^5	AlwS	66	GreyBeret111	Dr'sEnjyDollrs	10
24 May75	^{8}Del	6 f	:21^4	:45	1:11^{1}ft	4-5	▲124	2^h	2^h	2^h	1½	GallitnoG^4	AlwS	89	Gallant Bob 124	Bold Gun	7
22 Mar75	^{8}Pim	6 f	:22^4	:46^1	1:11^{1}ft	1	▲122	3½	2^h	1^1	2^h	GallitnoG^8	AlwS	90	BombayDuck122	GallantBob	9
15 Mar75	^{8}Aqu	7 f	:22^3	:45^3	1:23^{4}sy	2¾	▲119	2^h	2^h	1½	3¾	GallitnoG^8	AlwS	81	Lefty 113	Tass	8
1 Mar75	^{8}Aqu	6 f	:21^4	:45^2	1:09^{4}ft	3	117	1^h	1^1	2½	3$^{3\frac{1}{2}}$	GallitnoG^9	AlwS	90	Singh 114	Laramie Trail	10
22Feb75	^{8}Key	7 f	:22^1	:45	1:25^{3}ft	2-5	▲119	1^3	1^6	1^8	1^{10}	GallitnoG^1	AlwS	81	GallantBob119	WickedPark	11
15 Feb75	^{8}GS	6 f	:22^1	:45^4	1:11 gd	2-5	▲122	1^h	1^3	1^5	1^9	GallitnoG^6	AlwS	88	GallantBob122	LuckeyLeaf	7
1 Feb75	^{8}Bow	6 f	:22^4	:46^3	1:12 gd	4-5	▲124	1^3	1^5	1^5	1$^{4\frac{1}{2}}$	GallitnoG^6	AlwS	83	GallantBob124	PendulmSam	6
25 Jan75	^{8}Key	6 f	:22^2	:46^1	1:13^{2}sy	4-5	▲119	1½	1^h	1½	1^2	GallitnoG^6	AlwS	75	Gallant Bob 119	Sgt. Hunt	7

Nov 29 Key 4f ft :48⅘b

Give me an obviously sharp horse with a proven superiority over the contenders and I'll gladly support him carrying 120, 125, or 128 pounds, providing of course that he has successfully carried that kind of weight before. Give me a horse that is not in shape and I don't care what weight he carries.

A few years ago I remember getting 6–1 on a horse that had beaten the same field of starter handicap horses five straight times. The betting crowd was so afraid of the horse's 134-pound weight assignment that it failed to accept him at face value.

If the fans had bothered to look up his record, they might not have been so apprehensive. The season before the horse won a similar-class event under 136 pounds. To a certain extent the same kind of situation occurs several times a season at every racetrack in America.

Of course, common sense dictates paying some attention to large weight shifts or to heavy weight assignments, especially when two or more closely matched contenders are involved.

1¼ MILES—SUBURBAN HANDICAP, AQUEDUCT, JULY 20, 1974

True Knight * **127** Dk. b. or br. h (1969), by Chateaugay—Stealaway, by Olympia.
Breeder, J. W. Galbreath (Ky.). 1974 . . 8 3 3 0 $283,638
Owner, Darby Dan Farm. Trainer, T. L. Rondinello. 1973 . . 12 3 2 2 $200,858

Jly 13-74^{8}Mth	1 1-4	2:02	ft	8-5	▲124	9^{13}	4^{3}	$1^{1\frac{1}{2}}$	$1^{3\frac{3}{4}}$	Riv'aMA^{5}	HcpS 92	TrueKnight124 EcoleEtage HeyRube		9
Jun16-74^{9}Suf	1 1-8	1:48⅗	ft	3-5	▲121	7^{18}	7^{19}	$5^{8\frac{1}{2}}$	4^{3}	C'd'oAJr^{6}	HcpS 95	BillyComeLately109 Forage NorthSea		7
May27-74^{8}Bel	1	1:34⅖	ft	7	125	8^{22}	8^{13}	$7^{9\frac{3}{4}}$	$6^{8\frac{1}{4}}$	Riv'aMA^{5}	HcpS 88	ArbeesBoy112 Forego Timel'ssMom'nt		8
Apr 6-74^{8}GS	1 1-4	2:06	sl	6-5	125	$6^{8\frac{3}{4}}$	4^{3}	$2^{1\frac{1}{2}}$	$1^{\frac{3}{4}}$	C'd'oAJr^{4}	HcpS 70	TrueKnight125 ProveO't PlayTheF'ld		6
Mar23-74^{9}Hia	1 1-4	2:01⅕	ft	9-5	124	7^{19}	$7^{7\frac{1}{2}}$	$3^{2\frac{1}{2}}$	2^{1}	C'd'oAJr^{3}	HcpS 91	Forego 129 True Knight Play the Field		7
Mar 9-74^{8}Bow	1 1-4	2:05⅖	ft	3-5	▲123	14^{15}	10^{10}	$5^{4\frac{3}{4}}$	$1^{\frac{1}{2}}$	C'd'oAJr^{4}	HcpS 96	True Knight 123 Delay Ecole Etage		14
Feb23-74^{9}GP	1 1-4	1:59⅘	ft	1	▲123	6^{16}	$4^{5\frac{1}{2}}$	2^{h}	$2^{\frac{1}{2}}$	C'd'oAJr^{4}	HcpS 97	Forego127 TrueKnight GoldenDon		6
Feb 9-74^{9}GP	1 1-8	1:48⅗	ft	2¼	123	5^{16}	5^{16}	4^{6}	2no	C'd'oAJr^{3}	HcpS 91	Forego125 TrueKnight Proud andBold		5
Nov22-73^{8}Aqu	1$\frac{3}{16}$	1:55	ft	4¼	126	$11^{9\frac{1}{4}}$	$9^{7\frac{1}{2}}$	$3^{\frac{1}{2}}$	1^{2}	C'd'oAJr^{9}	HcpS 87	TrueKnight126 Triangular NorthSea		12
Oct27-73^{7}Aqu	2	3:20	ft	4½	124	5^{12}	3^{8}	3^{17}	4^{18}	C'd'oAJr^{2}	WfaS 78	Prove Out 124 Loud Twice A Prince		6
Oct15-73^{8}Aqu	1 1-8	1:47	ft	4	122	8^{11}	$5^{5\frac{1}{2}}$	3^{6}	$3^{4\frac{3}{4}}$	Cast'daM^{7}	HcpS 96	Riva Ridge 130 Forage True Knight		9
Sep22-73^{8}Bow	1 1-8	1:49⅘	ft	5½	120	9^{14}	8^{10}	1^{1}	1^{4}	C't'daM^{5}	HcpS 102	TrueKnight 120 Delay BurningOn		12

July 19 Bel 3f ft :39b   July 12 Bel 4f ft :50b   July 8 Bel 6f ft 1:16b

Forego **131** B. g (1970), by Forli—Lady Golconda, by Hasty Road.
Breeder, Lazy F Ranch (Ky.). 1974 7 5 2 0 $322,378
Owner, Mrs. Edward F. Gerry. Trainer, S. W. Ward. 1973 18 8 3 3 $188,909

Jly 4-74^{8}Aqu	1$\frac{3}{16}$	1:54⅘	ft	2-5	▲129	6^{15}	4^{8}	2^{h}	$1^{\frac{3}{4}}$	Gust'sH^{6}	HcpS 88	Forego129 BillyComeLately ArbeesBoy		7
Jun26-74^{8}Aqu	7 f	1:21⅕	ft	2-3	▲132	6^{12}	6^{12}	$5^{6\frac{1}{2}}$	$2^{\frac{1}{2}}$	G'tinesH^{2}	HcpS 94	Timel'ssM'm'nt112 Forego N'rthSea		6
May27-74^{8}Bel	1	1:34⅖	ft	6-5	▲134	6^{11}	2^{h}	$1^{1\frac{1}{2}}$	2^{2}	G'tinesH^{2}	HcpS 94	ArbeesBoy112 Forego Timel'ssMom'nt		8
May18-74^{8}Bel	7 f	1:22⅕	ft	7-5	▲129	8^{9}	$6^{3\frac{1}{2}}$	$1^{1\frac{1}{2}}$	$1^{2\frac{1}{4}}$	Gust'sH^{7}	HcpS 91	F'r'go129 Mr.Pr'sp'ct'r Tim'l'sM'm'nt		8
Mar23-74^{9}Hia	1 1-4	2:01⅕	ft	4-5	▲120	5^{10}	$1^{\frac{1}{2}}$	$1^{1\frac{1}{2}}$	1^{1}	G'tinesH^{5}	HcpS 92	Forego 129 True Knight Play the Field		7
Feb23-74^{9}GP	1 1-4	1:59⅘	ft	7-5	127	4^{8}	2^{2}	1^{h}	$1^{\frac{1}{2}}$	G'stinesH^{2}	HcpS 98	Forego127 TrueKnight GoldenDon		6
Feb 9-74^{9}GP	1 1-8	1:48⅗	ft	2-3	▲125	4^{6}	$3^{2\frac{1}{2}}$	2^{1}	1no	G'tinesH^{2}	HcpS 91	Forego125 TrueKnight Proud andBold		5
Dec 8-73^{8}Aqu	1 1-8	1:47⅕	ft	3-5	▲127	5^{6}	3^{4}	$1^{1\frac{1}{2}}$	$1^{\frac{3}{4}}$	G'tinesH^{6}	HcpS 99	For'go127 MyG'll'nt Key to theK'gd'm		7
Nov24-73^{8}Aqu	1$\frac{3}{16}$	1:54⅗	ft	2	▲123	4^{5}	$3^{2\frac{1}{2}}$	1^{3}	1^{5}	Gust'esH^{9}	HcpS 89	Forego123 MyGallant Twice aPrince		10
Nov10-73^{6}Aqu	7 f	1:22⅗	ft	4-5	▲122	$3^{5\frac{1}{2}}$	3^{6}	3^{4}	3^{4}	GustinesH^{2}	Alw 84	North Sea 115 Tap The Tree Forego		5

July 19 Bel 3f ft :35⅕b   July 15 Bel 7f ft 1:24h   July 13 Bel 3f ft :36⅘b

Two honest, hard-hitting stakes horses.

The difference between Forego and True Knight was never more than a length or two. In Florida during the winter of 1974 Forego won three straight races over True Knight, each by a narrow margin. In the spring Forego was twice unsuccessful in attempts to carry 130 or more pounds. And he was, in fact, meeting weaker horses than True Knight. Either he had lost some of his edge in condition or as a four-year-old was inhibited by such heavy weight loads. True Knight, on the other hand, was razor sharp; and on July 13, 1974, one week before the Suburban, True Knight put in his best lifetime race.

Given True Knight's obvious edge in condition, the spread in the Suburban weights and Forego's 131-pound impost were plus factors that deserved to be taken into account. Somehow, and I don't believe it yet, True Knight paid $10.60.

There is one special circumstance in which a rigid approach to the weight factor is supported by fact. Few people know about it.

Before the turn of the century the Jockey Club Scale of Weights was created as a concession to the natural maturation rate of horses. It is a common fact that a horse is not as well developed at age three as it is likely to be at age four.

Racing secretaries use the scale of age-linked weight concessions as a guide when carding races for horses of mixed age groups.

7th Arlington Park

INNER TURF COURSE
1 1-16 MILES
ARLINGTON PARK
START▲   ▲FINISH

1⅟₁₆ MILES (inner turf). (1:41⅘). CLAIMING. Purse $5,500. 3-year-olds and upward. 3-year-olds. 113 lbs.: older. 122 lbs. Non-winners of two races since May 20 allowed 2 lbs.; a race, 4 lbs. Claiming price, $13,000; 2 lbs. allowed for each $1,000 to $11,000. (Races where entered for $10,000 or less not considered.)

4th Detroit Race Course

Start ▼
6 FURLONGS
DETROIT
▲Finish

6 FURLONGS (chute). (1:08). CLAIMING. Purse $2,500. 3- and 4-year-olds, non-winners of two races. 3-year-olds. 115 lbs.: 4-year-olds. 120 lbs. Non-winners of a race in 1974 allowed 3 lbs.; a race since Nov. 10, 5 lbs. Claiming price, $2,500.

THE JOCKEY CLUB SCALE OF WEIGHTS

DISTANCE	AGE	JAN. & FEB.	MAR. & APR.	MAY	JUNE	JULY	AUG.	SEP.	OCT.	NOV. & DEC.
½ Mile	2	...	...	...	...	...	105	108	111	114
	3	117	119	121	123	125	126	127	128	129
	4	130	130	130	130	130	130	130	130	130
	5 & up	130	130	130	130	130	130	130	130	130
6 Furlongs	2	...	...	...	...	...	102	105	108	111
	3	114	117	119	121	123	125	126	127	128
	4	129	130	130	130	130	130	130	130	130
	5 & up	130	130	130	130	130	130	130	130	130
1 Mile	2	...	...	...	...	...	...	96	99	102
	3	107	111	113	115	117	119	121	122	123
	4	127	128	127	126	126	126	126	126	126
	5 & up	128	128	127	126	126	126	126	126	126
1¼ Miles	2	...	...	...	...	...	...	...	...	...
	3	101	107	111	113	116	118	120	121	122
	4	125	127	127	126	126	126	126	126	126
	5 & up	127	127	127	126	126	126	126	126	126
1½ Miles	2	...	...	...	...	...	...	...	...	...
	3	98	104	108	111	114	117	119	121	122
	4	124	126	126	126	126	126	126	126	126
	5 & up	126	126	126	126	126	126	126	126	126
2 Miles	3	96	102	106	109	112	114	117	119	120
	4	124	126	126	126	126	125	125	124	124
	5 & up	126	126	126	126	126	125	125	124	124

NOTE: *Fillies are entitled to a five-pound sex allowance in races against colts.*

For reasons I cannot fathom, there is a great deal of controversy in racing circles about the legitimacy of age-linked weight concessions. Every season there is talk of abolishing or amending the scale of weights. Most say that three-year-olds should not get automatic weight concessions in the late summer or fall. Nonsense. It seems to me the old-timers had a pretty good idea. The effectiveness of the scale and the need for the concessions are made abundantly clear in the following remarkable statement, checked out in a research project that included several thousand races.

When a three-year-old is assigned actual top weight in a race for horses three years and up, the three-year-old has little or no chance of winning. I suggest you read that again.

In all stakes and allowance races run at seven of the nation's most popular tracks during the mid-1970s, there were only ten total exceptions to this rule. In a spot check conducted during the first half of 1982 at three major Eastern tracks, there were but two exceptions.

All ten horses in the original study who defied the scale of age-linked weight concessions were curiously unable to repeat the feat at any other time, and only one managed to score a victory against weaker opposition during the next two months of competition. Ten exceptions from a sample of 400 top-weighted three-year-olds is pretty convincing evidence. Nothing has happened to change the situation.

SEX

In Europe fillies race against colts and win with absolute impunity. In America most trainers are reluctant to match the so-called weaker sex against males. Ruffian's tragic demise in the match race against Foolish Pleasure didn't help reverse the trend. But to his credit, it didn't change Frank Whiteley Jr.'s commitment to the experiment. Only two of Honorable Miss' races shown in the p.p.s below were against members of her own sex.

Honorable Miss **120** **B. m (1970), by Damascus—Court Circuit, by Royal Vale.**
Breeder, Mrs. T. Bancroft (Ky.). **1976 8 3 2 1 $100,148**
Owner, Pen-Y-Bryn Farm. Trainer, F. J. Whiteley, Jr. **1975 13 7 2 0 $183,857**

30 Aug76	^{8}Bel	6 f	:22^3	:45^4	1:10 ft	7-5	▲130	$9^{7\frac{1}{2}}$	$5^{3\frac{1}{2}}$	1^h	$1^{4\frac{1}{4}}$	ShmrW^{10}	HcpS	92	HonorableMiss130	Lachesis	10
25 Jly 76	^{8}Aqu	7 f	:23^2	:47	1:24^{2}ft	1	▲118	6^{12}	6^9	4^2	$3^{1\frac{1}{4}}$	VsquezJ^2	HcpS	78	El Fitirre 114	Nalee'sKnight	6
12 Jly 76	^{4}Atl	6 f	:22^1	:44^4	1:09 ft	1	▲119	10^{10}	10^{12}	9^{10}	5^6	VasqzJ^{10}	HcpS	91	North Call 115	Our Hero	10
4 Jly 76	^{8}Aqu	6 f	:22	:44^4	1:09^{2}ft	1	▲125	5^{14}	4^{11}	4^7	$5^{1\frac{1}{4}}$	VsquezJ^5	HcpS	95	Red Cross 118	Shy Dawn	5
27 May76	^{8}Bel	6 f	:22^3	:45^4	1:10^{2}ft	2-5e	▲123	6^{11}	6^5	2^1	$1^{3\frac{3}{4}}$	VasquezJ^1	Alw	90	Honorable Miss 123	Lachesis	6
15 May76	^{8}Bel	7 f	:22^2	:44^2	1:21 ft	9-5	▲121	9^{12}	$9^{9\frac{1}{4}}$	$5^{7\frac{1}{4}}$	$2^{6\frac{1}{4}}$	VsquezJ^1	HcpS	91	LordRebeau115	HonorbleMiss	9
1 May76	^{8}Aqu	7 f	:22^1	:44^2	1:22^{2}sy	$4\frac{3}{4}$	122	8^{11}	8^{13}	5^7	$2^{\frac{3}{4}}$	VasquezJ^5	HcpS	88	DueDiligence111	HnrbleMiss	8
23 Apr76	^{8}Aqu	6 f	:22^2	:45^4	1:10^{3}gd	1	▲123	6^{14}	6^{10}	3^3	$1^{\frac{3}{4}}$	VasquezJ^3	Alw	90	Ⓕ HonrbleMiss123	FltVictrss	6
1 Nov75	^{8}Bel	7 f	:22	:44^3	1:22^{4}ft	7-5e	▲125	11^{17}	10^{12}	$5^{8\frac{1}{2}}$	$4^{5\frac{1}{2}}$	VasqezJ^9	HcpS	82	No Bias 116	Step Nicely	11
13 Oct75	^{8}Bel	6 f	:22^3	:45^3	1:09^{4}ft	9-5e	▲133	14^{11}	$11^{6\frac{1}{2}}$	$5^{1\frac{1}{2}}$	1^2	VasqzJ^{15}	HcpS	93	Honorable Miss 133	No Bias	15
25 Sep75	^{8}Bel	7 f	:22^4	:45^3	1:23^{1}sy	1-2	▲119	$4^{8\frac{1}{2}}$	4^6	$3^{\frac{1}{2}}$	$2^{2\frac{3}{4}}$	VasquezJ^1	Alw	83	Ⓕ FltVictress112	HnrbleMiss	4

Sept 14 Bel 4f ft :46⅗h **Sept 10 Bel 4f ft :46⅘h** **Sept 5 Bel 4f ft :48b**

Of course in 1980 the filly Genuine Risk changed a lot of people's minds. Not since 1915 had a filly won the Kentucky Derby; not since 1959 had any owner or trainer elected to make the attempt. But through her gritty performances in all three Triple Crown races, Genuine Risk served notice to all chauvinistic types that the times are achanging.

Her victory was not simply a triumph of one rugged female over ordinary colts but a portent of things to come. Perhaps another filly will win a Triple Crown race within the next year or two or three to drive home the point. At the very least, more trainers and owners should be willing to make the attempt.

1980 Record of Genuine Risk

Genuine Risk

Own.—Firestone Mrs B R

Ch. f. 3, by Exclusive Native—Virtuous, by Gallant Man
Br.—Humphrey Mrs G W Jr (Ky)   1980   8 4 3 1 $503,742
Tr.—Jolley Leroy   1979   4 4 0 0 $100,245

27Sep80-8Bel	$1\frac{1}{4}$:48 1:12^2 1:49^{1}ft	*1-2 118	3$\frac{1}{2}$ 3^1 2^{hd} 1no	VsquezJ^1	ⒽRuffian H	81 GenuineRisk,MistyGllor,It'sInthAir 6
10Sep80-8Bel	1 :46^1 1:10^4 1:35^{2}ft	*6-5 118	4^5 3^1 1^{hd} 2no	VsquezJ^2	ⒻMaskette	91 Bold'NDtrmind,GnuinRisk,LovSign 5
7Jun80-8Bel	1$\frac{1}{2}$:50^1 2:04 2:29^{4}m	5 121	5^3 2$\frac{1}{2}$ 1^{hd} 2^2	Vasquez J^1	Belmont	69 TmprncHill,GnuinRisk,RockhillNtv 10
17May80-9Pim	1$\frac{3}{16}$:47^4 1:11^1 1:54^{1}ft	*2 121	4^4 43$\frac{1}{2}$ 2^1 24$\frac{3}{4}$	Vasquez J^5	Preakness	94 Codex, Genuine Risk,ColonelMoran 8
3May80-8CD	1$\frac{1}{4}$:48 1:37^3 2:02 ft	13 121	74$\frac{1}{2}$ 11$\frac{1}{2}$ 1^2 1^1	VasquezJ^{10}	Ky Derby	87 GenuineRisk,Rumbo,JaklinKlucmn 13
19Apr80-8Aqu	1$\frac{1}{8}$:47^2 1:11^3 1:50^{4}ft	8$\frac{1}{2}$ 121	3^2 31$\frac{1}{2}$ 3^2 31$\frac{1}{2}$	VsquezJ^3	Wood Mem	79 PfuggdNickl,ColonlMorn,GnunRsk 11
5Apr80-7Aqu	1 :46^4 1:12 1:38^{3}gd	*1-5 124	3^2 11$\frac{1}{2}$ 1^1 12$\frac{1}{2}$	Vasquez J^4	ⒻHcp0	73 GenuineRisk,TellASecret,SprucePin 4
19Mar80-7GP	7f :22 :44^4 1:22^{3}ft	*2-5 113	4^4 32$\frac{1}{2}$ 1$\frac{1}{2}$ 12$\frac{1}{2}$	Vasquez J^3	ⒻAlw	91 Genuine Risk, Sober Jig,PeaceBells 6

Because of a variety of economic factors, it is still true that a filly of $15,000 claiming class will usually run one- or two-fifths of a second slower than a colt of the corresponding claiming price. But if the filly is in a race with colts and is intrinsically the fastest horse in the field, my research shows that nothing linked to sex differences will prevent her from proving her superiority on the track. Simply put, a fast filly will beat a slow colt and a fast colt will beat a slow filly. It is not sex that is important but speed, staying power, and soundness.

One caution: During the late spring and early summer, female horses tend to go into heat. Occasionally that will bring out excessive kidney sweating and other nervous habits. A filly acting in that manner during the post parade is telling you she has other things besides racing on her mind. (This can happen in a race carded exclusively for fillies too.)

WORKOUTS

The racetrack is open for training in the early morning hours, and the *Daily Racing Form* clockers have a tough job. As many as thirty horses can be out on the racetrack at the same time, and there are no names or numbers on the saddlecloths to help identify the horses.

BELMONT PARK – Track Fast

Three Furlongs		Act Together	:48½ h	PrincetonScholr	:50¾ b	Gato Del Sol	1:00 h
BestndBrightest	:37 b	Balancing Act	:50⅗ b	Procurer	:48⅕ h	Gulf	1:01⅗ h
Bright Halo	:37⅗ b	Bedside	:50⅗ b	Roulette Wheel	:49⅗ b	Hush Dear	1:02⅗ h
Carefully Hidden	:35 h	Beneficense	:50⅗ b	Royal Hostage	:48 h	Laddy's Luck	1:02⅗ h
Drinks On Me	:37⅗ b	Castle Knight	:49⅗ b	Secret Sharer	:49⅗ b	**Muskoka Wyck**	:59⅗ h
Ducks in A Row	:37⅗ b	Cherry Sauce	:49⅗ b	Shador	:50½ b	Nahi	1:03⅗ h
Gail's Wish	:35⅗ h	Citius	:48 b	Shifty Sheik	:49 b	Promising Star	1:03 b
Granny Sack	:39⅗ b	ConquistdorCilo	:49⅗ b	Signal Nine	:49 b	Steady Naskra	1:06 b
Gravitation	:36⅗ h	D'Accord	:51 b	Stretch Dancer	:49⅗ h	WhoCouldForget	1:00⅘ h
Hab Dancer	:38⅗ b	D'Espirit	:48½ h	Sunny Sparkler	:49½ b	Wimbledon Star	1:03 b
Harlow	:38⅕ b	Damask Cheek	:49⅗ b	Thru A Straw	:49½ b	**Seven Furlongs—1:20⅗**	
Lord Darnley	:35 h	Disco Count	:49⅗ b	Winged Universe	:47⅗ h	Birch Bark	1:18⅗ b
Moment's Prayer	:38⅗ b	Dorinade	:48 h	**Winter's Tale**	:47⅗ b	Foolish Stunt	1:16 b
Mouthfull	:39⅗ b	Fever Pitch	:50½ b	**Five Furlongs—**	:57⅗	Jeffers West	1:16⅗ b
Oh Laurie	:39⅗ b	Fort Nightly	:50⅗ b	Baby Kobe	1:03⅗ h	NorthernBrbizon	1:15 h
Silver Buck	:37⅗ b	Maudlin	:48½ b	Beau Cougar	1:02⅗ h	Otter Slide	1:15⅗ h
T. Dykes	:37⅗ b	Mochila	:49⅗ b	Believable	1:00⅗ h	Ruling Gold	1:14⅗ h
Talish	:35 h	Mr. Milton	:52 b	Bysantine	1:00⅗ h	**Silver Supreme**	1:12⅗ h
The Time Is Now	:34⅗ h	My Yellow Bird	:49½ h	Campilan	1:00⅗ h	**1 Mile—1:33**	
Trenchant	:35⅗ h	No Mans Land	:50⅗ b	ChrgMyAccount	1:02⅗ h	Bucksplasher	1:41⅗ b
Four Furlongs		Pin Puller	:50 b	Creme de LaFete	1:00⅗ h		

LORD DARNLEY (3) is on edge. CONQUISTADOR CIELO (4) was hard held. WINTERS TALE (4) acts good. GATO DEL SOL (5) is doing well. SILVER SUPREME (6) went evenly. BUCKSPLASHER (8) had a useful trial with G. Martens in the irons.

ITEM: Because of typographical mistakes and omissions, workouts that appear in the daily tabulator listings are frequently more accurate than works appearing below the past performance profile. In addition, these tabular listings often contain the clocker's comments about some of the more noteworthy training drills of the day.

ITEM: When a horse ships from a section of the country serviced by one edition of the *Form* to another serviced by a different edition, the out-of-town workouts will frequently be omitted from the past performances. I have complained about this to the publisher of the *Daily Racing Form*, but aside from a smattering of California workouts that now make their way into the Eastern edition and vice versa, the response has not been satisfactory. Maybe if we all scream about this together we will get better results.

ITEM: The absence of workouts from any past performance profile does not mean the absence of training. Some works are missed, missing, or misidentified. A few trainers have access to private training tracks. Until all states adopt a rule requiring local workouts, the player is simply going to have to keep a record of the trainers who like to sneak their hot horses past the public.

For obvious reasons, this practice is most often attempted with first-time starters in cheap maiden claiming races and is particularly rampant in Maryland, a breeding state where the racing commission is not known for its compassion for the fan, and where there are almost fifty private training tracks within a 100-mile radius of Bowie, Laurel, and Pimlico.

ITEM: The times of workouts are as accurate as the clockers are skillful and honest. Because the vast majority of clockers are honest and skillful but not well paid, the player should expect a few of the best workouts to be misrepresented.

The most accurate clocking crews operate in New York (under the direction of Frenchie Schwartz), in California (where a workout identification system is used), and in Florida during the high-class winter meets. At all but a few racetracks, however, 95 to 99 percent of the workouts accorded to established stakes horses, and 70 to 80 percent of the rest are as accurate as a hand-held stopwatch can report them. In Maryland and Kentucky I would not be willing to stand by that statement.

ITEM: Some tracks offer an auxiliary training track to handle the overflow of horses on the grounds. These training tracks tend to be considerably deeper and slower than the main track, and the following table of times should be adjusted accordingly.

MAJOR-TRACK TABLE OF NOTEWORTHY
WORKOUT TIMES

DISTANCE	BREEZING (WITHOUT SERIOUS WHIPPING)	HANDILY	FROM GATE	MUD
3 Furlongs	.35⅘b	.35⅖h	Add ⅖ sec.	Add ⅘ sec.
4 Furlongs	.48b	.47⅗h	Add ⅖	Add 1
5 Furlongs	1:00⅗b	1:00⅕h	Add ⅖	Add 1⅕
6 Furlongs	1:13⅗b	1:13h	Add ⅖	Add 1⅖
7 Furlongs	1:27b	1:26⅖h	Add ⅖	Add 1⅗
1 Mile	1:41b	1:40⅖h	Add ⅖	Add 1⅘
1⅛ Miles	1:56b	1:55⅖h	Add ⅖ sec.	Add 2 sec.

Admittedly, the value of the above chart is limited. It is only a guide. On lightning-fast racetracks the standards should be adjusted by at least one full second, and at minor tracks few horses will ever work fast enough to spark the player's attention.

The value of workouts is not restricted to speed. Indeed, a fast workout is not often conclusive evidence of improved physical condition; nor is a series of short, speedy drills of any special import to a horse that consistently shows high early speed in its races. Instead the player should consider the value of workouts in the light of the following principles; they are the concepts many of the best trainers use, and the ones many of the best players use as well.

1. Pay special note to the frequency of workouts and give a horse extra credit for positive physical condition if it has several good workouts to its credit or has raced well recently and has worked four furlongs or longer at least once in the interim. This is especially true at minor racetracks and for horses that have been out of action sometime during the recent past.

Royal Rhett **115** Ch. g (1973), by Royal Union—Sweet Straw, by Jackstraw.
Breeder, Al Rossi (Ill.). 1976 4 3 0 0 $6,787

Owner, Lepere Stable. Trainer, Ron O. Goodridge.

10 Sep76 ^{10}Cka	5 f	:22^2	:46^2 :59^{2}ft	13	118	1^h	1^1	1$^{1\frac{1}{2}}$	1$^{1\frac{1}{2}}$	WolfC^5	Alw	90	RoyalRhett118	DarkAvenger	8
28 Jly 76 ^{8}FP	5½ f	:23^2	:48^{2}1:07^{4}ft	7-5	▴118	2½	3^2	4^2	5$^{2\frac{1}{2}}$	WolfC^4	Alw	80	MeanMr.Green114	SadiesMn	7
19 Jly 76 ^{5}FP	6 f	:23	:47 1:13^{2}ft	8-5	120	1$^{3\frac{1}{2}}$	1$^{3\frac{1}{2}}$	1$^{4\frac{1}{2}}$	1^5	WolfC^7	Alw	80	RoyalRhett 120	GreatPeach	8
29 May76 ^{3}FP	5½ f	:23	:47^{2}1:07 gd	8-5	▴120	1$^{1\frac{1}{2}}$	1$^{2\frac{1}{2}}$	1^4	1^3	WolfC^1	Mdn	87	RoylRhett120	AbleScrtaryJr.	10

Sept 9 Cka 4f ft :51⅖b   Sept 2 Cka 5f ft 1:00⅕hg   Aug 27 Cka 5f ft 1:02⅗bg

2. A recent fast workout at three or four furlongs is a positive sign if the horse has shown little early speed in its recent races (or has been racing in a route and is now attempting a sprint). Conversely, if the horse has been showing high early speed in its races or is attempting a significantly longer distance, a longer, slower workout would suggest the trainer's attempt to build staying power. In the first example below, Princely Song showed high speed in his training drill of July 11 and won a sprint off that work four days later. In the case of Bold Forbes, trainer Laz Barrera had employed several long slow workouts in his strategy to prepare the colt for a maximum effort in the Kentucky Derby. His workout prior to the Preakness, a blazing-fast half-mile, did nothing to advance the horse and may have put him too much on edge. For the Belmont, the workout line shows that trainer Barrera was very conscious of the stamina factor. A masterpiece of horsemanship on display.

Princely Song * **114** Dk. b. or br. c (1972), by Cornish Prince—Songster, by Jester.
Br., Warnerton Farm of Ky., Ltd. (Ky.). 1976 4 1 1 0 $12,150
Owner, A. & Christine Willcox. Trainer, L. Rettele 1975 3 2 0 0 $8,809

3Jly 76 ^{5}Hol	Ⓣ 1	:47^4	1:11^{3}1:36^{2}fm	3½	114	5^2	4$^{3\frac{1}{2}}$	6$^{2\frac{1}{2}}$	7^3	OlivaresF^7	Alw	85	Chindo115	EarlyCotton	7
26Jun76 ^{7}Hol	1	:45^4	1:10 1:35^{2}ft	40	114	3^2	2^h	2½	2½	OlivaresF^7	Alw	88	HomeJerome114	PrincelySong	7
4Jun76 ^{7}Hol	6 f	:22	:44^{2}1:08^{2}ft	2¾	115	6^4	6$^{6\frac{1}{2}}$	7^{11}	6^{11}	HawleyS^7	Alw	86	Maheras116	RestlessRestless	7
20May76 ^{7}Hol	6 f	:22	:44^{2}1:09^{3}ft	1	▴115	1½	1½	1½	1^{nk}	HawleyS^1	Alw	91	PrincelySng115	Chief'sHolday	7
22Nov75 ^{8}Key	6 f	:22^1	:45^{1}1:09^{4}gc	7	114	3$^{3\frac{1}{2}}$	3$^{1\frac{1}{2}}$	4^2	4^3	TrctteRL^8	AlwS	90	GallantBob119	BearerBond	8
10Nov75 ^{6}Key	7 f	:22^1	:45^{4}1:23^{3}sy	2-3	▴114	1½	1$^{1\frac{1}{2}}$	1^6	1^5	TurctteRL^1	Alw	91	PrincelySong114	Bee aTipper	7
27Oct75 ^{9}Key	6½ f	:23	:46^{2}1:17^{3}ft	3	119	1^h	1$^{1\frac{1}{2}}$	1^3	1^8	TrctteRL^8	Mdn	89	PrincelySong119	CourtRportr	10

*July 10 Hol 4f ft :46⅘h   June 20 Hol 6f ft 1:16h   June 17 Hol 5f ft 1:01h

Bold Forbes **126** Dk. b. or br. c (1973), by Irish Castle—Comely Nell, by Commodore M.
Br., Eaton Farms & Red Bull Stable (Ky.). 1976 . . 7 4 1 2 $318,890
Owner, E. R. Tizol. Trainer, L. S. Barrera. 1975 . . 8 7 0 1 $62,749

15 May76	^{8}Pim	1$\frac{3}{16}$	:45 1:09 1:55 ft	1e	126	1^2	1^2	2^h	3^4	CoroAJr^4	ScwS 91	Elocutionist126	Play theRed	6
1 May76	^{8}CD	1$\frac{1}{4}$	:45^{4}1:10^{2}2:01^{3}ft	3	126	1^5	1$\frac{1}{2}$	1$\frac{1}{2}$	1^1	CrdroAJr^2	ScwS 89	BoldForbes126	HonestPlesre	9
17 Apr76	^{8}Aqu	1$\frac{1}{8}$	:46 1:09^{4}1:47^{2}ft	2-5	▲126	1^3	1$^{1\frac{1}{2}}$	1^4	1$^{4\frac{3}{4}}$	CdroAJr^5	ScwS 98	Bold Forbes 126	On The Sly	7
20 Mar76	^{8}Aqu	7 f	:22^1 :44 1:20^{4}ft	8-5	119	2^h	1^2	1^7	1$^{7\frac{3}{4}}$	CdroAJr^7	AlwS 97	Bold Forbes 119	Eustace	8
28 Feb76	^{8}SA	1	:45^{3}1:09^{3}1:35 ft	2	117	1^2	2^1	1^4	1^3	PincyLJr^5	AlwS 94	BoldForbes117	Grandaries	7
14 Feb76	^{8}SA	7 f	:22 :44^{3}1:21^{4}ft	8-5	▲119	1^h	2$\frac{1}{2}$	1$^{2\frac{1}{2}}$	3$\frac{3}{4}$	PincyLJr^7	AlwS 93	ThrmlEnrgy117	StaindGlass	7
24 Jan76	^{8}SA	6 f	:22^1 :45 1:09^{3}ft	6-5	▲120	2$\frac{1}{2}$	2^2	2$\frac{1}{2}$	2no	PincyLJr^2	AlwS 91	Sure Fire 114	Bold Forbes	6
31 Dec75	^{4}SA	5$\frac{1}{2}$ f	:21^4 :44^{2}1:03 ft	1-3	▲122	1$\frac{1}{2}$	2$\frac{1}{2}$	2^h	3^5	PincayLJr^1	Alw 94	Sure Fire 114	Beau Talent	5
3 Aug75	^{8}Sar	6 f	:21^4 :44^{1}1:09^{4}ft	1-10	▲120	1^2	1^8	1^{10}	1^8	VlsquezJ^5	AlwS 91	BoldForbes120	FamilyDoct'r	5
23 Jly 75	^{8}Bel	6 f	:22^2 :45^{2}1:09^{2}ft	8-5	120	1$^{1\frac{1}{2}}$	1^2	1^4	1^5	PincyLJr^2	AlwS 96	Bold Forbes 120	Iron Bit	5
15 Jun75	^{7}PR	6 f	:22^2 :44^{3}1:10^{3}ft	1-6	▲118	1^2	1^4	1^5	1^{13}	HiraldoJ^2	Stk 101	Bold Forbes 118	Lovely Jay	4
4 Jun75	^{4}PR	6 f	:23 :45^{3}1:11^{2}ft	1-4e	▲114	1^2	1$^{3\frac{1}{2}}$	1^5	1^8	HiraldoJ^3	Alw 97	Bold Forbes 114	Lovely Jay	10
25 Apr75	^{1}PR	5 f	:22 :45^3 :59^{1}ft	1-6	▲116	1^4	1^5	1^6	1$^{8\frac{1}{2}}$	HiraldoJ^3	Alw 95	Bold Forbes 116	Lovely Jay	5
11 Apr75	^{1}PR	5 f	:22 :45^3 :58^{4}ft	1-3	▲115	1^5	1^5	1^5	1^5	HiraldoJ^4	Alw 97	Bold Forbes 115	Lovely Jay	5
12 Mar75	^{1}PR	5 f	:22 :45^4 :59^{2}ft	35	116	1^5	1^6	1^8	1^{17}	HiraldoJ^2	Mdn 94	BoldForbes116	MyDad'sBrdy	8

June 1 Bel 1m ft 1:50$\frac{3}{5}$bg   May 27 Bel 1$\frac{1}{2}$m ft 2:43$\frac{4}{5}$b   May 13 Pim 4f ft :45$\frac{2}{5}$h

3. A workout of any distance at any reasonable speed one or two days before a race is a useful "blowout" and can often be interpreted as a positive sign of trainer intention. To obtain Sunday workouts, which are not included in the Monday *Daily Racing Form* (published Saturday evening), check the racing secretary's office on entering the track. Some tracks announce these workouts over the public address system or post them in a designated location in the grandstand.

Speed Burgoo **116** B. f (1972), by Scotland—Queen Corona, by Bernburgoo.
Breeder, K. Blitsch (Ill.). 1976 . . 10 1 0 1 $2,010
Owner, S. Wheeler. Trainer, Rex Loney. $2,500 1975 . . 12 1 4 1 $3,3C0

9 Sep76	^{9}Lat	1$\frac{1}{16}$	:49^{1}1:18^{1}1:53^{4}sy	16	117	10^{31}	10^{22}	10^{17}	8^{17}	MurchisnJ^8	2500	ClassyCanuck109	KennyLeVn	1
2 Sep76	^{9}EIP	6 f	:24 :49 1:17 sl	26	120	7$^{8\frac{1}{2}}$	8$^{8\frac{1}{2}}$	5$^{7\frac{1}{2}}$	3^3	MurchsnJ^3	2500 62	J.Artest114	Day ofComfree	
23 Aug76	^{9}EIP	1	:48 1:13^{4}1:40^{3}ft	8e	117	5$^{5\frac{1}{4}}$	8$^{8\frac{3}{4}}$	9^{19}	8^{28}	MurchsnJ^7	2000 51	Quarnos 120	O Song	
12 Aug76	^{9}EIP	1$\frac{1}{4}$	:49^{2}1:52^{2}2:09^{2}ft	53	120	3$^{1\frac{1}{2}}$	6$^{7\frac{1}{4}}$	6$^{9\frac{1}{2}}$	6^{15}	MurchisnJ^1	2000 59	Phil's Regret 115	Controblss	
3 Aug76	^{6}EIP	1	:47^{4}1:33^{1}1:40^{3}ft	8$\frac{1}{4}$	115	3^5	4$^{5\frac{1}{2}}$	6^9	6^{22}	McDowlM^7	2000 57	JacCourt120	LilThermo	
26 Jly 76	^{2}EIP	1	:48^{3}1:42^{1}1:43 ft	5$\frac{3}{4}$	116	4$^{1\frac{1}{2}}$	3^1	3$\frac{1}{2}$	1$^{1\frac{1}{2}}$	MurchisnJ^1	2000 67	SpeedBurgoo116	HeACrook	10
19 Jly 76	^{6}EIP	6 f	:23^1 :46^{4}1:12^{2}ft	26	115	5$^{4\frac{1}{4}}$	5$^{4\frac{1}{4}}$	5^6	5$^{7\frac{1}{2}}$	CrtwrhtN^1	3500 78	FairDiamond115	BoxcrBetty	
13 Jly 76	^{2}EIP	6 f	:23 :47 1:14^{3}ft	27	112	5^7	6$^{6\frac{3}{4}}$	7$^{5\frac{3}{4}}$	9$^{5\frac{1}{4}}$	CwrightN^1	2500 72	Go Go Liza 112	Karen Lou	1
7 Jly 76	^{9}EIP	6 f	:23 :47 1:13 ft	26	118	5$^{3\frac{1}{4}}$	4$^{1\frac{1}{2}}$	5$^{2\frac{1}{2}}$	5^5	MurchisnJ^4	2000 80	ⒻOh Katy 113	Roy's Choice	
2 Jly 76	^{2}EIP	6 f	:23 :46^{1}1:12 ft	35	112	11^{13}	12^{14}	11$^{9\frac{1}{4}}$	11^{17}	CrtwrghtN^6	2500 73	Dr. Mills 114	Bixby Imp	1
8 Nov75	^{2}CD	6 f	:23^1 :47^{3}1:52^{2}sl	58	115	9$^{7\frac{3}{4}}$	9^{10}	8^9	8^{11}	BeechJJr^7	3000 58	Wa Tonka 117	Vent Du Sud	1

July 25 EIP 3f ft :38$\frac{1}{5}$b

4. Most stakes-class horses work fast, and with a well-trained horse every training drill has a purpose. The following past performance profile shows the great Kelso preparing for the Washington, D.C., International, a 1½-mile classic run each fall on Laurel's grass course. In this particular case, Kelso, who was

never 100 percent comfortable on the grass, lost by a narrow margin to Mongo, one of the top grass horses of the past twenty-five years. The defeat was surely no disgrace and certainly not the fault of trainer Carl Hanford, who made all the right moves.

Kelso ✕ **126** Dk. b. or br. g (1957), by Your Host—Maid of Flight, by Count Fleet.
Breeder, Mrs. R. C. duPont. 1963 . . 11 9 1 0 $544,762
Owner, Bohemia Stable. Trainer, C. H. Hanford. 1962 . . 12 6 4 0 $289,685

Oct19-63 7Aqu	2	3:22 ft	1-6	▲124	41¾	12	16	14	Val'z'lal1	WfaS 87	Kelso 124	Guadalcanal 124	Garwol	7
Sep28-63 7Aqu	1 1-4	2:00⅘ft	1-4	▲126	34	2½	1½	13½	Val'z'lal2	WfaS 96	Kelso126	NeverBend120	CrimsonSatan	5
Sep 2-63 7Aqu	1 1-8	1:49⅘ft	2-3	▲134	32	31	12	15½	Val'z'lal7	AlwS 92	Kelso134	CrimsonSatan129	Garwol	8
Aug 3-63 6Sar	1 1-8	1:50⅖ft	1-3	▲130	43	42½	11	12½	Val'elal2	SpwS 93	Kelso130	Saidam111	SunriseCounty	7
Jly 4-63 7Aqu	1 1-4	2:01⅘ft	2-5	▲133	32	31½	11½	11¼	Val'z'lal7	HcpS 91	Kelso 133	Saidam 111	Garwol	7
Jun19-63 7Aqu	1 1-8	1:48⅘ft	1-3	▲132	33½	31	12	11½	Val'uelal3	AlwS 97	Kelso 132	Lanvin 114	Polylad	5
Mar23-63 8Bow	1 1/16	1:43 ft	4-5	▲131	55	33	21½	1¾	Val''z'lal5	HcpS 98	Kelso131	CrimsonSat'n124	G'sh'gWind	6
Mar16-63 8G.P	1 1-4	2:03⅕ft	1-5	▲130	2h	12	12	13¼	Val'uelal2	HcpS 83	Kelso 130	Sensitivo 112	Jay Fox	6
Feb23-63 7Hia	1 1-4	2:01⅘ft	2-5	▲131	31	42½	23	22¼	Val'z'lal5	HcpS 87	BeauPurple125	Kelso131	Heroshogala	9
Feb 9-63 7Hia	1 1-8	1:48⅘ft	2¼	128	45	42	12	12¾	Val'z'lal1	HcpS 91	Kelso 128	Ridan 129	Sensitivo	6
Jan30-63 8Hia	7 f	1:22⅘ft	2½	128	2h	32	43½	45½	Val'z'lal4	HcpS 89	Ridan 127	Jaipur 127	Merry Ruler	5
Dec 1-62 8G.S	1 1-2	2:30⅕ft	2-5	▲129	1h	13	13	15	Val'z'lal2	AlwS 105	Kelso 129	Bass Clef 117	Polylad	5

Nov 5 Lrl tc 1 1-8m fm 1:50⅘h Nov 4 Lrl tc 3f fm :37⅖b Nov 1 Lrl 7f m 1:27⅗b

5. A horse that races regularly, particularly one in good form, does not necessarily need any workouts to stay in shape. A prior victory without workouts is sufficient proof of this.

Ego Image B. f. 4, by Banners Image—Ego Trip, by Park Trip
Br.—Nelson W C Jr (Wash) 1982 3 2 0 0 $10,615
Own.—Paul J **117** Tr.—Leonard Jack R **$16,000** 1981 22 0 2 2 $13,667

2Feb82-2BM	6f	:231	:472	1:122ft	6¼	114	78	43	32	1no	Wilburn J7	Ⓕ 14000	78	EgoImage,SunIndSuccess,Let'sPrty	7
22Jan82-7BM	6f	:224	:47	1:121sl	8½	114	614	67¾	55¼	42	Wilburn J3	Ⓕ 20000	77	Powerette,GulfBreeze,DreminLuck	6
7Jan82-2BM	6f	:231	:472	1:13 gd	8¾	114	712	77¼	33½	1½	Wilburn J3	Ⓕ 10000	75	EgoImage,MorePrevue,Escort'sJoy	7
24Dec81-2BM	1 1/16	:474	1:14	1:474ft	7	115	68½	89	812	713	Leonard J7	Ⓕ 10000	47	CurrentLine,PrevueLss,MorePrevu	9
8Dec81-5BM	1 1/16	:471	1:113	1:444ft	11	114	67½	68¾	57½	54½	Leonard J8	Ⓕ 12500	70	Taukouwee,PrevueLass,CariQueen	12
26Nov81-5BM	1 1/16	:474	1:131	1:47 m	16	114	66	44	43½	43¾	Wilburn J1	Ⓕ 12500	60	GoldnPolcy,Cognton,LovngThoght	9
18Nov81-5Hol	1 1/16	:454	1:11	1:453ft	54	114	59	412	510	67½	Leonard J3	Ⓕ 18000	59	Trppr'sBty,DwnsGoldnB.,OtrProms	7
12Nov81-9Hol	1 1/16	:463	1:113	1:44 ft	26	113	59	612	716	722	Leonard J6	Ⓕ 16000	53	AhNhHeed,JoyousLegcy,DerFrnchy	7
31Oct81-9LA	6½f	:211	:454	1:181ft	18	114	85¾	78½	47½	45¾	Leonard J4	Ⓕ 20000	80	LittlHooly,SunshinRoom,RingofErn	8
3Oct81-8Lga	1 1/16	:47	1:13	1:462m	5¼	112	55	31½	46½	47¾	Leonard J2	ⒻⓈ 20000	59	PikePlace,Tertzarima,NameItMndy	6

Dec 19 BM 6f sy 1:18 b (d) NO WORKOUTS SINCE DEC. 19.

6. To better determine the readiness of a first-time starter or an absentee, the player should review the daily tabular workout listings for additional clues. In maiden special-weight (nonclaiming) races at the top-class racetracks, very few first-timers win without showing snappy speed in one or more training trials or drawing at least one rave review from the clockers. Even

fewer win without showing at least one very good workout at five furlongs or longer among other trials that stretch back over four, six, or eight weeks of preparation. A good workout from the starting gate is also reassuring.

In California, where the tracks are very fast and the purse structure is the best in the nation, first-time starters in better-grade maiden races must show solid speed in at least two or more workouts to be considered as potential contenders. In addition, the player would do well to familiarize himself with the handful of trainers who have been schooled in quarter horse racing. Trainers like Wayne Lucas, for instance, are dealing from strength when they send out well-bred youngsters who have begun to show honest speed in their four- and five-furlong training trials.

Landaluce — Dk. b. or br. f. 2, by Seattle Slew—Strip Poker, by Bold Bidder
Br.—SpendthriftFm&KernnFrncis (Ky) 1982 1 1 0 0 $9,350
Own.—French & Beal **116** Tr.—Lukas D Wayne
Lifetime 1 1 0 0 $9,350
3Jly82-4Hol 6f :22 :44^{3} 1:08^{1}ft *4-5 117 1$^{1\frac{1}{2}}$ 1^{3} 1^{6} 1^{7} Pincay L Jr^{6} ⒻMdn 96 Lndluc,MidnightRptur,MissBigWig 7
Jun 27 Hol 4f ft :46^{4} h Jun 21 Hol 5f ft :59^{4} h Jun 11 Hol 4f ft :47^{3} h May 31 Hol 4f ft :53 h

---

The next two examples show the kind of training regimen necessary to get maiden claiming-class juveniles ready for a winning try. Note the subtle but real difference in workout times between the $20,000 and $30,000 colts. If these horses were entered in top-class maiden company, faster workouts would be required to accept them as contenders, unless they were trained by a known ace.

Elroy Braun **118** Dk. b. or br. c (1974), by Old Bag—Marcy Lynx, by Mount Marcy.
Breeder, R. E. Schleicher (Ky.). 1976 0 M 0 0 ——
Owner, R. E. Schleicher. Trainer, S. Martin. $20,000
July 11 Hol (TR) 5f ft 1:01⅕hg July 7 Hol 4f ft :50h July 2 Hol 4f ft :49⅖h
June 27 Hol (TR) 5f ft 1:02hg June 22 Hol 4f ft :48⅗h June 17 Hol 4f ft :48⅗hg

---

Devil's Bluff **114** Dk. b. or br. c (1974), by Big Bluffer—Witchy Norma, by Crimson Satan.
Breeder, Braugh Ranches (Texas). 1976 0 M 0 0 ——
Owner, Braugh Ranches. Trainer, L. Regula. $30,000
July 22 Hol 4f ft :48⅘h July 18 Hol 1(TR) 5f ft :59⅗hg July 14 Hol 4f ft :47⅘h
July 10 Hol 6f ft 1:15⅖h July 4 Hol 1(TR) 5f ft 1:00⅗h June 27 Hol (TR) 5f ft 1:02⅕hg

---

It may seem hard to believe but when Landaluce's daddy, the great Seattle Slew, made his debut at Belmont Park on September 20, 1976, he had no published workouts in the Western edition of the *Form*. A few mediocre works were listed in the Eastern *Form*, but they were no indication of his true ability. Only the heavy play he received on the tote board suggested he was ready for a solid performance. Trainer Billy Turner, who managed this incredible horse to a two-year-old Championship and a Triple Crown sweep, is nobody's fool.

Seattle Slew **122** Dk. b. or br. c (1979⁴), by Bold Reasoning—My Charmer, by Poker.
Breeder, B. S. Castleman (Ky.). 1976 0 M 0 0 (——)

Owner, Karen L. Taylor. Trainer, William H. Turner, Jr.

---

7. A workout on the turf course is an extremely valuable clue to trainer intention. A good drill on the turf is excellent evidence of the horse's ability to handle such footing. Sometimes the trainer will enter such a horse in a grass race immediately following a good turf work; sometimes he will wait until the workout is no longer listed in the past performances. As a rule, it makes good sense to keep a special record of all good turf works.

BELMONT PARK –
(Turf) Course Firm (Dogs Up)

Four Furlongs			**Thirty Years**	**:47⅘**	**h**	Hosanna II	1:04⅗	h	Our Doctor	1.15	b
Captain Max	:49⅕	b	Yvetot	:50⅖	b	Ode to Romeo	1:04⅖	b	PoliticalCoverup	1:18	b
Duveen	:48	h	**Five Furlongs**			**Spanish Dagger**	**1:00⅖**	**h**			
Inward Bound	:49⅘	b	Alibhai's Luck	1:02⅕	b	**Six Furlongs**			**Seven Furlongs—1:20⅘**		
Manifest	:48⅘	b	Carlogie	1:02⅗	h	**Go Double**	**1:14⅗**	**h**			
Ruling All	:48⅘	h	Close to Noon	1:01⅗	h	Herculean	1:15	h	**Barcas**	**1:32⅖**	**b**
Run Tara Run	:49⅖	h	Evening Dance	1:02⅕	h	I'm All	1:17	b	I Encircle	1:33	b

SPANISH DAGGER (5) looks good.

The following horse gave ample evidence of her ability to handle turf racing in two workouts prior to her winning turf race on July 13, 1976.

Miss Gallivant **113** B. f (1973), by Gallant Man—Year Around, by Hill Prince.
Breeder, L. R. Miller (Md.).
Owner, Dr. S. or L. Miller. Trainer, L. Rettele.

1976	7	2	1	1	$16,180
1975	0	M	0	0	——

18Jun76	^{6}Hol	$1\frac{1}{16}$	:47 1:11^{1}1:42^{2}ft	3½	116	1^h	1½	1^4	1^6	HawleyS^2	Alw	83	Ⓕ MissGallivnt116	Save aLtle	7
11Jun76	^{6}Hol	6 f	:22^1 :45^{1}1:09^{2}ft	5	114	3½	1½	1½	1^3	HawleyS^5	Mdn	92	Ⓕ MsGallivant114	Shanagoldn	7
5Jun76	^{4}Hol	6 f	:22^1 :45^{2}1:09^{4}ft	7¼	114	$5^{1\frac{3}{4}}$	2½	$3^{3\frac{1}{2}}$	3^8	HawleyS^5	Mdn	82	Ⓕ MadamGaylady114	Deploy	9
26Mar76	^{4}SA	1	:46^{2}1:12^{1}1:38^{4}ft	3¼	116	1½	1^1	6^7	9^{22}	ValdezS^3	Mdn	53	Ⓕ BidBoldly116	Shamara	9
13Mar76	^{3}SA	$1\frac{1}{16}$	:46^{3}1:22^{2}1:46^{3}ft	8-5	▴116	$1^{1\frac{1}{2}}$	5^3	9^{15}	9^{37}	ToroF^3	Mdn	32	Ⓕ Chavalarious116	BidBoldly	9
22Feb76	^{3}SA	6 f	:21^3 :44^{3}1:10^{4}ft	6-5	▴117	$4^{3\frac{1}{2}}$	$4^{4\frac{1}{2}}$	$4^{5\frac{1}{2}}$	$5^{5\frac{3}{4}}$	HawleyS^2	Mdn	79	Ⓕ ContingentFee117	Jaunting	10
25Jan76	^{3}SA	6 f	:22 :45 1:10^{3}ft	2	▴117	$8^{7\frac{1}{2}}$	6^5	$5^{4\frac{1}{2}}$	$2^{2\frac{1}{2}}$	PincayLJr^6	Mdn	83	Ⓕ Wandle117	MissGallivant	11

July 9 Hol (tc) fm 1:28⅕h *July 2 Hol 6f ft 1:13h *June 26 Hol (tc) 5f fm 1:00⅘h

8. Improving workouts generally denote improving physical condition. With the workout line below, all that Patriot's Dream needs is a slight drop in class.

Patriot's Dream **113** Ch. c (1973), by Gunflint—Ambitious Lady, by Petare.
Breeder, Ocala Stud, Inc. (Fla.).
Owner, H. Allen. Trainer, E. Jacobs.

1976	7	1	1	2	$10,590
1975	5	1	0	1	$6,769

18Jly 76	^{8}Aqu	6 f	:22^1 :45^{1}1:10^{3}ft	16	112	3^3	3^3	$5^{3\frac{1}{2}}$	$6^{4\frac{1}{4}}$	VelasqzJ^2	HcpS	86	ArabianLaw112	FullOut	7
8Jly 76	^{8}Aqu	6 f	:22^2 :45^{1}1:09^{2}ft	11	113	$4^{1\frac{1}{2}}$	$5^{2\frac{1}{4}}$	$4^{2\frac{1}{2}}$	$3^{6\frac{1}{4}}$	MontoyaD^2	Alw	90	SoyNumeroUno111	ArabanLw	6
30Jun76	^{8}Aqu	1	:45^{1}1:08^{4}1:34^{1}ft	40	114	$2^{\frac{1}{2}}$	2^1	5^6	$6^{9\frac{1}{2}}$	MontyaD^4	AlwS	85	DanceSpell 114	Zen	6
22Jun76	^{5}Mth	6 f	:22^1 :45^{2}1:11^{4}ft	3-5	113	3^4	$3^{1\frac{1}{2}}$	4^3	$3^{6\frac{3}{4}}$	EdwrdsJW^4	Alw	74	KindIndeed118	SecondTerm	5
15Jun76	^{7}Mth	6 f	:22^1 :44^{3}1:10 ft	2¾	115	2½	2^1	2^3	$2^{3\frac{1}{2}}$	EdwrdsJW^6	Alw	86	SunnyClime120	Patriot'sDrm	6
30May76	^{6}Bel	Ⓣ 1	:45^{4}1:10 1:34^{3}fm	10	115	3^1	9^{12}	10^{20}	10^{26}	HrnandzR^7	Alw	72	FifthMarine115	Burundi	10
21May76	^{7}Bel	6 f	:22^1 :45^{2}1:10 ft	2	114	1^1	$1^{1\frac{1}{2}}$	1^2	1¾	VeneziaM^1	Alw	92	Patriot'sDrm114	FinanclWhiz	7

July 23 Bel (trt) 5f ft :59⅖h July 14 Bel (trt) 5f ft 1:00⅕h July 5 Bel (trt) 4f ft :49b

9. A series of closely spaced workouts or workouts mixed with racing ordinarily points out a horse in sound physical health. Very often the average horseplayer eliminates an active horse with mediocre finishes in his past performance profile without realizing how fit the horse really is. On the other hand, a horse in apparent good form cannot be expected to hold that form if the trainer insists on working the horse hard and fast every few days between starts. Studying the strengths and weaknesses of trainers is the only reliable way to make accurate judgments about this type of training regimen.

This horse is racing fit. She has shown improved speed in her recent starts. Pretty soon she's going to get a field she can lead from wire to wire.

Cameo Girl **116** Ch. f (1972), by Dandy K.—Octopus Girl, by Octopus
Breeder, J. E. Sowards (Ky.). 1975 9 1 1 0 $2.440
Owner, J. E. Sowards. Trainer, J. E. Sowards. $3.500 1974 11 1 3 1 $3.774

7 Nov75	^{1}CD	6 f	:23 :47^{3}1:15^{3}sy	10	115	1^{1}	1^{1}	$7^{4\frac{1}{4}}$	9^{10}	McCllrJW^{6}	3500	58	(F)Mark theSpt115	GameFce	12
3 Nov75	^{2}CD	6 f	:22^{2} :46^{1}1:12^{3}ft	90	116	3^{1}	$6^{3\frac{3}{4}}$	$8^{3\frac{1}{2}}$	9^{12}	McCllrJW^{9}	5000	71	(F)ImprsiveMry114	Hln'sMsic	9
25 Oct75	^{2}Kee	6 f	:22^{3} :46^{1}1:12^{1}ft	20f	109	3½	$3^{5\frac{1}{2}}$	$5^{6\frac{1}{2}}$	6^{12}	McCllrJW^{1}	5000	69	Proud Spirit 112	Fuel	10
18 Oct75	^{2}Kee	6 f	:23 :48^{1}1:14^{2}sy	9¾	114	$1^{1\frac{1}{2}}$	1^{1}	$6^{7\frac{1}{4}}$	9^{19}	BrmfldD^{11}	5000	51	(F)May'sJwll 115	TooMchCrn	12
11 Oct75	^{7}Beu	6 f	:23 :46^{1}1:11^{3}ft	57	119	$7^{5\frac{1}{4}}$	11^{13}	11^{18}	11^{22}	UrrutiaJ^{6}	Alw	66	Darby Dale 114	Scott Man	11
17 Feb75	^{8}Lat	5½ f	:24^{1} :50^{2}1:10^{3}m	5	108	$2^{1\frac{1}{2}}$	2^{h}	1^{h}	1no	McCulrJW^{2}	Alw	65	Cameo Girl 106	Just Miss	8
8 Feb75	^{5}Lat	6 f	:23 :46^{2}1:11^{1}ft	5¼	114	3^{2}	4^{6}	4^{11}	4^{21}	McCurJW^{3}	Alw	71	Dr.Abs116	Holloway'sMistke	6
18 Jan75	^{4}Cwl	4½	:22^{3} :47^{2} :54^{4}m	2½	114	5	$4^{2\frac{1}{2}}$	2^{2}	2^{6}	McCurJW^{4}	7500	82	Clemstone 122	Cameo Girl	6
Jan 2-75	^{8}Cwl	6½ f	1:25⅘sm	64	117	2½	2½	2^{h}	$7^{8\frac{1}{2}}$	McCu'rJW^{9}	Alw	62	Donda'sMir'e122	CoolItB'e Jan't'sDe't	10

Nov 1 CD 5f ft 1:05b **Oct 24 Kee 3f ft :37b** **Oct 22 Kee 5f ft 1:04b**

This horse is crying for a rest. Instead, he was entered in a stakes race against For the Moment and other top-class juvenile colts.

Heidee's Pal **122** B. c (1974), by Tinajero—Debbys Charm, by Debbysman.
Breeder, M. M. Garren (N. Y.). 1976 11 1 2 1 $16,404
Owner, M. M. Garren. Trainer, Gilbert Puentes.

3 Sep76	^{6}Bel	6 f	:22^{4} :46^{2}1:10^{4}ft	13	115	$6^{3\frac{1}{2}}$	$5^{2\frac{3}{4}}$	$4^{5\frac{1}{2}}$	$4^{7\frac{3}{4}}$	MapleE^{6}	Alw	80	HeyHyJ.P.115	Albi'sTrckStp	6
19 Aug76	^{8}Sar	6 f	:22^{2} :46 1:12^{2}ft	10	119	12^{10}	$10^{8\frac{3}{4}}$	$6^{4\frac{3}{4}}$	2^{2}	MapleE^{6}	AlwS	76	FratelloEd115	Heidee'sPal	17
9 Aug76	^{3}Sar	6 f	:22^{3} :46^{3}1:12 m	6¾	120	2½	3^{nk}	2½	5^{3}	MapleE^{5}	27500	77	JollyQuill 119	Strtp'sGlitters	8
28 Jly 76	^{5}Aqu	6 f	:22^{3} :46^{4}1:13^{1}ft	20	122	7^{7}	9^{9}	9^{11}	9^{7}	SantgoA^{5}	35000	70	Plantaris 119	PrinceNoName	9
17 Jly 76	^{7}Aqu	5½ f	:22 :45^{2}1:04^{4}ft	13	115	7^{7}	$7^{9\frac{1}{2}}$	6^{12}	6^{12}	SantiagoA^{6}	Alw	77	Bucksaw 115	Hey Hey J. P.	7
10 Jly 76	^{3}Aqu	5½ f	:22^{3} :47 1:05^{4}sy	5½	122	$3^{1\frac{1}{2}}$	$2^{1\frac{1}{2}}$	1^{1}	1^{nk}	StgoA^{8}	M25000	84	Heidee'sPal 122	PrinceNoNe	8
2 Jly 76	^{4}Aqu	5½ f	:23 :47 1.06 ft	2¼	122	$4^{1\frac{1}{2}}$	4^{3}	3^{3}	$3^{2\frac{1}{2}}$	StgoA^{3}	M25000	80	Bucksaw 122	Dobrynin	7
24 Jun76	^{4}Bel	5½ f	:23^{2} :47^{3}1:06^{2}ft	20	118	3^{1}	3^{nk}	2½	2^{2}	SngoA^{9}	M20000	81	PeppyPeppis122	Heidee'sPal	
16 Jun76	^{3}Bel	5½ f	:23^{4} :44 1:07 ft	14	118	5^{5}	$9^{8\frac{3}{4}}$	$8^{8\frac{1}{4}}$	$7^{9\frac{3}{4}}$	SngoA^{8}	M20000	70	HawaiianWays120	Dky'sBlrc	
28 May76	^{4}Bel	5½ f	:22^{4} :46^{3}1:05^{3}ft	49	117^{5}	$8^{7\frac{1}{4}}$	$9^{8\frac{1}{2}}$	9^{13}	9^{17}	MartinJE^{4}	Mdn	70	MedievalMn122	FirstPretse	10
21 May76	^{4}Bel	5½ f	:23 :46^{4}1:05^{4}ft	5¾	122	4^{2}	$5^{5\frac{1}{4}}$	7^{13}	7^{16}	TrtteR^{5}	M35000	70	FlagOfficer122	WincomaLss	10

Sept 9 Bel trt 4f ft :47⅗h **Sept 1 Bel 4f ft :50⅖h** **Aug 26 Sar trt 5f ft 1:02h**

10. Consult the clocker's comments, where available, for special mention of noteworthy training drills, fractional times, workouts in company, and other important clues. Pay particular attention to the tone of the clocker's remarks. If the comment is a positive one, you might well expect improvement from the horse in the next race or two. A good "horses to watch" list can be compiled this way, depending of course on the reliability of the clocker in question.

SAMPLE CLOCKER COMMENTS, BELMONT PARK, SEPTEMBER 1976

SEATTLE SLEW is sharp. WARM FRONT had all his speed. DANCE SPELL acts good. HONORABLE MISS was full of run. ASHMORE AND MAITLAND II were in company. BOLD FORBES is doing well. FIGHTING BILL had Jockey Day up.

Most of the horses who drew the comments above were well-known stakes horses. However, there were two strangers who worked in company on even terms, and the player might not have paid attention to the modest comment they received. But the moment Ashmore was exposed as a contender for the $350,000 Jockey Club Gold Cup, the value of Maitland II's stock increased.

Workouts in company are particularly useful to the trainer and the horseplayer. Very often a trainer will not know which of two lightly raced horses is the faster. A workout in company may provide a definitive answer. As you might imagine, one of the most reliable workout clues is a victory by the slower of two horses that worked in company. From that moment onward, the faster worker becomes a four-star entry in my "horses to watch" list. A young maiden working on even terms with a known stakes horse is another key clue provided by workouts in company.

SAMPLE CLOCKER COMMENTS, BOWIE, SEPTEMBER 1976

(4) BACAYE still retains her speed. (4) SILVER FLORIN had a high turn of speed in his trial. (5) INCA ROCA with jockey Snell in the irons went in fractions of :22.1, :34, :46.1, :59.1 galloping out in 1:12.4. (5) ROYAL DRAFTSMAN is ready for another winning effort. (6) MUM BOLD had a useful trial. Additional Workout on Oct 6, 75, ALTO REBOT (4F) :50 B.

Most of the above comments are quite helpful and to the point, but I would tend to downgrade the clocker's note on Royal Draftsman unless prior results demonstrated the particular clocker's reliability as a tout.

RUNNING STYLE AND THE DISTANCE FACTOR

While most racehorses tend to have a preferred racing distance and some horses are incapable of winning a race when out of their element, there is great power in the training regimen to alter the distance capability of the horse. In addition, there is a most intriguing and predictable relationship between each different distance and running style.

A good trainer can increase or decrease the distance potential of a horse through workouts, special equipment, and actual races at longer and shorter distances. Allen Jerkens does it all the time; so do hundreds of other trainers of lesser talent. The following two principles illustrate the manner in which the vast majority of horses react to distance manipulations:

1. A horse that has been sprinting will most often race closer to the lead or will even set the pace in a longer, slower-paced route event.
2. A horse that has been on the pace in a longer, slower route may be unable to cope with the faster pace of a sprint but is nevertheless likely to show improved stretch punch.

The past performance profiles below demonstrate both principles at work.

A Kiss For Luck *

Dk. b. or br. f. 3, by Reflected Glory—Painted Flag, by Dusty Canyon
Br.—Rancho Jonata (Cal) 1981 11 4 3 2 $267,924
Own.—Singer C B **117** **Tr.—Fanning Jerry**

31Dec81-8SA	7f	:22 3	:46 1	1:27 2hy	2¼	122	3 3	32½	1 2	13¾	PcLJr 1	Ⓕ[S]Cal Brdrs	63	AKissforLuck,FirstAdvance,JenG.	10
21Nov81-8Hol	1 1/16	:45 4	1:10 4	1:43 1ft	3¼e	120	2½	2½	32½	47¾	PincyLJr 6	ⒻHol Strlt	71	SkillfulJoy,HeaderCrd,FlyingPrtner	8
7Nov81-8SA	1 1/16	:45 3	1:10 2	1:43 ft	4	117	1hd	1½	11½	21½	PincyLJr 1	ⒻOak Leaf	84	HeaderCrd,AKissforLuck,ModelTen	9
7Oct81-8SA	7f	:22	:45	1:22 ft	*8-5	120	2½	2 1	12½	12¾	PincayLJr 4	ⒻAnoakia	90	AKissforLuck,SkillfulJoy,BllofRinir	8
6Sep81-8Dmr	1	:45 2	1:11	1:37 2ft	5¾	117	2hd	11½	1½	33¾	PncyLJr 11	ⒻDmr Deb	77	SkillfulJoy,MrlLAnn,AKissforLuck	12
5Aug81-8Dmr	6f	:22 1	:45	1:09 4ft	*4-5	119	2½	21½	2 3	22½	Pincay LJr 4	ⒻJr Miss	86	BuyMyAct,AKissforLuck,FrstAdvnc	6
24Jly81-8Dmr	5½f	:22 1	:45	1:04 2ft	*4-5	117	1 2	12½	1 5	16½	McCrrCJ 5	Ⓕ[S]C T BA	89	AKssforLuck,AgttdLdy,SpryColognn	5
11Jly81-8Hol	6f	:21 3	:44 4	1:11 2ft	3	116	2½	1hd	1 2	42¾	OlivrsF 7	ⒻHol Lassie	77	Ticketed,Orphan'sArt,FirstAdvnce	11
1Jly81-8Hol	5½f	:21 3	:45 2	1:05 2ft	2½	119	1hd	1½	11½	2nk	ShomkrW 1	ⒻNursery	84	Ticktd,AKissforLuck,UnchinMyHrt	9
17Jun81-8Hol	5f	:22 1	:46	:58 4fr	7	119	53¼	3 1	32½	3 2	VlnzlPA 6	ⒻCinderella	83	Orphn'sArt,UnchnMyHrt,AKssfrLck	7
15May81-4Hol	5f	:22 1	:46 1	:58 4ft	4½	116	1½	1½	1 2	12½	ValenzuelaPA 3	ⒻMdn	85	AKissforLuck,NoPlanning,IronGold	6

Mr. President *

Ch. g. 6, by Amazing—Fennel, by Revoked
Br.—Rathbun Mr-Mrs H (Va) 1982 6 2 0 0 $12,050
Own.—Onzo-Lara-Smith **114** **Tr.—Marble James L** **$16,000** 1981 16 1 4 1 $12,135
Lifetime 38 6 5 4 $35,935

17Apr82-7GG	6f	:22 2	:45 2	1:10 2ft	8¼	114	52½	42½	31½	41¾	Pyfer R 4	16000	85	Commish,MauiBlade,ShurisBronze	12
20Mar82-7GG	6f	:22 2	:46 1	1:11 2gd	6½	114	8 11	8 9	88¾	7 10	Pyfer R 3	16000	72	BuenCentvo,Commish,MrketChmp	9
13Mar82-7GG	6f	:22 3	:46 1	1:11 3gd	9¾	114	52½	4 1	2 1	1½	Pyfer R 2	12500	81	Mr.Presidnt,MyDonDon,BunCntvo	12
29Jan82-9BM	1 1/16	:47 1	1:12 2	1:58 3m	*9-5	116	1 4	11½	2 6	48½	Pyfer R 4	A6500	71	KnghtlyAnsr,PrtnrsnTxs,SmmtDnc	5
19Jan82-6BM	1 1/16	:47	1:11 4	1:45 1sy	13	121	1 2	2 1	46½	4 9	Pyfer R 6	Aw13000	64	Native Sheik,Cheektowaga.TopFool	8
1Jan82-4BM	1⅛	:47	1:11 3	1:52 1m	4½	113	1 5	1 3	1 2	1 5	Pyfer R 3	A6500	70	Mr.Prsidnt,VictorE.,KnightlyAnswr	6
18Dec81-9BM	1⅛	:47 1	1:12 2	1:51 3m	3½	113	1 3	1½	2 4	2 8	Pyfer R 6	A6500	65	KnghtlyAnswr,Mr.Prsdnt,MrknRd	10
4Dec81-9BM	1⅛	:47	1:11 4	1:52 ft	8¼	113	1 2	1 2	2hd	4½	Pyfer R 12	A6500	70	KnghtlyAnswr,VctorE.,SummtDnc	13
21Nov81-7BM	6f	:22 1	:45 1	1:11 1sy	4½	114	31½	2 1	2 2	3 1	Pyfer R 6	10000	83	WhstlngEnvoy,Grg'sDc,Mr.Prsdnt	11
14Nov81-5BM	6f	:22 1	:45 1	1:10 1gd	7¼	114	54¾	42½	3 2	21¼	Pyfer R 2	8500	88	MightyBrzen,Mr.President,Orli'sJt	12

Apr 28 GG 3f ft :36 h **Apr 14 GG 4f gd :50 h** **Apr 8 GG 3f ft :35 4 h** **Mar 8 GG 5f ft 1:01 3 h**

Glamazon
Ch. m. 6, by Restless Native—Queen of the Seas, by Turn-to
Br.—Winer E (Md)
Own.—Winer Mrs R **114** Tr.—Ravich Hyman

1981	3	1	0	0	$14,350
1980	9	3	4	1	$36,920
Turf	6	2	2	1	$35,150

13Jun81-7Bel	1 1/16 [T]:48 1:11 1:42 fm	7	115	712	58½	411	57¾	Venezia M1	ⒻAlw	83	Hemlock,Ldy'sSlipperII,InRhythym	7
18May81-7Bel	1¼ [T]:50 1:39 2:04 fm	5½	115	1hd	11	11	17	♦Maple E4	ⒻAlw	74	Glamazon, Proud Barbara, Esdiev	7
♦18May81—Dead heat												
8May81-1Bel	7f :23 :462 1:242ft	15	119	53½	55	59	511	Maple E3	ⒻAlw	69	Stephanie Leigh, Sight, Explorare	5
7Sep80-8Del	1 1/16 Ⓣ:4721:1121:43 fm	21	110	2hd	2hd	22	32¼	WrightDR8	ⒻParlo H	87	T.V.Highlights,NativeWine,Glamzon	9
16Aug80-9Del	1 1/16 Ⓣ:4711:1111:44 fm	11	114	2½	11	2½	22½	Diaz J L3	ⒻHcp0	81	LdyRobert,Glmzon,LikelyExchnge	10
4Aug80-9Mth	a1 1/16 Ⓣ:49 1:1311:454gd	3	115	44	41½	22½	23½	Fann B3	ⒻAlw	—	Keeler, Glamazon, Riddle's Reply	6
9Jly80-8Mth	1 Ⓣ:49 1:1231:381fm	6¾	120	1½	12	11½	15	Fann B5	ⒻAlw	84	Glamazon,HurricneCrol,PrettyDoes	7
25Jun80-5Bow	6f :234 :474 1:122ft	2	117	52¾	41¼	21½	21	Wright D R5	ⒻAlw	77	Connie Knows, Glamazon,SpinTwin	5
16Jun80-7Bow	6f :233 :464 1:112sy	*7-5	117	1hd	2hd	31	23½	Barrera C5	ⒻAlw	79	DanceASpell,Glmzon,Slerno'sAngel	6
12Mar80-8Bow	1 1/16 :491 1:144 1:473ft	*2	119	41½	63½	59	59½	Passmore W J6	ⒻAlw	58	NorthernHlo,JennyKing,ProSupper	8

Feb 9 SA 5f ft :58 h ●Feb 3 SA 5f ft :582 h Jan 30 SA 5f ft 1:001 h Jan 25 SA 5f ft :592 hg

Time Holder *
Ro. g. 6, by Old Time Nonsense—Freehold, by Promised Land
Br.—Nolan Farms Inc (Cal)
Own.—Goldblatt H C **1125** Tr.—Knight Terry $11,000
Lifetime 43 9 9 5 $44,338

1982	8	3	3	2	$19,749
1981	23	4	4	2	$18,710

6Apr82-4GG	6f :223 :461 1:12 gd	2¾	117	46½	45½	44	1nk	Winland W M2	11000	79	TimeHoldr,‡Trondroy,OnShotHugh	6
20Mar82-3GG	6f :224 :462 1:122sl	2¾	1095	57	55	55½	1nk	Steiner J J2	11000	77	TimeHolder,RoundHead,HiltoLddie	8
13Mar82-5GG	1 1/16 :471 1:114 1:464gd	5¾	114	48	34	12	2½	Lamance C8	c8500	68	MightyFella,TimeHolder,GoneAgin	10
20Feb82-5GG	6f :223 :461 1:113ft	8¾	115	31½	2hd	21	21½	Lamance C9	11000	79	Who'sLeder,TimeHoldr,Pp'sMrtini	11
6Feb82-3BM	6f :223 :452 1:104ft	5¾	115	42½	44½	44	3¾	Schacht R1	Ⓢ c8500	85	Trondroy,NewStrdegy,TimeHolder	10
23Jan82-1BM	6f :23 :463 1:114gd	*3½	115	84¼	63¾	34	35	Schacht R10	8500	76	Fast Bill, CherubKing,TimeHolder	12
9Jan82-4BM	6f :231 :463 1:113gd	3	115	33	33	25	24	Schacht R5	8500	78	AmorLtino,TimeHolder,StylishCrer	8
2Jan82-1BM	6f :231 :47 1:124sy	*2¼	118	33½	22	21½	1¾	Krasner S8	c6500	76	TimeHoldr,NwStrdgy,OnShotHugh	10
12Dec81-5BM	6f :223 :454 1:111sy	*2¼	117	43	22	22	25	Pincay L Jr8	8500	79	AfroWr,TimeHolder,FitchMountin	10
28Nov81-3BM	6f :232 :472 1:131m	4½	114	88½	78¼	79¾	66	Johnson B G2	8500	68	FildFormn,McroniPrnc,TopDrgoon	10

Mar 6 GG 5f ft 1:04 h

Skipat
Ch. m. 8, by Jungle Cove—Conquian, by Primera
Br.—Grondin J A (Conn)
Own.—Beler C P **123** Tr.—Blusiewicz Leon

1981	6	2	0	0	$130,817
1980	6	4	0	0	$112,102
Turf	2	1	0	0	$18,297

8Apr81-9OP	1 1/16 :462 1:111 1:441ft	7½	118	3½	32	43½	46¾	AsssCB7	ⒻApplBlmH	80	Bold'NDtrmnd,LBonzo,Krl'sEnough	7
14Mar81-9Bow	1¼ :48 1:373 2:043ft	6	115	1hd	2hd	32	46½	Black K2	Campbell H	90	Relaxing, Irish Tower, Peat Moss	9
7Mar81-9Bow	7f :222 :443 1:23 ft	3	124	21½	22	12	17½	AsssCB1	ⒻBFritchiH	90	Skipat,Whispy'sLss,SecretEmotion	8
22Feb81-8SA	1⅛ :444 1:084 1:471ft	59	118	22½	22	41	55	McHrDG9	ⒻStMrgIH	88	PrncssKrnd,GlorosSong,Ack'sScrt	10
24Jan81-8Aqu	1 1/16 ⊡:4711:1211:452ft	9-5	125	33½	33	53	67	Fell J4	ⒻAffect'ly H.	80	Plnkton,SweetMid,TheWheelTurns	6
10Jan81-7Aqu	6f ⊡:223 :4641:121ft	4¾	124	63¾	64½	2hd	12	AsssCB1	ⒻIntrboroH	83	Skipat, Soft Colors, No Joke	6

BREEDING

I am not what you might call a student of breeding. Over the years I have found that it makes better sense to study the horse's racing record and pay attention to the trainer's techniques. Nevertheless, I learned rather early in my handicapping adventures to pay more than a little attention to the bloodlines of horses in certain clear-cut situations. So I forced myself and learned to recognize the top two-year-old sires, the top mud sires, and of course the top turf sires. I did that because it was impossible to handicap certain races without knowing which newcomer to the turf or which first-time starter would be more likely to cope with a five-furlong race in April, a muddy track, or a grass race. I now find that there are fewer and fewer cases where breeding knowledge is the significant factor. Consider turf racing.

For the first sixty years of this century turf racing was not very popular in the United States. Few racetracks had turf courses and those that did scheduled perhaps one grass race every two or three days. Those were the good old days for a student of turf breeding, days when a few European-born sires produced virtually every turf race winner this side of the Atlantic.

During the 1960s American racetrack owners built dozens of turf courses. Belmont Park has two turf courses, as do Arlington Park and a few other tracks. Indeed three out of every five racetracks now card an average of six turf races a week, weather permitting. That's change number one. Change number two is the influence of breeding itself. Fifteen years ago there were only a handful of established turf sires; at present the number is well past 300 and counting.

As more and more horses are imported from Europe and as more and more are trained and raced over turf courses, the signal importance of breeding as a turf-racing indicator will continue to be diluted. In the meantime, I have compiled a list of the sixty most potent turf course sires, which may prove useful in evaluating two-year-olds and other first-time grass runners. Asterisks denote extraordinary turf potency. Get them while they last.

THE NEARCO FAMILY
Ambernash
Blushing Groom
Buffalo Lark
Diplomat Way
Drone
Explodent
Good Counsel
Hail to Reason
Halo
Hawaii
* Icecapade
Mill Reef
Mr. Leader
Mongo
* Naskra
Neartic
Never Bend
Nijinsky II
* Northern Dancer
One for All
Quack
* Roberto
* Royal Charger
* Secretariat
Sir Gaylord
* Sir Ivor
Stop the Music
Tell
T.V. Lark

THE RIBOT FAMILY
Arts and Letters
Graustark
Ribocco

Sir Ribot
* Tom Rolfe

THE HYPERION FAMILY
Assagai
Forli
Khaled
Swaps
* Vaguely Noble
Your Alibhai

THE PRINCEQUILLO FAMILY
* Advocator
* Prince John
* Round Table
* Speak John
**Stagedoor Johnny
* Tambourine

OTHER DOMINANT TURF SIRES
FROM ASSORTED FAMILIES
* Affirmed
* Alydar
Bagdad
Bolero
Cougar II
* Dr. Fager
Exclusive Native
* Gallant Man
* Herbarger
* Mac Diarmedia
Mr. Prospector
Raise a Native
Sea Bird
The Axe II

NOTE: *The best turf sire in the world is Stagedoor Johnny. That's particularly interesting because Stagedoor Johnny never raced on a grass course in his life.*
Speculating on turf-breeding success, data not yet available.

Mud

Although previous form in the mud (including strong workouts) is the best indication of ability to handle an off-track, a few sires and sire families tend to transmit the trait to nearly all their offspring. The most prominent of these are Bagdad, Better Bee, and the entire Bold Ruler line (especially What a Pleasure and the Bold Commander–Dust Commander wing of that line).

Cinteelo, a son of Jacinto, who in turn was a son of Bold Ruler, is a case in point. I think he was just about the best mud runner I've ever seen.

Cinteelo **119** **B. c (1973), by Jacinto—Teela, by Cockrullah.**
Breeder, J. M. Schiff (Ky.). **1976 6 2 0 2 $24,600**
Owner, J. M. Schiff. Trainer, T. J. Kelly. **1975 7 2 0 1 $13,260**

19 May76	^{8}Bel	$1\frac{1}{16}$	:46^{2}1:11^{3}1:43^{1}	sy	2-3	▲106^{5}	1^{2}	1$^{1\frac{1}{2}}$	1^{5}	1$^{7\frac{1}{2}}$	VelezRI^{3}	Alw	86	Cinteelo106	BabyFaceBeau	8
1 May76	^{6}Aqu	1	:45 1:09 1:34^{3}	sy	6-5e	▲104^{5}	2h	1^{1}	1^{5}	1$^{8\frac{1}{2}}$	VelezRI^{4}	Alw	93	Cinteelo 104	El Portugues	7
17 Apr76	^{6}Aqu	1	:45^{2}1:09^{4}1:35^{1}	ft	2	▲104^{5}	2h	2h	1$^{\frac{1}{2}}$	3$^{2\frac{3}{4}}$	VelezRI^{1}	Alw	87	RoughPunch112	BrownCat	7
27 Mar76	^{6}Aqu	1	:46 1:09^{4}1:35^{2}	ft	14	112^{5}	1h	1h	2h	3^{4}	VelezRI^{4}	Alw	85	MountSterlng119	NwCollctn	9
3 Mar76	^{6}Aqu	7 f	:23^{1} :46^{3}1:23^{4}	ft	3	115	3$^{2\frac{1}{2}}$	3^{3}	7^{11}	8^{14}	VelasquzJ^{5}	Alw	68	GabeBenzur117	PlayTheRed	8
24 Jan76	^{5}Hia	Ⓣ $1\frac{1}{16}$	1:43^{2}	fm	$4\frac{1}{2}$	119	4^{2}	3^{4}	3$^{5\frac{1}{2}}$	5$^{7\frac{1}{4}}$	CruguetJ^{1}	Alw	74	ControllerIke122	GrstarkLad	8
21 Nov75	^{7}Aqu	1	:44^{4}1:08^{4}1:34	sy	$1\frac{1}{2}$	117	1^{3}	1^{5}	1^{4}	1^{6}	CruguetJ^{4}	Alw	92	Cinteelo 117	Play the Red	9
15 Nov75	^{5}Aqu	7 f	:23 :46 1:23^{2}	ft	37	115	4$^{1\frac{1}{2}}$	5$^{1\frac{1}{4}}$	3^{nk}	4$^{2\frac{3}{4}}$	CruguetJ^{2}	Alw	81	JumpOvr theMn122	Wn'tYld	8
28 Aug75	^{4}Bel	7 f	:23^{1} :47 1:25^{1}	ft	3-2	▲120	5$^{3\frac{1}{2}}$	2$^{\frac{1}{2}}$	1$^{1\frac{1}{2}}$	1^{1}	CrugtJ^{6}	M35000	76	Cinteelo 120	Ahoy John	9

June 3 Bel 3f ft :35b **May 30 Bel trt 5f ft 1:01⅗h** **May 26 Bel trt 4f ft :52b**

Speed Sires

In early season two-year-old races at three, four, and five furlongs the emphasis is on speed and precocious physical development. If the get of Loom, Mito, Mr. Washington, and other one-dimensional sprint specialists are going to win any top-grade races, they will usually do so in these abbreviated dashes. Many win at first asking. Few hold their form beyond six furlongs.

Stamina Sires

Over the past dozen years, Leon Rasmussen, breeding columnist for the *Daily Racing Form*, has written extensively about

"Chef-de-Race Sires." Without going into a detailed explanation pro or con on the usefulness of this reference list, I should like to point out that Conquistador Cielo's Belmont Stakes win was a bit of a shock to the breeding community. Nevertheless, it didn't take them long to figure out a way to take advantage. In August, Cielo was syndicated for a staggering $36.4 million and everybody with a good broodmare would love to get in on that deal. The Chef-de-Race list is the original work of Dr. Franco Varola and is periodically updated by Rasmussen and a panel of breeding experts. It is reproduced here through the courtesy of the *Daily Racing Form* and Dr. Franco Varola.

CHEF-DE-RACE SIRES

BRILLIANT

Abernant	Gallant Man*	Noholme II*	Raise a Native
Black Toney*	Grey Sovereign	Northern Dancer*	Reviewer*
British Empire	Heliopolis	Olympia	Roman*
Bold Ruler*	Hyperion*	Orby	Royal Charger
Bull Dog	Intentionally	Panorama	Sir Cosmo
Cicero	My Babu	Peter Pan	Tudor Minstrel
Court Martial	Nasrullah	Phalaris	Turn-to*
Double Jay	Nearco*	Pharis	Ultimus
Fair Trial	Never Bend*	Pompey	What a Pleasure
Fairway			

INTERMEDIATE

Ben Brush	Equipoise*	Never Bend*	Star Shoot
Big Game	Full Sail	Petition	Sweep
Black Toney*	Gallant Man*	Pharos	The Tetrarch
Bold Ruler*	Havresac II	Polynesian	Ticino
Broomstick	Khaled	Princequillo*	Tom Fool*
Colorado	King Salmon	Roman*	Traghetto
Congreve	Mahmoud*	Sir Gaylord*	Turn-to*
Djebel	Nashua	Sir Ivor	T. V. Lark
Eight Thirty	Native Dancer*	Star Kingdom*	

CLASSIC

Alibhai	Gainsborough	Noholme II*	Sir Gallahad III
Aureole	Graustark*	Northern Dancer*	Sir Gaylord
Bahram	Gundomar	Persian Gulf	Star Kingdom*
Blandford	Hail to Reason	Pilate	Swynford
Blenheim II*	Herbager*	Prince Bio	Tom Fool*
Blue Larkspur	Hyperion*	Prince Chevalier	Tom Rolfe*
Brantome	Mahmoud*	Prince John	Tourbillon*
Buckpasser	Midstream	Prince Rose	Tracery
Bull Lea	Mossborough	Reviewer*	Vieux Manoir
Clarissimus	Native Dancer*	Ribot*	War Admiral
Count Fleet	Navarro	Rock Sand*	
Equipoise*	Nearco*	Sicambre	
Exclusive Native	Never Say Die	Sideral	

SOLID

Asterus	Discovery	Princequillo*	Tantieme
Bachelor's Double	Fair Play*	Right Royal	Teddy
Ballymoss	Graustark*	Rock Sand*	Vatout
Blenheim II*	Herbager*	Round Table	Worden
Bois Roussel	Man o' War	Sea-Bird	
Chaucer	Oleander	Sunstar	

PROFESSIONAL

Admiral Drake	Dark Ronald	Mieuxce	Spearmint
Alcantara II	Donatello II	Ortello	Sunny Boy
Alizier	Fair Play*	Precipitation	Tom Rolfe*
Alycidon	Foxbridge	Rabelais	Tourbillon*
Bayardo	Hurry On	Ribot*	Vaguely Noble
Bruleur	La Farina	Sardanapale	Vandale
Chateau Bouscaut	Le Fabuleux	Solario	Vatellor
Crepello	Massine	Son-in-Law	Wild Risk

Brilliant: speed potency of the highest order, with most stakes winners up to one mile.

Intermediate and **Classic:** *potency up to and including the true Derby distance of 1½ miles, by European standards.*

Solid and **Professional:** sire lines for stayers and marathon runners.

NOTE: *An asterisk following a sire's name indicates he has been placed in two separate classes. Therefore, his influence in any generation is likely to be divided equally between those two classes.*

OPTIONAL EQUIPMENT

BLINKERS: There is nothing like a pair of blinkers (eye cups) to help keep a horse's mind on its business, particularly a young horse that has had a difficult time running a straight course. Blinkers also tend to improve a horse's gate-breaking ability or early speed; and as a tool of last resort blinkers sometimes help the quitter type—the kind that stops in its tracks the moment another horse challenges it for the lead. If the quitter can't see the competition, it just might hold on long enough to get a piece of the purse.

Although more than half of the 70,000 horses racing in America go to the post with blinkers, "blinkers on" for the first time is generally a very positive sign of trainer intention. "Blinkers off" is not so easy to interpret.

In the case of a speedball, or perhaps a quitter type, the removal of blinkers may help the horse relax a bit and conserve some of its energy for the stretch. A few horses also run better when they see the competition. For obvious reasons, some trainers remove blinkers when they send a sprinter into a longer race or, conversely, put them on when a router is seriously meant in a sprint.

In the East the oversized edition of the *Daily Racing Form* carries blinker information in the past performance profile, but elsewhere players must rely on result charts to learn about this important piece of equipment.

MUD CAULKS: If the track is muddy, heavy, or slow or the turf course is anything but firm or hard, the addition of mud caulks is a sign of trainer intent; it is also often helpful to the horse itself.

Mud caulks are horseshoes with small prongs for better traction. On fast or hard racing surfaces these shoes can do damage to the horse's ankle or hoof, but on a soggy surface, especially on a soggy turf course, mud caulks are a distinct advantage.

The trainer is a cheapskate or a fool if he consistently avoids spending the extra few dollars for mud-caulked horseshoes when conditions are bad enough to warrant them. And the player is taking a big risk if he pays no attention to this information when it is available.

STEEL SHOES AND BAR SHOES: The player takes a bigger risk investing money on horses equipped with steel shoes or bar shoes, unless the horse in question has won with that kind of equipment before. Both types are danger signals. The horse usually has foot problems, and the shoe is an attempt to give more secure footing at the cost of extra, unfamiliar weight.

I am sorry to report that at present there are a number of racetracks that do not care about the fan sufficiently to provide a working shoe board on the grounds. Please yell at the general manager of any such racetrack for me too.

BANDAGES: Many trainers apply bandages on the rear legs as a matter of course to keep a horse from hitting itself in close quarters. But the presence of front leg bandages may have distinctly negative implications: a minor injury or a weak ankle or a sore muscle. Front leg bandages are chiefly used for extra support, and unless the player knows that the horse has raced well with them before (Forego, for example) or is expert at evaluating the horse in motion during the post parade, it is wise to be suspicious.

On muddy racetracks I will not bet a horse with front leg bandages because of the extra weight that is bound to adhere to these wrappings. Try running 100 yards yourself with an ounce of bandages taped to each ankle if you doubt my point. This act of temperance has cost me only nine otherwise qualified winners in twenty-two years.

PHYSICAL APPEARANCE

It takes a trained eye and many years of experience to reach valid conclusions about physical fitness on sight. A few basics should help; but I caution you to pay close attention to the clues in the *Racing Form* until you have mastered the art.

NEGATIVE SIGNS: Excessive kidney sweat between the flanks. And on cool days, heavy sweating of any kind in the paddock or post parade. Fractious, uncontrollable behavior during the post parade and warm-up period. Unusual swelling at the knee joints. Stiff-leggedness. A gimpy stride, favoring one leg. Cantankerous or listless behavior. A dull coat.

POSITIVE SIGNS: Aggressive but controllable behavior in the post parade and warm-up. A fluid transition from a walking gait to the gallop to the run. Attentive, alert behavior nearing the gate (watch the ears and head). A well-groomed, shiny coat.

JOCKEYS

Most trainers have alliances with one or more jockeys. Some jockeys ride every race for the trainer; others ride only when the trainer is serious. The player should learn who the top jockeys are, who rides for what stable, and who can't ride a merry-go-round.

Some trainers like to use apprentice jockeys because of the three-, five-, seven-, or ten-pound weight concession permitted during their apprenticeship.

My standards for jockeys may not be your standards, but I will play a well-qualified contender ridden by a hot apprentice, by an established veteran or star, by a rider who has won with the horse before, or by a stable favorite. Under no circumstances will I play a horse ridden by a ten-pound apprentice or a proven incompetent.

I do not discriminate against women jockeys, but there are few I am currently impressed with. Mary Alligood is by far the best, while Julie Krone and Amy Rankin seem worthy of support under most circumstances. Karen Rogers is also very good, but she has suffered so many serious injuries in her brief career that I worry about her and wonder if she shouldn't apply herself to training, or else take a long vacation before attempting her eighty-eighth comeback. Most of the rest you can keep, although I am sure the day isn't too far away when a woman apprentice will wind up leading the nation in victories.

In handicapping, the jockey factor is not one that reduces itself to simple dos or don'ts. The player simply has to watch races very carefully to assess the strengths and weaknesses of the prominent riders on the local circuit.

Some of the best of them wind up boxed, blocked, or hopelessly outfoxed without rhyme or reason. And we have also seen prominent names dragged through court testimony about fixed or suspiciously run races. It is a tough, exacting life to be a 115-pound horserider and it is the rare jockey who makes a full career without arousing controversy.

All too many of them—like Ron Turcotte—wind up in wheelchairs. Others, like Alverdo Pineda and his brother Robert, have lost their lives on the job. That's no joke. The risks are enormous and the unwritten code of macho ethics that comes with the territory can exert an unhealthy influence on a slumping rider's judgment. And there are always a few trainers willing to play loose with the rules.

I have a lot of admiration and respect for jockeys who conduct themselves honestly, trying to win as many races as possible.

Put controversial Angel Cordero Jr. on a horse and you know you will get an intelligent, aggressive ride, especially if he's got a fair chance. Put Jean Luc Samyn on a grass runner and watch how he saves all possible ground on the clubhouse turn, easing outside for a late run when that is the only way to get clear.

Eddie Maple and Chris McCarron are as steady as they come and Laffit Pincay Jr. has the strongest finishing technique in the game.

Jorge Velasquez is also a solid finisher who knows his way home at any distance on any course. And before he got hurt in a spill at Saratoga in 1978, Steve Cauthen was as good as Willie Shoemaker, Eddie Arcaro, or Bill Hartack at their best.

Cauthen's rides aboard Affirmed in the 1978 Triple Crown chase were Hall of Fame material. But after his injury, he lost all of his timing and needed to go to England to regain his confidence. Which brings up one last point about jockeys.

At one time or another, all of them hit slumps. Terrible slumps. Like zero for thirty-five, or two for sixty. (Cauthen was zip for 110 in California during the winter of 1979.) Not only should the player avoid these jockeys when they are losing, but he should expect improvement from the horses they rode when a switch to another rider takes place.

A decade ago, Johnny Rotz, a solid twenty-year veteran, was riding so poorly that the "Rotz off" angle produced six longshot winners in two weeks and a dozen or more during the next two months. Mr. Rotz apparently got the message and retired gracefully the following winter.

14.
The Drug Factor

SEVENTH RACE CD 34634 May 4, 1968

1 1-4 MILES. (Northern Dancer, May 2, 1964, 2:00, 3, 126.) Ninety-fourth running KENTUCKY DERBY. Scale weights. $125,000 added. 3-year-olds. By subscription of $100 each in cash which covers nomination for both the Kentucky Derby and Derby Trial. All nomination fees to Derby winner, $500 to pass the entry box, $1,000 additional to start, $125,000 added, of which $25,000 to second, $12,500 to third, $5,000 to fourth. $100,000 guaranteed to winner (to be divided equally in event of a dead heat). Weight, 126 lbs. The owner of the winner to receive a gold trophy. A nomination may be withdrawn before time of closing nominations. Closed Thursday, Feb. 15, 1968, with 191 nominations.
Value of race $165,100. Value to winner $122,600; second, $25,000; third, $12,500; fourth, $5,000.
Mutuel Pool, $2,350,470.

Index	Horses	Eq't	A	Wt	PP	¼	½	¾	1	Str	Fin	Jockeys	Owners	Odds to $1
34451Aqu1	—Dancer's Image		3	126	12	14	14	$10^{\frac{1}{2}}$	8^{h}	1^{1}	$1^{1\frac{1}{2}}$	R Ussery	Peter Fuller	3.60
34402Kee1	—Forward Pass	b	3	126	13	3^{2}	4^{4}	3^{4}	2^{2}	$2^{\frac{1}{2}}$	2^{nk}	I Valenz'ela	Calumet Farm	2.20
34402Kee3	—Francie's Hat		3	126	10	11^{3}	11^{2}	7^{2}	7^{2}	4^{2}	$3^{2\frac{1}{2}}$	E Fires	Saddle Rock Farm	23.50
34402Kee2	—T. V. C'mercial	b	3	126	2	$9^{\frac{1}{2}}$	8^{1}	9^{1}	$6^{\frac{1}{2}}$	5^{h}	4^{1}	H Grant	Bwamazon Farm	24.00
34307CD4	—Kentucky Sherry		3	126	4	$1^{\frac{1}{2}}$	1^{2}	1^{2}	1^{h}	3^{2}	5^{1}	J Combest	Mrs Joe W Brown	f-14.70
34325CD2	—Jig Time	b	3	126	3	$7^{1\frac{1}{2}}$	$6^{\frac{1}{2}}$	$6^{\frac{1}{2}}$	4^{h}	6^{h}	$6^{\frac{1}{2}}$	R Brouss'rd	Cragwood Stable	36.30
34425GG2	—Don B.		3	126	7	5^{2}	5^{2}	5^{1}	$5^{1\frac{1}{2}}$	7^{4}	7^{5}	D Pierce	D B Wood	35.50
34307CD2	—Trouble Brewing		3	126	5	$12^{\frac{1}{2}}$	9^{1}	11^{2}	13^{4}	12^{4}	8^{nk}	B Thornb'rg	Coventry Rock Farm	f-14.70
34325CD1	—Proper Proof		3	126	11	13^{3}	12^{1}	12^{2}	11^{2}	$8^{1\frac{1}{2}}$	9^{4}	J Sellers	Mrs Montgomery Fisher	9.90
34325CD4	—Te Vega	b	3	126	6	8^{h}	13^{h}	13^{1}	12^{2}	9^{2}	$10^{\frac{3}{4}}$	M Mang'llo	F C Sullivan	f-14.70
34307CD1	—Captain's Gig		3	126	9	2^{h}	2^{h}	2^{1}	3^{2}	10^{2}	$11^{1\frac{1}{2}}$	M Ycaza	Cain Hoy Stable	6.10
34451Aqu2	—Iron Ruler		3	126	1	$10^{\frac{1}{2}}$	$7^{\frac{1}{2}}$	$8^{\frac{1}{2}}$	9^{h}	11^{1}	12^{3}	B Baeza	October House Farm	5.70
34325CD3	—Verbatim	b	3	126	8	6^{h}	10^{h}	14	14	14	13no	A Cord'o Jr	Elmendorf	37.40
34402Kee5	—Gl'ming Sword	b	3	126	14	$4^{\frac{1}{2}}$	$3^{\frac{1}{2}}$	4^{h}	10^{2}	13^{1}	14	E Belmonte	C V Whitney	31.20

f-Mutuel field.

Time, :22⅕, :45⅘, 1:09⅘, 1:36⅕, 2:02⅕. Track fast.

$2 Mutuel Prices:			
9-DANCER'S IMAGE	9.20	4.40	4.00
10-FORWARD PASS		4.20	3.20
7-FRANCIE'S HAT			6.40

Gr. c, by Native Dancer—Noors Image, by Noor. Trainer, L. C. Cavalaris, Jr. Bred by P. Fuller (Md.).

IN GATE—4:40. OFF AT 4:40½ EASTERN DAYLIGHT TIME. Start good. Won driving.

DANCER'S IMAGE, void of speed through the early stages after being bumped at the start, commenced a rally after three-quarters to advance between horses on the second turn, cut back to the inside when clear entering the stretch at which point his rider dropped his whip. Responding to a vigorous hand ride the colt continued to save ground to take command nearing the furlong marker and was hard pressed to edge FORWARD PASS. The latter broke alertly only to be bumped and knocked into the winner, continued gamely while maintaining a forward position along the outside, moved boldly to take command between calls in the upper stretch and held on stubbornly in a prolonged drive. FRANCIE'S HAT, allowed to settle in stride, commenced a rally after three-quarters and finished full of run. T. V. COMMERCIAL closed some ground in his late rally but could not seriously menace. KENTUCKY SHERRY broke in stride to make the pace under good rating, saved ground to the stretch where he drifted out while tiring. JIG TIME faltered after making a menacing bid on the second turn. PROPER PROOF was always outrun. CAPTAIN'S GIG tired badly after prompting the issue for three-quarters. IRON RULER failed to enter contention. GLEAMING SWORD broke alertly but sharply to the inside to bump with FORWARD PASS, continued in a forward position for five furlongs and commenced dropping back steadily.

NOTE: DANCER'S IMAGE DISQUALIFIED FROM PURSE MONEY BY ORDER OF CHURCHILL DOWNS STEWARDS, MAY 15, 1968 AND RULING SUSTAINED BY THE KENTUCKY STATE RACING COMMISSION

On the first Sunday in May 1968 the ninety-fourth running of the Kentucky Derby was decided in the laboratory of the state chemist. A small trace of the prohibited painkilling drug phenylbutazone was found in the urine sample of Dancer's Image, the winner of the world's most famous horserace. Thoroughbred racing in America hasn't been the same since.

Today phenylbutazone ("Bute") and the controversial diuretic furosemide (Lasix) are legal in a dozen racing states (including Kentucky) and are used promiscuously nearly everywhere else. What this means to the future of racing I can only guess, but in the 1980s there remain serious questions about the sport's willingness to adopt an open, well-defined policy toward curbing drug use for racing purposes.

Bute tends to reduce swelling in the joints and dulls the horse's sensory apparatus. Lasix, an effective treatment to curb bleeding in the nasal passages, flushes out watery substances with amazing efficiency. The sudden widespread use of these and other drugs, detectable and undetectable, have changed the nature of the sport and threaten to undermine the essence of handicapping. So long as racing commissioners and track owners refuse to join together in a nationwide program to fund research for sophisticated drug detection, the sport faces the prospect of more scandals during the coming decade.

I have personally conducted studies on horse performance where drug information was made available to the public, and in 1974 and 1975 I published reports in *Turf and Sport Digest* and in *The New York Times*. A special research commission working at the request of the New York State Racing and Wagering Board also delved into this subject and shared similar concerns. It has been nearly six years since this information was brought to the public's attention and despite a lot of speeches and a lot of correspondence, there is still much fundamental work to be done.

The key facts about drugs as they affect the horseplayer are as follows:

1. Because drugs interfere with the horse's warning system (pain), more horses are breaking down with drugs than without them.

2. Administering Lasix for the first time can and often does create a wake-up effect.

3. Although the regular use of Bute is widespread, it is impossible to measure its value as a handicapping factor.

4. In some cases either or both drugs can act as a screen to the detection of other drugs.

5. The public disclosure of drug information has improved in a few scattered states. But most states prefer to keep horseplayers in the dark and have only themselves to blame for the loss of public confidence.

6. The testing procedures used to protect against drug abuse are not sufficient to cope with the variety of sophisticated drugs currently on the market. A multimillion dollar, nationwide, industry-run testing laboratory is the only realistic answer to this problem, but there is presently little interest in that proposal.

7. It is not possible to tell whether trainers who persistently put over dramatic form reversals are in fact training their horses from the bottle. But the player should keep a record of all such horsemen for future reference.

8. If the player is suspicious of the drug factor to the extent that he begins to blame defeats on it, he has probably lost touch with other aspects of his game. Nevertheless, he could do a tremendous service to racing if he saved the past performance profiles of such suspicious defeats and took them up with a competent steward or racing writer at his favorite track. Contrary to typical racetrack cynicism, most racing officials are sensitive to this issue and would appreciate a sincere, well-documented complaint.

A little fan pressure is the best way to keep these folks on the ball. If all else fails, write to me, care of the publisher. I'm no crusader, but this is one issue worth caring about.

15.
To Bet or Not To Bet,
and How Much?

When a gambler goes to Las Vegas for a weekend of roulette, craps, or blackjack, he should know in advance that the percentages constantly favor the house. Before the payoff odds are calculated, approximately 3 to 6 cents is raked off the top of every dollar wagered and the payoff odds are always lower than the actual mathematical odds.

This of course is the house take, and except for the one-in-a-million blackjack memory expert, no amount of skill will change the odds to the player's favor. I'm sorry folks, but the only way to beat the house is through unabashed luck—the longer one plays craps or roulette, the greater the probability for a wipeout.

A good casino gambler, then, is simply one who knows to quit if he's lucky enough to be ahead.

In betting on pro football and other team sports, the point spread theoretically balances out the action between supporters of two competing teams, and the player usually pays a 10 percent charge, or "vigorish," for the privilege of betting with a bookie. I won't go into the theories of proper football betting strategy in this book other than to say that racetrack bettors should only have it so easy. Consider the following:

By flipping a coin to determine which team should be played, anyone can expect approximately 50 percent winners. With any degree of skill at all 55 to 65 percent of spot-play winners is not only possible, but anyone calling himself a professional should be ashamed if he can't do that well. (Are you there Jimmy the Greek?)

At the racetrack the average field has nine horses, most of which have never faced each other before and never will again. The best horse in the race may get into trouble, step on a pebble, lose its jockey, jump a puddle, or decide to go for a swim in the infield lake. The jockey may have a toothache or commit a terrible mistake, or the stewards may have or do the same.

Meanwhile, for all his trouble in researching the complexities of racing, the horseplayer is told that the state and the track will take away some 20 cents per dollar on straight win bets and that much and more on most combination bets like the exacta or big triple. That's a tough nut to overcome. Good handicapping and thorough research help, but sound money management is just as important.

Whether you are a four-time-a-year novice or a once-a-week regular, the way you play your money at the track will determine whether you win or lose and how much you win or lose. Through skill, the odds can be turned to the player's favor, but it takes intelligent handling of betting capital to be in a position to take advantage. At 20 cents on the dollar, you can get wiped out pretty fast if you do not have a healthy respect for your money.

If you know something about two-year-old sprint racing but lack an understanding of stakes, claimers, or routes, it would be smart to concentrate your strongest bets on your specialty. If you use speed figures and know how to recognize a speed-figure standout, it would be foolish to bet the same amounts on races when you have no reason to be so confident. And if you do not know *what* you know, you should spend some time finding out.

Keep a record of your bets. Be honest with yourself.

Do you know how to spot a track bias when you see one? Do you have a feel for turf racing or stakes? Are claiming-class sprints easier than allowance-class routes? Do you have special insights about the winning and losing tendencies of the top trainers in your area? Perhaps you find it easy to narrow the field to live contenders but very difficult to separate the winner from the second- or the third-best horse. Can you pass up a race or an entire card, or must you have a bet every half-hour?

Asking questions like those above will do wonders for your profit-and-loss statement. They will also bring to light the strengths and weaknesses in your game.

When I go unprepared to a strange racetrack, I do not bring very much money. Without the necessary insights about the track, the trainers, and all the other fundamentals that influence results, I am no more likely to win than thousands of other players in the crowd. I have my winning days at such race-tracks—I do pay attention—but I have to be lucky and extremely cautious with my money.

When I do prepare for a serious assault on a track, I do the research necessary to uncover any prevailing track bias and learn as much as I can about the trainers, jockeys, and horses I will be asked to compare. At most racetracks that kind of preparation takes about thirty to fifty hours of advance work, requires two hours of daily follow-up, and yields approximately one to three good bets a day; but that is not enough action for me and I know it.

Most racing fans, myself included, like something to root for in almost every race. It's tough to sit through a whole card waiting around for the ninth-race goodie. So most of the time I don't.

Instead, and as a concession to my personality, I separate my money into serious *prime* bets and *action* bets. Nothing would upset my concentration more than a $40 winner that I liked well enough to think about but didn't bet a dime on. Perhaps you feel the same way.

I have two very stiff requirements for a serious prime bet. Bitter experience has taught me that holding to these requirements is the safest way to guard my capital and maximize my skill.

When I think the horse deserves a 50 percent or better chance to win the race, I expect to be right at least 50 percent of the time. That's my first requirement. The second is a payoff price of 8–5 ($1.60–$1.00) or higher.

Fifty percent may seem to be an outrageously high win percentage to achieve, but with the tools and insights I have been detailing in this book it really isn't all that difficult.

King Leatherbury dropdowns coming back after a month's rest win 60 percent of the time. Front runners on the rail in 1¹/₁₆-mile races at Pimlico win almost as often. Other high-percentage strategies and tools include Van Berg repeaters going up in class, fast Calder front runners shipping into Gulfstream, Tony Basile–trained first-time starters at Keenland, fit Jerkens–trained horses right back or stretching out in distance, minor track classification codes, hidden class dropdowns in allowance races, speed horses ready to get the lead for the first time, post position studies, Key Races, trainer patterns, clocker's comments, result charts, class pars, speed figures, track bias, and so on. Anyone willing to put in the necessary research time can pick 50 percent spot-play winners with these tools and insights. And the prices will astound you.

I have personally taught much of this material to nine of my friends, including two absolute novices. Within one year all were able to approach or exceed 50 percent results. Nothing is stopping you from achieving as much. If, however, you find your winning average is lower—35 percent, for example—you must adjust your minimum-odds requirement to compensate.

Logically, 35 percent winners would require payoff odds of 5–2 or better, but frankly I am not at all sure it is possible to win at the races without being able to pick a higher percentage of winners. A lower win percentage is an invitation to long losing streaks. I further believe my criteria help create enough selectivity to provide safe but profitable betting opportunities. By these standards an odds-on favorite can never be a prime bet, unless I am playing it to place and getting a bargain minimum of 80 cents on the dollar.

An exacta or daily double can never be a prime bet unless the total investment needed to cover the selected combinations yields a 50 percent chance of cashing a winning ticket at an expected 8–5 or better. To fulfill the two requirements in the case of a key horse wheel, it is sometimes necessary to buy extra combinations on the lowest anticipated payoffs. And in those cases where I am confident to play one horse as a key with two, three, or four others, I reduce my total investment in the exotic bet and place at least some money in the win pool to protect myself. I may also be inclined to use my key horse underneath the three contenders for additional protection. For solid crisscross plays using three or four live contenders, I will rarely invest more than half of my typical prime betting unit. Exactas often present inflated payoff possibilities, but the risk is usually increased as well (see Appendix).

I repeat, a prime bet is an estimated 50 percent chance to cash a winning ticket at 8–5 or better. All other bets are action bets and I separate the two categories in the following manner:

PRIME BETS: A maximum of 5 to 8 percent of total betting capital for the meet per play; 8 percent reserved for superconfident plays. Maximum of three prime bets allowed in one day, unless first two out of three win.

ACTION BETS: A maximum of 2 to 3 percent of total betting capital for the meet per day. On a day with three prime bets, no action bets are permitted beyond a token $2 to $5 per race.

EXPENSES: Deduct 1 percent per day.

For example, if my total available betting capital for the meet is $2,000, a prime bet would be $100 to $160, depending on how well I have been doing at the meet and how much more than a 50 percent edge the horse really has. On that scale I would feel free to play the rest of the card with $40 to $60 on contenders lacking prime betting qualifications, on wild stabs, daily doubles, or exactas.

As capital increases (or decreases) the amount of the bet changes, but not the percentages.

I expect to lose money with my action bets and I do. But I have a lot of fun with them; I watch races more carefully because of them, and they help keep my equilibrium. A small price to pay for peace of mind.

I realize of course that not many racing fans can afford to put aside $2,000 to bet on horseraces. Not many should either. But the truth is many horseplayers lose that much and more in a season, and if you go to the racetrack regularly and want to improve your chances of success, you must take care to plan your betting activity along similar guidelines.

Whether your typical daily capital is $100 or you bring considerably more to the track, the point is to consolidate the power of your money on the races in which you have some insight.

Betting odds-on favorites is taking the worst of it. Betting a large percentage of your capital in the daily double or big triple is a sure-fire way to put yourself in the hole to stay. Betting a disproportionate amount of your money on any one race places too much emphasis on the luck factor. Doubling up your bet to "get even" on the last race is a way to triple your losses in track record time.

Every horseplayer has losing streaks. But there is no reason why a player should lose serious money during such streaks.

Losing three or four prime bets in a row is a warning sign, a sign to cut down all serious play until the problem is solved. Maybe you have lost touch with the track or have failed to note the presence of a hot trainer. Maybe you are bothered by personal problems, or a tough defeat has upset you more than you thought.

Take a day or two off. Go to a ballgame. Rediscover your family and friends. Watch TV, and if that doesn't work, try a few exercises in fundamentals.

Rather than trying to pick the race winner, try instead to pick the worst horse in the race or the horse most likely to be in front ten strides out of the gate. Check the past three days of racing. Has there been a subtle change in the bias? Has the bias disappeared? It happens.

These exercises can be fun, and like a baseball player who needs to take extra batting practice, you will find they help straighten out many a weakness. Try some of them, or invent others to suit your fancy. Lighten up. It's only a game.

16.
La Prevoyante to Win, My Wife to Place

With the advent of the big triple and other popular, exotic forms of wagering, very few racing fans have been schooled in the finer points of place and show betting. While no argument will be presented here to suggest an emphasis on the minor payoff spots, there are times at the track when it pays handsomely to think second best.

In the early 1960s I remember being at a New York racetrack when so much money was bet on the mighty Kelso to win and so little was bet on him to place that he paid $2.40–$3.60–$2.40 across the board. By thinking win, and win only, the crowd in attendance that day offered one of the safest bets of modern times, an overlay of gigantic proportions. If Kelso was worth 20 cents on the dollar to win the race, which I will not debate, he was surely worth 80 cents on the dollar to finish second or better. It's doubtful Lloyds of London could have offered a better deal.

Of course, most racetrack crowds do not let such absurd situations occur every day, but I've seen enough $3.60 win, $4.00 place payoffs in my lifetime to give the tote board a close look before parting with my money. And if in truth I wasn't always careful to do that, my wife, Laurie, gave me ample cause to do so a few years ago.

At Saratoga during the 1972 racing season Laurie thought it would be a good idea if she came out to the track to see Robyn Smith, a pretty tough cookie and one of the best female jockeys in America. My friend Andy Beyer and I traded in our two reserved seats plus a dollar for three seats together. Andy and I were enjoying a spectacular meeting but didn't know we were about to miss out on the easiest bet of the year.

During the first six races on the card Robyn won one and lost one; so did Laurie. Andy and I had won the one Robyn and Laurie lost and had lost the one they both had won. Not that we were prejudiced against female jockeys or anything; we just figured one race *right* and one race *wrong*. So the day went. Andy and I had shoved almost half a thousand through the windows to be plus $40 apiece. Laurie had bet maybe $8 and was ahead $50.

I wasn't depressed, far from it, but was glad to see her

winning; maybe she would get hooked or something. After all, it would be nice to talk about horses with someone besides Andy. In any case, the point of this setting was the race on deck: the $50,000-added Spinaway Stakes.

La Prevoyante, undefeated and on her way to a two-year-old championship, was the odds-on favorite. Yet in spite of her unblemished record, neither of us thought she was very much horse. She had never run a truly fast race, and she had been beating up on the worst bunch of stakes-class juvenile fillies we had ever seen. She had beaten them pretty badly, though, and she figured to do so again; but there was a new challenger in the field—Princess Doubleday—a shipper from Chicago.

Although Princess Doubleday had finished last in her most recent race in the slop, she had raced strongly in Chicago throughout the summer, winning two races and finishing a close third in a stakes. After checking some out-of-town result charts to determine the quality of the Midwestern juvenile fillies and after one last review of the *Form*, Andy and I concluded independently that Princess Doubleday had a great chance to win the Spinaway at 40–1.

Now it isn't too often that a sound piece of handicapping turns up a 40–1 shot that should really be a solid second choice in the betting, and naturally we were excited. We didn't want to go overboard; we still knew that we had to beat an undefeated 1–5 shot. We each decided to make a maximum-limit action bet— $60—and with just five minutes to post Laurie returned from the saddling area to share in the good news. I was surprised by her response. "It all sounds great," she said, "but shouldn't you bet your money to place?" Almost instinctively my stomach grumbled its reply to this heresy. I agreed that it would certainly be safer to bet to place but patiently explained to her that since the money bet to place on a heavy favorite like La Prevoyante would be returned to her supporters in the place pool, she would deflate the place prices on every other horse in the race. I argued that the value of this longshot was only in the win pool.

"As it is," I said, "we have to beat a filly that has slaughtered her opposition half a dozen times just to win our bet. For us to get a big place price on Princess Doubleday, La Prevoyante would have to run third or worse. Besides," I added, "40–1 on this filly is a tremendous overlay." Convinced by my own logic, my stomach relaxed. Laurie said she understood my position but insisted we would be better off if we followed her advice.

By that time I began to feel that Laurie should have stayed out by the trees or gone to talk to Robyn. Shaking our heads in unison, Andy and I gave up on the talking and headed for the win windows. He went upstairs and I went downstairs.

At the windows, after I had traded serious money for pasteboard, a sudden impulse crossed my brain. I ran as fast as I could to the place line and just did get in a small bet before the bell rang. "And they're off," the PA system said. But I knew exactly what was going to happen.

La Prevoyante breezed to victory as Princess Doubleday rallied to get second money.

Back at the seats, we watched the prices go up on the board. La Prevoyante paid $2.80 to win, $3.00 to place, $2.60 to show. Princess Doubleday paid $15.20 in the middle—at least $6 more than an early reading of the tote board had indicated. Laurie didn't say a word, but just counted her money and smiled. Andy, I found out, had made the same play I had, and our impulsive saver wagers to place gave us each a slight profit on the race. But some fifteen minutes later, while scooping some of Saratoga's great homemade ice cream, I nearly choked on the reality of what had happened.

"We're both idiots," I screamed abruptly, causing Andy to spill his sundae on the floor. "Supposing we had been told La Prevoyante was a late scratch and wouldn't be in the Spinaway. What price would we then have made Princess Doubleday to beat the rest of that weak field? Even money? Seven to five? Well, by ignoring the place pool, by being so longshot conscious, we just passed up the sweetest 6–1 prime bet of the year." We could have made an action bet on her to win and quadrupled the place bet with absolute confidence.

Strangely, my stomach never bothers me anymore when I talk horses with Laurie, and ever since that eye-opening experience I have had no trouble remembering to check the place and show pools very carefully. You just never know when the track is going to give it away.

17.
More on Betting

There are many lessons to be learned about betting, many traps that await the reckless, overconfident player. What follows in this chapter are some additional facts of life that every handicapper should find profitable to recognize.

Above all other repetitious mistakes, the average racetrack crowd will seriously overbet the chances of horses whose records resemble the past performances below. I can't stress enough the folly of playing horses to win when everything in their records says they don't want to do that. Experienced horseplayers have a pet name for horses like these. They call them "sucker" horses. The term applies just as well to the players who bet on them.

Santo's Joe — Gr. h. 5, by Northern Jove—Maria L, by Mystic II
Own.—Luca S — **117** — Br.—Luca S (Fla) — Tr.—Luca Santo
Lifetime 54 2 8 10 $85,800 | 1982 6 0 2 2 $14,160 | 1981 22 1 3 3 $36,560 | Turf 20 1 3 5 $40,640

31Mar82-7Aqu	7f :22 :44^3 1:23^{1}ft	6½	117	5^{7½}	4^{6½}	4^4	3^5	Samyn J L^6	Aw17000	80	Feel Good, Rigid, Santo's Joe	8
17Mar82-6Aqu	1 :48^1 1:13^2 1:39^{2}gd	4¼	117	1^{½}	1^{1½}	2^{½}	2^{½}	Cordero AJr^6	Aw18000	68	HailEmperor,Santo'sJoe,Kryptonite	7
13Mar82-5Aqu	6f ⊡:22^4 :46^{2}1:11^{1}ft	9	121	8^{6¼}	6^{4½}	5^5	3^{3½}	Santagata N^4	Aw17000	85	OldTestment,CtchMtthew,Snto'sJo	8
25Feb82-5Aqu	1$\frac{1}{16}$ ⊡:48^{2}1:13^{3}1:45^{4}ft	3¼	117	3^2	3^{2½}	4^{3½}	4^{4¾}	Cordero AJr^6	Aw18000	79	DscoCont,RtrnForGlory,Dsn'tEvryn	7
15Feb82-7Aqu	1$\frac{3}{16}$ ⊡:48^{2}1:13 1:58 ft	3¾	117	1^{½}	2^{½}	3^{½}	4^{8½}	MacBeth D^6	Aw18000	79	NicePirt,Dosn'tEvryon,Lrking'sRun	8
28Jan82-8Aqu	1⅛ ⊡:47^{4}1:11^{2}1:51^{1}ft	8	117	3^{nk}	3^{1½}	1^{1½}	2^{¾}	Cordero AJr^4	Aw18000	89	Agilemont,Snto'sJoe,Dosn'tEvryon	8
16Dec81-7Aqu	170 ⊡:46^{3}1:11^{4}1:42^{3}sy	13	117	6^{12}	5^6	7^7	7^{7¼}	Maple E^1	Aw18000	82	BestCnnon,DiscoCount,WsHeFuzzy	7
30Nov81-8Aqu	1 :47^3 1:12 1:36^{3}ft	14	117	2^{½}	4^{6½}	5^{13}	6^{21}	Santagata N^2	Aw22000	62	JohnCsy,CountrEspiong,Bucksplshr	6

●Apr 15 Aqu 4f ft :48^2 h   Mar 30 Aqu 3f ft :37 b   Mar 10 Aqu ⊡ 4f ft :50^2 b   Feb 23 Aqu ⊡ 4f ft :49^2 b

---

***Friedenau** — Dk. b. or br. f. 3, by Faraway Son—Freizeit, by Neckar
Own.—Luro Frances W — **113** — Br.—Bresges Mrs W (Fra) — Tr.—Luro Horatio A
Lifetime 6 0 4 0 $9,390 | 1982 5 M 4 0 $9,300 | 1981 1 M 0 0 $90 | Turf 2 0 2 0 $4,680

22Mar82-5GP	1$\frac{1}{16}$:49^2 1:14 1:46^{1}ft	9-5	121	4^{1½}	2^{½}	2^{1½}	2^2	Maple E^3	ⒻMdn	68	Trust Account,Friedenau,KindRex	12
5Mar82-10Hia	1⅛ Ⓣ 1:49^{2}fm	*3-2	120	3^{4½}	2^1	1^1	2^1	Brumfield D^9	ⒻMdn	86	Malapropism,Friedenau,TreatyOak	12
23Feb82-4Hia	a1⅛ Ⓣ 1:49^{3}fm	3½	120	5^{4½}	3^{3½}	3^3	2^2	Brumfield D^2	ⒻMdn	82	HatTbGirl,Friedenu,PretentiousNn	12
1Feb82-6Hia	1$\frac{1}{16}$:48^2 1:13^3 1:45^{1}ft	7¼	120	5^{1¾}	2^3	2^6	2^{11}	Maple E^4	ⒻMdn	66	ChristmasPast,Friedenau,Sidmzelle	9
11Jan82-6Hia	7f :23^3 :47^4 1:25^{4}ft	23	120	10^{10}	10^{11}	8^{12}	6^{14}	Bailey J D^8	ⒻMdn	60	Blongng,NvrNvrQun,DchssofVndy	12
19Dec81-4Crc	7f :23^4 :47^2 1:24^{4}ft	13	119	10^{13}	10^{19}	8^{24}	7^{26}	Castaneda K^{11}	ⒻMdn	66	ReglActress,SvedGround,Dejeuner	11

May 19 Bel 3f ft :37^1 b   ●May 14 Bel 7f ft 1:26 h   May 7 Bel 4f ft :49 b   ●Apr 21 Hia 4f ft :49^4 h

---

Very Valid — B. f. 4, by Valid Appeal—Lentil Soup, by Ponder
Own.—Feiner I — **113** — Br.—Fuller P (Fla) — Tr.—Campo John P — $70,000
Lifetime 31 2 7 6 $42,587 | 1982 8 0 1 0 $11,120 | 1981 18 2 6 5 $30,357 | Turf 6 0 3 1 $12,160

21May82-1Bel	1¼ Ⓣ:51 1:39^{4}2:04^{3}fm	4¾	113	1^1	1^{½}	2^{½}	2^{nk}	Lovato F Jr^1	Ⓕ 70000	71	Anjuli, Very Valid, Latka	5
14May82-3Aqu	1$\frac{1}{16}$ Ⓣ:48^{2}1:13^{1}1:44^{4}fm	25	113	2^{1½}	2^{½}	2^{hd}	4^{nk}	Lovato F Jr^1	Ⓕ 70000	81	AlwaysPretty,Prtridgeberry,Bedzzle	7
21Mar82-5Aqu	6f :23 :46^3 1:11^{3}ft	13	117	6^{4½}	6^{7½}	4^{6½}	4^{11}	Skinner K^5	Ⓕ 50000	72	MdmMischif,HrlmQun,IllustriousLs	7
12Mar82-3Aqu	170 ⊡:47^{3}1:12^{4}1:43 gd	21	113	2^4	3^{2½}	5^{6½}	6^{12}	Santagata N^2	Ⓕ 70000	75	GoodHevn'sGirl,StormPtrl,Nor'sLss	7
2Mar82-3Aqu	1⅛ ⊡:49 1:13^{2}1:53 ft	9¼	114	3^{2½}	3^{4½}	6^{7½}	5^8	Skinner K^6	Ⓕ 75000	73	GallantRuby,‡GoodMusicl,Nor'sLss	6
2Mar82—Placed fourth through disqualification												
21Feb82-7Aqu	1$\frac{1}{16}$ ⊡:47^{3}1:12^{4}1:45^{4}ft	14	117	3^2	3^2	2^2	4^{2½}	Skinner K^3	ⒻAw22000	81	SheerFntsy,HvnnhLke,Hunter'sDrm	8
21Jan82-4Aqu	1⅛ ⊡:48 1:13^{4}1:53 ft	8	117	2^4	2^{1½}	4^{3½}	4^8	McCarron G^3	Ⓕ c50000	73	ThirdWife,HaloAgain,HarlemQueen	7
16Jan82-2Bow	7f :23^2 :46^3 1:24^{3}ft	13	113	—	—	—	—	Wright DR^1	ⒻAw11500	—	RingDncer,CopyConni,Fildr'sChoic	9

Wise Colleen

Own.—Hextonia Stable

121

Ro. f. 3, by Wise EXchange—Nalgana, by Nade
Br.—DuPont Mrs S F (Md)
Tr.—Small Richard W

1982	13	2	6	2	$48,184
Turf	1	0	1	0	$2,090
Lifetime	13	2	6	2	$48,184

12Jun82-8Lrl	$1\frac{1}{16}$:46¹ 1:11⁴ 1:45²ft	4½	112	8²¹ 6¹⁸ 3⁸ 2ⁿᵏ	MrsL⁷	⒫ⓈPearlNkIce	81	GoldenWge,WiseColleen,PltinumBll 8
28May82-8Lrl	$1\frac{1}{16}$⑦:46 1:11¹1:42⁴fm*8-5	109	6⁹ 5¹⁰ 3¹ 2ⁿᵏ	Moyers L⁶	⒫Aw9500	89	MorningQueen,WisColln,FunEvning 7
14May82-8Pim	$1\frac{1}{16}$:47¹ 1:11⁴ 1:44³ft	17	114	89½ 9¹⁴ 6¹¹ 6¹²	MrsL⁴	⒫Blk Eyed Su.	70	Delicate Ice, Trove, Milingo 10
4May82-6Pim	$1\frac{1}{16}$:47⁴ 1:13¹ 1:46 ft	9-5	112	4¹³ 47¹ 34½ 2³	Moyers L⁴	⒫Aw27000	72	Martie'sDouble,WiseColleen,Chrsky 5
22Apr82-6Pim	$1\frac{1}{16}$:46² 1:11³ 1:43⁴ft	*1-2	117	7¹³ 76¾ 43½ 2ʰᵈ	BrccileVJr⁷	⒫Aw11900	86	GoldenWage,WiseColleen,Pipparoo 7
12Apr82-8Pim	$1\frac{1}{16}$:46³ 1:10³ 1:43³ft	4½	115	9¹⁹ 9¹⁵ 46½ 2²	BrccilVJr⁴	⒫⒮Hilltop	85	Mrt'sDoubl,WsColln,SwftAttrcton 10
2Apr82-8Pim	$1\frac{1}{16}$:47² 1:11² 1:44 ft	*1	115	65½ 45½ 32½ 2ʰᵈ	BrccileVJr⁴	⒫Aw25000	85	Mrtie'sDouble,WiseColln,Inclvtting 7
22Mar82-8Pim	$1\frac{1}{16}$:45³ 1:11² 1:44¹ft	*9-5	120	10²⁰ 6⁶ 1³ 1³	BrccileVJr⁸	⒫Aw10000	84	WiseCollen,WssoWsso,PrincssJov 12

Jun 8 Pim 5f m 1:07 b

Sometimes the act of wagering on a horse is more than a simple process of translating one's own opinion into cash. At times it becomes a test of will power. Tipsters, touts, and the blinking lights of the tote board can exert an amazing influence on the rational decision-making process, and any player who doesn't have a basic knowledge of the reliability of these enticing sources of information will be busted out of the game every time.

There is such a thing as "smart money," but it is not likely to be aligned with the tipsters and touts who advertise their "expertise" and sell it for a buck. Nor is it likely to be represented by the wildest spenders in the crowd.

Although most players get caught up in the tidal wave of enthusiasm generated by strong late play on the tote, very few moves of that kind are worth any consideration. Let's take the exceptions:

1. A shipper.
2. A first-time starter or absentee with no positive workouts.
3. A stable that has a history of such doings.

Generally speaking, the winning potential of a horse that gets excessive play is logically limited to the winning capacity of the people behind it. Most often there will be ample clues in the past performance profile to suggest an all-out performance. However, certain trainers—people like Kaye Belle in Kentucky and M. C. Preger in New York—rarely win a race unless the tote board says tilt.

On the other hand, the lack of convincing betting action on a seemingly superior, apparently sharp horse, except in stakes races, is a powerful tote board clue to a probable subpar performance. If the horse has won a few recent races or has been in excellent form and is now dropping to a seemingly easy spot, he should attract heavy play. If he does not, if he flirts with 2–1 or 5–2 odds when he should be 4–5, the player would do well to examine the rest of the field closely. Tepidly played standouts seldom run to their prior good form.

According to long-standing tradition, the morning line—the odds posted on the tote board before the betting begins—is supposed to provide an estimate of the probable post-time odds for each horse in the race. The theoretical value of this line is to enable the player to spot overlays as well as to isolate those horses getting excessive betting action. I'm afraid it rarely does that.

In the days before pari-mutuel betting the morning line was a matter of professional pride. If an operating bookmaker in the track's betting ring didn't make a first-class morning line, the best bettors in the crowd would pounce on his mistakes. In those days a good morning line had to have value. It had to reflect a balanced book of percentages and reflect the realities of the race at hand. Frankly, I envy the players who had a chance to play the game in the age of the trackside bookmaker. It must have been great fun.

Today at the racetrack, in the age of pari-mutuel betting, the morning line is usually put together by a member of the mutuel department. Rarely does it do any more than suggest the probable betting favorites, although in "blind" betting situations—the daily double and exacta—it does exert an influence on the betting habits of uninformed bettors. Almost automatically the average horseplayer will include the top two or three morning-line choices in his double and exacta combinations. This has three predictable effects: (1) it tends to create lower double and exacta payoffs on morning-line choices regardless of their merits; (2) it forces higher payoffs on overlooked longshots; and (3) it sometimes helps to single out a betting stable's serious intentions with an otherwise lightly regarded horse.

Considering the reliability of low payoff possibilities for all morning-line choices in daily doubles and exactas, the player can conclude with reasonable certainty that a horse getting substantially greater play than his morning-line odds in these "blind" betting pools is getting play from informed sources. I know several professional handicappers who pay careful attention to the flow of money in daily doubles and exactas, and all of them say that the morning-line angle is fundamental to their calculations. Naturally, these players put their own money on the line only when a stable with a good winning history is involved.

One of the things that separates professional horseplayers from the rest of the crowd is the ability to assign approximate yet realistic odds values to the horses in the race. This has nothing to do with post-time odds.

For example, when Riva Ridge, winner of the 1972 Kentucky Derby, went to Pimlico two weeks later for the Preakness Stakes, it was a foregone conclusion that his overall record and TV popularity would make him a prohibitive odds-on favorite. A good morning line would have surely pegged him at 1–2. A good value line might have been willing to accept 4–5 as a fair estimate of his winning chances—that is, until the rains began to fall on the eve of the Preakness.

Riva Ridge was no mud runner, by any stretch of the term. He had already been beaten in the Everglades Stakes by a common sort named Head of the River and had always worked below par on sloppy tracks. A professional handicapper who knew that about Riva Ridge could hardly have made him anything but third choice in the Preakness to No Le Hace and Key to the Mint, two horses that eventually did finish in front of him (Bee Bee Bee won).

Three weeks later Riva Ridge tackled most of these horses again on a fast racetrack in the 1½-mile Belmont Stakes. A good value line on the race would have established the horse at even money or 4–5. There was nothing wrong with Riva Ridge. He was still in top form, far and away the best three-year-old in America. And he had trained brilliantly for the race. The only potential danger was Key to the Mint, who was on the comeback trail. With or without some fine-line handicapping of Key to the Mint's credentials (he worked much too fast for the race and, in a rare mistake for Elliott Burch, was somewhat short on distance preparation), the 8–5 post-time odds on Riva Ridge were a gift presented by national TV coverage of the Derby winner's horrible Preakness performance. Although horses are not robots, and it is dangerous to think that every race on paper will be run exactly to specifications in the flesh, there is money to be made betting the best horse in the race at generous odds. That is, in fact, the heart and soul of the game.

"If they ran this race 100 times, how many times would Riva Ridge win?" That's the kind of question that helps to establish the value line. On Belmont's fast racetrack Riva Ridge seemed strong enough and fit enough to have at least 50 percent of the race all to himself. That's the kind of answer that sets up prime betting possibilities, and it happens every day.

Had Andy Beyer and I been thinking in terms of the value line, Princess Doubleday to place would certainly have qualified as a value-line prime bet. And there are several other instances when the value-line concept works to the advantage of players who are capable of thinking second best.

The setting is an exacta event and there is an overwhelming odds-on favorite, a horse that deserves its lofty ranking, a horse that has every advantage over the competition. Although there are some players in the crowd who bet huge amounts of money on such "stickouts," only the very best handicappers among them will avoid betting the occasional phony that will break a bankroll in one shot. Those who have the skill to back 90 percent or more short-priced winners would do far better in the long run betting less money on good horses going to the post at good odds. But that's their problem. When I see a standout odds-on favorite in an exacta event, I will commit myself to a small action bet on it or perhaps bet another horse that I think might have a chance to spring an upset. There are two extremely important exceptions.

In some exacta races the betting public has trouble evaluating the contenders for second money. If sound handicapping turns up two, three, or four logical contenders for second place, a check of the exacta payoff possibilities on the closed-circuit TV system will sometimes open up the door to a maximum bet.

On the other hand, the public sometimes bets most of its exacta money on the dominant race favorite linked with one other apparently fit horse. In such circumstances it pays to take a close look at this "second-best" horse. If it lacks convincing credentials, if there are sound reasons to bet against it, a wheel on the rest of the field could produce exciting payoffs. Indeed, this phenomenon occurs many times over in a season and produces a betting pattern that is extraordinarily predictable. Hundreds of illustrations could be given here, none more dramatic than the one facing the player lucky enough to have been at Belmont Park for the greatest performance in the history of Thoroughbred racing, Secretariat's 1973 Belmont Stakes.

Going into the Belmont, Secretariat was lord and master of the three-year-old division, a solid 1–10 shot to become the first Triple Crown winner in twenty-five years. Unlike Carry Back, Northern Dancer, Kauai King, Canonero II, and Majestic Prince—the five horses that failed to complete the Derby-Preakness-Belmont sweep—Secretariat came up to the 1973 Belmont at the peak of his powers, working faster and more energetically for the race than for any other race in his life. The same could not be said for Sham, the second-best three-year-old of 1973.

Sham had tried Secretariat twice and had failed both times. In the Derby Secretariat went very wide on both turns and with power in reserve outdrove Sham from the top of the stretch to the wire.

In the Preakness, while under no special urging, Secretariat made a spectacular move around the clubhouse turn—from last to first—passing Sham in the backstretch. For the final half of the race Pincay slashed his whip into Sham with wild fury. Turcotte, aboard Secretariat, never moved a muscle. But Sham never gained an inch. At the wire he was a tired horse.

Coming up to the 1973 Belmont, Sham had begun to show signs of wear and tear. He showed fewer workouts and they were not as brisk; this horse had been through a rough campaign. Five route races in top company in less than eight weeks. Trips to California, Kentucky, Maryland, and New York. Actually, the only thing keeping Sham in the Triple Crown chase was trainer Frank Martin's stubbornness. A more objective view of his chances in the Belmont said that he would never beat Secretariat and could even go severely off form.

These were the win odds quoted on the race:

Secretariat	$ .10–$1.00
Sham	$ 5.10–$1.00
Private Smiles	$14.30–$1.00
My Gallant	$12.40–$1.00
Twice a Prince	$17.30–$1.00

These were the exacta payoff possibilities as they were flashed on the closed-circuit TV system prior to post time:

Secretariat with Sham	$ 3.40
Secretariat with Private Smiles	$24.60
Secretariat with My Gallant	$19.80
Secretariat with Twice a Prince	$35.20

Eliminating Sham from the exacta play meant an investment of $6 (three combinations) and a minimum payoff of $19.80 (My Gallant). What all this means is that the track was offering three horses and excellent payoffs to beat a tired Sham for second place. In fact, the payoffs were almost identical to the odds in the win pool, the odds being offered on each of these three horses to beat Sham *and* Secretariat. By conceding the race to Secretariat, the player had a chance to collect the same odds merely by beating Sham. Now that's what I call value.

Through the weakness of the second betting favorite and the availability of exacta wagering, an exciting but seemingly unplayable race was turned into a very logical, very promising prime bet. In a very real sense, it was like being offered a bonus dividend for understanding the subtleties of a great moment in racing history. It's times like that when a horseplayer knows he is playing the greatest game in the world.

105TH RUNNING—1973—SECRETARIAT

EIGHTH RACE
Belmont
JUNE 9, 1973

1 ½ MILES. (2.26⅗) 105th Running THE BELMONT $125,000 added. 3-year-olds. By subscription of $100 each to accompany the nomination; $250 to pass the entry box, $1,000 to start. A supplementary nomination may be made of $2,500 at the closing time of entries plus an additional $10,000 to start, with $125,000 added, of which 60% to the winner, 22% to second, 12% to third and 6% to fourth. Weights, Colts and Geldings 126 lbs. Fillies 121 lbs. Starters to be named at the closing time of entries. The winning owner will be presented with the August Belmont Memorial Cup to be retained for one year, as well as a trophy for permanent possession and trophies will be presented to the winning trainer and jockey. Closed Thursday, February 15, 1973 with 187 Nominations.
Value of race $150,200, value to winner $90,120, second $33,044, third $18,024, fourth $9,012. Mutuel pool $519,689, OTB pool $688,460.

Last Raced	Horse	Eqt	A	Wt	PP	¼	½	1	1¼	Str	Fin	Jockey	Odds $1
19May73 ⁸Pim¹	Secretariat	b	3	126	1	1^{hd}	1^{hd}	1^{7}	1^{20}	1^{28}	1^{31}	Turcotte R	.10
2Jun73 ⁶Bel⁴	Twice A Prince		3	126	5	4^{5}	4^{10}	3^{hd}	2^{hd}	3^{12}	2½	Baeza B	17.30
31May73 ⁶Bel¹	My Gallant	b	3	126	3	3^{3}	3^{hd}	4^{7}	3^{2}	2^{hd}	3^{13}	Cordero A Jr	12.40
28May73 ⁸GS²	Pvt. Smiles	b	3	126	2	5	5	5	5	5	4¾	Gargan D	14.30
19May73 ⁸Pim²	Sham	b	3	126	6	2^{5}	2^{10}	2^{7}	4^{8}	$4^{1½}$	5	Pincay L Jr	5.10

Time, :23⅗, :46⅕, 1:09⅘, 1:34⅕, 1:59, 2:24, (Against wind in backstretch.). Track fast.
New Track Record.

$2 Mutuel Prices:				
	2-(A)-SECRETARIAT	2.20	2.40	—
	5-(E)-TWICE A PRINCE		4.60	—
	(No Show Wagering)			

Ch. c, by Bold Ruler—Somethingroyal, by Princequillo. Trainer Laurin L. Bred by Meadow Stud Inc (Va).
IN GATE AT 5:38; OFF AT 5:38, EDT. Start Good. Won Ridden out.

SECRETARIAT sent up along the inside to vie for the early lead with SHAM to the backstretch, disposed of that one after going three-quarters, drew off at will rounding the far turn and was under a hand ride from Turcotte to establish a record in a tremendous performance. TWICE A PRINCE, unable to stay with the leader early, moved through along the rail approaching the stretch and outfinished MY GALLANT for the place. The latter, void of early foot, moved with TWICE A PRINCE rounding the far turn and fought it out gamely with that one through the drive. PVT. SMILES showed nothing. SHAM alternated for the lead with SECRETARIAT to the backstretch, wasn't able to match stride with that rival after going three-quarters and stopped badly.

$2.00 EXACTA (2–5) PAID $35.00

18.
The Winning Horseplayer

Ideally, the most instructive way to illustrate the practical applications of the material in this book would be to present thousands of actual races, playable and nonplayable.

We would select several different racetracks, do post position studies for each, save and read result charts, compare the past performance records of all the important trainers, and be careful to note and measure the relative power of the racing surface as it influences the action on the track.

To get a fix on the local horses, we could construct classification codes, keep a record of purses, pay attention to the daily tabular workout listings, generate class pars, compute speed figures, hunt for Key Races, and watch whatever races we are privileged to see with eyes geared to detect the unusual as it happens.

Not all professional-class players do all of that.

Some rely strictly on speed figures or generally broad insights to uncover sound betting propositions. Some watch races with such skill that they are able to build a catalogue of live horses for future play. And some concentrate all serious play on one specific type of race—turf events, claiming races, sprints, routes, maidens, or stakes.

Frankly, I have no argument with players who are able to solve more than their share of racetrack riddles through a single window or two. Indeed, specialization according to individual strength makes excellent sense. Different strokes for different folks. On one level that is precisely what this book has been about. But on another level that is not the case at all.

I have been very fortunate. During my years around the racetrack I have been continuously exposed to the varied menu only an extensive itinerary can bring. Five years at Rutgers University, Garden State Park division. Two years of handicapping fifty races a day at five or more tracks for the *Daily Racing Form*. Triple Crown coverage for Mutual Radio and the *Philadelphia Inquirer*. Five hundred daily five-minute seminars on handicapping for WLMD radio in Maryland. The editorship of *Turf and*

Sport Digest. Daily columns and picks at Atlantic City, Delaware Park, and Keystone for the *Philadelphia Journal.* Trips to forty-eight different racetracks and conversations with some of the best thinkers and players in the game. People like Andy Beyer and Clem Florio in Maryland, Jules Schanzer and Saul Rosen at the *Form*, John Pricci of *Newsday* in New York, and Tom Ainslie, the man who gave me special encouragement to commit to print all the insights I have thus far gained.

It has taken me almost 200 pages to do that. But I think it would help your focus if I reduced the essence of it all to a few key principles and a few key examples.

There are only two kinds of playable prime betting situations: easy ones and hard ones. The easy ones practically leap off the pages of the *Racing Form;* the hard ones require a bit of digging.

To the student of track bias, an easy one may come any time the bias is strong enough to prejudice the outcome of the race. The Travers Stakes on page 38 is a classic illustration of that. So is the Schuylerville Stakes on page 126.

To students of class, easy ones come in many forms. A hidden class dropdown like Caspar Milquetoast on page 104. A Key Race standout like Gay Gambler on page 95. A Shredder, a Secretariat, a Laplander, or a horse with significantly faster speed figures. (Yes, that too is an edge in class.)

Likewise, for those who pay attention to trainers and their methods, there is nothing very complicated about spotting a Mack Miller first-timer on the grass; much the same can be said for dozens of other horses whose past performance records signal the confidence of a winning horseman's best work.

Upsets? Of course. They happen every day. Horses and the humans who handle them are always capable of throwing in a clunker or improving beyond previous limits of performance. Mistakes? Certainly. The player is no less governed by the same laws of nature. But to win at the racetrack, the player must not only learn from his own mistakes but avoid the trap of punishing himself for having made them. Usually, that kind of genuine confidence comes only from knowing that other straightforward opportunities will not be long in coming.

With no hestitation I can assure you that the tools, concepts, and research techniques contained in this book will isolate the probable race winner with minimum difficulty in hundreds of races each and every season. And two of the most frequently encountered betting situations will bear a striking resemblance to the following pair of examples.

There are many reasons why most players would not want to touch the above race with a ten-foot pole. Despite the grossly inflated purse—put up to encourage the New York State breeding industry—it would be difficult to find a weaker field of nonwinners at any major-class track. Nevertheless, there is a standout, maximum-limit prime bet in this race—the filly Flylet, a horse that embodies a classic winning pattern (see page 189).

In each of her prior races Flylet has shown considerably more early speed than any of her rivals has ever shown. Twice she even took a narrow lead at the first quarter call. On August 11 she met every member of today's field with the exception of No Empty Pocket and First Proof, and she was no less than half a dozen lengths in front of them all for much of the race. I'm sure you can imagine the ease with which she will therefore be able to sail to the front in today's race. And therein lies the heart and power of the pattern.

Except on a stretch-running track, whenever a horse figures to get a clear, uncontested lead on the field for the first time, the player should expect dramatic improvement over recent performances. If the horse already rates close to the competition, as Flylet certainly does, the expected improvement is odds-on to result in victory. Odds-on is what I said and odds-on is what I meant. Give a horse like that a slow-breaking field or a front-running racetrack, and the only thing that will beat it is an act of god or war.

1st Saratoga

AUGUST 26, 1976

6 FURLONGS. (1:08). MAIDENS. CLAIMING. Purse $10,000. 2-year-olds, foaled in New York State and approved by the New York State-bred registry. (All purse money from New York Breeders' Fund). Weight, 122 lbs. Claiming price, $20,000; for each $1,000 to $18.000, allowed 2 lbs.

COUPLED: JOSH GOLDNER, RANDY'S CIL and NO EMPTY POCKET.

Listed According to Post Positions

Heidee's Cousin 118
B. c (1974), by Flaneur II.—Buccanette, by Black Beard.
Breeder, Murray M. Garren (N. Y.). 1976 9 M 1 0 $3,090
Owner, Murray M. Garren. Trainer, Gilbert Puentes. $18.000

11 Aug76	1Sar	5½ f :223 :4631:054m	6½	122	1011	86½	810	916	VelezRI2	Mdn	72	RedSam 122	RagT meBelle	12
3 Aug76	3Sar	5½ f :223 :4631:053ft	6¼	122	88	710	815	726	MapleE9	Mdn	63	VandySue119	TakeItAlong	9
25 Jly 76	9Aqu	5½ f :24 :49 1:083ft	3	120	62½	53¾	55½	45½	MpleE1	M22500	64	Tacitus 122	Mad Jack	9
18 Jly 76	4Aqu	5½ f :232 :4741:063ft	6½	122	95	95¾	79	58¼	StgoA8	M25000	72	PrinceNoNme117	PictreShw	10
12 Jly 76	4Aqu	5½ f :232 :48 1:074ft	4½	122	44	32	32½	2nk	MapleE6	Mdn	74	Ducky'sBolero122	Hdee'sCsn	8
30 Jun76	3Aqu	5½ f :223 :4631:06 ft	4	8	53	421	54	53½	StgoA2	M20000	79	HasAFuture120	ChairmanOx	8
27 Jun76	4Bel	5½ f :232 :4621:044ft	19	1135	41½	58	68½	68	MtnJE4	M40000	83	Peak Top 122	Proud Arion	9
11 Jun76	4Bel	5½ f :234 :48 1:064ft	30	118	75¾	711	711	714	StgoA3	M 0000	67	Lancer'sPride122	PrizeNtive	9
31 May76	4Bel	5½ f :224 :4641:052ft	49	1175	98¾	911	920	923	MartinJE9	Mdn	65	DukeWayne122	Turn ofCoin	9

Aug 24 Sar trt 4f ft :49⅗h   Aung 19 Sar trt 5f ft 1:03b   July 17 Bel trt 3f sy :36h

Ruddy Duck 118
Ch. c (1974), by High Rank—Meadow Mole, by Egotistical.
Breeder, Mrs. Ann K. Morse (N. Y.). 1976 2 M 0 0 (——)
Owner, Ann K. Morse. Trainer, Thomas M. Waller. $18.000

11 Aug76	1Sar	5½ f :223 :4631:054m	2e	*122	1111	118½	911	815	TurcotteR5	Mdn	73	RedSam 122	RagT meB le	12
12 Jly 76	4Aqu	5½ f :232 :48 1:074ft	4½e	122	56	59	58	57	TurctteR5	Mdn	67	Ducky'sBolero122	Hdee'sCsn	8

Aug 21 Sar 5f ft 1:05b   Aug 15 Sar trt 4f ft :54b   Aug 9 Sar 4f sy :48⅗h

First Proof 122
Dk. b. or br. c (1974), by Only Once—Flora Bonda, by Auditing.
Breeder, Maxion Farms (N. Y.). 1976 2 M 0 0 (——)
Owner, William J. Maxion. Trainer, Everett F. Schoenborn. $20.000

19 Aug76	8Sar	6 f :222 :46 1:122ft	93	115	1617	1315	1110	109	TurcteR13	AlwS	69	FratelloEd115	Heidee'sPal	17
12 Jly 76	4Aqu	5½ f :232 :48 1:074ft	35	122	823	830	825	819	VeneziaM2	Mdn	55	Ducky'sBolero122	Hdee'sCsn	8

Aug 2 LD 3f ft :38bg   July 23 LD 49f ft :50⅖bg   July 9 FL 4f ft :50⅖bg

Flylet 117
B. f (1974), by Flying Error—Whiglet, by Whig.
Breeder, Saverio Cardile (N. Y.). 1976 6 M 0 1 $1,440
Owner, Saverio Cardile. Trainer, Saverio Cardile. $19.000

19 Aug76	8Sar	6 f :222 :46 1:122ft	38	112	33	98¼	1213	1112	SmithRC4	AlwS	66	FratelloEd115	Heidee'sPal	17
11 Aug76	1Sar	5½ f :223 :4631:054m	8¼	119	33	33	66½	69½	BaezaB11	Mdn	78	RedSam 122	RagT meBe e	12
3 Aug76	3Sar	5½ f :223 :4631:053ft	28	119	1½	32	48	620	RujanoM1	Mdn	69	VandySue119	TakeItAlong	9
19 Jly 76	4Aqu	5½ f :223 :47 1:062ft	20	115	52¼	86¼	913	1016	RjnoM5	M35000	65	Ⓕ Regal Jay119	Vandy Sue	10
12 Jly 76	4Aqu	5½ f :232 :48 1:074ft	16	119	11	2h	21½	33¾	RujanoM4	Mdn	70	Ducky'sBolero122	Hdee'sCsn	8
6 May76	4Bel	5½ f :231 :4731:073ft	11	115	2h	64	716	822	DayP7	M45000	55	Ⓕ Sly Grin 119	Rethread	8

July 18 Bel trt 3f ft :38⅘b   July 10 Bel trt 3f m :40b   July 3 Bel 5f ft 1:01hg

Randy's Cil 119
B. f (1974), by Thomasville—Brimstar, by Mielleux.
Breeder, Dr. L. D. Star (N. Y.). 1976 3 M 0 1 $1,440
Owner, Winifred Star. Trainer, Adrien Gauthier. $20.000

19 Aug76	8Sar	6 f :222 :46 1:122ft	5½e	112	1717	1214	109¾	98¾	VelqezJ15	AlwS	69	FratelloEd115	Heidee'sPal	17
11 Aug76	1Sar	5½ f :223 :4631:054m	4e	119	99¾	97	46	36	VelasqezJ9	Mdn	82	RedSam 122	RagT meBelle	12
3 Aug76	3Sar	5½ f :223 :4631:050ft	15	119	911	911	69¾	617	VelasqzJ3	Mdn	72	VandySue119	TakeItAlong	9

July 29 Bel 5f ft 1:00⅗h   July 24 Bel 4f sy :49⅗bg   July 18 Bel trt 3f ft :36⅖h

Big Albert 118
Ch. c (1974), by O'Hara—Lisl's Favor, by Noholme II.
Breeder, Dr. D. J. DeLuke (N. Y.). 1976 2 M 0 0 (——)
Owner, Assunta Louis Farm. Trainer, Ramon M. Hernandez. $18.000

11 Aug76	1Sar	5½ f :223 :4631:054m	7½	122	1213	129½	1011	1016	HerndzR7	Mdn	72	RedSam 122	RagT meBe e	12
15 Jly 76	4Aqu	5½ f :224 :4711:054ft	36	122	1114	1114	1113	1013	HerndezR2	Mdn	71	Turn of Coin 122	Red Rolfe	12

Aug 21 Sar 4f ft :48⅖hg   Aug 7 Sar 3f ft :38h   Aug 5 Sar 5f ft 1:03⅘b

No Empty Pocket 118
B. c (1974), by Zip Pocket—May Boss, by Boss.
Breeder, Dr. L. D. Star (N. Y.). 1976 7 M 1 0 $976
Owner, L. D. Star. Trainer, Adrien Gauthier. $18.000

19 Aug76	1Key	5½ f :224 :47 1:063ft	9½	118	76¾	78	510	57½	LogioA4	M10000	79	LimestoneCowby120	Lry'sLk	7
11 Aug76	4Mth	5½ f :23 :4631:054ft	5	114	42½	55	55	57	MiceliM4	M8000	81	Night Games 118	Stangley	8
23 Jly 76	3Key	5½ f :224 :4721:071ft	4¾	120	42½	34½	33½	22½	LogcioA3	M5000	81	Manza117	NoEmptyPocket	6
18 Jly 76	4Aqu	5½ f :232 :4741:063ft	23e	118	1010	108¾	1015	1017	RhdsC1	M20000	63	PrinceNoNme117	PictreShw	10
11 Jly 76	4Aqu	5½ f :222 :47 1:07 ft	10e	122	911	911	87½	86½	RchdsC4	M10000	71	BrghtJade122	Hl tothePrnce	10
21 May76	4Bel	5½ f :23 :4641:054ft	34	118	108	99¾	915	816	RdsCH7	M30000	70	FlagOfficer122	WincomaLss	10
27 Apr76	4Aqu	5 f :234 :472 :591ft	11	118	68	610	718	722	RodrzJA4	20000	67	I Got Em 122	Translation	7

June 30 Bel trt 4f sy :50b

In the actual race Flylet went wire to wire, scoring a handy three-length victory, and paid a juicy $15.60.

MAY 3, 1975

9th Churchill Downs

1 1/16 MILES. (1:41⅗). ALLOWANCES. Purse $25,000. 3-year-olds. Weight, 122 lbs. Non-winners of a race of $9,775 at a mile or over allowed 3 lbs.; a race of $6,000 at any distance, 5 lbs.; a race of $4,875 at any distance, 7 lbs.; a race of $3,900 at a mile or over in 1975, 9 lbs. (Maiden, claiming and starter races not considered.)

Jim Dan Bob 113

B. c (1972), by Wa-Wa Cy—Legayle, by Bar Le Duc.
Breeder, G. Begley (Ky.). 1975 10 0 3 3 $7,754
Owner, G. Begley. Trainer, A. Montano. 1974 11 4 2 2 $9,265

26 Apr75	7CD	7 f	:234 :4711:25	ft	52	117	77¼	714	615	512	ArroyoH1	Alw	70	Greek Answer122 Gatch	7
17 Apr75	7Kee	7 f	:23 :46 1:234	ft	92	1075	913	99¾	910	96¾	TrsclairAJ7	Alw	80	HoneyMark114 Brent'sPrnce	11
3 Apr75	7Lat	1	:4711:1241:402	ft	8-5e	114	78¾	410	210	37½	McKnghtJ9	Alw	69	Some Dude 115 Count Paco	9
29 Mar75	7Lat	1	:48 1:1321:40	gd	7¼	112	52½	34½	34½	38	McKnhtJ2	AlwS	71	NaughtyJke119 PromndeLft	8
18 Mar75	8Lat	1	:4831:1441:433	gd	3¾	113	35	44½	37	22	McKnghtJ6	Alw	59	ClarenceHenry120 JimDan	9
7 Mar75	7Lat	6 f	:24 :4811:151	gd	8-5	▲116	2h	15	11½	2no	VasqzG1	A—	72	MowingJoe113 JimDanBob	5
21 Feb75	7Lat	1 1/16	:4841:1441:494	ft	2½	113	33	2h	21	21½	VasquezG3	Alw	59	ClarenceHnry116 JmDanBob	6
1 Feb75	6Key	170	:4711:1441:47	gd	11	119	59	412	58½	511	OrtizI3	Alw	54	Go Go Treniers 119 Prfct Gn	6
25 Jan75	8Key	6 f	:222 :4611:132	sy	11	112	58½	48	511	619	OrtizI4	AlwS	56	Gallant Bob 119 Sgt. Hunt	7
17 Jan75	8Key	6 f	:222 :4611:12	ft	17	117	66½	51¾	31½	3¾	OrtizI3	Alw	81	SneakyWin 117 Dr.FrankB.	8
Dec28-74	7Cwl	6½ f	1:23⅘	sy	1	▲119	12	12	11	11	VasquezG2	Alw	79	JimDanBob119 Clar'nceH'ry B.J.King	6

April 24 CD 4f sy :52b March 27 Lat 3f ft :39b March 5 Lat 3f ft :37h

Ruggles Ferry 117

Gr. c (1972), by Drone—Trotta Sue, by Promised Land.
Breeder, F. Preston (Ky.). 1975 5 2 1 0 $12,075
Owner, Mrs. F. Preston. Trainer, H. Trotsek. 1974 13 2 2 6 $26,884

24 Apr75	7Kee	1⅛	:4711:12 1:49	sy	53	117	59	44	37	57¾	ArroyoH8	AlwS	84	MasterDerby123 HoneyMark	9
15 Apr75	7Kee	1 1/16	:47 1:11 1:423	gd	6	115	56	54	23	25	ArroyoH5	Alw	88	MasterDerby123 RugglsFrry	6
22 Mar75	9FG	1⅛	:4611:1021:493	ft	14	115	1020	914	911	98¼	BarrowT2	AlwS	88	MasterDrby123 ColonelPowr	11
14 Mar75	9FG	6 f	:221 :46 1:104	ft	1-2	▲120	67¼	54½	22	11	BarrowT4	Alw	94	RugglesFrry120 ElectnSpecl	6
15 Feb75	6Hia	7 f	:23 :4521:232	ft	7	117	108¼	79½	32	1h	BarrowT7	Alw	88	RgglsFerry117 BravestRman	11
Nov16-74	8CD	1	1:36	ft	5¾	116	88½	75	52½	35¼	BarrowT2	HcpS	84	CircleHome116 MasterD'rby R'gl'sF'ry	9
Nov 6-74	8CD	7 f	1:25⅖	sy	9	115	1118	1014	55	32½	BarrowT9	Alw	77	MasterD'rby122 W'yw'rdR'd R'gl'sF'y	11
Oct19-74	7Kee	a 7 f	1:25⅘	ft	8½	122	109¾	88½	35	35½	BarrowT9	ScwS	88	Pack'rC'pt'n122 M'st'rD'by R'gl'sF'ry	11
Oct 9-74	7Kee	6 f	1:09⅗	ft	5½	115	65¾	66½	41½	11½	BarrowT4	Alw	94	RugglesFerry115 Ga'ntBob Pack'rCa'n	6
Aug28-74	7AP	6 f	1:11⅗	gd	2¼	▲119	77	43½	22½	2¾	BarrowT6	Alw	84	CraftyD'ne119 R'gglesFerry DonOman	7

April 30 CD 5f ft 1:03⅖b April 23 Kee 3f ft :36b April 20 Kee 5f ft 1:04b

Dixmart 122

B. g (1972), by Swoon's Son—Liz Piet, by Piet.
Breeder, Copelan & Thornbury (Ky.). 1975 7 2 3 2 $29,800
Owner, C. O. Viar & R. Holthus. Trainer, R. Holthus. 1974 13 2 2 3 $11,085

22 Apr75	6Kee	7 f	:23 :4541:23	ft	6½	122	78	66½	24	22	CampbllRJ1	Alw	89	Paris Dust 116 Dixmart	9
5 Apr75	7OP	170	:4611:1141:414	ft	8	113	79	63¾	2½	1¾	CampbllRJ3	Alw	87	Dixmart 113 Doug	6
31 Mar75	5OP	6 f	:22 :4541:112	ft	6-5	▲118	41¾	52	41	32	CampbllRJ3	Alw	86	Jay'sGig114 BourrePadnah	9
26 Mar75	6OP	6 f	:22 :4511:104	ft	5¾	113	32	23½	22½	2no	CmpblRJ10	Alw	91	Pleasure Prize 113 Dixmart	10
11 Mar75	6OP	6 f	:221 :4611:131	sl	8¾	112	86¾	77½	43	11½	CmpblRJ3	22500	79	Dixmart 112 Kayjo	11
4 Mar75	6OP	6 f	:214 :4511:12	ft	3¼	114	54	54¼	3nk	2nk	RiniA9	15000	85	Warrior Knight 112 Dixmart	10
18 Feb75	6OP	5½ f	:222 :4641:053	ft	4¾	116	84	53¼	41½	36½	RiniA9	15000	83	BourrePadnh111 GrtRhythm	12
Oct19-74	5Haw	6½ f	1:16⅕	ft	8-5e	▲114	87½	814	714	711	LivelyJ1	Alw	81	Str'teMiss114 J'dgeBol'm'r Hon'yM'rk	9

April 29 CD 6f ft 1:18b Mar 25 OP 3f ft :37⅗b Mar 20 OP 5f ft 1:02⅗b

Marauding

119 Gr. c (1972), by Warfare—Juliet, by Nearctic.
Breeder, Barrett M. Morris & Virginia M. Morris (Ky.). 1975 . . 8 2 2 2 $32,450
Owner, Bromagen Cattle Co. Trainer, G. P. Bernis. 1974 10 1 3 0 $7,955

22 Apr75 6Kee 7 f :23 :4541:23 ft 3¾ 122 32 54½ 34½ 33 LouvereGE7 Alw 88 Paris Dust 116 Dixmart 9
5 Apr75 9OP 1⅛ :4641:1021:514ft 17 123 53½ 94½ 85½ 85½ McHrgeD7 AlwS 79 PrmisedCity126 BldChapeau 14
15 Mar75 9OP 170 :4721:1311:442gd 2e 119 31 2h 41¾ 54¾ MelncnL2 HcpO 69 PromisedCity120 Me n'Mine 12
8 Mar75 7OP 170 :23 :4721:42 ft 4½ 117 1½ 1h 1h 1h MelanconL1 Alw 86 Maraudng117 CountryByJim 7
28 Feb75 8OP 6 f :213 :4511:111ft 4¾ 122 51¾ 44 53¾ 22¾ MelnconL8 Alw 86 PoorOldJoe 114 Marauding 8
14 Feb75 8OP 6 f :214 :4431:102ft 2½e*120 53¼ 47 31 31 MelconL4 HcpO 92 King Jody 112 Untwine 11
7 Feb75 8OP 5½ f :221 :4621:06 gd 27 117 52¼ 42¼ 31½ 1¾ MelnconL4 Alw 88 Marauding 117 Peto'sFellow 12
24 Jan75 8LaD 6 f :231 :4821:142m 9-5 *1155 11½ 16 13 2½ WolfCG6 Alw Hot Paque 111 Marauding 6
Nov30-749FG 6 f 1:13⅘gd 68 112 42½ 33 58½ 511 Mel'onL6 HcpO 70 HoneyM'k117 RusticRuler MidniteR'o 14
April 28 CD 1m ft 1:45⅗b April 21 Kee 3f ft :37⅗b April 16 Kee 5f ft :59h

Naughty Jake

122 Dk. b. or br. c (1972), by Gallant Romeo—Matrona, by Terra Firma.
Breeder, S. Turner (Ky.). 1975 . . 8 2 0 1 $25,650
Owner, Mildred Bachelor. Trainer, J. Bachelor. 1974 . . 7 3 1 0 $17,675

29 Apr75 8CD 1 :4641:11 1:362ft 4½ 122 21½ 2½ 31½ 33¼ VasqzG4 AlwS 94 RoundStake122 RushingMan 5
15 Apr75 7Kee 1 1/16 :47 1:11 1:423gd 9½ 123 33½ 43½ 55½ 412 VasquezG1 Alw 81 MasterDerby123 RugglsFrry 6
29 Mar75 7Lat 1 :48 1:1321:40 gd 1-3 *119 1½ 13 1½ 11 VasqzG3 AlwS 79 NaughtyJke119 PromndeLft 9
22 Mar75 5Lat 6 f :23 :4711:124sy 2-3 *122 26 23 11 14 VasquezG7 Alw 84 NaughtyJake122 ColonialPnt 7
20 Feb75 3Hia 1 1/16 :4631:11 1:424sy 5½ 117 711 511 48 49¾ ValdizanF1 Alw 79 CircleHome119 Administratr 7
29 Jan75 9Hia 7 f :222 :4441:22 ft 30 115 68 58 58 65½ ValdiznF5 AlwS 89 Ascetic 115 Ellora 11
18 Jan75 9Hia 6 f :22 :4431:101sy 74 115 75¾ 56½ 45 41¾ ValdiznF6 AlwS 90 Ricks Jet 114 Prevailer 11
Jan 9-759Crc 6½ f 1:19⅗ft 15 122 67 68¾ 67 45½ ValdizanF4 Alw 87 Strateaway113 Prevailer IrishRing 6
April 27 CD 3f ft :35h

Mr. Snow Cap

113 B. g (1972), by One More Chorus—Orange Ice, by Iceberg II.
Breeder, H. G. Tilson (Ky.). 1975 . . 6 2 2 1 $9,210
Owner, Audley Farm Stable. Trainer, D. Smith.

24 Apr75 4Kee 6 f :22 :45 1:101sy 4 114 68 56½ 49 514 DelahyeE10 Alw 77 BearerBond112 CmmrclFilot 11
18 Apr75 6Kee 7 f :233 :4631:242ft 6-5 *112 21½ 2½ 2½ 12½ DelahsyeE2 Alw 84 Mr. Snow Cap 112 Easabaya 10
9 Apr75 7Kee 6 f :222 :4541:103ft 8-5 *114 43 43 21 2¾ DelahsyeE3 Alw 88 RushingMan118 Mr.SnwCap 9
12 Mar75 7FG 6 f :222 :4641:122ft 3-2 120 54¾ 44 31½ 2no DelahsyeE1 Alw 86 FlwlssFinish120 Mr.SnwCap 7
26 Feb75 8FG 6 f :214 :4531:111ft 1-2e*120 4¾ 1h 21 34½ AndersnJR8 Alw 87 Tailor'sTack120 BoldChapau 9
16 Feb75 2FG 6 f :224 :4811:141sl 3-2 *120 1½ 11 12 15 DsyeE11 M10000 77 Mr.SnwCap120 BrtherBadBy 12
April 17 Kee 3f ft :35⅖b April 7 Kee 3f ft :36b March 28 FG 3f ft :37b

Victory Judge

113 B. c (1972), by Traffic Judge—Choiseul, by Victory Morn.
Breeder, R. C. Kyle (Can.). 1975 . . 8 1 0 0 $1,452
Owner, Sacred Stable. Trainer, A. Battaglia. 1974 4 M 1 1 $1,050

17 Apr75 9GP Ⓣ a 1 1:392fm 90 114 813 811 813 823 RamosR6 Alw 61 TooCordial 114 StepForward 8
10 Mar75 9GP 7 f :22 :4411:213ft 239 110 55½1016 1023 1128 DennieD10 AlwS 68 GreekAnswer122 FashinSale 11
1 Mar75 6Hia 6 f :222 :4541:102ft 54 119 97¼ 810 914 913 ArroyoH7 Alw 78 SwingLbrSwing117 Zinglng 10
5 Feb75 8Hia 7 f :231 :4531:224ft 66 122 32½ 54½ 917 1118 BrumfelcD9 Alw 73 Directory 117 Jimbosanda 11
29 Jan75 9Hia 7 f :222 :4441:22 ft 299 112 57 915 1120 1117 ArroyoH11 AlwS 78 Ascetic 115 Ellora 11
18 Jan75 3Cwl 6½ :242 :4831:234m 2 *120 15 16 15 19 SaylerB5 Mdn 79 VictoryJudge120 ZperGgette 8
Jan10-758Cwl 5½ f 1:08⅖sy 5 105 614 511 54¼ 41½ ClinchT1 Alw 81 Mike'sPal 116 PrinceArc NoDate 7
Jan 2-758Cwl 6½ f 1:25⅖m 13 116 63¼ 31½ 31½ 818 GastonR6 Alw 53 Donda'sMir'e122 CoolItB'e Jan't'sDe't 10
Dec21-743Cwl a1 1:42⅘gd 2-3 *120 14 11 2h 35½ SaylerB1 Mdn 61 Cool ItBabe117 BrightM'ch V't'ryJ'ge 10
Dec 7-748Cwl 1 1/16 1:54⅘sy 29 111 21½ 1h 1h 21½ SaylerB4 Alw 65 Clar'ceH'ry113 Vict'yJ'ge JimDanBob 6
April 21 GP 7f ft 1:28⅘h

Greek Answer

122 B. c (1972), by Northern Answer—Greek Victress, by Victoria Park.
Breeder, E. P. Taylor (Can.). 1975 5 3 0 1 $57,707
Ownr, W P. Gilbride. Trainer, F. H. Merrill. 1974 . 11 5 2 2 $187,261

26 Apr75 7CD 7 f :234 :4711:25 ft 1-3 *122 1½ 12½ 12 1¾ SolomneM7 Alw 82 Greek Answer122 Gatch 7
19 Mar75 9GP 1 1/16 :46 1:1011:424ft 6-5 *122 15 16 13 14 SolmneM6 AlwS 87 Greek Answer 122 Decipher 8
10 Mar75 9GP 7 f :22 :4411:213ft 3-5 *122 1½ 1½ 14 15 CstdaM11 AlwS 96 GreekAnswer122 FashinSalc 11
29 Jan75 9Hia 7 f :222 :4441:22 ft 3½ 122 11 11½ 22 44¾ CastaM10 AlwS 90 Ascetic 115 Ellora 11
18 Jan75 9Hia 6 f :22 :4431:101sy 3-5 *122 1h 1h 2h 31 CstndaM4 AlwS 91 Ricks Jet 114 Prevailer 11
Oct19-748Bow 7 f 1:24⅘ft 2-3 *119 22½ 22 1h 2¾ Hin'j'saH6 AlwS 80 Gall'tBob113 Gr'kAnswer ParvaHasta 10
Sep15-748WO 1-70 1:42⅕ft 7-5 122 11½ 11 22½ 36½ C'st'daM7 HcpS 85 L'Enjol'r122 N'r t'eHighS'a G'kAnsw'r 11
Sep 2-748AP 6½ f 1:17⅘ft 3½ 122 12½ 11 11½ 1¾ C'st'daM2 ScwS 86 Gr'kAnsw'r122 Col'lP'w'r TheB'g'lPr'e 7
Aug24-748Sar 6½ f 1:15 ft 13 121 12½ 12 1½ 2¾ Cas'daM8 ScwS 92 F'lishPl's're121 G'kAnsw'r OurT'lism'n 8
Aug 5-746FE 6½ f 1:21⅕sl 2-5 *120 1h 2h 1h 48 GreenW2 AlwS 65 Col'sCl'rion115 OnaP'dSt'l'g P'sleyPal 8
Jly 21-746FE 6½ f 1:17 ft 1-3 *122 1½ 12 13 1¾ GreenW2 AlwS 94 Greek Answer 122 L'Enjoleur Hagelin 5
Jun28-746WO 6 f 1:10⅗ft 4-5 *120 2h 1½ 13 17 GreenW4 AlwS 90 Gr'kAnswer120 N'r t.HighSea R'lS'ari 6
Jun 9-746WO 6 f 1:10⅖ft 1-2 *114 1h 12 13½ 15½ GreenW7 AlwS 91 GreekAnswer114 Sgt.Hunt RunJay 7
April 21 CD 1m ft 1:41h

As I explained in Chapter 4, the position of the starting gate relative to the first turn is very important in middle-distance route races at most racetracks. Churchill Downs is one of those tracks.

The favorite in this race—the Twin Spires Purse, an annual fixture on the Derby Day program—is Greek Answer at 3–5. There are several reasons why this choice is outrageously out of line with reality.

One of those reasons is named Ruggles Ferry, who has run only one subpar race (March 22) while meeting some of the best three-year-old routers in America (Master Derby, Colonel Power, Honey Mark, Circle Home). He has also shown enough speed in several of his races to suggest he can take advantage of his inner post position.

The other reasons lie with Greek Answer himself. This is a colt that has shown a tendency to tire in the late stages at 6½ furlongs and beyond; a colt whose lone win around two turns was scored on Gulfstream Park's notorious front-running track; a colt that will have to use much of his early speed to get clear of this field in the short run to the first turn. These are serious problems for a 3–5 shot to overcome. I make him 6–1.

The crowd made Ruggles Ferry 5–2. I make him even money, a 250 percent overlay. The key to this betting situation is more subtle than that of a Flylet-type front runner, but it is nevertheless there for all to see. The favorite is breaking from a disadvantageous post position, and his past performance history suggests he can ill afford to race under a handicap. The chief competition is easily identified and is set to race from a favorable post.

In the race Greek Answer raced four wide in the run to and through the clubhouse turn, struggled to get the lead on the backstretch, and tired steadily thereafter to finish fourth. Ruggles Ferry saved ground, held a striking position to the far turn, and rallied in the upper stretch to win by seven widening lengths. Had the post positions been reversed, I am sure Greek Answer would have given a much better account of himself.

Learning to recognize the straightforward betting opportunity is fundamental to the player's ambitions for profit. There will be countless other times, however, when the player will have to use all the tools in his bag to uncover the probable race winner. As often as 80 percent of the time, the only conclusion to be drawn from the effort is that no single horse in the field deserves a significant edge. There is great joy, however, in the exception.

SEPTEMBER 24, 1976

7th Tdn

$3 PERFECTA WAGERING ON THIS RACE

6 FURLONGS (chute). (1:09⅘). CLAIMING. Purse $2,300. Fillies and mares. 3-year-olds and upward. 3-year-olds, 115 lbs.; older, 121 lbs. Non-winners of three races since June 30 allowed 2 lbs.; two races since then. 4 lbs.; a race since then, 6 lbs. Claiming price. $2,500; if for $2.250. allowed 2 lbs.

Sultan Sue Sis **112** Ro. f (1972) by Venetian Jester—Sultan s Sue, by Strokkr.
Br. Edward & J. Armstrong. Jr (Okla.) 1976 15 5 3 1 $8,642
Owner, R. F. Zupanc. Trainer. Ida Zupanc. $2.500 1975 6 M 3 2 $1 680

11 Sep76 4Tdn	6 f	:233 :4821:142sl	2½	1085	42	41	3nk	11½	BordenD2	c2000	77	SultanSueSis108	TurningShy	8
3 Sep76 7Tdn	6 f	:23 :4811:151ft	6-5	▴1115	86¼	41¼	31½	21½	BordenD4	2000	71	ⒻAmberComt116	SltnSeSis	8
19 Aug76 6Tdn	6 f	:23 :47 1:124ft	2½	▴1115	34	23	33½	36	BordenD7	2500	79	ⒻAprilFrost120	MissJeerful	7
15 Aug76 3Tdn	5½ f	:223 :4741:08 m	7½	1125	86¼	86¼	74	64½	BordenD2	2500	74	JazzDancer111	BridgePatrl	8
24 Jly 7610Tdn	6 f	:224 :4711:142ft	6½	117	51¾	31	41½	2nk	GraellA3	2500	77	WrkAndTrn120	SltanSueSis	10
15 Jly 7610Tdn	6 f	:222 :4611:13 ft	5½	117	86¼	65½	53½	45½	FelinoBR8	2500	78	ClayPigeon122	GreekWhiz	12
17 Jun76 2Tdn	6 f	:224 :4721:144sl	3½	117	74½	57	41½	24	FelicoBR1	2500	71	OverlandWay120	SltnSueSis	10
11 Jun76 6Tdn	6 f	:232 :4741:134gd	12	117	96¾	87	55	57½	KelleyBA4	3500	72	Blocklamur 122	Count Adam	9
3 Jun76 5Tdn	6 f	:222 :4611:131ft	3	117	32	21½	1h	12	FelicoBR2	2500	83	SultanSueSis117	HevnlyRosa	9
26 May76 5Tdn	6 f	:223 :4721:133ft	5	120	43	22	15	110	FelicoBR1	2000	91	ⒻSultanSueSis120	HwieToo	11

Shad Pac **110** B. m (1971), by Clem Pac—Star Shadow, by Stella Aurata.
Breeder. C. P. Blake & S. Laser (Ark.). 1976 15 3 1 1 $6,141
Owner, Lela Mellinger. Trainer, Edward H. Mellinger III. $2.500 1975 21 2 1 2 $4.287

19 Sep76 1Tdn	5½ f	:224 :4731:071ft	18	1085	83¼	63¾	66	57½	FranscoD8	2500	75	GallowayBay116	ShrLovelins	8
5 Sep76 8Com	4½ f	:233 :473 :54 ft	10	114	4	53½	67½	44¼	AntusLJ5	2500	89	Hollie'sPaxton115	HenryH.	7
29 Jun76 6Com	6½ f	:23 :47 1:193ft	2½	114	614	513	411	47¼	LydaR2	2500	84	EasyMission117	G.J.Frmlwy	6
6 Jun76 5RD	170	:48 1:1341:464ft	3	109	45½	42½	3½	31¾	NewkirkT7	2500	64	Humbjo 116	Make Me Gone	8
31 May76 3RD	6 f	:221 :4631:133m	3	1077	310	37½	31½	11½	TalricoM1	2500	75	Shad Pac 107	Althen	7
22 May76 3RD	6 f	:221 :4621:123ft	17	1087	88½	87½	74½	61¼	TalaricoM1	2500	79	Liberal Man 116	Hesourpet	12
14 May76 2RD	6 f	:222 :4621:114ft	41	119	85½	90½	97½	011	WingoR9	3500	73	ⒻAnthorPluck116	Buxomby	10
13 Apr76 5HP	1	:4921:1521:424ft	30	115	98¼	109	916	915	GilbtCJJr5	3200	54	HotShotDor115	AkepotSask	10
5 Apr76 6HP	6½ f	:23 :48 1:202ft	9¾	1105	57½	58	69½	67	RodgzJD3	3200	72	CocntRow115	Kg of theOzks	10
29 Mar76 5Lat	1	:4741:15 1:44 m	10	1127	45	22½	11½	15	NewkirkT4	2500	58	ⒻShadPac112	QueerVashti	9

Crafty Vodelia **115** Dk. b. or br. f (1972), by Noble Commander—Crafty Love, by Crafty
Admiral. Breeder, F. Wiercioch (Fla.). 1976 24 3 2 2 $5,954
Owner, L. R.Benshoff, lessee. Trainer, L. R. Benshoff. $2.500 1975 22 0 0 1 $2,529

18 Sep76 3Tdn	6 f	:231 :4741:141m	31	114	43	33½	21½	22	RiniA4	2000	76	Rick'sBuckeye120	CrftyVdlia	8
11 Sep76 4Tdn	6 f	:233 :4821:142sl	67	114	83¼	77	53¾	45½	RiniA3	2000	71	SultanSueSis108	TurningShy	8
14 Aug76 5Tdn	6 f	:224 :4711:141sl	63	114	42	75½	66½	69¼	RiniA3	2000	69	King's Levy 122	Fast Arab	8
4 Aug76 7Tdn	6 f	:232 :4731:144ft	93	118	52¾	45	66	67½	InfanteF8	2000	67	ⒻTouchO'Ri113	April Silvrs	8
28 Jly 76 5Tdn	5½ f	:221 :48 1:083ft	21	1117	74¾	87	710	68	StaffordA7	2000	68	ⒻConfetti 118	Lady's Hat	8
8 Jly 76 7Tdn	140	:4911:1541:47 sl	25	115	21½	44½	86½	813	RiniA4	2000	47	EarlyLady117	CertnlyMntrip	9
30 Jun76 4Tdn	6 f	:24 :49 1:163sy	2½	115	21	1h	11	12	RiniA7	2000	66	CraftyVodelia115	FirstBurst	7
24 Jun76 5Tdn	140	:4811:1541:482sy	5¾	117	12	21	53	610	CooperG3	2000	43	PrceBravos122	StlTheRoses	7
17 Jun76 7Tdn	6 f	:222 :4621:142sl	39	117	87¼	76½	64¼	48½	CooperG2	2500	68	Greek Whiz 118	Our Pirate	8

Sept j Tdn 5f ft 1:03⅘b

Kin O Mine 115

Ch. m (1969), by Mighty Mine—Kimeo, by Ozbeg.
Breeder, J. A. Davis (Cal.). 1976 12 4 1 1 $6,345
Owner, Bunny Coatney. Trainer, Bunny Coatney. $2,250 1975 14 2 3 2 $5,020

4 Aug76	7Tdn	6 f	:232 :4731:144ft	4½	120	42½	65½	43	44½	MunsterL3	2000	70	ⒻTouchO'Ri113	April Silvrs	8
24 Jly76	2Tdn	6 f	:224 :4721:142ft	2½	117	32½	31	42	78½	MunsterL5	2000	68	Part Western 120	Fleet Pac	8
8 Jly 76	6Tdn	6 f	:231 :4731:142sl	8-5	•118	21	1h	1h	11	SosaR8	2000	77	ⒻKin O Mine 118	Tiz A Joy	8
23 Jun76	7Tdn	6 f	:223 :4641:14 ft	8-5	•116	73¾	41½	3½	11	SosaR9	2000	79	ⒻKinOMine 116	MissJeerful	9
5 Jun76	5Tdn	6 f	:232 :4711:131ft	8	115	3½	2½	21	14	SosaR1	2000	83	Kin O Mine 115	Extinguisher	12
26 Mar76	6Tdn ⊡	a 5 f	:234 :4841:014ft	2¾	118	1h	2h	2½	43½	CooperG6	2000	83	ⒻIndianCojo120	AtollsMiss	6
20 Mar76	7Tdn ⊡	a 5 f	:224 :48 1:011ft	3½	118	54½	53½	33	24½	GraellA5	2500	84	ⒻTrafficGun113	KinOMine	7
13 Mar76	10Tdn ⊡	a 5 f	:24 :49 1:02 gd	9-5	113	85¼	34½	32½	11	GraellA5	2000	85	Kin O Mine 113	Alfie O	10
6 Mar76	3Tdn ⊡	a 5 f	:242 :4831:012ft	5	115	22½	31½	33½	34	PlackeD9	2000	84	Hub 118	Smart David	9

Sheer Loveliness 112

B. m (1971), by Molino—Mischief Miss, by Don Mike.
Breeder, Mrs. J. P. Strain (Ohio). 1976 13 3 1 1 $3,492
Owner, J. P. Strain, Jr. Trainer, J. P. Strain, Jr. $2,500 1975 5 M 0 0 $161

19 Sep76	1Tdn	5½ f	:224 :4731:071ft	28	1087	11	11	12	22	ShewellJ1	2500	81	GallowayBay116	ShrLovelins	8
29 Aug76	2Tdn	6 f	:231 :4721:124gd	19	115	62¾	56½	47	616	D'AmicoA9	2500	69	Angl'sPlsre118	Freemn'sMn	9
12 Aug76	9Tdn	6 f	:224 :4641:131ft	54	117	1½	21	66½	615	VaughnJ5	6000	68	ⒻBaryVible115	VincesDr'm	7
31 Jly 76	5Com	6½ f	:243 :4841:214ft	16	117	1h	22½	13	11½	PhillipsD10	2000	80	SheerLoveliness117	MsPnRn	10
22 Jly 76	5Com	4½ f	:232 :471 :534ft	2½	117	1	21½	24	36½	†HussrMW9	2000	88	Time ofEmprrs122	MissLrgrs	9
†Disqualified and placed seventh.															
15 Jly 76	4Com	6½ f	:234 :4731:211ft	4½	117	12	11	1½	45	HussrMW2	2000	78	JolliPassage114	MissPanRun	7
1 Jly 76	10Tdn	6 f	:231 :4821:16 m	39	118	11½	1h	1h	45½	HussrMW4	2500	63	SandyLathe102	CrtyDestino	10
1 Jly 76	10Tdn	6 f	:231 :4821:16 m	39	118	11½	1h	1h	45½	†HussrMW4	2500	63	SandyLathe102	CrftyDestino	10
†Placed third through disqualification.															
21 Jun76	2Com	5 f	:233 :4731:011ft	2¾	118	11½	12	11	11½	HussrMW1	1500	82	ShrLovelinss118	GenrlMateo	8

Bibi Mine 115

Ch. m (1971), by O'Bibi—Condamine, by Deliberator.
Breeder, J. W. Mecom (Tex.). 1976 16 3 4 1 $10,521
Owner, Miller Farm. Trainer, Edward Collins. $2,500 1975 14 1 2 3 $4,285

11 Sep76	6Lat	6½ f	:24 :48 1:211ft	6½	116	41½	42½	54½	65	TennbmM8	5000	70	Tosoro 113	Circus Act	10
5 Sep76	10RD	6 f	:221 :4541:113ft	8¼	111	42	42	35	45½	TnnbmM5	05000	79	ResJudicada113	MmySowrd	11
28 Aug76	6Tdn	140	:4711:1341:45 sl	6¾	113	22	23	86	811	MunsterL8	6000	59	Reasontodare113	BritishRed	8
12 Aug76	9Tdn	6 f	:224 :4641:131ft	3	116	41	31	32	31½	MunsterL6	6000	82	ⒻBaryVible115	VincesDr'm	7
1 Aug76	7Tdn	6 f	:223 :4631:13 ft	27	115	31	52½	42	53½	MunsterL1	7000	81	Dad'sReflction116	BrlyVsble	10
24 Jly 76	7RD	5½ f	:223 :4621:063sy	7½	117	87½	912	68½	68¾	SorezW5	A2500	73	Triptique 116	Shaded Silver	10
27 Jun76	8Tdn	6 f	:23 :4621:12 ft	19	116	42½	54	55½	510	MunsterL2	Alw	79	ⒻGoOnDrmng116	Mrge'sPck	7
9 Jun76	9Tdn	6 f	:223 :46 1:122ft	8½	114	22	23	2½	13	MunsterL2	Alw	87	ⒻBibi Mine 114	Lark Star	10
1 Jun76	5CD	6 f	:223 :4541:122ft	31	117	31½	1½	11½	2nk	SoirezW8	5000	84	ⒻHelen'sMusic117	BibiMine	9
2[illegible] May76	8Tdn	6 f	:231 :47 1:131ft	3½	116	1h	1h	1h	11	MunsterL3	3500	83	ⒻBibiMine116	GoDancerGo	7

Pajone's Hostess 115

Ch. f (1972), by Pajone—Anchorette, by My Host.
Breeder, W. J. Kosterman (Wash.). 1976 13 0 0 1 $558
Owner, W. Kosterman. Trainer, John Myers. $

15 Sep76	10Tdn	6 f	:23 :47 1:132ft	33	115	62½	43	98¾	1014	PlackeD5	3500	68	SkyLock111	Work and Turn	11
5 Sep76	3Tdn	140	:4741:1331:43 ft	42	1085	43½	69	817	836	BordenD8	3500	44	LookWho'sHere 122	DuroT	[illegible]
26 Aug76	6Tdn	6 f	:23 :4631:13 ft	5	1095	51½	22	54½	612	KelleyBA9	3500	72	ⒻGrandElm116	April Frost	9
19 Aug76	9Tdn	6 f	:222 :4541:124ft	19	1085	33½	21	4¾	65½	KelleyBA9	3500	80	InfieldHomer117	AbilityPls	10
6 Aug76	7Tdn	6 f	:223 :4611:123ft	23	113	32½	34	67	715	SackettR3	4500	71	LookWho'sHere118	SkyLock	8
28 Jly 76	7Tdn	6 f	:222 :4621:131ft	15	1085	63¾	43½	43½	78	KelleyBA5	4500	75	Urticante116	Whatawaytogo	8
22 Jly 76	9Tdn	6 f	:222 :4631:133ft	18	1095	42	1h	1h	34½	KelleyBA6	4500	76	ⒻMillennum115	Wally'sSisr	9
15 Jly 76	9Tdn	6 f	:224 :4631:121ft	26	115	31½	2h	75	714	GraellA5	5000	74	IndianSpeed 120	EarlsMeldy	7
19 Jun76	7Tdn	6 f	:224 :4711:14 m	22	117	71½	31½	52¾	610	FelicnoBR6	Alw	69	BoldTom122	Great[illegible]bridge	7

Aug 2 Tdn 3f ft :37⅘bg

Foolish Lola 117

Ch. m (1970), by Venetian Jester—Lassa Gal, by Gallahadion.
Breeder, C. Sawyer (Okla.). 1976 10 2 1 1 $2,689
Owner, G. Mancuso. Trainer, Joseph Mazur. $2,500 1975 25 6 4 5 $10,446

10 Sep76	5Tdn	6 f	:233 :4821:152sl	2	•114	1h	11½	13	14½	D'AmicoA1	2000	72	ⒻFoolishLola114	IndianLil	7
27 Aug76	7Tdn	6 f	:231 :47 1:141sl	28	113	2½	73¾	55	55½	D'AmicoA4	2500	72	DriveJoy122	LadofPrtsmuth	10
31 Jly 76	6Com	5 f	:232 :4731:002ft	4½	117	31½	33	35	35¼	RamosW5	2500	84	Sharpsville 115	Base Fiddle	7
17 Jly 76	6Com	5 f	:23 :4731:001ft	3	117	54¼	68	67	65	RamosW7	2500	82	OpenWind122	KamsinWind	7
26 Jun76	8Com	6½ f	:233 :4731:212ft	2¾	•112	1½	1½	21	22½	RamosW4	2500	79	Wild Boss 117	Foolish Lola	7
18 Jun76	9Com	6½ f	:241 :4821:22 ft	3¾	•115	12	12	15	112	RamosW1	2000	79	FoolishLola115	RennieBee	10

Confetti 112

Dk. b. or br. f (1972), by Roman Line—Starstruck, by Dark Star.
Breeder W H. May (Ky.). 1976 16 4 0 4 $6,147
Owner, K. E. Strickler. Trainer, Homer Dewey. $2,500 1975 16 0 2 3 $2,148

29 Aug76	7RD	6 f	:22 :4611:121ft	21	1107	87	811	813	819	MysJRJr8	02500	63	TriplicateCopy 111	BushHoc	8
28 Jly 76	5Tdn	5½ f	:221 :48 1:083ft	9¾	118	54½	34	32	13	InfanteF6	2000	76	ⒻConfetti 118	Lady's Hat	8
9 Jly 76	zFL	5½ f	:233 :48 1:081ft	6	114	31½	3½	13	13¼	VedilgoW4	2000	81	Confetti 114	Northen Proof	7
3 Jly 76	7FL	5½ f	:224 :4641:081ft	7	115	63¾	65¼	66¼	56½	VedilgoW6	2000	74	Tisha Bell 115	Grossecat	7
26 Jun76	5FL	6 f	:223 :4641:142ft	4	114	42½	2h	2h	44	VedilgoW1	2000	78	Prove It Su 106	Easy Mike	6
15 Jun76	6FL	6 f	:23 :4611:122ft	13	112	67	57½	67	76¼	WingoR5	A1750	85	Barborian 112	Petit Homme	8
5 Jun76	6FL	5½ f	:222 :4631:061ft	29	111	74¾	76½	76	65½	WingoR7	3000	85	Misget 111	Anar Kali	7
22 May76	6FL	5½ f	:223 :47 1:071ft	18	111	77¾	67	65	78	RinconR7	3500	78	RuthlessCount116	ShoeTax	8

Using only the past performance records above, the handicapper would have a hard time justifying a confident selection. Several horses in the field appear to be in good form, while a few others are ostensibly dropping in class. Yet the past performance records do not contain sufficient clues to make conclusive comparisons. The same is true for the majority of claiming races run throughout the country.

There is no trick bias, no known trainer pattern, and no unusual betting activity to consider. But there are result charts, and classification codes, and speed figures.

Using speed figures or result-chart time comparisons, we would begin our detective work by determining that Sultan Sue Sis ran the fastest recent race.

On September 11, in an open-grade $2,000 claiming race, Sultan Sue Sis completed six furlongs in 1:14²/₅, not very impressive time on first glance. But compared with several other races that day, the time was extraordinary. These were some of the other six-furlong times posted:

$5,000 claiming 1:14¹/₅
$4,500 claiming 1:14⁴/₅
$3,500 claiming 1:14²/₅
$3,000 claiming 1:14³/₅

Obviously, Sultan Sue Sis ran a big race last time out and is ready to step up sharply in class. But what about the rest of the field? What about 4–5 favorite Bibi Mine, who is getting play mostly on the basis of her sharp drop in claiming price?

In my judgment, this is not a negative class drop in the classic sense. Considering Bibi Mine's inability to win at the higher claiming level, the drop in class may be what she needs to get back on the winning track. In order to make a clearer determination of that judgment we need to discover more information about the caliber of horses she faced at Latonia. Again, result charts and comparative race times will prove very useful to this end.

The first race on the September 11 Latonia card was a $3,500 maiden claiming race. The functions and final time were identical to Bibi Mine's $5,000 claiming race, a race for proven winners: .24 . . . .48 . . . 1:14⅕ . . . 1:21⅕. Two conclusions are possible: Either the maiden race was run very fast or Bibi Mine's race was run very slow.

Two other races run that day say Bibi Mine was in a slow field:

$3,500 claiming. 1:14⅖
$3,500 claiming. . . . . .1:14 . . . 1:20⅘

Indeed, Bibi Mine may once have been a much better horse and will probably appreciate the drop in class today, but at present she is not faster than Sultan Sue Sis and has no right to be favored over her.

Crafty Vodelia was recently trounced by Sultan Sue Sis and then came back to race very creditably in an open-grade $2,000 claimer. Another meeting with Sultan Sue Sis will not be what the doctor ordered.

Shad Pac recently returned to competition but gave no indication that she is fit enough to catch these horses in a six-furlong race.

Kin O' Mine has been absent from competition for seven weeks and is stepping up in claiming price. A good performance is likely, considering the interval that preceded her win over a weak field on June 5; but it would be asking too much to have her step into this field of multiple winners to win first crack out of the box.

Sheer Loveliness has shown good early speed on several occasions, but she couldn't hold onto a clear lead in a shorter race last time out. A time-comparison study of the races run that day will also show that Sheer Loveliness was in a slow $2,500 race.

Pajone's Hostess is winless this year and desperately needs a drop in class. Signs of early lick in her recent past performances are valid indicators of improving physical condition; but a win seems unlikely.

Foolish Lola won her last race the same way she scored her only other victory this season: wire to wire. A review of the Thistledown charts for September 10 will make light of her chances to repeat that today. Although she had the rail from start to finish on a track that was extremely biased toward the inside, her fractional times were slower than those for most of the other races on the card. Moreover, she is stepping up sharply in company from a C-class $2,000 claimer to an open-class $2,500 race.

Confetti was in top form at the tail end of July but spent a month in the barn before making her next start. That's a clear sign of physical problems, fully confirmed by her August 29 performance, the worst race on her chart. She now returns with another four-week vacation behind her. If this horse wins, the knowledgeable horseplayers in the crowd should give trainer Homer Dewey a standing ovation; but few if any of them will wager on her chances. Short of clear-cut evidence in the post parade, there is no logical reason to conclude that this horse is back in top competitive form.

EXACTA PAYOFF FOR SULTAN SUE SIS WITH	
Bibi Mine	$ 52
Shad Pac	$ 96
Foolish Lola	$158
Pajone's Hostess	$190
Crafty Vodelia	$210
Sheer Loveliness	$275
Kin O'Mine	$275
Confetti	$390

On the basis of the material that our detective work has uncovered, we may now conclude that Sultan Sue Sis has a decided edge over every horse in the race. Indeed, she need only run within two lengths of her most recent race to win in a walk. For added confidence, her honest record, including five prior wins, suggests that she is likely to do that and more. Given 7–2 odds on Sultan Sue Sis, we should forgive the player who is now making a mad dash to the win windows, but anyone contemplating a wager larger than $30 would be better off investing in the exacta pool.

At $3 per ticket, a straight wheel would cost $24, but it would also leave the player open to two less profitable results (Bibi Mine or Shad Pac). However, there are other alternatives to consider, and the following is only the simplest.

By purchasing two *extra* combinations with Bibi Mine and one with Shad Pac, the player would automatically increase the minimum odds on Sultan Sue Sis to 4–1 ($33 invested, $156 minimum possible payoff) and give himself a chance for considerably greater rewards without additional risk. In a game that taxes the player 20 cents for every dollar wagered, 50 cents extra profit on the dollar is nothing to sneeze at. (See betting strategies in Appendix.)

SEVENTH RACE
Tdn
Sept'ber 24, 1976

6 FURLONGS (chute). (1:09⅗). CLAIMING. Purse $2,300. Fillies and mares. 3-year-olds and upward. 3-year-olds, 115 lbs.; older, 121 lbs. Non-winners of three races since June 30 allowed 2 lbs.; two races since then, 4 lbs.; a race since then, 6 lbs. Claiming price, $2,500; if for $2,250, allowed 2 lbs.

Value to winner $1,380; second, $460; third, $230; fourth, $115; fifth, $69; sixth, $46. Mutuel Pool, $14,296. Perfecta Pool, $32,082.

Last Raced	Horse	EqtAWt	PP	St	¼	½	Str	Fin	Jockeys	Owners	Odds to $1
11 Sep76 4Tdn1	Sultan Sue Sis	b4 117	1	7	2h	2h	11	13	RSackett	R F Zuanc	3.60
11 Sep76 6Lat6	Bibi Mine	b5 115	6	8	6½	3½	2¹	2¹	LMunster	Miller Farm	.80
15 Sep76 10Tdn10	Jajone's Hostess	b4 115	7	2	4h	4½	41	3no	DPlacke	W Kosterman	16.80
4 Aug76 7Tdn4	Kin O Mine	7 115	4	4	7h	5¹	3½	4½	BMWilson	Bunny Coatney	21.30
18 Sep76 3Tdn2	Crafty Vodelia	b4 115	3	9	8h	9	5h	5¹	ARini	L R Benshoff lessee	12.70
19 Sep76 1Tdn5	Shad Pac	b5 110	2	5	3r	61	61	61	BAKelley5	Mrs L Mellinger	5.60
10 Sep76 5Tdn1	Foolish Lola	6 117	8	3	5¹	7h	8½	7¹	AD'Amico	G Mancuso	12.50
19 Sep76 1Tdn2	Sheer Loveliness	b5 112	5	6	9	82	9	82	JShewell7	J P Strain Jr	23.30
29 Aug76 7RD8	Confetti	b4 112	9	1	13	1h	7½	9	RJMyres7	K E Strickley	82.40

OFF AT 4:08 EDT. Start good. Won driving. Time, :23, :47⅖, 1:14. Track slow.

$2 Mutuel Prices:

1-SULTAN SUE SIS	9.20	3.60	2.80
6-BIBI MINE		3.40	2.80
7-PAJONE'S HOSTESS			6.00

$3 PERFECTA (1-6) PAID $52.80.

Ro. f, by Venetian Jester—Sultan's Sue, by Strokkr. Trainer, Ida Zupanc. Bred by Edward and J. Armstrong, Jr. (Okla.).

SULTAN SUE SIS, with the pace all the way while saving ground along the rail, had to be steadied at the five-sixteenths pole while waiting for an opening, got through along the rail to make the lead and won under steady pressure. BIBI MINE circled horses on the middle of the turn to go up to challange for the lead, then finished evenly. PAJONE'S HOSTESS lacked the needed response. KIN O' MINE closed some ground late. SHAD PAC was through early. FOOLISH LOLA had brief speed. CONFETTI set the pace for a half and stopped to a walk.

Before we leave this step-by-step illustration—indeed, before we part company altogether—I would like to point out that Sultan Sue Sis was not preordained to win the above race. There was, in fact, one major clue that could well have destroyed all our expectations. The little *c* next to Sultan Sue Sis' claiming price on the September 11 past performance line indicates she was claimed by the trainer of record—Ida Zupanc.

Considering the extraordinary impact trainers have on the performance potential of all horses, it would be a mistake to bet serious money on a horse whose trainer had given any evidence of incompetence. In the case of Ida Zupanc, no such evidence is revealed in a review of recent result charts. Moreover, her excellent judgment in claiming this improving racehorse ten or fifteen minutes prior to the September 11 race is reason enough to give her the benefit of the doubt. I am not that conservative to pass up 4–1 odds on a 50–50 proposition. But I am also not that foolish to forget that 50 percent winners means 50 percent losers as well. To win at the racetrack the player has to be alert, flexible, and fully in touch with his own limitations. The future may be predictable, but it is never predetermined.

Appendix

Guide to

PAST PERFORMANCES

WITH FRACTIONAL TIMES

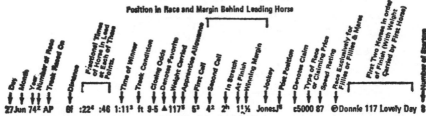

Position in Race and Margin Behind Leading Horse

27 Jun 74² AP   6f :22⁴ :46 1:11³ ft 9-5 ▲117⁵ 5³ 4² 2ʰ 1¹⁄₂ JonesJ⁶   c5000 87 ⊕Donnie 117 Lovely Day 8

Note: In past performances the position in the race for "first call" is as follows: In races less than 5 furlongs the first call is the start; at 5 furlongs the first call is the three-sixteenths; from 5¼ to 7¼ furlongs the first call is the quarter mile; at 1 mile or more the first call is the half.

		Points of Call				Fractional Times Given At These Points of Call		
	Distance of Race	1st Call	2nd Call	3rd Call	4th Call			
2	Furlongs	Start	—	Stretch	Finish	—	—	Finish
5/16	Mile	Start	—	Stretch	Finish	—	—	Finish
3	Furlongs	Start	—	Stretch	Finish	1/4	—	Finish
3 1/2	Furlongs	Start	1/4	Stretch	Finish	1/4	3/8	Finish
4	Furlongs	Start	1/4	Stretch	Finish	1/4	—	Finish
4 1/2	Furlongs	Start	1/4	Stretch	Finish	1/4	1/2	Finish
5	Furlongs	3/16	3/8	Stretch	Finish	1/4	1/2	Finish
5 1/2	Furlongs	1/4	3/8	Stretch	Finish	1/4	1/2	Finish
6	Furlongs	1/4	1/2	Stretch	Finish	1/4	1/2	Finish
6 1/2	Furlongs	1/4	1/2	Stretch	Finish	1/4	1/2	Finish
7	Furlongs	1/4	1/2	Stretch	Finish	1/4	1/2	Finish
1	Mile	1/2	3/4	Stretch	Finish	1/2	3/4	Finish
1	Mile, 70 yards	1/2	3/4	Stretch	Finish	1/2	3/4	Finish
1 1/16	Miles	1/2	3/4	Stretch	Finish	1/2	3/4	Finish
1/8	Miles	1/2	3/4	Stretch	Finish	1/2	3/4	Finish
1 3/16	Miles	1/2	3/4	Stretch	Finish	1/2	3/4	Finish
1 1/4	Miles	1/2	1 mile	Stretch	Finish	1/2	3/4	Finish
1 5/16	Miles	1/2	1 mile	Stretch	Finish	1/2	3/4	Finish
1 3/8	Miles	1/2	1 mile	Stretch	Finish	1/2	3/4	Finish
1 1/2	Miles	1/2	1 1/4	Stretch	Finish	1/2	3/4	Finish
1 5/8	Miles	1/2	1 3/8	Stretch	Finish	1/2	3/4	Finish
1 3/4	Miles	1/2	1 1/2	Stretch	Finish	1/2	3/4	Finish

Key to Symbols, Abbreviations in Past Performances

FOREIGN-BRED HORSES

An asterisk (*) preceding the name of the horse indicates foreign-bred. (No notation is made for horses bred in Canada and Cuba.)

MUD MARKS

✱--Fair mud runner   X--Good mud runner
         ⊛--Superior mud runner

COLOR

B--Bay   Blk--Black   Br--Brown   Ch--Chestnut
Gr--Gray   Ro--Roan   Wh--White
Dk b or br--Dark bay or brown

SEX

c--colt   h--horse   g--gelding   rig--ridgling
     f--filly   m--mare

PEDIGREE

Each horse's pedigree lists, in the order named, color, sex, age, sire, dam and grandsire (sire of dam).

BREEDER

Abbreviation following breeder's name indicates the state, place of origin or foreign country in which the horse was foaled.

TODAY'S WEIGHT

With the exception of assigned-weight handicap races, weights are computed according to the conditions of the race. Weight includes the rider and his equipment: saddle, lead pads, etc., and takes into account the apprentice allowance of pounds claimed. It does not include a jockey's overweight, which is announced by track officials prior to the race. The number of pounds claimed as an apprentice allowance is shown by a superior (small) figure to the right of the weight.

TODAY'S CLAIMING PRICE

If a horse is entered to be claimed, the price for which he may be claimed appears in bold face type to the right of the trainer's name.

RECORD OF STARTS AND EARNINGS

The horse's racing record for his most recent two years of competition appears to the extreme right of the name of the breeder and is referred to as his "money lines." This lists the year, number of starts, wins, seconds, thirds, and earnings. The letter "M" in the win column of the upper line indicates the horse is a maiden. If the letter "M" is in the lower line only, it indicates the horse was a maiden at the end of that year.

TURF RECORD

The horse's Turf Record shows his lifetime starts, wins, seconds, thirds and earnings on the grass and appears directly below his money lines.

DISTANCE

a--preceding distance (a6f) denotes "about" distance (about 6 furlongs in this instance.)

FOREIGN TRACKS

◆--before track abbreviation indicates it is located in a foreign country.

RACES OTHER THAN ON MAIN DIRT TRACK

(·)--following distance denotes inner dirt course.
①--following distance indicates turf (grass) course race.
⑪--following distance indicates inner turf course.
[S]--following distance indicates steeplechase race.
[H]--following distance indicates hurdle race.

TRACK CONDITIONS

ft--fast   fr--frozen   gd--good   sl--slow   sy--sloppy
     m--muddy   hy--heavy
Turf courses, including steeplechase and hurdles
    hd--hard   fm--firm   gd--good
    yl--yielding   sf--soft

SYMBOLS ACCOMPANYING CLOSING ODDS

* (preceding)--favorite   e (following)--entry
   f (following)--mutuel field

APPRENTICE OR RIDER WEIGHT ALLOWANCES

Allowance indicated by superior figure following weight--117⁵

ABBREVIATIONS USED IN POINTS OF CALL

no--nose   hd--head   nk--neck

DEAD-HEATS, DISQUALIFICATIONS

♠--following the finish call indicates this horse was part of a dead-heat (an explanatory line appears under that past performance line.)

†--following the finish call indicates this horse was disqualified. The official placing appears under the past performance line. An explanatory line also appears under the past performance of each horse whose official finish position was changed due to the disqualification.

‡--before the name of any of the first three finishers indicates the horse was disqualified from that position.

POST POSITION

Horse's post position appears after jockey's name—Smith T³

FILLY OR FILLY-MARE RACES

Ⓕ--preceding the race classification indicates races exclusively for fillies or fillies and mares.

STATE-BRED RACES

Ⓢ--preceding the race classification indicates a race restricted to horses foaled in a specific state.

RACE CLASSIFICATIONS

10000--Claiming race (eligible to be claimed for $10,000). Note: The letter c preceding claiming price (c10000) indicates horse was claimed.
M10000--Maiden claiming race (non-winners--eligible to be claimed)
10000H--Claiming handicap (eligible to be claimed)
⊙10000--Optional claiming race (entered NOT to be claimed)
10000⊙--Optional claiming race (eligible to be claimed).
Mdn--Maiden race (non-winners).
AlwM--Maiden allowance race (for non-winners with special weight allowances).
Alw--Allowance race.
HcpO--Overnight handicap race
SplW--Special weight race
Wfa--Weight-for-age race
Mtch--Match race
A10000--Starter allowance race (horses who have started for claiming price shown, or less, as stipulated in the conditions).
H10000--Starter handicap (same restriction as above)
S10000--Starter special weight (restricted as above)
Note: Where no amount is specified in the conditions of the "starters" race dashes are substituted, as shown below
    A----   H----   S----
50000S--Claiming stakes (eligible to be claimed)

STAKES RACES

In stakes races, with the exception of claiming stakes, the name or abbreviation of name is shown in the class of race column. The letter "H" after name indicates the race was a handicap stakes. The same procedure is used for the rich invitational races for which there are no nomination or starting fees. The letters "Inv" following the abbreviation indicate the race was by invitation only.

SPEED RATINGS

This is a comparison of the horse's final time with the track record established prior to the opening of the racing season at that track. The track record is given a rating of 100. One point is deducted for each fifth of a second by which a horse fails to equal the track record (one length is approximately equal to one-fifth of a second). Thus, in a race in which the winner equals the track record (a Speed Rating of 100), another horse who is beaten 12 lengths (or an estimated two and two-fifths seconds) receives a Speed Rating of 88 (100 minus 12). If a horse breaks the track record he receives an additional point for each one fifth second by which he lowers the record (if the track record is 1:10 and he is timed in 1:09⅘, his Speed Rating is 102). In computing beaten-off distances for Speed Ratings, fractions of one-half length or more are figured as one full length (one point). No Speed Ratings are given for steeplechase or hurdle events, for races of less than three furlongs, or for races for which the horse's speed rating is less than 25.

When Daily Racing Form prints its own time, in addition to the official track time, the Speed Rating is based on the official track time.

Note: Speed Ratings for new distances are computed and assigned when adequate time standards are established.

WORKOUTS

Each horse's most recent workouts appear directly under the past performances. For example, Jly 20 Hol 3 ft :36b indicates the horse worked on July 20 at Hollywood Park. The distance of the work was 3 furlongs over a fast track and the horse was timed in 36 seconds, breezing. A "bullet" ● appearing before the date of a workout indicates that the workout was the best of the day for that distance at that track.

Abbreviations used in workouts:
   b--breezing   d--driving   e--easily   g--worked from gate   h--handily   bo--bore out
              ①--turf course   Tr--trial race
   tr.t following track abbreviation indicates horse worked on training track.

Abbreviations for North American Tracks

The following table may be used as an adjunct to Daily Racing Form's past performance feature of showing the value of allowance race purses. The number in bold face type following the name of each track (except hunt meets) represents the average net purse value per race (including stakes and overnight races), rounded to the nearest thousand.

AC — (Agua) Caliente, Mexico—**3**	GrP — *Grants Pass, Ore.—**1**	ShD —*Shenand'h Downs, W. Va.
Aks — Ak-Sar-Ben, Neb.—**10**	GS — †Garden State Park, N. J.	SLR —†San Luis Rey Downs, Cal.
Alb — Albuquerque, N. Mex.—**6**	Haw — Hawthorne, Ill.—**10**	Sol — *Solano, Cal.—**6**
AP — Arlington Park, Ill.—**13**	Hia — Hialeah Park, Fla.—**8**	Spt — *Sportsman's Park, Ill.—**12**
Aqu — Aqueduct, N.Y.—**19**	Hol — Hollywood Park, Cal.—**27**	SR — *Santa Rosa, Cal. —**7**
AsD — *Assiniboia Downs, Canada—**3**	HP — *Hazel Park, Mich.—**6**	Stk — Stockton, Cal.—**4**
Atl — Atlantic City, N.J.—**7**	Imp —*Imperial, Cal.	StP — *Stampede Park, Canada—**4**
Ato — *Atokad Park, Neb—**1**	JnD —*Jefferson Downs, La—**4**	Suf — Suffolk Downs, Mass.—**7**
BD — *Berkshire Downs, Mass.	Jua — Juarez, Mexico	SuD — *Sun Downs, Wash.—**1**
Bel — Belmont Park, N.Y.—**24**	Kee — Keeneland, Ky.—**17**	Sun — Sunland Park, N. Mex.—**2**
Beu — Beulah Race Track, Ohio—**4**	Key — Keystone Race Track, Pa.—**8**	Tam — Tampa Bay Downs, Fla.—**3**
Bil — *Billings, Mont.—**1**	LA —*Los Alamitos, Cal.—**15**	(Formerly Florida Downs)
BM — Bay Meadows, Cal.—**10**	LaD — Louisiana Downs, La.—**13**	Tdn — Thistledown, Ohio—**4**
Bmf — Bay Meadows Fair, Cal.—**10**	LaM — *La Mesa Park, N. Mex.—**1**	Tim — *Timonium, Md.—**5**
Bml — Balmoral Park, Ill.—**4**	Lat — Latonia, Ky.—**4**	TuP — Turf Paradise, Ariz.—**3**
Boi — *Boise, Idaho—**1**	Lbg — *Lethbridge, Canada	Vic — *Victorville, Cal.
Bow — Bowie, Md.—**9**	Lga — *Longacres, Wash.—**7**	Was — Washington Park, Ill.
CD — Churchill Downs, Ky.—**11**	LnN — *Lincoln State Fair, Neb.—**4**	Wat — Waterford Park, W. Va.—**2**
Cda — *Coeur d'Alene, Idaho—**1**	Lrl — Laurel Race Course, Md.—**10**	WO —Woodbine, Canada—**10**
Cen — Centennial Race Track, Colo.—**3**	MD — *Marquis Downs, Canada—**2**	YM — Yakima Meadows, Wash.—**1**
Cka — *Cahokia Downs, Ill.	Med — Meadowlands, N.J.—**12**	
Cls — *Columbus, Neb.—**2**	Mex — *Mexico City, Mexico	**HUNT MEETINGS**
Com — *Commodore Downs, Pa.—**2**	MF — *Marshfield Fair, Mass.—**1**	
Crc — Calder Race Course, Fla.—**8**	Mth — Monmouth Park, N. J.—**10**	Aik — Aiken, S. Carolina
CT — *Charles Town, W. Va.—**3**	Nmp —*Northampton, Mass.—**2**	AtH — Atlanta, Ga.
DeD — *Delta Downs, La.—**3**	NP — *Northlands Park, Canada—**4**	Cam — Camden, S. Carolina
Del — Delaware Park, Del.—**7**	OP — Oaklawn Park, Ark.—**14**	Clm — Clemmons, N. Carolina
Det — Detroit Race Course, Mich.—**5**	Pen — Penn National, Pa.—**4**	Fai — Fair Hill, Md.
Dmr — Del Mar, Cal.—**19**	Pim — Pimlico, Md.—**10**	Fax — Fairfax, Va.
Dmf — Del Mar Fair, Cal.—**9**	PJ — *Park Jefferson, S. D.—**1**	FH — Far Hills, N. J.
Elm — *Elma, Wash.	Pla — *Playfair, Wash.—**2**	Fx — Foxfield, Va.
EIP — Ellis Park, Ky.—**5**	Pln — Pleasanton, Cal.—**7**	Gln — Glyndon, Md.
EnP — †Enoch Park, Canada	PM — Portland Meadows, Ore.—**3**	GN — *Grand National, Md.
EP — *Exhibition Park, Canada—**6**	Pmf — Portl'nd M'd'ws Fair, Ore.	Lex — Lexington, Ky.
EvD — *Evangeline Downs, La.—**4**	Poc — *Pocono Downs, Pa.	Lig — Ligonier, Pa.
FD — Florida Downs, Fla.	Pom — *Pomona, Cal.—**11**	Mal — Malvern, Pa.
FE — Fort Erie, Canada—**6**	PR — Puerto Rico (El Com'te)	Mid — Middleburg, Va.
Fer — *Ferndale, Cal.—**1**	Pre — *Prescott Downs, Ariz.—**1**	Mon — Monkton, Md.
FG — Fair Grounds, La.—**9**.	RD — River Downs, Ohio—**4**	Mor — Morven Park, Va.
FL — Finger Lakes, N. Y.—**5**	Reg — *Regina, Canada—**2**	Mtp — Montpelier, Va.
Fno — Fresno, Cal.—**4**	Ril — *Rillito, Ariz.—**1**	Oxm — Oxmoor, Ky.
Fon — *Fonner Park, Neb.—**3**	Rkm — Rockingham Park, N. H.	Pro — Prospect, Ky.
FP — Fairmount Park, Ill.—**4**	Rui — *Ruidoso, N. Mex—**4**	PW — Percy Warner, Tenn.
GBF — *Great Barrington, Mass.—**2**	SA — Santa Anita Park, Cal.—**26**	RB — Red Bank, N. J.
GD — †Galway Downs, Cal.	Sac — Sacramento, Cal.—**5**	SH — Strawberry Hill, Va.
GF — *Great Falls, Mont.—**2**	Sal — *Salem, Ore. (Lone Oak)—**1**	SoP — Southern Pines, N. C.
GG — Golden Gate Fields, Cal.—**11**	San — *Sandown Park, Canada—**2**	Try — Tryon, N.C.
GP — Gulfstream Park, Fla.—**15**	Sar — Saratoga, N.Y.—**26**	Uni — Unionville, Pa
Grd — *Greenwood, Canada—**8**	SFe — *Santa Fe, N. Mex.—**3**	War — Warrenton, Va
		Wel — Wellsville, Pa.

Tracks marked with (*) are less than one mile in circumference. †Training facility only.

'Points of Call' in Thoroughbred Charts

Following is a tabulation listing the "points of call" for the various distances in charts of thoroughbred racing:

3	Furlongs	PP	Start					Str	Fin
3½	Furlongs	PP	Start	¼				Str	Fin
4	Furlongs	PP	Start	¼				Str	Fin
4½	Furlongs	PP	Start	¼				Str	Fin
5	Furlongs	PP	Start	3-16	⅜			Str	Fin
5½	Furlongs	PP	Start	¼	⅜			Str	Fin
6	Furlongs	PP	Start	¼	½			Str	Fin
6½	Furlongs	PP	Start	¼	½			Str	Fin
7	Furlongs	PP	Start	¼	½			Str	Fin
7½	Furlongs	PP	Start	¼	½			Str	Fin
1 Mile		PP	Start	¼	½	¾		Str	Fin
1 Mile, 30 Yards		PP	Start	¼	½	¾		Str	Fin
1 Mile, 70 Yards		PP	Start	¼	½	¾		Str	Fin
1 1/16 Miles		PP	Start	¼	½	¾		Str	Fin
1 1/8 Miles		PP	Start	¼	½	¾		Str	Fin
1 3/16 Miles		PP	Start	¼	½	¾		Str	Fin

Note: In races at 1 1/4 Miles to 1 11/16 Miles, the Start call is eliminated and the ¼ mile call is substituted (as shown below):

1 1/4 Miles	PP	¼	½	¾	1		Str	Fin
1 5/16 Miles	PP	¼	½	¾	1		Str	Fin
1 3/8 Miles	PP	¼	½	¾	1		Str	Fin
1 7/16 Miles	PP	¼	½	1	1¼		Str	Fin
1 1/2 Miles	PP	¼	½	1	1¼		Str	Fin
1 9/16 Miles	PP	¼	½	1	1¼		Str	Fin
1 5/8 Miles	PP	¼	½	1	1⅜		Str	Fin
1 11/16 Miles	PP	¼	½	1	1⅜		Str	Fin

In races at 1 3/4 Miles or more, the first call is at the ½ mile (as shown below):

1 3/4 Miles	PP	½	1	1¼	1½	Str	Fin
1 13/16 Miles	PP	½	1	1¼	1½	Str	Fin
1 7/8 Miles	PP	½	1	1⅜	1⅝	Str	Fin
1 15/16 Miles	PP	½	1	1⅜	1⅝	Str	Fin
2 Miles	PP	½	1	1½	1¾	Str	Fin
2 Miles, 70 Yards	PP	½	1	1½	1¾	Str	Fin
2 1/16 Miles	PP	½	1	1½	1¾	Str	Fin
2 1/8 Miles	PP	½	1	1½	1¾	Str	Fin
2 3/16 Miles	PP	½	1	1½	1¾	Str	Fin
2 1/4 Miles	PP	½	1	1½	2	Str	Fin
2 5/16 Miles	PP	½	1	1½	2	Str	Fin
2 3/8 Miles	PP	½	1	1½	2	Str	Fin
2 1/2 Miles	PP	½	1	1½	2	Str	Fin

SAMPLE PAST PERFORMANCES *DAILY RACING FORM* EASTERN EDITION

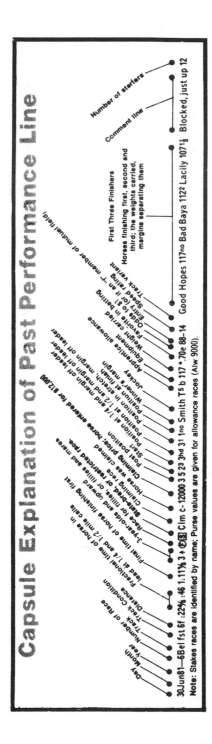

***Perrault** — Ch. h. 5, by Djakao—Innocent Air, by Court Martial
Br.—Sasse & Sheed (Eng)
Own.—Fradkoff & Vanzuylen Baron — Tr.—Whittingham Charles

126 — Lifetime 23 8 5 5 $889,942 — 1982 6 3 1 2 $597,400 — 1981 8 3 2 1 $203,566 — Turf 21 7 4 5 $514,942

15Aug82- 8Dmr fm 1⅛ Ⓣ:48⅘ 1:12⅕ 1:48⅖ 3↑Eddie Read H 6 3 2½ 1¹ 3¹ 3¹ Pincay L Jr b 129 *.70 95-06 Wickerr 119½ Spence Bay 122½ Perrault 129¼ Sluggish, bore out 7
13Jun82- 8Hol fst 1¼ :45⅖ 1:33⅘ 1:59⅕ 3↑Gold Cup H 4 4 4³ 2hd 1½ 1¹ Pincay L Jr b 127 *.70 95-15 Perrault 127¹ Erins Isle 118½ It's The One 125² Driving 8
18Apr82- 8SA fm *1¾ Ⓣ:23 1:58⅘ 2:45⅗ Capistrano H 9 2 2⁵ 2hd 2½ 3¾ Pincay L Jr b 129 *.40e 90-06 Lemhi Gold 121⁷ Exploded 118¼ Perrault 129½ Weakened 9
28Mar82- 8SA fm 1½ Ⓣ:46⅖ 2:00 2:24 S. Luis Rey 5 1 1½ 1½ 1¹ 1¾ Pincay L Jr b 126 1.70e 95-05 Perrault 126¾ Exploded 126½ John Henry 126no Ridden out 5
7Mar82- 8SA fst 1¼ :45 1:34⅖ 1:59 S Anita H 4 5 5⁷ 4¼ 1½ 1no Pincay L Jr b 126 4.20e🄳 94-07 🄳Perrault 126no John Henry 130¾ It's The One 120nk Drifted out 11
7Mar82-Disqualified and placed second
10Feb82- 8SA yl 1¼ Ⓣ:47⅗ 2:04⅗ Arcadia H 7 4 4½ 1½ 1½ 1⁵ Pincay L Jr b 124 *1.60 64-36 Perrault 124⁵ Silveyville 117¹¹ Le Duc De Bar 111⁵ Handily 7
8Nov81- 8SA fm 1½ Ⓣ:47⅖ 1:59⅗ 2:23⅖ 3↑Oak Tree 5 5 4½ 5½ 7¹¹ 7¹⁵ Saint-Martin Y b 126 7.70e 83-02 John Henry 126nk Spence Bay 126¼ The Bart 126no Tired 7
4Oct81♦4Longchamp(Fra) sf*1½ 2:35⅕ Ⓣ Arc de Triomphe(Gr.1) 4¾ Samani H b 130 27.00 — — GoldRiver 127¾ Bikala 123no AprilRun 120² Well up thruout 24
30Aug81♦4Deauville(Fra) fm*1¹⁄₁₆ 2:58⅗ Ⓣ GrandPrix deDeauville(Gr2 1hd StMartin Y b 131 *1.20 — — Perrault 131hd CastleKeep 126¾ Glenorum 131½ Bid, up late 11
14Jly81♦6StCloud(Fra) gd*1⅞ 2:38⅖ Ⓣ PrixMaurice deNieuil(Gr2) 1½ StMartin Y b 130 *1.30 — — Perrault 130½ RoiGuillaume 113nk DomMenotti 128² Going away 10
LATEST WORKOUTS Aug 26 AP Ⓣ 5f fm :59 h — Aug 21 Dmr 3f fst :35 h — Aug 9 Dmr Ⓣ 1 fm 1:41 h (d) — Aug 5 Dmr Ⓣ 1 fm 1:39⅗ h (d)

Capsule Explanation of Past Performance Line

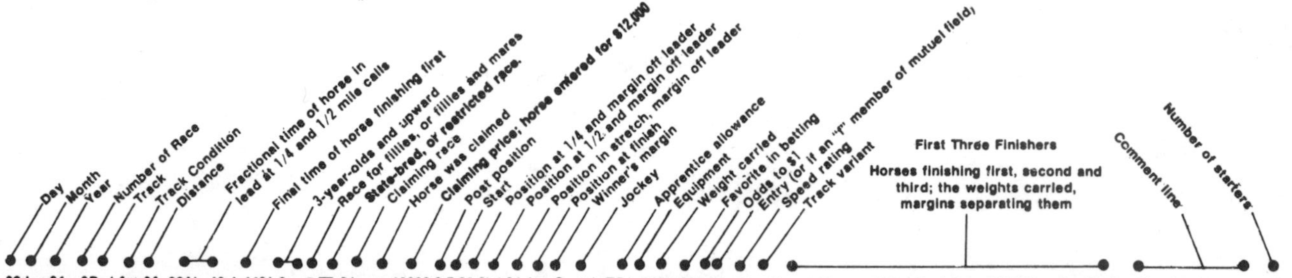
Day
Month
Year
Number of Race
Track
Track Condition
Distance
Fractional time of horse in lead at 1/4 and 1/2 mile calls
Final time of horse finishing first
3-year-olds and upward
Race for fillies, or fillies and mares
State-bred, or restricted race.
Claiming race
Horse was claimed
Claiming price; horse entered for $12,000
Post position
Start
Position at 1/4 and margin off leader
Position at 1/2 and margin off leader
Position in stretch, margin off leader
Position at finish
Winner's margin
Jockey
Apprentice allowance
Equipment
Weight carried
Favorite in betting
Odds to $1
Entry (or if an "f" member of mutuel field)
Speed rating
Track variant
First Three Finishers
Horses finishing first, second and third; the weights carried, margins separating them
Comment line
Number of starters

30Jun81—6Bel fst 6f :22⅘ :46 1:11⅘ 3↑ Ⓕ🅂 Clm c-12000 3 5 2³ 3hd 3¹ 1no Smith T⁵ b 117 *.70e 88-14 Good Hopes 117no Bad Baya 112² Lacily 107½ Blocked, just up 12

Note: Stakes races are identified by name; Purse values are given for allowance races (Alw 9000).

POST POSITIONS AND ODDS

THE PROPER WAY TO SET UP A POST POSITION SURVEY

For the period involved, note at each distance charted: (1) the number of races from each post position, (2) the number of wins per post, and (3) the win percentage per post. A separate category should be maintained for "outside post position" for all races. *Optional:* At the same time, record the number of wire-to-wire winners.

Several sample post position surveys appear below.

POST POSITION
TURF RACES (all distances)

Post Position	Starters	Wins	Win Percentage
1	69	18	26.1
2	69	12	17.4
3	69	8	11.6
4	69	8	11.6
5	69	7	10.1
6	68	10	14.7
7	54	1	—
8	43	3	—
9	21	1	—
10	5	1	—
11	2	0	0.0
12	1	0	0.0
outside	69	4	5.8

Wire-to-wire winners — 20.3%

POST POSITION
SPRINTS (6 furlongs)

Post Position	Starters	Wins	Win Percentage
1	203	33	16.3
2	203	27	13.3
3	203	26	12.8
4	203	25	12.3
5	203	27	13.3
6	200	9	4.5
7	178	22	12.4
8	143	13	9.1
9	95	8	8.4
10	74	3	4.1
11	54	6	11.1
12	28	4	14.3
outside	203	18	8.9

Wire-to-wire winners — 30.5%

POST POSITION
ROUTES (1 mile — abt. 1¼ miles)

Post Position	Starters	Wins	Win Percentage
1	115	15	13.0
2	115	13	11.3
3	115	13	11.3
4	115	22	19.1
5	115	16	13.9
6	114	15	13.2
7	99	9	9.1
8	69	8	11.6
9	35	1	—
10	21	3	—
11	9	0	0.0
12	3	0	0.0
outside	115	12	10.4

Wire-to-wire winners — 26.1%

PERCENTAGE TABLE FOR COMPUTING
A MORNING LINE

The following table provides a reference for computing a morning line. The percentage totals for the field should equal 118 to 125 points. This allows for the pari-mutuel tax.

ODDS	PERCENTAGE POINTS	ODDS	PERCENTAGE POINTS
1–5	83	2–1	33
1–4	80	5–2	28
1–3	75	3–1	25
1–2	67	7–2	22
3–5	62	4–1	20
2–3	60	9–2	18
3–4	57	5–1	16
4–5	55	6–1	14
even	50	8–1	11
6–5	45	10–1	9
7–5	41	12–1	8
3–2	40	15–1	6
8–5	38	20–1	4
9–5	35	30–1	3

Below are two sample morning lines with percentage points.

HYPOTHETICAL RACE 1—1¼ MILES

HORSE	ODDS	POINTS
Kelso	9–5	35
Damascus	5–2	28
Buckpasser	7–2	22
Dr. Fager	9–2	18
Carry Back	8–1	11
Intentionally	15–1	6
Mongo	20–1	4

124 *points*

HYPOTHETICAL RACE 2—1¼ MILES

HORSE	ODDS	POINTS
Secretariat	6–5	45
Seattle Slew	7–2	22
Affirmed	6–1	14
Forego	6–1	14
Spectacular Bid	8–1	11
Conquistador Cielo	12–1	8
Alydar	15–1	6
Canonero II	30–1	3
		123 points

COMPUTING APPROXIMATE PLACE AND SHOW PAYOFFS

Short of using the most sophisticated electronic equipment, no player can hope to generate all the possible place and show payoffs in a race. Place and show payoffs are determined by the order of finish itself, or more correctly, by the money bet in the place pool and the money bet in the show pool on each horse involved in the top two and three finishing positions. The player's best course is to compute the lowest possible place and show payoff—a single calculation—because the lowest possible payoff is statistically the most likely payoff. It is the one produced by the favorites in the race finishing in the money. The following example shows how this is done.

HORSE	PLACE POOL	SHOW POOL
Carry Back	$ 4,000	$ 2,500
Buckpasser	$ 8,500	$ 6,000
Count Fleet	$12,000	$ 7,000
Tom Fool	$ 9,000	$ 4,000
Native Dancer	$10,000	$ 5,000
Round Table	$ 5,500	$ 1,500
Swaps	$10,000	$ 8,000
Silky Sullivan	$ 1,000	$ 1,000
Totals	$60,000	$35,000

QUESTION: *How much will Native Dancer pay to place?*

ANSWER: Minimum payoff is computed in four steps.

> STEP 1: Deduct 20 percent pari-mutuel takeout tax from place pool total (20 percent of $60,000 or $12,000). Net pool = $48,000.

> STEP 2: Combine the amount of money bet on Native Dancer to place with the amount of money bet on the horse getting the most play in the race. In this case, Count Fleet with $12,000 is the favorite in the place pool; thus the combined total equals $22,000.

> STEP 3: Subtract the $22,000 from the $48,000 net place pool to determine the amount of money available for profit. In this case, $48,000 − $22,000 = $26,000 profit.

> STEP 4: Divide the $26,000 profit into two equal parts to determine the amount of profit available to Native Dancer place pool bettors. In this case

$$\frac{\$26,000}{2} = \$13,000$$

> THUS: The odds on Native Dancer to place are $13,000 profit to $10,000 invested, or 13–10 ($1.30–$1.00). Native Dancer will pay a minimum place price of $4.60 (includes original $2 investment).

QUESTION: *How much will Tom Fool pay to show?*

ANSWER: Minimum show payoff is computed in four steps.

> STEP 1: Deduct 20 percent pari-mutuel takeout tax from show pool total (20 percent of $35,000, or $7,000). Net pool = $28,000.

> STEP 2: Combine the amount of money bet on Tom Fool to show ($4,000) with the amount of money bet on the two horses getting the most play in the race. In this case, Swaps is getting $8,000; Count Fleet, $7,000. Thus the combined total for all three horses is $19,000.

STEP 3: Subtract $19,000 from the $28,000 net show pool to determine the money available for profit. In this case, $28,000 − $19,000 = $9,000 net profit.

STEP 4: Divide the net profit into three equal parts to determine Tom Fool's show pool profit. In this case

$$\frac{\$9,000}{3} = \$3,000$$

THUS: The odds on Tom Fool to show are $3,000 profit to $4,000 invested, or 3–4 ($.75–$1.00). Tom Fool will pay a minimum show price of $3.40 (includes breakage to nearest dime and original $2 investment).

With some practice, the place and show payoffs for any horse can be computed in this manner in a matter of seconds. *Hint:* Round off to convenient whole numbers.

SPEED FIGURES

CLASS PARS AND PARALLEL TIME CHARTS

The Beyer-Kovitz speed-figure method is a means to compare the final times of all main-track races with a workable set of standards (or par times). The parallel time chart which appears below is an essential tool in this process. The time values incorporated in the chart were developed through class-par research at New York racetracks. With some important exceptions, described in the following material, this parallel time chart may be used at any racetrack with a circumference of one mile or more.

PARALLEL TIME CHART

SPEED FIG-URE	5½ FUR-LONGS	6 FUR-LONGS	7 FUR-LONGS	1 MILE	BEL-MONT (ONE TURN) 1⅛ MILES	AQUE-DUCT (TWO TURNS) 1⅛ MILES
136	1:02⅘	1:09	1:21⅖	1:33⅘	1:46⅖	1:48⅕
132	1:03	1:09⅕	1:21⅗	1:34⅕	1:46⅘	1:48⅗
128	1:03⅕	1:09⅗	1:22	1:34⅗	1:47⅕	1:49
124	1:03⅗	1:09⅘	1:22⅖	1:35	1:47⅗	1:49⅖
120	1:03⅘	1:10⅕	1:22⅘	1:35⅖	1:48	1:49⅘
116	1:04	1:10⅖	1:23	1:35⅘	1:48⅖	1:50⅕
112	1:04⅖	1:10⅗	1:23⅖	1:36⅕	1:49	1:50⅘
108	1:04⅗	1:11	1:23⅘	1:36⅗	1:49⅖	1:51⅕
104	1:04⅘	1:11⅕	1:24⅕	1:37	1:50	1:51⅘
100	1:05⅕	1:11⅗	1:24⅗	1:37⅗	1:50⅗	1:52⅕
96	1:05⅖	1:11⅘	1:24⅘	1:37⅘	1:50⅘	1:52⅗
92	1:05⅗	1:12⅕	1:25⅕	1:38⅕	1:51⅕	1:53
88	1:06	1:12⅖	1:25⅖	1:38⅗	1:51⅗	1:53⅖
84	1:06⅕	1:12⅘	1:25⅘	1:39	1:52⅕	1:54
80	1:06⅖	1:13	1:26⅕	1:39⅖	1:52⅗	1:54⅖
76	1:06⅘	1:13⅕	1:26⅗	1:39⅘	1:53⅕	1:55
72	1:07	1:13⅗	1:27	1:40⅕	1:53⅗	1:55⅖
68	1:07⅕	1:13⅘	1:27⅕	1:40⅗	1:54	1:55⅘
64	1:07⅗	1:14⅕	1:27⅗	1:41	1:54⅖	1:56⅕
60	1:07⅘	1:14⅖	1:28	1:41⅖	1:55	1:56⅗

The above chart offers a speed-rating system consistent with the value of one-fifth of a second at all rates of speed at all distances. These relationships between different distances and different rates of speed were developed mathematically and adjusted through practical use.

ITEM: There is a natural, mathematical relationship between final times at various distances. For example, if a horse travels six furlongs in 1:13, it will have to travel the seven-furlong distance in 1:26⅕ to earn equal credit. This additional 13⅕ seconds for the extra furlong is based on considerable research, is mathematically sound, and incorporates the normal loss of speed we would expect for the added difficulty of a longer distance. Given a faster rate of speed, say 1:10 for six furlongs, the equivalent seven-furlong time would be 1:22⅗, or a difference of 12⅗ seconds. Given a slower rate of speed, say six furlongs in 1:14⅗, the equivalent seven-furlong time would be 1:28, or a difference of 13⅖ seconds.

ITEM: The above relationship assumes the presence of only one turn at each distance, and a similar mathematical relationship could be shown to exist for all other one-turn distances. For example, at Belmont Park, where a chute extends the track's ability to card one-turn races up to 1¼ miles, the following times are approximately equal to each other:

6 FURLONGS		7 FURLONGS		1 MILE		1⅛ MILES
1:14⅗	=	1:28	=	1:41⅖	=	1:55
1:13	=	1:26⅕	=	1:39⅖	=	1:52⅘
1:10	=	1:22⅗	=	1:35⅕	=	1:48

ITEM: The equivalent time for a race involving a half-furlong (i.e., 6½ furlongs or 1¹⁄₁₆ miles) can be interpolated from the above table. For instance, 1:39⅖ at one mile equals 1:46⅕ at 1¹⁄₁₆ miles.

ITEM: The presence of an extra turn destroys the mathematical relationship as represented by the table. Thus at Aqueduct, where 1⅛-mile races are contested around two turns, the only way to establish equivalent times is to conduct class-par research. To refresh your memory (Chapter 11), that means finding the average winning time (fast tracks only) for each class of race at each distance. What I am suggesting below is a shortcut.

STEP 1: For the most popular sprint distance (one turn), find the average winning time for every major race classification. At Belmont Park and Aqueduct, for instance, the class pars for older horses traveling six furlongs are as follows. The approximate speed-figure ratings can be obtained by consulting the parallel time chart.

CLAIMING RACES			
$50,000+	1:10⅗	$11,000+	1:11⅗
$35,000+	1:10⅘	$ 8,000+	1:11⅘
$25,000+	1:11	$ 6,000+	1:12
$20,000+	1:11⅕	$ 5,000+	1:12⅕
$15,000+	1:11⅖		

MAIDEN CLAIMING		ALLOWANCE RACES	
$30,000+	1:12	$25,000 purse	1:10⅕
$20,000+	1:12⅖	$20,000 purse	1:10⅖
$12,000+	1:12⅘	$15,000 purse	1:10⅗
$ 8,000+	1:13	$12,000 purse	1:11
		$10,000 purse	1:11⅖

MAIDEN SPECIAL WEIGHT			
All ages	1:11⅘	Stakes races	1:10

STEP 2: Repeat the above class-par research for as many two-turn distances as you wish to include in the parallel time chart. Because the relationship between final time and class is an orderly one, someone handy with numbers may reduce the required research by skipping several class levels and filling in the missing time values through interpolation.

STEP 3: Using the following example as a guide, match the class pars for each distance so that each horizontal line represents an equivalent measure of speed. It is in this manner that the parallel time chart can be adjusted to reflect the true value of the extra turn.

AQUEDUCT—$25,000 CLAIMING

6 FURLONGS   1⅛ MILES

1:11   =   1:51⅕

AQUEDUCT—$15,000 CLAIMING

6 FURLONGS   1⅛ MILES

1:11⅖   =   1:52

TRACK VARIANTS

Using class pars and the parallel time chart on page 212, we are now ready to compute a track variant.

PAR	ACTUAL SPEED FIGURE	VARIANT
88	91	−3
83	88	−5
90	92	−2
96	96	0
108	112	−4
turf	no figure	no variant
1½ miles	no figure	no variant
120	126	−6
108	109	−1
		Average variant = −3 (−21 for 7 races)

STEP 1: After today's races are run, compare the final times with the par time for the distance and class. At Belmont the par time for a $25,000 claiming race is 1:11 for six furlongs. On the parallel time chart that is worth 108 speed-figure points. If, however, the race was run in 1:10⅗, the winner has actually earned 112 speed-figure points. What we want to find out is whether the horse actually earned the high figure or whether he was helped to some extent by the speed conduciveness of the racetrack. For this we will need to

compare all the speed figures and par times for main-track races at Belmont Park that day.

STEP 2: At this point, deduct 3 speed-figure points from each horse's earned figure. It is obvious that the track contributed to the final times. When we enter the net speed figures in our permanent record, we will note the variant and the adjusted speed figures in the following manner:

		RACES								
DATE	VARIANT	1	2	3	4	5	6	7	8	9
6/11	−3	88	85	89	93	109	T	none	123	106

Of course, not every racing day is so easily compared. Sometimes the times will be much faster than par for the first few races and not as fast for the remainder of the card. Sometimes the one-turn races will be faster or slower than the two-turn races. It is for this reason that the player should set up the par time comparisons in the following manner (S = sprint, R = route).

PAR	ACTUAL SPEED FIGURE	VARIANT
90 – S	95	−5
84 – S	90	−6
100 – R	100	0
106 – S	112	−6
80 – R	77	+3
turf	no figure	no variant
94 – S	100	−6
120 – R	118	+2
88 – R	85	+3
		Sprints = −6 (−23 for 4 races)
		Routes = +2 (+ 8 for 4 races)

Deduct 6 speed-figure points from each sprint race speed figure. Add 2 speed-figure points to each route race speed figure. Enter the adjusted speed figures on the permanent record.

STEP 3: After a few weeks of compiling speed-figure ratings, you will be able to employ speed figures for handicapping purposes. To determine the speed figure of any horse, consult the permanent record and adjust the figure according to the beaten-lengths chart below.

STEP 4: (Optional) Andy Beyer's advanced speed-figure method eliminates the par times as a standard once the permanent record becomes functional. Instead of par times, Andy substitutes *projected* times based on the actual speed figures earned by the horses in prior races. In other words, if a race is run in 1:11 flat, instead of comparing the time to the expected par Andy compares the actual speed figure to the speed figure the horse's prior record indicates it should have run. Indeed, he projects speed figures for several horses in each race in order to get a valid standard. Obviously, this procedure is more accurate, but it is difficult to master. It should not be attempted until the player has complete familiarity with the class-par version of the method, which by itself provides an adequate *track* variant.

The interested handicapper should note these additional facts about speed figures:

1. Speed figures may be generated for turf races only at those racetracks where an electronic timing device is known to be accurate and in regular use.
2. The class pars for races carded exclusively for fillies are usually one-fifth of a second slower for each class at six furlongs.
3. The six-furlong class pars for three-year-olds are three-fifths of a second slower in January, two-fifths slower in June, and one-fifth slower in September.
4. Speed figures earned on severely biased racetracks should be regarded suspiciously for handicapping purposes.

BEATEN-LENGTHS CHART
(*Deduct Points from Winner's Rating*)

MARGIN	5 FUR-LONGS	6 FUR-LONGS	7 FUR-LONGS	1 MILE	1⅛ MILES
neck	1	1	1	0	0
½	1	1	1	1	1
¾	2	2	2	1	1
1	3	2	2	2	2
1¼	4	3	3	2	2
1½	4	4	3	3	3
1¾	5	4	4	3	3
2	6	5	4	4	3
2¼	7	6	5	4	4
2½	7	6	5	4	4
2¾	8	7	6	5	5
3	9	7	6	5	5
3¼	9	8	7	6	5
3½	10	9	7	6	6
3¾	11	9	8	7	6
4	12	10	8	7	7
4¼	12	10	9	8	7
4½	13	11	9	8	8
4¾	14	11	10	9	8
5	15	12	10	9	8
5½	16	13	11	10	9
6	18	15	12	11	10
6½	19	16	13	12	11
7	20	17	14	13	12
7½	22	18	15	13	13
8	23	20	17	14	13
8½	25	21	18	15	14
9	26	22	19	16	15
9½	28	23	19	17	16
10	29	24	20	18	17
11	32	27	23	20	18
12	35	29	25	21	20
13	38	32	27	23	22
14	41	34	29	25	23
15	44	37	31	27	25

OFF-TRACK BETTING AND EXOTIC WAGERING

OFF-TRACK BETTING

In the 1980s, many tracks around the country offer out-of-town feature races as part of their Saturday or Sunday betting programs. This unique form of off-track betting is made possible through closed-circuit television simulcasts.

In New York, where there are hundreds of Off-Track Betting parlors scattered throughout the state, play is possible on dozens of races at two or more racetracks every day, but the punter pays for the privilege with an exorbitant 5 percent surcharge deducted from winning bets.

Off-Track Betting is not without its merits. It does contribute a lot of money to the purse structure at participating tracks and it also raises badly needed cash for the city and state. But for the serious-minded horseplayer, OTB is something to appreciate for other reasons: at times it helps to inflate the odds of logical contenders.

Even with piped-in television, the OTB player can't see the horses in the paddock, or in their pre-race warm-ups. He can't evaluate the up-to-the-minute flow of cash in the daily double or exacta pools; he can't watch races carefully enough to see the way contenders are ridden, or why they never made a move, or if they got blocked in the rear of the pack. Occasionally, these difficulties do not matter enough to keep a good player's opinions in his pocket. But if he wants to win consistently, he must limit his OTB play to circumstances where he knows he is backing a solid contender at a square price.

In such instances, the 5 percent loss in profit may be partially offset by the reduction in overall expenses. After all, a trip to the track even with a free admission pass is likely to cost $12, $15, or $20.

In addition there is something to be said for playing OTB steadily for a few days as a warm-up, to prepare for an extended on-track assault at Saratoga or Belmont. Keeping such play to the barest minimum will sometimes help put oil in the thinking cap by allowing the player to refine his handicapping at limited cost.

And also, there are some betting opportunities that are offered only to OTB patrons. Playing the Kentucky Derby, the Preakness, or the Arlington Million is more for fun than profit, but that's not always the case.

For instance, if you liked Perrault's chances to beat a field of international grass runners in the 1982 Arlington Million, you could have had $6.20 at OTB, while bettors at Arlington settled for even money! This kind of betting opportunity occurs primarily because OTB usually breaks stable couplings into separate betting interests. (In the Arlington race at the track, Perrault and Erin's Isle raced under one pari-mutuel ticket as the Whittingham-trained entry.)

Likewise, OTB occasionally features a special exacta or daily double involving races at different tracks, which may afford a strong player a good chance at bonus profits. This, of course, is dangerous business for most people, but I would be remiss if I didn't offer a few practical ways to approach exotic wagering.

DAILY DOUBLES, EXACTAS, AND TRIFECTAS

One of the most common approaches to betting the daily double is the basic wheel, or betting a single horse in one race with all the horses in the other. To put this bet into perspective, the player should treat his total investment in the wheel as a straight win bet on the key horse.

If the total investment to lock up all entries in the second race is $20 (for a ten-horse field), the player should compare the *lowest possible payoff* in the daily double with the straight payoff for a $20 win bet. Most often a few payoffs will be under the probable gain from a straight win bet, but in that case *extra tickets* on the two or three lowest payoffs will bring things into better balance. (A practical example of this rudimentary betting tool is shown using an exacta wheel in the final section.)

Obviously, a wheel forces the player to use seemingly unworthy contenders in the second half of the double. And there will be times when some of the field can be safely eliminated. But for every $2 saved by virtue of such fine line handicapping, the player must be willing to accept the added risks of a total loss. Nothing is more frustrating than to pick a solid winner in the first half of the double, only to see the unexpected, unplayed long shot come romping home in front. Of such omissions are losers made.

To guard against developing a self-destructive pattern, the player must be his own best friend and critic. If he persistently makes trouble for himself by leaving out winners in his combination bets, he should recognize the need to cut back sharply on exotic play. Buying two, three, or four horses in a single exacta race or in both halves of the daily double will frequently put a player in the hole to stay.

These betting opportunities must be approached with discipline. They are extremely useful devices for boosting profits, but they can be seductive.

A solid-looking contender coupled in the exactas with several contenders is a good betting strategy, provided the bulk of the bet is put on the horse's nose.

A horse used as a key to win and/or run second with a handful of potential upset possibilities is also a way to make good money even if the key horse turns out to be second best.

Unfortunately, the majority of horseplayers are mesmerized by daily doubles, exactas, and trifectas. Time after time, they will play too much money on too many combinations, giving themselves no real chance to stay in control of their game. This happens periodically to experienced horseplayers, including professionals, but there is no reason why the player cannot stop a losing strategy as it begins to threaten his overall approach.

The bottom line is this: If bonus profits come from these wagering opportunities, that is a valid license to continue. If the player is not winning, he must accept the results and concentrate on straightforward betting strategies matched to his level of skill.

Experiments in exotic wagering should be done privately, at the track but without actual money, *before* one attempts to include them in regular play. Otherwise, the player is just giving away any edge he may have gained through careful research.

But for those players who feel justifiably confident of their basic tote board play, I would recommend several specific betting approaches in exotic wagering situations. Each tool is designed to add extra profits without requiring disproportionately large betting units, but none of these tools will do anything for the $5 or $10 bettor. Of course, everyone has a right to take a shot at a big score for a couple of bucks, but if the casual player concentrates his limited capital into daily doubles, exactas, and trifectas, he can expect a quick trip to Tap City. I think there are better ways to enjoy a day at the races than to chase rainbows in the dark.

Betting Strategies in Daily Doubles

1. *The Key Horse Wheel.* The basic strategy. To be used when a qualified prime bet occurs in a daily double race.

    STEP A: Buy $2 tickets on the key horse with all the horses in the second half of the daily double.

    STEP B: Buy extra tickets using the key horse with the *lowest* payoff possibilities in the second half of the D.D.

    STEP C: Buy extra tickets using the key horse with two or three *selected contenders* in the second half of the D.D.

    The above steps frequently provide a balanced range of payoffs greater than the net payoff from a straight win bet on the key horse. The example below demonstrates a logical distribution of play involving such a key horse with a field of nine in the second half of the daily double.

Example of Key Horse Wheel

STEP A: $2 tickets on the KH with a, b, c, d, e, f, g, h, i. $18.

STEP B: $6 tickets on the KH with a, d, e (lowest payoffs). $18.

STEP C: $8 tickets on the KH with a, c, f (selected contenders). $24.

Totals: 30 daily double tickets bought = $60 investment.

NOTES: The KH-a combination was a $16 investment.
The KH-d and KH-e combinations were $8 investments.
The KH-c and KH-f combinations were $10 investments.
All the other combinations were $2 investments.

2. *A Partial Wheel.* Using the key horse with selected contenders in the second half of the D.D. To be used in tandem with a straight win on the key horse.

STEP A: Bet 50 percent of intended investment on the key horse to win.

STEP B: Buy multiple daily double tickets on the key horse with selected contenders in the second race.

This strategy is employed when there are very few probable contenders in the second half of the daily double.

Example of a Partial Wheel

STEP A: $30 win bet on the key horse.

STEP B: $10 daily doubles on KH-a, KH-c, and KH-f. $30.

Totals: $30 win + $30 in daily doubles = $60 investment.

3. *A Crisscross Saver.* Using the key horse *and* an alternate selection in the same race with selected contenders in the second half of the daily double. To be used in tandem with a win bet on the key horse.

STEP A: A 50 percent win bet on the KH.

STEP B: A partial wheel using the KH.

STEP C: A partial wheel using an alternate selection as a secondary KH.

To be used if there is a dangerous contender in the KH race and there are but a few legitimate contenders in the second half of the double.

Example of a Crisscross Saver

STEP A: $30 win bet on the KH.

STEP B: $6 D.D.s on KH-a, KH-c, and KH-f. $18.

STEP C: $4 D.D.s on Alt. Sel.-a, Alt. Sel.-c, and Alt. Sel.-f. $12.

Totals: $30 win bet + $18 KH D.D.s + $12.00 Alt. Sel. D.D.s = $60 investment.

4. *Daily Double–Exacta Combine.* Using the key horse in a partial D.D. wheel and in tandem with a crisscross, *plus* extra play on the KH in exactas if the opportunity is there.

STEP A: 50 percent win bet on KH.

STEP B: Partial D.D. wheel using the KH.

STEP C: Partial D.D. wheel using an alternate selection as a secondary KH.

STEP D: Exacta tickets using the KH to win over one, two, or three probable contenders for second place.

STEP E: Exacta tickets using the KH in the *place* position under one, two, or three probable contenders (including the alternate selection).

Example of Daily Double–Exacta Combine

STEP A: $30 win bet on the KH.

STEP B: $4 D.D.s on KH-a, KH-c, and KH-f. $12.

STEP C: $2 D.D.s on Alt. Sel. = a, Alt. Sel. = c, and Alt. Sel. = f. $6.

STEP D: $2 exacta tickets on KH over Alt. Sel., plus KH over two other probable contenders in the race. $6.

STEP E: $2 exacta tickets on KH in the *place* position under the alternate selection and two other probable contenders. $6.

Totals: $30 win bet + $12 KH D.D.s + $6 Alt. Sel. D.D.s + $6 + $6 in exactas = $60 investment.

Betting Strategies in Exactas

1. *The Key Horse Wheel.* Using a qualified prime bet as a key horse in exacta play.

    STEP A: Buy $2 exacta tickets on KH over the rest of the field.

    STEP B: Buy extra tickets on KH over the lowest payoff possibilities.

    STEP C: Buy extra tickets on KH over selected contenders. The example below is based on a ten-horse field.

Example of Basic Strategy

STEP A: $2 exacta tickets on KH over a, b, d, e, f, g, h, i, j. $18.

STEP B: $6 exacta tickets on KH over a, KH over i, and KH over j. $18.

STEP C: $6. exacta tickets on KH over d, e, f, j. $24.

Totals: $18 for basic wheel + $18.00 (lowest payoffs) + $24 (selected contenders) = $60.

2. *Top and Bottom Wheel.* Using key horse as an exacta wheel in the win and place positions. For better value than straight win-place betting.

    STEP A: $2 tickets on KH over the field.

    STEP B: $2 tickets on KH under the field.

    STEP C: Extra tickets on KH over lowest possible payoffs.

STEP D: Extra tickets on KH under lowest possible payoffs.
STEP E: Extra tickets on KH over selected contenders.
STEP F: Extra tickets on KH under selected contenders.

Example of Top and Bottom Wheel

STEP A: $2 tickets on KH over a, b, d, e, f, g, h, i, j. $18.
STEP B: $2 tickets on KH under a, b, d, e, f, g, h, i, j. $18.
STEP C: $2 tickets on KH over a, i, j. $6.
STEP D: $2 tickets on KH under a, i, j. $6.
STEP E: $2 tickets on KH over d, e, f, j. $8.
STEP F: $2 tickets on KH under d, e, f, j. $8.

Totals: $18 + $18 + $6 + $6 + $8 + $8 = $64 investment.

3. *A Partial Exacta Wheel.* Using key horse with selected contenders in exacta play. To be used in tandem with a straight win bet.

STEP A: 50 percent win bet on KH.
STEP B: A partial exacta wheel.
STEP C: Saver exactas in the place position (optional).

Example of Partial Exacta Wheel

STEP A: $30 win bet on KH.
STEP B: $5 exacta tickets on KH over d, e, f, j. $20.
STEP C: $2 exacta tickets on KH under d, e, f, j. $8.

Totals: $30 win + $20 + $8 in exactas = $58 investment.

NOTE: Without saver exactas, STEP C, increase STEP B to $8 exactas

4. *Straight Top and Bottom.* A partial wheel, using KH in the win and place positions with three (or fewer) selected contenders. To be used in tandem with a saver win wager.

STEP A: A 25 percent win wager.
STEP B: $10 exactas KH over three selected contenders.
STEP C: $5 exactas KH under three selected contenders. This strategy is only valuable when the contention is clearly defined.

Example of Straight Top and Bottom
STEP A: $15 win bet on key horse as a saver.
STEP B: $10 exactas on KH over d, f, j. $30.
STEP C: $5 exactas on KH under d, f, j. $15.

Totals: $15 win + $30 + $15 in exactas = $60 investment.

5. *Key Horse-Exacta Box.* Using key horse in all possible combinations with two or three other contenders in the same race.
STEP A: 50 percent win bet on key horse.
STEP B: KH in win position over three contenders.
STEP C: KH in place position under three contenders.
STEP D: Tickets on other contenders in all possible combinations with each other.

Example of Key Horse-Exacta Box
STEP A: $30 win bet on KH.
STEP B: $4 exactas on KH over d, f, j. $12.
STEP C: $4 exactas on KH under d, f, j. $12.
STEP D: $2 exactas on a over f, j. $4.
            $2 exactas on a under f, j. $4.
            $2 exactas on f over and under j. $4.

Totals: $30 win bet + $24 + $12 = $66 investment.

NOTE: If necessary to keep play at or below $60 total investment, reduce STEP A to $24.

6. *Seconditis Wheel.* Using key horse in a wheel underneath the rest of the field. To be used in tandem with a saver win wager.

STEP A: 20 percent win wager on key horse.

STEP B: A full wheel using the KH underneath the rest of the field.

STEP C: Extra tickets on lowest payoffs.

STEP D: Extra tickets on selected contenders.

This strategy is extremely potent when the key horse is obviously sharp, but is burdened by a persistent history of finishing second.

Example of Seconditis Wheel

STEP A: $12 win bet on key horse as saver.

STEP B: $4 exactas on KH underneath a, b, d, e, f, g, h, i, j. $36.

STEP C: $2 exactas on KH under a, i, j. $6.

STEP D: $2 exactas on KH under d, f, j. $6.

Totals: $12 win bet + $36 + $6 + $6 in exactas = $60 investment.

Betting Strategies in Trifectas

There are many different ways to buy into the trifecta, including a complete win wheel of a key horse over the rest of the field and assorted boxes and partial wheels. The objective is to pick the correct 1–2–3 order of finish, which is far more difficult than picking a clear-cut winner or an exact 1–2 order of finish. But even so, and despite its reputation as a "sucker's bet," the trifecta sometimes offers intriguing possibilities, especially if play is kept in perspective as part of a sound betting strategy. The primary emphasis in such a strategy is on the win position. The trifecta is a profit booster, a home-run hitter's delight, but it can also be the quickest ticket to a losing season if the player fails to keep his eye on the ball.

1. *Partial Wheel.* Using key horse in the win position over a three-, four-, or five-horse box for the place and show posi-

tions. To be used in tandem with a realistic win wager on the KH.

STEP A: 66 percent win bet on KH.

STEP B: Partial wheel of KH over five selected contenders. At most tracks, it is possible to buy into the trifecta with $1 betting units, even though the full trifecta payoff is calculated on the basis of a $2 or $3 unit wager. Using this and other suggested strategies, it will cost $6 to partial wheel the KH over three horses, $12 to partial wheel the KH over four horses, and $20 to cover five horses under the KH.

Example of Partial Wheel

STEP A: $40 win bet on KH.

STEP B: Partial trifecta at $1 tickets of KH over a, d, e, f, j. $20

Totals: $40 win bet + $20 trifecta = $60 investment.

NOTE: If the KH wins, the trifecta is won if any two of the five selected contenders finish second and third.

2. *Partial Wheel Win and Place.* Using key horse in the win and place positions with four contenders. To be used in tandem with a realistic win wager.

STEP A: 66 percent win bet on KH.

STEP B: Partial wheel using KH in win position over four contenders.

STEP C: Partial wheel using KH in place position with four contenders.

Example of Partial Wheel Win and Place

STEP A: $40 win bet on KH.

STEP B: $1 trifecta tickets KH over a, e, f, j box. $12.

STEP C: $1 trifectas a, e, f, j box over KH over a, e, f, j box. $12.

Totals: $40 win bet + $12 win trifectas + $12 place trifectas = $64 investment.

3. *Partial Wheel and Alternate.* Using KH in the win position in a partial wheel and using an alternate selection in another partial wheel. To be used in tandem with a win bet on key horse.

STEP A: 66 percent win bet on KH.

STEP B: Partial KH win wheel over four contenders.

STEP C: Partial alternate selection win wheel over four contenders.

Example of Partial Wheel and Alternate

STEP A: $40 win bet on KH.

STEP B: $1 trifecta tickets on KH over (a, e, f, j) box. $12.

STEP C: $1 trifectas on Alt. Sel. over a, e, f, KH box. $12.

Totals: $40 win bet + $12 KH win trifecta wheel + $12 Alt. Sel. trifecta wheel = $64.

NOTE: Hypothetically, the alternate selection in these examples is horse j.

4. *Full Wheel plus Place.* Using key horse to win and an alternate selection to place over the rest of the field. To be used in tandem with a win wager on KH.

STEP A: 66 percent win bet on KH.

STEP B: Playing the KH and Alt. Sel. on top of the rest of the field.

To be used only when the first two contenders seem very solid, a rare occurrence.

Example of Full Wheel plus Place

STEP A: $40 win bet on KH.

STEP B: $2 trifectas on KH with Alt. Sel. over a, b, c, d, e, g, h, i. $16.

Totals: $40 win bet + $16 in trifectas = $56 investment.

5. *Full Wheel plus Place and Show*. Using the key horse in the win position and using the alternate selection in the place and show positions. To be used in tandem with a win bet on KH.

STEP A: 66 percent win bet on KH.

STEP B: A full wheel using KH to win and Alt. Sel. to place.

STEP C: A full wheel using KH to win and Alt. Sel. for show.

Example of Full Wheel plus Place and Show

STEP A: $40 win bet on KH.

STEP B: $1 tickets on KH over Alt. Sel. over a, b, c, d, e, g, h, i. $8.

STEP C: $1 tickets on KH over a, b, c, d, e, g, h, i, over Alt. Sel. $8.

Totals: $40 win bet + $8 + $8 trifecta wheels = $56 investment.

6. *Trifecta Box*. No key horse, but possible three- or four-horse exacta box. To be used when there is no bona fide key horse and the pre-race favorite is distinctly eligible to go off form.

STEP A: No win bet.

STEP B: $1 tickets on a three-, four-, or five-horse box.

Example of Trifecta Boxes

A three-horse box at $1 betting units involves 6 combinations.

A four-horse box at $1 betting units involves 24 combinations.

A five-horse box at $1 betting units involves 60 combinations.

NOTE: I do not recommend boxing trifecta contenders as a substitute for a prime bet. Such play is intended only for light action, or in special cases when the pre-race favorites are highly suspect. I shall have more to say on this subject in a future work.

RECOMMENDED READING LIST

STATISTICS AND GENERAL RACING INFORMATION

The American Racing Manual, published annually by the *Daily Racing Form*.

The Blood Horse's annual statistical review.

The Thoroughbred Record's annual statistical review.

BREEDING AND TRAINING

The Blood Horse (weekly magazine).

Breeding the Racehorse, by Federico Tesio; tr. Marchese E. Spinola. British Book Center, 1973. $12.50.

Training Thoroughbred Horses, by Preston M. Burch. The Blood Horse Library, revised edition, 1973. $10.75.

Typology of the Racehorse, by Franco Varola. J. A. Allen Sporting Book Center, 1974. $29.75.

RACING HISTORY

Big Red of Meadow Stable: Secretariat, The Making of a Champion, by William Nack. Arthur Fields Books, 1975. $10.00.

The History of Thoroughbred Racing in America, by William H. Robertson. Bonanza Books, 1964. $25.00.

In the Winner's Circle, by Joseph A. Hirsh and Gene Plowden. Mason Charter, 1974. $7.95.

Run for the Roses: 100 Years of the Kentucky Derby, by Jim Bolus. Hawthorn Books, 1974. $12.95.

This Was Racing, by Joe H. Palmer. Henry Clay, 1973. $7.95.

HANDICAPPING

Ainslie's Complete Guide to Thoroughbred Racing, by Tom Ainslie. Simon and Schuster, 1968. $17.95.

Picking Winners, by Andrew Beyer. Houghton Mifflin, 1975. $8.95.

I have been very fortunate. During my years around the race-track I have been continually exposed to the varied menu only an extensive itinerary can bring: Five years at Rutgers University, Garden State Park division; two years of handicapping fifty races a day at five or more tracks for the *Daily Racing Form;* Triple Crown coverage for Mutual Radio and the *Philadelphia Inquirer;* five hundred daily five-minute seminars on handicapping for WLMD radio in Maryland; the editorship of *Turf and Sport Digest;* daily columns and picks at Atlantic City, Delaware Park, and Keystone for the *Philadelphia Journal;* visits to forty-eight different racetracks and conversations with some of the best thinkers and players in the game. People like Andy Beyer and Clem Florio in Maryland, Jules Schanzer and Saul Rosen at the *Form*, John Pricci of *Newsday* in New York, and Tom Ainslie, the man who gave me special encouragement to commit to print all the insights I have thus far gained.